ENERGY IN INT
TRADE .

Against the backdrop of energy markets that have radically changed in recent decades, this book offers an in-depth study of energy regulation in international trade law. The author seeks to clarify what we define as 'energy' in the context of the applicable international trade rules, and gives the reader a thorough analysis of the concepts, history and law of the various legal frameworks underpinning international energy trade. In addition, several case studies address the ongoing quest for energy security and show how the existing rules relate to some of the vast challenges that energy markets face today, notably the decentralization and decarbonization of energy markets.

ANNA-ALEXANDRA MARHOLD is Assistant Professor at the Grotius Centre for International Legal Studies at Leiden University Law School, where she researches and teaches in the area of international law, including international economic law. Her specialization is international trade law at the intersection of energy and environmental regulation.

CAMBRIDGE INTERNATIONAL TRADE AND ECONOMIC LAW

Series editors

Dr Lorand Bartels
University of Cambridge
Professor Thomas Cottier
University of Berne
Professor Tomer Broude
Hebrew University of Jerusalem
Professor Andrea K. Bjorklund
McGill University, Montréal

Processes of economic regionalization and globalization have intensified over the last decades, accompanied by increases in the regulation of international trade and economics at the levels of international, regional and national laws. At the same time, significant challenges have arisen with respect to economic liberalization, rule-based systems of trade and investment, and their political and social impacts. The subject matter of this series is international economic law in this contemporary context. Its core is the regulation of international trade, investment, finance and cognate areas such as intellectual property and competition policy. The series publishes books on related regulatory areas, in particular human rights, labour, environment and culture, as well as sustainable development. These areas are horizontally interconnected and vertically linked at the international, regional and national levels. The series also includes works on governance, dealing with the structure and operation of international organizations related to the field of international economic law, and the way they interact with other subjects of international and national law. The series aims to include excellent legal doctrinal treatises, as well as cutting-edge interdisciplinary works that engage law and the social sciences and humanities.

Books in the series

ENERGY IN INTERNATIONAL TRADE LAW

Concepts, Regulation and Changing Markets

ANNA-ALEXANDRA MARHOLD

Leiden University

CAMBRIDGE
UNIVERSITY PRESS

Shaftesbury Road, Cambridge CB2 8EA, United Kingdom

One Liberty Plaza, 20th Floor, New York, NY 10006, USA

477 Williamstown Road, Port Melbourne, VIC 3207, Australia

314–321, 3rd Floor, Plot 3, Splendor Forum, Jasola District Centre, New Delhi – 110025, India

103 Penang Road, #05–06/07, Visioncrest Commercial, Singapore 238467

Cambridge University Press is part of Cambridge University Press & Assessment, a department of the University of Cambridge.

We share the University's mission to contribute to society through the pursuit of education, learning and research at the highest international levels of excellence.

www.cambridge.org
Information on this title: www.cambridge.org/9781108445917

DOI: 10.1017/9781108551526

First published 2021
First paperback edition 2023

A catalogue record for this publication is available from the British Library

Library of Congress Cataloging-in-Publication data
Names: Marhold, Anna-Alexandra, 1983– author.
Title: Energy in international trade law : concepts, regulation and changing markets / Anna-Alexandra Marhold, Leiden University.
Description: Cambridge, United Kingdom ; New York, NY : Cambridge University Press, 2021. | Series: Cambridge international trade and economic law | Based on author's thesis (doctoral - European University Institute, 2016) issued under title: Energy in international trade law from GATT to TTIP. | Includes bibliographical references and index.
Identifiers: LCCN 2021008912 | ISBN 9781108427227 (hardback) | ISBN 9781108445917 (paperback) | ISBN 9781108551526 (ebook)
Subjects: LCSH: Power resources – Law and legislation. | Foreign trade regulation.
Classification: LCC K3981 .M358 2021 | DDC 343.08/7533379–dc23
LC record available at https://lccn.loc.gov/2021008912

ISBN   978-1-108-42722-7   Hardback
ISBN   978-1-108-44591-7   Paperback

To my mother Eduarda, my husband Vasyl
and our son Arthur Samuel

CONTENTS

TABLES

FOREWORD

Dr Marhold's work serves as a comprehensive and rigorous introduction to the norms of the international trading order as they apply to and affect energy markets. As such, it serves admirably as a text or treatise for students, practitioners and scholars who need to grasp international trade law's regulation of this crucial field of economic activity. But the book offers much more than this; it contains in-depth examinations of some of the most difficult legal and political questions entangled with contemporary controversies over energy, including government policies to promote renewables, the impact of the unbundling of energy production and supply on trade, the issue of fossil fuel subsidies, allegedly anti-competitive practices such as dual pricing and cartel-like behaviour, and what promises to be the overarching or meta-issue in the new world of what Anthea Roberts and her colleagues call 'geoeconomics' – namely, energy security.

One should begin by asking why it has taken this long to produce scholarship on international trade law and energy of this quality and ambition. As Dr Marhold points out, energy was long regarded as a non-issue for GATT and the World Trade Organization. One reason may be that many of the world's leading energy producers, Russia and most of the Gulf states, only recently became members of the multilateral trading regime. Another may be the considerable uncertainty as to how trade rules might or might not apply to some of the most pertinent, and contested, features of global energy markets, in particular the OPEC price and supply cartel. In the face of such uncertainty, and perhaps for other (geopolitical?) reasons, other forums emerged as choices for responding to these realities, above all the International Energy Agency (IEA) and, as Dr Marhold discusses, the Energy Charter Treaty (which, however, as she deftly analyses, overlaps in some areas with important norms of the WTO, especially on the issue of energy transit). Moreover, as Marhold reminds us, competition or anti-trust rules are largely excluded from the WTO legal order (even if some may exist in regional agreements), leading to an impression of the WTO's limited relevance in tackling a range of arguably significant anti-competitive practices, especially those of enterprises whose conduct could not be unproblematically attributed to the state(s) concerned (whether under special rules for state enterprises or more general attribution norms in the law of state responsibility). Acknowledging this, Marhold nevertheless shows that WTO norms have more to say about some such practices than is typically appreciated.

When I began writing about trade, climate change and renewable energy nearly two decades ago (and eventually in collaboration with Antonia Eliason), the reaction from the 'old hands' in the WTO and trade policy worlds was that, while an interesting intellectual exercise, such scholarly inquiry had little practical importance – there would never, for instance, be a WTO dispute about renewable energy. Now, of course, there have been a number of such disputes, including the high-profile *Canada – Renewables* case, as well as the *India – Solar Cells* dispute. These cases raise squarely the issue of the policy space that states have under WTO rules to incentivize the emergence of domestic renewable energy markets, enabling a shift to energy sources with low or lower carbon emissions. The context is a world where fossil fuel energy was cheaper than renewable alternatives – that is, as long as the carbon externalities generated by fossil fuels were not internalised into the prices (this context has now changed, especially in the case of solar energy). In *Canada – Renewables* the WTO's Appellate Body (whose operation, as Marhold explains, has now been suspended due to a blockage on new appointments by the United States) found that the benchmark against which government intervention was to be judged under the WTO subsidies rules must take into account the government's policy choice to create a renewables market. Government pricing mechanisms and other incentives to establish a renewables market do not necessarily constitute an anti-competitive benefit for renewables just because they do not apply to fossil fuel producers. They constitute part of a separate market structure determined by public policy. This was a doctrinally imaginative move, which arguably signals considerable deference to governments that create comprehensive schemes establishing renewables markets on a significant scale.

But the limit to policy space that states continue to push against in the WTO is non-discrimination. As Marhold discusses, in the *India – Solar Cells* dispute India attempted to make an 'energy security'-type argument for favouring domestic inputs in the production of solar energy. India invoked, in particular, Article XX(j) of GATT, which refers to situations of shortages in supply, claiming that, given the ambition and needs of the country's renewables programme, incentives were needed to ensure the country was not entirely dependent upon foreign sources of supply. On the evidence, the Appellate Body rejected India's argument, upholding the panel's finding that the domestic content requirements violated GATT. Another instance where a WTO adjudicator rejected an Article XX(j) energy security defence was the EU-Russia natural gas dispute. In that case the EU had sought to justify certain aspects of the restructuring of the EU natural gas market that allowed discrimination against non-EU operators. Again, the panel found that discrimination against non-EU actors could not be justified as necessary for reasons of security of supply.

I believe Marhold is entirely right to imply that these 'energy-security' (and, in some sense, geopolitical energy sovereignty) claims are not going to go away. After decades of avoiding activating what could be seen as a huge loophole in WTO obligations, some WTO members have now been bringing into play the broad and at least partly self-judging general security exception in Article XXI of GATT (and the equivalent in other WTO agreements). Panels have decided two cases so far under Article XXI, the Russia-Ukraine transit dispute and an intellectual property rights dispute between Saudi Arabia and Qatar. The panel rulings make it clear that Article XXI is far from a limitless carve-out or fully self-judging. But these cases come in the context of a non-functioning Appellate Body, and if more tailored exceptions such as XX(j) continue to prove unavailing with respect to energy security arguments, eventually Article XXI is likely to be invoked, one would imagine.

The IMF and others have documented the significant impact of fossil fuel subsidies on climate change. As Marhold discusses, there is quite limited momentum in the WTO to work towards effective disciplines on such subsidies. She also notes that there has been reluctance to use dispute settlement under the existing subsidies rules to attack fossil fuel subsidies, as opposed to renewable energy incentives. From a climate mitigation perspective that, of course, seems entirely perverse. It seems entirely possible to make good arguments that some of the fossil fuel measures are illegal under the existing rules (even if efforts to explicitly outlaw them have stalled): Marhold shows this with respect to dual pricing, where her analysis is to my mind entirely convincing. She refers not only to the WTO subsidies rules, but also to the possibility that dual pricing (establishing a lower energy price for domestic consumers than for export) may in fact be an export restriction within the meaning of

Article XI of GATT, and therefore prohibited (though, as she says, this would depend on the actual design and operation of the particular dual-pricing scheme being challenged). Since upstream and downstream subsidies are challengeable under WTO rules, dual-pricing schemes that, for example, disproportionately benefit industries that are large consumers of fossil fuel energy as production inputs might well be attacked as specific and actionable under WTO dispute settlement.

Marhold's enterprise is animated by a spirit of hopefulness about the possibility of evolving better international cooperation on trade and energy, including more adequate legal norms to address the controversies and policy imperatives of the present and future. But she is at the same time rightly cautious about grandiose approaches that seem oblivious to institutional and geopolitical constraints – such as the idea of negotiating a comprehensive agreement on trade and energy at the WTO. Much more plausible is the evolution of norms through dispute settlement, geopolitical conflict and self-interested bargaining among states and perhaps other stakeholders. Marhold's book is indispensable guidance for all those who might be engaged in, or by, such developments.

Robert Howse
Lloyd C Nelson Professor of International Law
New York University School of Law
New York, August 2020

ACKNOWLEDGEMENTS

Keep reading books, but remember that a book's only a book, and you should learn to think for yourself.

Maxim Gorky

Anyone who takes himself too seriously always runs the risk of looking ridiculous; anyone who can consistently laugh at himself does not.

Václav Havel

We live in a globalized world. The very realization of this book reflects that. My interest in the topic was developed during studies in Amsterdam. The application to undertake a PhD at the European University Institute (EUI) on the topic was made from Yerevan. I started working on the thesis, the basis for this book, in Florence and continued in New York. With many writing stops in between (including in Prague and Kyiv), the thesis was completed in Geneva – and it is no coincidence that the city is home to one of the institutions at the centre of my dissertation, the World Trade Organization. More time was then needed to rework the thesis into a monograph, and it was interrupted by the arrival of our wonderful son. The book was finalized in Rotterdam, Europe's largest seaport, at the time of the corona pandemic.

The conceptualization of this book has benefited from many helpful hands along the way. First and foremost, I extend my gratitude to my supervisor Petros C. Mavroidis. His encouragement, sharp mind, positive outlook, sense of humour and flexibility were what made this project possible in the first place. I also wish to thank Catherine Redgwell, Bernard Hoekman and Robert Howse for serving on my PhD defence committee.

My time at the EUI was inspiring, unique and both great fun and highly challenging. I particularly wish to thank Dennis Patterson for his support. On a personal level, I had the privilege of becoming acquainted with some wonderful colleagues at the EUI. These include, but are not limited to, Johanna Jacobsson, Emma Linklater, Jacobien van Dorp,

Diana Natermann, Marijn van der Sluijs, Sanna Salo, Yuting Hua, Jan Zglinksi, Alexandra Ortolja-Baird, Marion Guerrero and Marianna Karttunen-Saint Bris.

I should, however, go back to my pre-PhD days and thank those who introduced me to international law and legal academia in the first place: my former colleagues at the University of Amsterdam. Without them, I would not be where I am now. They are André Nollkaemper, Catherine Brolmann, Janne Nijman, Yvonne Donders, Hege Elisabeth Kjos, James Mathis, Pieter Jan Kuijper and Isabelle Swerissen.

Further away from home, the generous contribution of the EU-US Fulbright-Schuman Program enabled me to work on my book as a visiting scholar at New York University. I am grateful to the kind people of the NYU Law JSD Program, especially Karen Loevy, for including me in their meetings and giving me the opportunity to present my work. I am also greatly indebted to Robert Howse, who so caringly welcomed me. Both he and Alan Sykes took time to read and comment extensively on my draft.

In Geneva, I had the opportunity to be part of the Marie Curie DISSETTLE project at the Graduate Institute, which gave me a deeper insight into the world of law and economics, from which this book has undoubtedly benefited. I had the pleasure of working in a stimulating environment with motivating people such as Joost Pauwelyn, Damien Neven and Theresa Carpenter. I was honoured to become acquainted with Gabrielle Marceau, who is always an inspiration and has been very generous to our family. In addition, I thoroughly enjoyed working with my colleagues and friends, both lawyers and economists, at the Centre for Trade and Economic Integration and beyond, including Stela Rubínová, Viktor Kümmritz, Yuan Zi, Aksel Erbahar, Andrea Barrios Vidal, Weiwei Zhang, Chuck Wu, Klara Polackova-Van der Ploeg, Katrin Fernekess and Vitaliy Pogoretskyy.

The supportive environment at the Grotius Centre of Leiden Law School truly enabled me to finalize and publish the monograph. Thank you to Eric de Brabandère for taking me on board, and to a team of passionate, hard-working colleagues, who are dearly missed in times of working from home. Special thanks go out to my colleague and office mate Daniëlla Dam-de Jong, who shared valuable insights into the regulation of natural resources that have been incorporated into this monograph.

On the personal front, my family were there long before I started the book and I am not sure I can even express my gratitude and what they mean to me in words. What I can say is that I am grateful for my mother's resilience, perseverance, optimism, curiosity, depth and thoughtfulness, which I hope I have inherited somewhat. I owe a lot to her tireless encouragement. My father's unconventional thinking, on the other hand, has always forced me out of my comfort zone – indispensable when undertaking a PhD, as I discovered. My brother Nathan and Aunt Viki have also always cheered me on.

Then there is, of course, my husband Vasyl. Aside from everything else, he was an enormous support during all the ups and downs inherent in realizing this book. Vasyl was always ready to carefully debate any issue with keen and supportive interest. This is rare luxury and one that has to be treasured. The book has certainly benefited from his expertise.

* * *

This book is based on an EUI PhD and has been published with a financial subsidy from the EUI.

All errors in this monograph are mine alone and the views expressed in this study should not be attributed to any of the institutions with which I have been affiliated.

TABLES OF CASES

World Trade Organization

Short Form	Full Citation
Argentina – Hides and Leather	Panel Report, Argentina – Measures Affecting the Export of Bovine Hides and the Import of Finished Leather, WT/DS155/R and Corr 1, adopted 16 February 2001, DSR 2001:V, p 1779
Australia – Automotive Leather II	Panel Report, Australia – Subsidies Provided to Producers and Exporters of Automotive Leather, WT/DS126/R, adopted 16 June 1999, DSR 1999:III, p 951
Australia – Automotive Leather II (Article 21.5 – US)	Panel Report, Australia – Subsidies Provided to Producers and Exporters of Automotive Leather – Recourse to Article 21.5 of the DSU by the United States, WT/DS126/RW and Corr 1, adopted 11 February 2000, DSR 2000:III, p 1189
Brazil – Retreaded Tyres	Appellate Body Report, Brazil – Measures Affecting Imports of Retreaded Tyres, WT/DS332/AB/R, adopted 17 December 2007, DSR 2007:IV, p 1527
Canada – Renewable Energy / Canada – Feed-In Tariff Program	Appellate Body Reports, Canada – Certain Measures Affecting the Renewable Energy Generation Sector / Canada – Measures Relating to the Feed-In Tariff Program, WT/DS412/AB/R, WT/DS426/AB/R, adopted 24 May 2013, DSR 2013:I, p 7
Canada – Renewable Energy / Canada – Feed-In Tariff Program	Panel Reports, Canada – Certain Measures Affecting the Renewable Energy Generation Sector / Canada – Measures Relating to the Feed-In Tariff Program, WT/DS412/R and Add 1, WT/DS426/R and Add 1, adopted 24 May 2013, as modified by Appellate Body Reports WT/DS412/AB/R, WT/DS426/AB/R, DSR 2013:I, p 237

(*cont.*)

(*cont.*)

Short Form	Full Citation
Colombia – Ports of Entry	Panel Report, Colombia – Indicative Prices and Restrictions on Ports of Entry, WT/DS366/R and Corr 1, adopted 20 May 2009, DSR 2009:VI, p 2535
Colombia – Textiles	Appellate Body Report, Colombia – Measures Relating to the Importation of Textiles, Apparel and Footwear, WT/DS461/AB/R and Add 1, adopted 22 June 2016, DSR 2016:III, p 1131
EC – Asbestos	Appellate Body Report, European Communities – Measures Affecting Asbestos and Asbestos-Containing Products, WT/DS135/AB/R, adopted 5 April 2001, DSR 2001:VII, p 3243
EC – Bananas III	Appellate Body Report, European Communities – Regime for the Importation, Sale and Distribution of Bananas, WT/DS27/AB/R, adopted 25 September 1997, DSR 1997:II, p 591
EC – Bananas III	Panel Reports, European Communities – Regime for the Importation, Sale and Distribution of Bananas, WT/DS27/R/ECU (Ecuador), WT/DS27/R/GTM, WT/DS27/R/HND (Guatemala and Honduras), WT/DS27/R/MEX (Mexico), WT/DS27/R/USA (US), adopted 25 September 1997, as modified by Appellate Body Report WT/DS27/AB/R, DSR 1997:II, p 695 to DSR 1997:III, p 1085
EC – Seal Products	Appellate Body Reports, European Communities – Measures Prohibiting the Importation and Marketing of Seal Products, WT/DS400/AB/R, WT/DS401/AB/R, adopted 18 June 2014, DSR 2014:I, p 7
EU – Biodiesel (Argentina)	Appellate Body Report, European Union – Anti-Dumping Measures on Biodiesel from Argentina, WT/DS473/AB/R and Add 1, adopted 26 October 2016, DSR 2016:VI, p 2871
EU – Biodiesel (Argentina)	Panel Report, European Union – Anti-Dumping Measures on Biodiesel from Argentina, WT/DS473/R and Add 1, adopted 26 October 2016, as modified by Appellate Body Report WT/DS473/AB/R, DSR 2016:VI, p 3077

(*cont.*)

Short Form	Full Citation
EU – Biodiesel (Indonesia)	Panel Report, European Union – Anti-Dumping Measures on Biodiesel from Indonesia, WT/DS480/R and Add 1, adopted 28 February 2018, DSR 2018:II, p 605
EU – Cost Adjustment Methodologies II (Russia)	Panel Report, European Union – Cost Adjustment Methodologies and Certain Anti-Dumping Measures on Imports from Russia (Second Complaint), WT/DS494/R and Add 1, circulated to WTO members 24 July 2020 [adoption/appeal pending]
EU – Energy Package	Panel Report, European Union and Its Member States – Certain Measures Relating to the Energy Sector, WT/DS476/R and Add 1, circulated to WTO members 10 August 2018 [appealed by EU 21 September 2018; the division suspended its work on 10 December 2019]
India – Autos	Panel Report, India – Measures Affecting the Automotive Sector, WT/DS146/R, WT/DS175/R, and Corr 1, adopted 5 April 2002, DSR 2002:V, p 1827
India – Quantitative Restrictions	Panel Report, India – Quantitative Restrictions on Imports of Agricultural, Textile and Industrial Products, WT/DS90/R, adopted 22 September 1999, upheld by Appellate Body Report WT/DS90/AB/R, DSR 1999:V, p 1799
India – Solar Cells	Appellate Body Report, India – Certain Measures Relating to Solar Cells and Solar Modules, WT/DS456/AB/R and Add 1, adopted 14 October 2016, DSR 2016:IV, p 1827
India – Solar Cells	Panel Report, India – Certain Measures Relating to Solar Cells and Solar Modules, WT/DS456/R and Add.1, adopted 14 October 2016, as modified by Appellate Body Report WT/DS456/AB/R, DSR 2016: IV, p 1941
Japan – Alcoholic Beverages II	Appellate Body Report, Japan – Taxes on Alcoholic Beverages, WT/DS8/AB/R, WT/DS10/AB/R, WT/DS11/AB/R, adopted 1 November 1996, DSR 1996: I, p 97

(cont.)

Short Form	Full Citation
Japan – Film	Panel Report, Japan – Measures Affecting Consumer Photographic Film and Paper, WT/DS44/R, adopted 22 April 1998, DSR 1998:IV, p 1179
US – Countervailing and Anti-Dumping Measures (China)	Appellate Body Report, United States – Countervailing and Anti-Dumping Measures on Certain Products from China, WT/DS449/AB/R and Corr 1, adopted 22 July 2014, DSR 2014:VIII, p 3027
US – Countervailing and Anti-Dumping Measures (China)	Panel Report, United States – Countervailing and Anti-Dumping Measures on Certain Products from China, WT/DS449/R and Add 1, adopted 22 July 2014, as modified by Appellate Body Report WT/DS449/AB/R, DSR 2014:VIII, p 3175
US – FSC	Panel Report, United States – Tax Treatment for 'Foreign Sales Corporations', WT/DS108/R, adopted 20 March 2000, as modified by Appellate Body Report WT/DS108/AB/R, DSR 2000:IV, p 1675
US – Gambling	Appellate Body Report, United States – Measures Affecting the Cross-Border Supply of Gambling and Betting Services, WT/DS285/AB/R, adopted 20 April 2005, DSR 2005:XII, p 5663 (and Corr 1, DSR 2006:XII, p 5475)
US – Gasoline	Appellate Body Report, United States – Standards for Reformulated and Conventional Gasoline, WT/DS2/AB/R, adopted 20 May 1996, DSR 1996:I, p 3
US – Gasoline	Panel Report, United States – Standards for Reformulated and Conventional Gasoline, WT/DS2/R, adopted 20 May 1996, as modified by Appellate Body Report WT/DS2/AB/R, DSR 1996:I, p 29
US – Poultry (China)	Panel Report, United States – Certain Measures Affecting Imports of Poultry from China, WT/DS392/R, adopted 25 October 2010, DSR 2010:V, p 1909
US – Renewable Energy	Panel Report, United States – Certain Measures Relating to the Renewable Energy Sector, WT/DS510/R and Add 1, circulated to WTO members 27 June 2019 [appealed by US 15 August 2019; the division suspended its work on 10 December 2019]

(*cont.*)

Short Form	Full Citation
US – Shrimp	Appellate Body Report, United States – Import Prohibition of Certain Shrimp and Shrimp Products, WT/DS58/AB/R, adopted 6 November 1998, DSR 1998:VII, p 2755
US – Shrimp	Panel Report, United States – Import Prohibition of Certain Shrimp and Shrimp Products, WT/DS58/R and Corr 1, adopted 6 November 1998, as modified by Appellate Body Report WT/DS58/AB/R, DSR 1998:VII, p 2821
US – Softwood Lumber IV	Appellate Body Report, United States – Final Countervailing Duty Determination with Respect to Certain Softwood Lumber from Canada, WT/DS257/AB/R, adopted 17 February 2004, DSR 2004:II, p 571
US – Softwood Lumber V	Appellate Body Report, United States – Final Dumping Determination on Softwood Lumber from Canada, WT/DS264/AB/R, adopted 31 August 2004, DSR 2004:V, p 1875
US – Softwood Lumber VI	Panel Report, United States – Investigation of the International Trade Commission in Softwood Lumber from Canada, WT/DS277/R, adopted 26 April 2004, DSR 2004:VI, p 2485

WTO Requests for Consultations/Ongoing Cases

Case No	Title	Complainant	Date	Status
DS593	European Union – Certain Measures Concerning Palm Oil and Oil Palm Crop-Based Biofuels	Indonesia	9 December 2019	Panel established 29 July 2020.
DS592	Indonesia – Measures Relating to Raw Materials	European Union	22 November 2019	Consultations

(*cont.*)

Case No	Title	Complainant	Date	Status
DS575	Colombia – Measures Concerning the Distribution of Liquid Fuels	Venezuela	9 January 2019	Consultations
DS572	Peru – Anti-Dumping and Countervailing Measures on Biodiesel from Argentina	Argentina	29 November 2018	Consultations
DS562	United States – Safeguard Measures on PV Products	China	14 August 2018	Panel composed 24 October 2020. Panel process ongoing.
DS563	United States – Certain Measures Related to Renewable Energy	China	14 August 2018	Consultations
DS545	United States – Safeguard Measures on PV Products	Korea	14 May 2018	Panel established 26 September 2018, but not yet composed.
DS521	EU – Anti-Dumping Measures on Certain Cold-Rolled Flat Steel Products from Russia	Russia	27 January 2017	Panel established 16 March 2020.
DS519	China – Subsidies to Producers of Primary Aluminium	United States	12 January 2017	Consultations
DS508	China – Export Duties on Raw Materials	United States	13 July 2016	Panel established 8 November 2016.
DS459	European Union and Certain Member States – Certain Measures on the	Argentina	15 May 2013	Consultations

(*cont.*)

General Agreement on Tariffs and Trade

(cont.)

Short Form	Full Citation
	Recourse to Article XXIII:2 by the United States (L/ 5142) (panel report not adopted)
US – Sugar	US – Imports of Sugar from Nicaragua (L/5607 – 31S/ 67) (panel report adopted 13 March 1984)
US – Superfund	US – Taxes on Petroleum and Certain Imported Substances (L/6175 – 34S/136) (panel report adopted 17 June 1987)
US – Taxes on Automobiles	US – Taxes on Automobiles (DS 31/R) (11 October 1994, panel report not adopted)
US – Tuna	US – Prohibition of Imports of Tuna and Tuna Products from Canada (L/5198 – 29S/91) (panel report adopted 22 February 1982)
US – Trade Measures	US – Trade Measures Affecting Nicaragua (L/6053) (13 October 1986, panel report not adopted)

International Court of Justice

Armed Activities on the Territory of the Congo (Democratic Republic of the Congo v Uganda) [2005] ICJ Rep 168

Anglo-Iranian Oil Co Case (UK v Iran) [1952] ICJ Rep 93

Permanent Court of Arbitration

Texaco Overseas Petroleum Co v Government of the Libyan Arab Republic (Award of 19 January 1977) (1978) 17 ILM

Hulley Enterprises Limited v Russian Federation (PCA Case No AA226), Yukos Universal Limited v Russian Federation (PCA Case No AA227) and Veteran Petroleum Limited v Russian Federation (PCA Case No AA228), Interim Awards on Jurisdiction and Admissibility (30 November 2009)

Hulley Enterprises Limited v Russian Federation (PCA Case No AA226), Yukos Universal Limited v Russian Federation (PCA Case No AA227) and Veteran Petroleum Limited v the Russian Federation (PCA Case No AA228), Final Awards (18 July 2014)

Court of Justice of the European Union

Case C-393/92 Almelo v Energiebedrijf IJsselmij [1994] ECR I-1477

Case C-158/94 Commission v Italy [1997] ECR I-5789

Case C-439/06 Citiworks AG (22 May 2008)

ACRONYMS AND ABBREVIATIONS

AB	Appellate Body
ADA	Anti-Dumping Agreement
AoA	Agreement on Agriculture
ASEAN	Association of Southeast Asian Nations
BIT	bilateral investment treaty
CPC	Central Product Classification
CVD	countervailing duty
DCFTA	Deep and Comprehensive Free Trade Agreement
DCR	domestic content requirement
DDA	Doha Development Agenda
DSB	Dispute Settlement Body
DSU	Dispute Settlement Understanding
EC	European Community/European Communities
ECS	Energy Charter Secretariat
ECT	Energy Charter Treaty
EEZ	Exclusive Economic Zone
EGA	Environmental Goods Agreement
EU	European Union
Euratom	Treaty Establishing the European Atomic Energy Community
FFS	fossil fuel subsidies
FIT	feed-in tariff
FTA	free trade agreement
GATS	General Agreement on Trade in Services
GATT	General Agreement on Tariffs and Trade
GECF	Gas Exporting Countries Forum
GHG	greenhouse gas
GPA	Agreement on Government Procurement
HS Convention	Harmonized System Convention
IAEA	International Atomic Energy Agency
ICCPR	International Covenant on Civil and Political Rights
ICJ	International Court of Justice
IEA	International Energy Agency

IEC	International Energy Charter
IEM	internal energy market
IGO	intergovernmental organization
IMF	International Monetary Fund
ISDS	investor-state dispute settlement
ISO	independent system operator
ITO	International Trade Organization
ITO	independent transmission operator
JNNSM	Jawaharlal Nehru National Solar Mission
LNG	liquefied natural gas
MFN	most favoured nation
NAFTA	North American Free Trade Agreement
NDC	nationally determined contribution
NT	national treatment
OECD	Organisation for Economic Co-operation and Development
OPEC	Organization of Petroleum Exporting Countries
OS	observer status
OU	ownership unbundling
PCA	Permanent Court of Arbitration
PCI	project of common interest
PEEREA	Protocol on Energy Efficiency and Related Environmental Aspects
PSNR	permanent sovereignty over natural resources
PTA	preferential trade agreement
QR	quantitative restriction
SCM Agreement	Agreement on Subsidies and Countervailing Measures
SITC	Standard International Trade Classification
STE	state trading enterprise
TBT	technical barriers to trade
TEN-E Regulation	Trans-European Networks for Energy Regulation
TEP	Third Energy Package
TEU	Treaty on European Union
TFEU	Treaty on the Functioning of the European Union
TPA	third-party access
TPRM	Trade Policy Review Mechanism
TRIMs Agreement	Trade-Related Investment Measures Agreement
TRIPs Agreement	Trade-Related Intellectual Property Rights Agreement
TSO	transmission system operator
TTIP	Transatlantic Trade and Investment Partnership
UN	United Nations
UNCTAD	United Nations Conference on Trade and Development
UNDP	United Nations Development Programme

UNECE	United Nations Economic Commission for Europe
UNFCCC	United Nations Framework Convention on Climate Change
UNGA	United Nations General Assembly
UNSD	United Nations Statistics Division
UN SDGs	United Nations Sustainable Development Goals
US	United States
USMCA	United States-Mexico-Canada Agreement
VCLT	Vienna Convention on the Law of Treaties
VIU	vertically integrated undertaking
WCO	World Customs Organization
WTO	World Trade Organization

~

Introduction and Objectives

Energy is all around us. It comes in many forms and, just as much as the air we breathe and the water we drink, is essential for our survival. Energy is also ever-changing and in transition. Up until the end of the nineteenth century we were burning wood and peat as the main fuels to keep our houses warm and our economies going.[1] Industrialization transported us into the age of coal, which lasted until the middle of the twentieth century. This energy transition was soon followed by yet another one: oil overtook coal as our primary fuel after large discoveries of petroleum at the close of the nineteenth and start of the twentieth centuries.[2] The ensuing establishment of huge multinationals extracting oil caused a steep increase in its global consumption and trade.[3] The oil age placed us under the spell of 'black gold' from the second half of the twentieth century onwards. Added to which, the 1970s oil crises made it painfully clear how dependent the world was on oil and what turmoil follows if supplies are hampered.

At the beginning of the twenty-first century, large shale gas discoveries, especially in North America, heralded the dawn of the natural gas era we are experiencing today.[4] At the same time, we have become confronted with the fact that the fossil fuels we have so eagerly burned over the past

---

[1] V Smil, *Energy Transitions: History, Requirements, Prospects* (Praeger 2010) 25ff; see also US Energy Information Administration, 'Energy sources have changed throughout the history of the United States' (*Today in Energy*, 3 July 2013) <www.eia.gov/todayinenergy/detail.php?id=11951> accessed 20 July 2020.

[2] See D Yergin, *The Prize: The Epic Quest for Oil, Money and Power* (Free Press 2008) ch 6 'The Oil Wars: The Rise of Royal Dutch, the Fall of Imperial Russia'.

[3] See eg US Energy Information Administration, Data on US imports of crude oil 1920–2020 <www.eia.gov/dnav/pet/hist/LeafHandler.ashx?n=PET&s=MCRIMUS1&f=M> accessed 20 July 2020.

[4] See D Yergin, *The Quest: Energy Security and the Remaking of the Modern World* (Penguin Press 2011) ch 16 'The Natural Gas Revolution'.

century have brought a negative externality: climate change.[5] As a consequence, our collective ambitions compel us to transition once more into an era of clean energy and to provide for our needs in a competitive, secure, sustainable and CO_2 neutral way.

These energy transitions have changed our stance towards energy. Industrialization was primarily focused on ever-growing production and consumption, but in 2020 the need for a new approach oriented towards sustainable development and climate change mitigation can no longer be ignored. Yet, the rise in the global population means that the world's energy consumption keeps on increasing, despite our ongoing efforts to curb emissions.[6] What is more, as globalization increases, so does international trade in energy, causing international trade rules to come into play.

The relevance of multilateral energy trading rules was for a long time overlooked, downplayed and underestimated. One explanation for this may be that for many years energy was almost exclusively traded by international, vertically integrated and often state-owned companies. However, the above-mentioned transitions have changed the global energy trading landscape significantly. The energy trade is no longer confined to oil tankers transporting barrels from the Gulf; it now extends to wind turbines and solar panels. The last three decades have indeed brought revolutionary advancements in renewable and clean energy. The clean energy transition has been accompanied by increasing regulation, which in turn has triggered disputes in the context of the World Trade Organization (WTO).[7] And this rise in international trade disputes relating to both renewable and non-renewable energy has led to a growing awareness of the importance of regulating international trade in energy. Moreover, an increasing number of major energy producing, exporting and transporting countries are joining the WTO,

---

[5] The Preamble to the COP21 Paris Agreement states: 'Recognizing that climate change represents an urgent and potentially irreversible threat to human societies and the planet and thus requires the widest possible cooperation by all countries, and their participation in an effective and appropriate international response, with a view to accelerating the reduction of global greenhouse gas emissions'. United Framework Convention on Climate Change (UNFCCC), 'Report of the Conference of the Parties on its twenty-first session, held in Paris from 30 November to 13 December 2015' (29 January 2016) UN Doc FCCC/CP/2015/L9/Rev 1, 2.

[6] IEA, 'World Energy Outlook 2019: Executive Summary' (2019) 1.

[7] See eg *Canada – Renewable Energy / Canada – Feed-In Tariff Program*, panel and Appellate Body reports.

acceding to the Energy Charter Treaty (ECT) and/or concluding preferential trade agreements (PTAs) that include provisions relevant to
energy.

This book offers an in-depth study of energy regulation in international trade law against the backdrop of energy markets that have
radically changed over recent decades. In Part I, through a thorough
discussion of the concepts, history and law of various legal frameworks
applicable to international energy trade, it seeks to clarify what we mean
by 'energy' in the context of international trade rules. Part II then
addresses the relationship between the existing rules and the huge challenges faced by energy markets today – notably, their decentralization
and decarbonization – in the light of the ongoing quest for energy
security. Through several case studies, it will demonstrate that current
international rules are often unable to meet the challenges faced by
today's changing energy markets.

Chapter 1 discusses energy as a concept that has transformed over time
and explains how the rules of international trade law are relevant to the
energy sector, paying particular attention to the challenges of decarbonization, decentralization and energy security. Chapter 2 examines the
treatment of energy from the inception of the General Agreement on
Tariffs and Trade (GATT) in 1947 to the present time. Chapter 3
continues by discussing the current legal framework of the WTO, providing an overview of WTO agreements relevant to energy. It is here that
we expose some challenges – such as export restrictions and fossil fuel
subsidies in the energy sector in the light of international trade law –
which will be further elaborated upon in Part II. Chapter 4 enquires into
energy commitments beyond the WTO, namely in the ECT and in
selected PTAs. By means of a comparative study, the chapter scrutinizes
the nexus between the WTO and the ECT. It looks at the interplay
between these international treaty regimes, including their overlap and
potential conflict. Chapter 5 introduces the second part of the book and
considers the challenge of decentralizing energy markets. It lays bare the
difficulties WTO law has with respect to strategic, unevenly distributed
natural resources and cartels maintained by states. It does so by taking
the practices of the world's best-known energy cartel, the Organization of
Petroleum Exporting Countries (OPEC), as an example. It additionally
looks at decentralization policies put in place by the European Union
(EU) and how international trade rules enable or constrain such policies.
Chapter 6 examines the challenge of decarbonizing energy markets by
looking at the treatment of environmentally harmful fossil fuel subsidies

under WTO law. Lastly, Chapter 7 sheds light on the growing relevance of energy security in international trade law, including its use as a defence in WTO dispute settlement. By way of conclusion, Chapter 8 considers some policy options for enhanced energy governance at the institutional level.

At the time of writing, the multilateral trading system is undergoing a deep crisis. Energy is by no means the only subject in need of revision within the global trading system but is certainly a topic that, given today's changing markets, can no longer be overlooked.

PART I

Energy in International Trade Law: Concepts,
History and Legal Framework

Energy in the Context of International Trade Law: Concepts and Changing Markets

1.1 Introduction

This book studies the regulation of energy in international trade law in the light of changing markets. To understand how the rules of international trade law are relevant to energy, it is first necessary to conceptualize what is meant by the elusive term 'energy' used throughout this monograph. The purpose of this introductory chapter is therefore threefold: (1) to explain energy as a concept that has transformed over time and highlight the difference between primary, secondary, renewable, clean and non-renewable energy sources; (2) to describe how the rules of international trade law are relevant for the energy sector in general including how various types of energy are classified in the Harmonized System Convention[1]; and finally (3) to explores what major changes energy markets have undergone in recent decades, focusing on decarbonization, decentralization and the eternal quest for energy security.

1.2 Framing Energy: Defining an Evolving Concept

The term 'energy' has many meanings. In everyday language it covers many things, from globally traded fossil fuels such as crude oil and natural gas to the heat and electricity those fuels generate and on which our cities depend.[2] This, however, is rather a crude description of

---

[1] The HS Convention (International Convention on the Harmonized Commodity Description and Coding System (adopted 14 June 1983, entered into force 1988) 1503 UNTS 167) is the system according to which all schedules are structured; see World Customs Organization <www.wcoomd.org/home.htm> accessed 20 July 2020.

[2] The Oxford English Dictionary defines energy, inter alia, as '[p]ower or force derived from the exploitation of physical and chemical resources in order to operate machines and devices, to provide light and heat, etc., and frequently regarded as a resource or commodity' <www.oed.com> accessed 2 October 2019.

a process that in reality is not so straightforward. The generation of energy in the conventional sense involves, first, the extraction of some natural resources or raw materials, which are then traded as fossil fuels (such as crude petroleum or natural gas), after which they undergo a combustion process to create energy (power and heat) by the laws of physics.[3] The question, then, is at what stage in this process we should label something as 'energy'. Can fossil fuels, for instance, be considered as 'energy' before they are extracted from the ground? Or is 'energy' rather the electricity generated by these raw materials and distributed through grids to power our homes and offices?

Furthermore, energy is an evolving concept; what we understand by it has been shifting over time. Before industrialization, wood – a renewable, though not very clean, source of energy – was the primary fuel used by mankind.[4] From industrialization to the moment when the first modern-day renewables arrived on the scene in the 1970s or thereabouts, energy generally meant fossil fuels such as crude petroleum, coal and natural gas, and the electricity, power and heat generated from them.[5] Since then, our understanding of 'energy' has changed yet again, as it now extends to clean and renewable sources from which energy can be generated, such as wind, water and sunshine.

To unravel the legal questions raised by energy regulation in international trade, we therefore first need to find a common understanding of the defining concept of energy. For the purpose of this study, it is important to explain and dissect the concept of energy and classify its different forms into workable definitions for two reasons. Identifying the different types of energy that exist and their distinctive characteristics enables us, first, to better understand how this influences the various aspects of their tradability and, second, to associate the different types of energy with the appropriate agreements in international trade law. For example, does a particular type of energy qualify as a good or rather

---

[3] In physics, energy is defined as '[t]he potential or capacity of a body or system to do work by virtue of its motion, position, chemical structure, etc., frequently regarded as a quantifiable attribute or property which can be acquired, transferred, and expended' <www.oed.com> accessed 2 October 2019.

[4] See Food and Agriculture Organization of the United Nations (UNFAO), 'Wood Energy' <www.fao.org/forestry/energy/en/> accessed 20 July 2020.

[5] The (renewed) interest in renewable energy technologies only arose during the 1973–74 oil embargo, when several technically viable solutions emerged; see B Sørensen, 'A History of Renewable Energy Technology' (1991) 19 Energy Policy 8, 10.

a service?[6] Do the processes of extracting and selling a tradable product, typical of the energy sector, contain aspects of both?[7] And, with regard to non-discrimination, do we consider two particular energy products as like or unlike each other? Can natural gas be equated with liquefied natural gas (LNG), and fossil fuels with renewables?[8] Similar questions arise in relation to electricity generated by different means (eg from coal or through solar power).[9] The first part of this chapter will therefore seek to provide a better understanding of energy (and terms often used interchangeably with 'energy' like 'natural resources' and 'raw materials').

In the discipline of energy statistics, the term 'energy' traditionally refers to heat and power generated through combustion, as in the burning of fossil fuels[10]. However, the term is also commonly used more broadly to refer to fuels, gas and electricity. 'Energy commodities' would therefore seem to be a more precise way of referring to heat and power and the means used to produce them.[11]

In this book, in keeping with common usage, 'energy' will refer to the means by which the power and heat we rely on in our everyday lives are generated, and will cover both renewable, clean and non-renewable sources. It should also be pointed out that this study focuses on energy as a commodity tradable across international borders and for commercial

---

[6] This is pertinent to the divide between the General Agreement on Tariffs and Trade 1994, Marrakesh Agreement Establishing the World Trade Organization, Annex 1A (signed 15 April 1994) 1867 UNTS 187, 33 ILM 1153 (1994) (GATT) and the General Agreement on Trade in Services, Marrakesh Agreement Establishing the World Trade Organization, Annex 1B (signed 15 April 1994) 1869 UNTS 183, 33 ILM 1167 (1994) (GATS).

[7] WTO, Council for Trade in Services – Energy Services – Background Note by the Secretariat' (9 September 1998) Doc S/C/W/52, 1–4.

[8] On the likeness of LNG and pipeline transport services and service suppliers, see *EU – Energy Package*, panel report, paras 7.1398–7.1439. See also DC Crosby, 'Energy Discrimination and International Rules in Hard Times: What's New This Time Around, and What Can Be Done?' (2012) Journal of World Energy Law and Business 1, 9.

[9] These are complex questions, to which the answers may vary depending on the case and context. See Crosby (n 8) 9–11, pointing out that this debate remains open since some process and production matters can differ widely yet result in the same end product (electricity). On cross-border electricity trade generally, see also T Cottier and I Espa (eds), *International Trade in Sustainable Electricity* (CUP 2017).

[10] The second law of thermodynamics imposes limitations on the capacity of a system to transfer energy by performing work, since some of the system's energy might necessarily be consumed in the form of heat instead; see eg RL Lehrman, 'Energy Is Not the Ability to Do Work' (1973) 11 Physics Teacher 15, 15–18.

[11] OECD, IEA and Eurostat, *Energy Statistics Manual* (OECD/IEA 2005) 17.

gain. It will follow the classifications of energy sources developed by the International Energy Agency (IEA) in cooperation with the United Nations Statistics Division (UNSD),[12] while also making use of the more elaborate definitions and explanations found in the data and reports of several international organizations dealing in detail with the topic, such as the United Nations Conference on Trade and Development (UNCTAD), the Organisation for Economic Co-operation and Development (OECD), Eurostat, the World Trade Organization and the World Customs Organization (WCO).

Below we focus in particular on primary and secondary energy commodities and the related concepts of natural resources and raw materials. These four expressions closely interrelate and overlap with each other and are frequently confused through being used interchangeably. We will also consider another, parallel divide, namely between non-renewable, renewable and clean energy.

1.2.1   Natural Resources and Raw Materials

Natural resources are relevant to energy, as they ultimately are to all goods, whose production depends on them or can be traced back to them in one way or another.[13] Natural resources are the starting point of all products we use, and thus for all forms of energy, too. Taking this line of argument to the extreme, all goods could thus logically be labelled natural resources. However, it would be unworkable to do so and of little practical use.[14] Although manufactured goods are made of natural resources, we generally do not consider them as such in themselves. The opposing argument would be to say that the resources we use are truly natural resources only when they are found in their natural state, in other words not yet harvested or processed for economic gain.[15] Yet this view, too, falls short, since natural resources do have to be processed in one way or another before they can be used for economic gain, as when they are traded, for example. It follows that the dividing line between what is to be considered a natural resource and what not will at times be subjective and have to be decided on a case-by-case basis.[16] There is no strict legal definition of the term 'natural resources', although the

---

[12] See <www.iea.org> and <https://unstats.un.org/> accessed 20 July 2020.
[13] WTO, *World Trade Report 2010: Trade in Natural Resources* (WTO 2010) 46.
[14] ibid.
[15] ibid.
[16] ibid.

definition of the related term 'biological diversity' can help to give us a better understanding of what natural resources are.[17] According to Article 2.1 of the 1992 UN Convention on Biological Diversity, this term refers to 'the variability among living organisms from all sources including, inter alia, terrestrial, marine and other aquatic ecosystems and the ecological complexes of which they are part'. Beyerlin and Holzer correctly submit that the expression 'natural resources' is broader than 'biological diversity', as natural resources cover 'not only the total of living organisms, in particular the variety of species of flora and fauna, but also non-living organisms which are not part of "biological diversity", such as water, soil and land'.[18] Dam-de Jong cites definitions that describe natural resources as 'those materials and substances of a place which can be used to sustain life or for economic exploitation' and as 'any material from nature having potential economic value or providing for the sustenance of life'.[19]

The World Trade Organization's *World Trade Report 2010*, whose focus was trade in natural resources, likewise adopts a perspective oriented towards consumption and economic gain, describing natural resources in terms of their tradability as 'stocks of material that exist in the natural environment that are both scarce and economically useful in production or consumption, either in their raw state or after a minimal amount of processing'.[20] The main product groups the WTO identifies as natural resources are fish, forestry products, fuels, ores and other minerals, and non-ferrous metals (the last two groups are jointly referred to as mining products).[21] Similarly, the OECD describes natural resources as 'natural assets (raw materials) occurring in nature that can be used for

---

[17] Several authors have attempted to define the concept; see U Beyerlin and V Holzer, 'Conservation of Natural Resources' in R Wolfrum (ed), *Max Planck Encyclopedia of Public International Law* (OUP 2008) online edn.

[18] ibid.

[19] D Dam-de Jong, *International Law and Governance of Natural Resources in Conflict and Post-Conflict Situations* (CUP 2015) 24. The definitions are respectively from the Oxford English Dictionary Online and *Black's Law Dictionary*, which also describes them as 'raw or unprocessed material[s] that [are] extracted or harvested and also require very little processing before consumption'. See also N Schrijver, *Development without Destruction: The UN and Global Resource Management* (UN Intellectual History Project Series, Indiana University Press 2010) 2–3.

[20] The WTO further explains that 'scarce and economically useful' means that the natural resources 'must command a positive price in markets and can be used either as inputs in production or directly as a source of utility to consumers'; see *World Trade Report 2010* (n 13) 46, 71.

[21] ibid.

economic production or consumption', and divides them into four categories: mineral and energy resources, soil resources, water resources and biological resources.[22]

The *World Trade Report 2010* further lists several key features of natural resources (note that the list is merely illustrative and not final):

a) **Exhaustibility**. Natural resources tend not to increase in quantity or otherwise renew themselves over a very short, economically relevant time.[23] Any amount consumed today will reduce their availability tomorrow. An obvious example is energy products like crude petroleum.[24] The term exhaustible is thus often understood as being synonymous with non-renewable. However, even renewable sources such as fish stocks and forests may be considered exhaustible if they are over-exploited.[25]

b) **Uneven distribution across countries**. A given state may have abundant natural resources within its territory, while others may have limited domestic supplies and be overly dependent on imports. When it comes to crude oil, for instance, 90 per cent of the world's proven reserves are located in a mere fifteen countries.[26]

c) **Negative externalities**. An externality (as understood in economics) occurs when the actions of one economic agent indirectly affect other agents in a positive or negative way.[27] Natural resource economics focuses mainly on the negative externalities arising from the extraction and consumption of natural resources (such as the pollution that accompanies the extraction of crude oil, or CO_2 emissions resulting from the burning of fossil fuels).

d) **Dominance of natural resources**. Certain natural resources occupy a dominant position in some national economies, causing those countries to become overly dependent on the export of a particular

---

[22] 'The naturally occurring assets that provide use benefits through the provision of raw materials and energy used in economic activity (or that may provide such benefits one day) and that are subject primarily to quantitative depletion through human use.' OECD, Glossary of Statistical Terms, Glossary of Environment Statistics, Studies in Methods, Series F, No 67, (UN 1997) <http://stats.oecd.org/glossary/detail.asp?ID=1740> accessed 20 July 2020.

[23] *World Trade Report 2010* (n 13) 47.

[24] ibid. Many petroleum experts believe that world oil production has reached, or soon will reach, its maximum point, known as 'peak oil'. Once oil production peaks, it is believed that future supplies will become more and more difficult to obtain.

[25] *World Trade Report 2010* (n 13) 47.

[26] ibid 48.

[27] ibid 49.

product.[28] This is especially true of countries that are rich in fuels and mining products.

e) **Volatility**. Natural resources are often marked by occasional (and extreme) price volatility, which may be a consequence of their uneven distribution and dominance in national economies. Price volatility is especially characteristic of fuels, minerals and metals, which, as strategic commodities, are susceptible to trading crises.[29]

It should be mentioned that several leading GATT/WTO cases have addressed the question of whether or not a particular commodity could be considered as an *exhaustible* natural resource in the sense of paragraph (g) of Article XX GATT ('General Exceptions'). Clean air, for instance, as well as sea turtles, have been regarded as exhaustible natural resources subject to this provision.[30]

Another concept worth discussing in this context is raw materials, often also referred to as feedstock, unprocessed materials or primary commodities. Raw materials are basic materials derived from natural resources and can be considered a subcategory of natural resources that includes a number of cultivated agricultural products such as raw hides and crude animal and vegetable materials.[31] In contrast to the notion of biological diversity, which chiefly covers living organisms, raw materials consist rather of non-living organisms that can be traded for economic gain.[32] In its *World Trade Report 2010*, the WTO arrived at a workable definition of natural resources, including raw materials, by combining three product groups drawn from the WTO's *International Trade Statistics* and having regard to revision 3 of the UN Standard International Trade Classification (SITC),[33] the result of which is summarized in Table 1.1.

---

[28] ibid 48.

[29] Such as those in the 1970s between the United States and the members of OPEC when the latter announced a trade embargo in 1973; see D Yergin, *The Prize: The Epic Quest for Oil, Money and Power* (Free Press 2008) ch 29 ('The Oil Weapon').

[30] *US – Shrimp*, Appellate Body (AB) report, para 134; *US – Gasoline*, panel report, para 6.37.

[31] *World Trade Report 2010* (n 13) 204.

[32] See UN Convention on Biological Diversity, art 2.1.

[33] *World Trade Report 2010* (n 13) 204, 207–208; and United Nations Standard International Trade Classification (UNSITC) Revision 3, Statistical Papers Series M, No 34/Rev 3, ST/ESA/STAT/SER.M/34/Rev 3 (2006). Note that non-monetary gold is excluded from natural resources altogether. It is listed under 'commodities not elsewhere specified' in the UNSITC, but is not recorded systematically by all countries in the *World Trade Report 2010*.

Table 1.1 *Natural resources, including raw materials*

1. Fish (SITC division 03)
2. Raw materials (SITC divisions 21, 23, 24, 25, 26, 29)
of which:
- Raw hides, skins and fur skins (21)
- Crude rubber (23)
- Cork and wood (24)
- Wood pulp (25)
- Textile fibres (26)
- Crude animal and vegetable materials, not elsewhere specified (29)
3. Fuels and mining products (SITC section 3 and divisions 27, 28, 68)
of which:
- Ores and other minerals (SITC divisions 27, 28)
- Fuels (SITC section 3)
- Non-ferrous metals (SITC division 68)

Source: WTO, *World Trade Report 2010*, 204.

It should be noted that raw materials have featured prominently in WTO dispute settlement, for example in the much-discussed *China – Raw Materials* and *China – Rare Earths* cases.[34] That said, the titles used in the disputes do not always correspond to WTO's own categorization. Here, the materials involved – cobalt, copper, tungsten ... – belong rather to the natural resources subgroup 'fuels and mining products' than to the sub-group 'raw materials'.[35]

1.2.2   Primary and Secondary Energy Commodities

Primary and secondary energy commodities are considered subcategories of natural resources.

According to the classifications developed by the IEA and the UNSD, energy commodities can be divided between these two groups. Primary energy commodities are either extracted or captured directly from natural resources.[36] The main examples of primary energy commodities are crude

---

[34] See *China – Raw Materials*, panel and AB reports; *China – Export Duties on Raw Materials*, WT/DS508/6, 14 October 2016 (panel established, but not yet composed) (*China – Raw Materials II*); *China – Rare Earths*, panel and AB reports.

[35] See Table 1.1.

[36] *Energy Statistics Manual* (n 11) 18.

petroleum, coal and natural gas. Secondary energy commodities are not extracted directly from natural resources but produced from primary energy commodities, as is the case with electricity generated from burning a fossil fuel (a primary energy commodity). Electricity and heat can be produced from both primary and secondary energy commodities. The former happens when primary heat is captured directly from natural resources (eg the sun through solar panels), and the latter when we burn gas to generate heat that is then used to generate electricity. Put differently, primary energy commodities represent new energy entering the system, while secondary commodities have already been transformed within the system.[37]

1.2.3   Non-Renewable, Renewable and Clean Energy

Another important distinction to make is between non-renewable, renewable and clean energy sources. It is unrelated to the primary or secondary nature of the energy commodity. Rather, it points to the extent to which a source of energy can be depleted and considered clean.[38] In the extreme, it could be argued that all energy sources are 'renewable', though some (eg crude petroleum) over very long periods of time. In common usage, however, we apply a human timescale and consider fossil fuels (and fuels manufactured from fossil fuels) such as coal, crude petroleum and natural gas as non-renewable (and thus exhaustible).[39] These products are derived from the biomass formed in the geological past, and they deplete over time through use.[40] Renewable energy commodities, on the other hand, are drawn from constantly available flows of solar and gravitational energy. An example is electricity generated from sources such as wind, sunshine, biomass, biofuels, waste, tidal forces and hydro energy. Table 1.2, based partly on UNSD information, gives an overview of primary and secondary energy commodities and their renewable or non-renewable nature.[41]

The concept of clean energy calls for additional comment in relation to the distinction between non-renewable and renewable energy sources. The term 'clean energy' is often used interchangeably with 'renewable energy'. However, it would be precarious to assume they are identical.

---

[37] S Øvergaard, 'Definition of Primary and Secondary Energy' (September 2008) Oslo Group on Energy Statistics Issue Paper.
[38] 'Clean' here means free of, or with only minimal, CO_2 emissions.
[39] On exhaustibility, see Section 1.2.1.
[40] *Energy Statistics Manual* (n 11) 19.
[41] United Nations Statistics Division, 'Manual of the Basic Set of Environmental Statistics of the FDES 2013' (28 December 2016) 12.

Table 1.2 *Primary and secondary energy products*

	Primary energy products	Secondary energy products
Non-renewable	■ Hard coal ■ Brown coal ■ Peat ■ Oil shale ■ Natural gas ■ Conventional crude oil ■ Liquefied natural gas (LNG) ■ Additives and oxygenates ■ Industrial waste ■ Municipal waste (in part) ■ Nuclear heat ■ Heat from chemical processes	■ Coal products ■ Peat products ■ Refinery feedstocks ■ Oil products ■ Electricity and heat from combusted fuels of fossil origin ■ Electricity derived from heat from chemical processes and nuclear heat ■ Any other product derived from primary/secondary non-renewable energy products
Renewable	■ Biofuels (except charcoal) ■ Municipal waste (in part) ■ Heat from renewable sources, except from combusted biofuels ■ Electricity from renewable sources, except from geothermal, solar thermal or combusted biofuels	■ Charcoal ■ Electricity and heat from combusted biofuels ■ Electricity from geothermal and solar thermal ■ Any other products derived from primary/secondary renewable products

When we refer to clean energy, we generally refer to energy sources free of, or with only very little, CO_2 emissions or other negative environmental externalities.[42] Yet, what we consider as clean may in fact be non-renewable. Take the rather controversial example of nuclear energy. While nuclear energy, which uses uranium in its generation process, is considered a non-renewable source of energy, it has zero carbon emissions in its generation cycle. Therefore, many consider it to be a clean source of energy, at least as far as CO_2 emissions are concerned.[43] For this

[42] See UN Sustainable Development Goals, Goal 7, Targets and Indicators <https://sdgs.un.org/goals/goal7> accessed 19 March 2021.
[43] JB Eisen and others, *Energy, Economics and the Environment: Cases and Materials* (4th edn, Foundation Press 2015) 395–96.

reason, many governments include nuclear power in their plans for a cleaner energy mix and emission reductions.[44] However, the emphasis placed on zero carbon emissions overlooks the waste generated by the cycle of nuclear energy production, which, for obvious reasons, cannot be qualified as clean, but is rather a negative environmental externality.[45]

Nor is energy that is derived from renewable sources necessarily clean. This becomes painfully clear when one considers the complete life cycle of certain renewable energy sources. Biofuels like biodiesel and bioethanol, for example, which are derived from specially grown crops, are regarded as renewable, yet they can hardly be considered as clean, as the cultivation of those crops displaces food crops and encroaches on lands used for other purposes, such as wetlands, forests and peatlands.[46] The entire production cycle for biofuels is energy-intensive. It is for these reasons that biofuel production has to comply with high sustainability criteria in the European Union, for instance.[47]

1.3   The Relevance of International Trade Rules for Energy

1.3.1   The World Trade Organization, Energy Charter Treaty and Preferential Trade Agreements

All goods and services that are traded across borders are subject to the rules governing international trade. Consequently, such rules become applicable to energy, insofar as it can be regarded as a good or a service. Crude petroleum, for example, is amongst the most traded commodities in the world.[48] Three corpuses of international trade rules are relevant to trade in energy: (1) the laws of the World Trade Organization; (2) the framework of the Energy Charter Treaty; and (3) the energy-relevant disciplines in preferential trade agreements. The rationale behind each of these frameworks will be briefly explained below.

---

[44] IEA, 'Nuclear Power in a Clean Energy System' (2019) 6–7.

[45] For a discussion of the catastrophes in Chernobyl, Ukraine and Fukushima, Japan, see Eisen (n 43) 407–12.

[46] See eg SK Chauhan and A Shukla, 'Environmental Impacts of Production of Biodiesel and Its Use in Transportation Sector' in MA Dos Santos Bernardes (ed), *Environmental Impact of Biofuels* (In Tech Open 2011) 5ff.

[47] Directive (EU) 2018/2001 of the European Parliament and of the Council of 11 December 2018 on the promotion of the use of energy from renewable sources (recast) [2018] OJ L328/82.

[48] After a slowdown between 2014 and 2016, the petroleum market picked up again between 2017 and 2019 due to a rise in energy prices; see WTO, *World Trade Statistical Review* (WTO 2019) 58.

1.3.1.1   The World Trade Organization

The General Agreement on Tariffs and Trade (GATT) 1947 was originally set up to regulate trade in goods. The World Trade Organization took on a broader set of responsibilities in 1995, adding services (GATS), investment measures (TRIMs) and intellectual property (TRIPs) to its portfolio.[49] Overall, the WTO has an economic focus, as it governs trade relations amongst its members (164 at present).[50] The objective of the organization is to promote free trade by reducing tariffs and other trade barriers and eliminating discriminatory treatment in international trade relations.[51] It serves as an institutional forum for trade negotiations and as such addresses various trade-related issues. Besides setting international trade rules, it also administers a specialized dispute settlement system.

The core aim of the WTO system is to achieve non-discrimination in trade, which is reflected in Articles I and III GATT relating respectively to most-favoured-nation (MFN) treatment and national treatment (NT).[52] MFN prohibits members from discriminating against foreign products, while NT requires that foreign products should be given the same treatment as like domestic products once they have entered the domestic market.[53] Import tariffs on foreign products are the only form of trade protectionism allowed by GATT.[54] Although not illegal under WTO rules, tariffs are nevertheless considered a serious obstacle to trade, and

---

[49] GATS (n 6); Agreement on Trade-Related Investment Measures, Marrakesh Agreement Establishing the World Trade Organization, Annex 1A (signed 15 April 1994) 1868 UNTS 186; Agreement on Trade-Related Aspects of Intellectual Property Rights, Marrakesh Agreement Establishing the World Trade Organization, Annex 1C (signed 15 April 1994) 1869 UNTS 299, 33 ILM 1197 (1994). All three instruments can be found in WTO, *The Legal Texts: The Results of the Uruguay Round of Multilateral Trade Negotiations* (WTO 1999).

[50] Marrakesh Agreement Establishing the World Trade Organization (signed 15 April 1994) 1867 UNTS 154, 33 ILM 1144 (1994), art II:1: 'The WTO shall provide the common institutional framework for the conduct of trade relations among its Members in matters related to the agreements and associated legal instruments included in the Annexes to this Agreement.'

[51] ibid, preamble.

[52] See B Hoekman and PC Mavroidis, *The World Trade Organization: Law, Economics and Politics* (Routledge 2007) 16.

[53] ibid.

[54] Reference is made in its preamble to the signatory states 'being desirous of contributing to [their] objectives by entering into reciprocal and mutually advantageous arrangements directed to the substantial reduction of tariffs and other barriers to trade and to the elimination of discriminatory treatment in international commerce'. See also Hoekman and Mavroidis (n 52) 15.

the WTO's long-term objective is therefore to ensure that they are as low as possible, or, preferably, eliminated altogether. Once a member has agreed to a particular tariff in order to obtain market access for a product, it must grant all other members the same tariff. In other words, it must be applied without discrimination to all foreign like products imported into the domestic market. This is the essence of the MFN principle applicable under WTO rules.[55] Although there are no WTO disciplines specific to energy, the MFN principle, as part of WTO rules, applies to trade in energy and services, just as it does to any other goods and services.[56]

1.3.1.2 The Energy Charter Treaty

The Energy Charter Treaty (ECT) is a specialized instrument covering trade and investment in the energy sector.[57] It originated as separate branch of the GATT/WTO regime in the early 1990s and continues to operate as a (semi-)distinct treaty-based system today.[58] In a certain sense, the ECT is a development of GATT specifically conceived for energy. The two frameworks – WTO and ECT – partially overlap with each other in respect of their constituent elements, objectives and membership. At the same time, each has distinct functions and mechanisms, which do not always accord with each other.[59]

The ECT was signed in Lisbon in 1994, just before the establishment of the WTO in 1995. It entered into force in 1998.[60] In 2017, the Energy Charter Secretariat launched official discussions to modernize and renegotiate the treaty.[61] The ECT's treaty regime is similar to that of the WTO, but besides regulating energy trade also deals extensively with investment and contains an environmental protocol.[62] In essence, the

---

[55] GATT (n 6) art I.

[56] See Chapter 2.

[57] Energy Charter Treaty (adopted 17 December 1994, entered into force 16 April 1998) 2080 UNTS 100.

[58] The ECT was inaugurated in 1994, just before the establishment of the WTO in 1995. The term semi-distinct is used here because the treaties are partly connected in substance through the ECT's Articles 4 ('Non-Derogation from WTO Agreement') and 32 ('Transitional Arrangements'). The ECT incorporates WTO rules by reference and can be seen as a 'stepping-stone' treaty for countries on the path to WTO accession.

[59] See Chapter 4.

[60] ECT (n 57).

[61] See ECT, 'Approved Topics for the Modernization of the Energy Charter Treaty' <www .energychartertreaty.org/modernisation-of-the-treaty/> accessed 20 July 2020.

[62] Investment and dispute settlement are regulated in parts III and V of the ECT. The ECT also incorporates a Protocol on Energy Efficiency and Related Environmental Aspects (PEEREA).

ECT came into being as an alternative to concluding an energy-specific agreement within the GATT/WTO framework after the end of the Cold War. Its trade provisions draw largely on those of GATT, but are better adapted to the needs of energy trade. For instance, they include detailed definitions of energy products ('Energy Materials and Products') and services ('Economic Activity in the Energy Sector') and, in Article 7 on transit, include gas pipelines as a means of transport.[63] The purpose of the treaty is to provide a stable and predictable framework, based on GATT/WTO rules, for trade in energy materials, products and energy-related equipment.[64]

1.3.1.3   Preferential Trade Agreements

The third corpus of energy trade rules is found in preferential trade agreements (PTAs) between countries concluded on a bilateral or multi-lateral basis. Countries that conclude PTAs are also likely to be members of the WTO, whose membership extends to around 75 per cent of all countries in the world. One reason for countries entering into PTAs is to promote deeper integration among themselves.[65] Article XXIV GATT allows WTO members to enter into customs unions and free trade areas.[66] While the conclusion of a PTA may appear contrary to the principle of MFN treatment, it can be justified by the argument that it promotes closer cooperation amongst its members and thereby furthers the WTO's goal of eliminating trade barriers (provided it does not backtrack on commitments made by WTO members). In addition to trade rules, PTAs often contain rules on investment protection and cover matters that go beyond trade in the narrow sense, such as trade and sustainable development. Several PTAs contain chapters specifically on energy trade, alongside their chapters on trade in goods and services generally.[67]

---

[63] Energy materials and products are listed in Annex EM of ECT; Article 1(5) ECT defines 'Economic Activity in the Energy Sector'; and Article 7(10)(b) ECT classifies gas pipelines as 'Energy Transport Facilities'.

[64] Energy Charter Secretariat, *Applicable Trade Provisions of the Energy Charter Treaty* (ECS 2003); Energy Charter Secretariat, *Trade in Energy: WTO Rules Applying under the Energy Charter Treaty* (ECS 2001).

[65] See H Gnutzmann and A Gnutzmann-Mkrtchyan, 'The Silent Success of Customs Unions' (2019) 52 Canadian Journal of Economics 178.

[66] GATT (n 6) art XXIV ('Territorial Application – Frontier Traffic – Customs Unions and Free Trade Areas').

[67] See Chapter 4, Section 4.3.

1.3.2   The Legal Classification of Energy Resources in International Trade Law

1.3.2.1   The World Trade Organization

Article II GATT ('Schedules of Concessions') provides that members 'shall accord to the commerce of the other contracting parties treatment no less favourable than that provided for in the appropriate Part of the appropriate Schedule annexed to this Agreement'.[68] Members' schedules of concessions record specific tariff commitments for particular products (so-called tariff lines).[69] Schedules consists of four parts covering, successively, MFN tariffs (part I), preferential concessions (part II), concessions on non-tariff measures (part III) and specific commitments on agricultural products (part IV).[70] Each member has its own national schedule, which is annexed either to the results of the different rounds of trade negotiations or to the member's accession protocol.[71] Schedules form an integral part of the WTO agreements.[72]

Tariff lines may be bound or unbound (free).[73] If they are bound, a member cannot apply *ad valorem* (specific or composite) duties above the level agreed in the schedule (the so-called tariff ceiling),[74] but may, if it wishes, use applied rates, which can be lower than the bound rates.[75] If a tariff is free or unbound, the member did not make any commitment to bind its tariff in the earlier round of multilateral trade negotiations, be it due to the sensitivity of the issue or because other members did not request a tariff binding.[76] In theory, this means that a member can impose a customs duty as high as it pleases on the imported good. That

---

[68]   See GATT (n 6) art II:1(a).

[69]   See WTO, 'Goods Schedules – Member's Commitments' <www.wto.org/english/tra top_e/schedules_e/goods_schedules_e.htm> accessed 20 July 2020.

[70]   ibid. Not all schedules contain all parts; this depends on the negotiation round in question.

[71]   See A Hoda, *Tariff Negotiations and Renegotiations under the GATT and the WTO: Procedures and Practices* (CUP 2002) 111.

[72]   GATT (n 6) art II:7. This is not the case, however, when a member is part of a customs union, in which case the members of the union share a common schedule. See P van den Bossche and W Zdouc, *The Law and Policy of the World Trade Organization* (4th edn, CUP 2017) 420.

[73]   See C Mavroidis, G Bermann and M Wu, *The Law of the World Trade Organization* (West 2010) 85ff.

[74]   ibid, also 89 (*ad valorem* duties imply that a certain percentage of the product's value is levied).

[75]   ibid.

[76]   MJ Trebilcock and R Howse, *The Regulation of International Trade* (3rd edn, Routledge 2002) 679.

said, WTO members are not allowed to agree in their schedules on treatment that is inconsistent with basic GATT obligations; hence, both bound and unbound tariff lines must comply with Articles I (MFN) and III (NT), except where the Article III:8 exclusions apply.[77]

Concerning trade in primary energy commodities, it is generally in the interests of importing members to keep import tariffs as low as possible, so as to secure their national energy supplies. For this reason, import tariffs are actually not the greatest concern in relation to energy trade barriers. To the contrary, export duties are a much bigger concern and one of the idiosyncrasies of international energy trade (GATT's so-called market access bias).[78]

Virtually all goods that are traded globally, including energy products and commodities, are registered and classified in the Harmonised Commodity Description and Coding System (HS) managed and regularly updated by the World Customs Organization (WCO).[79] Products are classified as raw materials, semi-finished goods or finished products. For instance, mineral fuels and oils are grouped under chapter 27.[80] They are then broken down into different types of oils and fuels (eg crude vs refined) in subcategories 2701–2716.[81] Derivative products are classified under their respective HS codes; for example, crude oil has the code 2709.00).[82] At present, energy goods, whether renewable or non-renewable, and energy-related equipment are found in different parts of the HS Convention. They are found in different product categories and are not grouped under one heading dedicated to energy. For traditional energy resources, the main categories of importance in the HS Convention are nuclear energy (HS headings 26.16, ex28.44 and ex28.45), coal, natural gas, petroleum and petroleum products, electrical energy as a good (HS chapter 27) and wood as a fuel (eg logs, HS headings ex44.01 and 44.02).[83]

---

[77] This was first touched on by the GATT panel *US – Sugar*, GATT panel report, para 5.2, and later confirmed in *EC – Bananas III*, AB report, para 154. See also Mavroidis, Bermann and Wu (n 73) 101.

[78] See Chapter 5, Section 5.2.

[79] HS Convention (n 1). The current version dates from 2017.

[80] HS Convention (n 1) ch 27 ('Mineral fuels, mineral oils and products of their distillation; bituminous substances; mineral waxes').

[81] ibid. See heading 27.10 ('Petroleum oils and oils obtained from bituminous minerals, other than crude; preparations not elsewhere specified or included, containing by weight 70% or more of petroleum oils or of oils obtained from bituminous minerals, these oils being the basic constituents of the preparations; waste oils').

[82] ibid.

[83] ibid.

Services relating to the energy sector are classified together in the WTO, and will be discussed in Chapter 3.

1.3.2.2 The Energy Charter Treaty

As a specialized instrument covering trade and investment in the energy sector, the Energy Charter Treaty went a step further and, pursuant to Article 1(4) and (4bis), brought together energy materials and products in Annexes EM I and EM II and energy-related equipment in Annexes EQ I and EQ II. Although still based on the HS Convention and the Combined Nomenclature of the European Union, the classification has the advantage of serving as a common listing for ease of reference. The categories listed have been refined over time and will likely change further in keeping with technological advancements.[84] ECT Annexes EM cover energy products and materials but are limited to the fossil fuels discussed in relation to the HS Convention and the WTO above. They do not expressly cover biofuels or other renewable forms of energy, nor do they differentiate between electrical energy generated by clean and not-so-clean means (the production processes and methods are not considered). Annex EQI of the ECT contains an extensive list of energy-related equipment, such as steel pipes, tubes, etc.

Energy services are also covered in the Energy Charter Treaty under the term 'Economic Activity in the Energy Sector' (as defined in Article 1(5)), which covers the exploration, extraction, refining, production, storage, land transport, transmission, distribution, trade, marketing, or sale of energy materials and products. According to Annex NI, the category of fuel wood is excluded for the definition of economic activity in the energy sector.

1.3.3 When Do International Trade Rules Kick In?

The logical follow-up question, after explaining the classification of energy in international trade law, is at what stage do these resources become subject to its disciplines. One of the problems posed by fixing the point at which international trade rules start to apply to trade in natural

---

[84] It was last updated in 2014; see ECS, 'Correspondence Table: Changes made by the Energy Charter Conference to Annexes EM I, NI and EQ I pursuant to changes of the Harmonized Commodity Description and Coding System, (HS) of the World Customs Organisation' (18 June 2014) <www.energychartertreaty.org/fileadmin/Correspondence_table_-_HS_nomenclature.pdf> accessed 19 March 2021.

resources is the difficulty of determining when a natural resource ceases to be in its natural state and becomes a tradable good. We will examine this question by testing it against the rules of the multilateral trading framework (WTO). As already pointed out, all goods incorporate natural resources, are dependent upon them when manufactured, or can be traced back to them in one way or another.[85] Although the WTO regulates the terms of trade between its members, it is not primarily concerned with the ownership of, and sovereignty over, the products that are being traded.[86] With respect to natural resources, of which primary energy commodities are a part, the general international law principle of Permanent Sovereignty over Natural Resources (PSNR) is the authoritative rule. PSNR is relevant for those energy resources located within the territory of a state and over which it can assert its sovereignty. Typically, these are non-renewable, primary energy commodities such as fossil fuels. The principle is thus relevant to coal, crude oil and natural gas in all possible forms in the territory of a state, including its territorial waters and exclusive economic zones.[87]

It is important to highlight the interplay between these principles and international trade law. PSNR protects the right of states and their peoples to dispose freely of their natural resources.[88] It is enshrined in various political declarations from the decolonization era onwards, the most important of which is the 1962 United Nationals General Assembly (UNGA) Resolution 1803 (XVII). The resolution consists of eight clauses, the second of which states as follows:

> The exploration, development and disposition of such resources, as well as the import of the foreign capital required for these purposes, should be in conformity with the rules and conditions which the peoples and nations freely consider to be necessary or desirable with regard to the authorization, restriction or prohibition of such activities.

---

[85] *World Trade Report 2010* (n 13) 46.

[86] *World Trade Report 2010* (n 13) 177.

[87] However, one can also include the sources of renewable energy within a state's territory, such as water reserves, wind and sun, to the extent that they qualify as both an energy commodity and a natural resource. See eg Y Lifshitz, 'Gone with the Wind? The Potential Tragedy of the Common Wind' (2010) 28 UCLA Journal of Environmental Law and Policy 435.

[88] See generally N Schrijver, 'Natural Resources, Permanent Sovereignty over' in R Wolfrum (ed), *The Max Planck Encyclopedia of Public International Law* (OUP 2008) online edn; SR Chowdhury, 'Permanent Sovereignty over Natural Resources' in K Hossain and SR Chowdhury (eds), *Permanent Sovereignty over Natural Resources in International Law* (Frances Pinter 1984).

The strict obligation upon states and international organizations to respect the sovereignty of peoples and nations over their natural wealth and resources mirrors this right of nations to explore their natural resources.[89] Other issues covered in the resolution include nationalization and expropriation, foreign investment and the sharing of profits.

The emergence of the PSNR principle, through several interrelated UNGA resolutions in the 1950s and 1960s, is directly connected to the struggle of colonial peoples for self-determination.[90] Understandably, the principle relates to both the general notion of sovereignty (ie a state's supreme authority within a territory) and the state's competence to exercise that authority over the territory (and thus its natural resources), whether by legislative, executive or judicial means.[91] In the years following the 1962 UNGA resolution, developing countries actively pursued the implementation of the principle through cooperation in the field of natural resources, which led to the first UN Conference on Trade and Development (UNCTAD).[92] During 1960s, the core ideas underlying the PSNR principle's core ideas were materialized in the establishment of the

---

[89] Schrijver (n 88).

[90] See Audiovisual Library of International Law, 'Permanent Sovereignty over Natural Resources: General Assembly resolution 1803 (XVII)' <http://legal.un.org/avl/ha/ga_1803/ga_1803.html> accessed 20 July 2020 ('Procedural History'); Schrijver (n 88); UNGA Res 523 (VI) (12 January 1952); UNGA Res 626 (VII) (21 December 1952). Following the nationalization by Iran of the Anglo-Iranian Oil Company in 1952 (see *Anglo-Iranian Oil Co Case (UK v Iran)* 1952 ICJ Rep 93), Uruguay submitted a draft resolution recommending that member states recognize 'the right of each country to nationalize and freely exploit its natural wealth, as an essential factor of independence' (UNGA 'Economic Development of Under-Developed Countries: Uruguay: Draft Resolution', preamble, para 5). Although in the final text the phrase 'nationalize and freely exploit' was replaced with 'freely use and exploit' (UNGA Res 626 (VII) para 1), it remains known as the 'nationalization' resolution. International Covenant on Civil and Political Rights (adopted 19 December 1966, entered into force 23 March 1976, rectified 25 October 1977) 999 UNTS 171, 1057 UNTS 407, art 1.2: 'All peoples may, for their own ends, freely dispose of their natural wealth and resources without prejudice to any obligations arising out of international economic cooperation, based upon the principle of mutual benefit, and international law. In no case may a people be deprived of its own means of subsistence.' See also SM Schwebel, 'The Story of the UN's Declaration on Permanent Sovereignty over Natural Resources' (1963) 49 American Bar Association Journal 463.

[91] BH Oxman, 'Jurisdiction' and S Besson, 'Sovereignty' in R Wolfrum (ed), *The Max Planck Encyclopedia of Public International Law* (OUP 2008) online edn.

[92] Schrijver (n 88). General Principle Three recommended by UNCTAD affirmed that '[e]very country has the sovereign right freely to trade with other countries, and freely to dispose of its natural resources in the interest of the economic development and well-being of its own people'. Proceedings of the United Nations Conference on Trade and Development (Geneva, 23 March–16 June 1964) UN Doc E/CONF.46/141, vol I, 10.

Organization of Oil Exporting Countries (OPEC). Then came oil crises of the 1970s, with a US oil embargo and a wave of (fossil fuel) nationalizations in developing countries.[93] Although PSNR was a product of the decolonization era and was mainly invoked by developing countries, the ideas it articulates are relevant for all states today, whether former colonies or not.

Despite its importance, PSNR is a controversial issue in international law, not least because of the way it came into being.[94] As Schrijver explains, the creation of international law through resolutions of political organs, rather than through traditional means such as treaty-making or evolving state practices, is a cause of dissension.[95] The principle has nonetheless been incorporated in several treaties, such as the International Covenant on Civil and Political Rights,[96] and has been invoked in international arbitrations and judicial decisions.[97]

PSNR's relevance to international trade rules lies in part in its ability to help us determine when these rules start applying with respect to trade in natural resources (and the state in which those resources must exist). Although the preamble of the GATT 1947 lists as one of its objectives 'developing the full use of the resources of the world', there is no provision in WTO law that deals directly with the issue of their ownership.[98] The reason for this is that international trade rules are designed mainly to regulate access to *markets* for producers, but not necessarily to facilitate access to *supplies* for consumers. With respect to trade in natural resources, it would seem to be generally accepted that WTO rules kick in only after the natural resources in question have been extracted and are tradable for economic gain.[99] This implies that once a natural resource has been extracted, WTO Members must abide by the rules governing multilateral trade in respect of that resource. States consequently tend to

---

[93] eg Libya's oil industry between 1971 and 1974; see Schrijver (n 88) paras 4, 12.

[94] Schrijver (n 88) para 1.

[95] ibid, para 3.

[96] International Covenant on Civil and Political Rights (n 90) arts 1.2, 47.

[97] Notably in the ICJ case *Armed Activities on the Territory of the Congo (Democratic Republic of the Congo v Uganda)* [2005] ICJ Rep 168. See also *Texaco Overseas Petroleum Co v Government of the Libyan Arab Republic (Award of 19 January 1977)* (1978) 17 ILM 1.

[98] In the preamble to the WTO Agreement this was modified to 'allowing for the optimal use of the world's resources in accordance with the objective of sustainable development'.

[99] cf *Canada – Herring*, GATT panel report, paras 3.31–3.32. The parties and the panel apparently agreed that GATT rules did not apply to measures restricting the catching of fish (ie upstream measures), but only to measures restricting the export of fish once caught.

consider that according to PSNR, what they do with their natural resources before extraction is a policy matter over which they have exclusive sovereignty.

It is worth noting, however, that nowhere in WTO texts is it stated in black and white when trade rules start governing natural resources. Moreover, there are exceptions to the generally accepted position described above, as when the Appellate Body in *US – Softwood Lumber IV* determined that trees are tradable goods before they are harvested.[100]

1.4 The Challenge of Changing Energy Markets: Decentralization, Decarbonization and Energy Security

Global energy markets have changed radically over the past century. Their centre of gravity has shifted with the opening-up of markets (decentralization), the growing emphasis on climate change mitigation (decarbonization) and a growing focus on energy security in the context of increasingly globalized geopolitics. Changing markets and technological developments over recent decades have shed new light on the increasingly present trilemma of decentralization, decarbonization and energy security. These three concepts are inherently intertwined and, in turn, they greatly impact cross-border energy regulation. This transformation is key to understanding the evolving nature of energy regulation in the WTO. The following section will briefly highlight each of these developments, which will be leitmotifs throughout this book.

---

[100] See *World Trade Report 2010* (n 13) 162:

> Nevertheless, in some circumstances, WTO rules may have implications for products in their 'natural' state. For example, in the *US – Softwood Lumber IV* dispute, one of the issues that arose was whether the provision by provincial governments of harvesting rights for timber at less than adequate remuneration could be considered a subsidy within the meaning of the Agreement on Subsidies and Countervailing Measures (SCM Agreement). More specifically, the question was whether the term 'goods' as used in Article 1.1 of the SCM Agreement could include 'trees before they are harvested, that is, standing timber attached to the land (but severable from it) and incapable of being traded as such' (Appellate Body Report, *US – Softwood Lumber IV*, para 57). Ultimately, it was decided that there was no basis to exclude 'tangible items – such as standing, unfelled trees – that are not both tradable as such and subject to tariff classification' from the scope of the term 'goods' in Article 1.1 (Appellate Body Report, *US – Softwood Lumber IV*, para 67).

1.4.1   Decentralization: Opening-Up a Vertically Integrated Sector

Industrialization coincided with the discovery of the first oil wells in the mid-nineteenth century, whence a constant supply of energy in the form of fossil fuels quickly became indispensable for our economies to function. As the production of fossil fuels was inherently connected to the geographical location of the available supplies, the energy sector developed in a vertically integrated manner, being closely tied to the state and its political economy and (energy) security interests.[101] Consequently, the electricity and gas industries, for example, have traditionally been either completely state-owned or operated by vertically integrated companies, often operating as a natural monopoly owing to the sunk costs connected to energy production and infrastructure investments.[102] The vertical integration of the sector usually implied that a state-owned company was in charge of exploring the fossil fuel, transporting it (including managing infrastructures) and selling energy to both industrial and household consumers. Little to no competition existed.[103] There was limited cross-border energy trade; besides, it was not explicitly regulated by international law but rather took the form of ad hoc contractual arrangements.

In many parts of the world the energy sector remains vertically integrated even today. This is especially true of the major energy producing and exporting countries, such as those that are members of OPEC or the Gas Exporting Countries Forum (GECF). Some of these countries, however, are gradually opening up their markets to foreign players (eg the Saudi state-backed oil company Saudi Aramco).[104] Other countries or regions (notably the United States and the European Union) have been gradually decentralizing their energy markets since around the 1980s, in some instances vigorously pursuing strategies to introduce a large degree of competition into the market.[105] Originating in the United Kingdom

---

[101] See A-A Marhold, 'The Interplay between Liberalization and Decabornization in the European Internal Energy Market for Electricity' in K Mathis and BR Huber (eds), *Energy Law and Economics* (Springer 2018) 63–64.

[102] See generally T Daintith and L Hancher, *Energy Strategy in Europe: The Legal Framework* (De Gruyter 1986).

[103] Marhold (n 101) 64.

[104] See J Jolly and J Ambrose, 'Saudi Aramco Becomes Most Valuable Listed Company in History' *The Guardian* (11 December 2019).

[105] President Reagan first aggressively attempted to deregulate the US energy sector, after which President Carter tried to correct that policy's failings, but both approaches proved unsuccessful; see JP Tomain and RD Cudahy, *Energy Law in a Nutshell* (3rd edn, West Academic 2016) 86–90. In the late 1980s, the Federal Energy Regulatory Commission

and the United States, the breaking-up of vertically integrated energy markets and introduction of competition represented an extension of the benefits of competition policies pursued in others areas of the economy.[106] The ultimate beneficiary of competition is the consumer: when companies are allowed to compete fairly with one another, efficiency is improved, quality and innovation increases, prices decrease and consumers have a wider range of choices.[107]

A prime example of a major economy decentralizing and liberalizing its energy market is the European Union, which will be studied in Chapter 5. The EU's internal energy market (IEM) is the result of having gradually introduced more coherent, EU-wide energy legislation and policy from the 1980s onwards. Since the Treaty of Lisbon, EU energy law and policy is based on Article 194 TFEU.[108] Its overall objective is to achieve a fully interconnected EU energy market, which at the same time is liberalized and decarbonized and can guarantee energy security of supply for Europe's citizens (yet another reference to the interconnectedness of these concepts). Through IEM legislation, two policy goals are merged into one: realization of the EU single market through the extension of competition policy to the energy market on the one hand, and the introduction of a coherent, Union-wide and increasingly integrated energy policy on the other.[109]

The move towards the liberalization and interconnection of network industries reached the energy sector later than it did most other goods and services sectors in the EU, due to the aforementioned link between the energy sector and the state and its industrial policy. Historically, there were few cross-border interconnections between electricity grids and gas pipelines across Europe. The extension of the European single market to the energy sector was realized progressively by breaking up vertically

---

(FERC) started to restructure the electric utility industry, while leaving the 'natural monopoly' elements of the US energy sector heavily regulated; see Eisen (n 43) 13–14.

[106] M Pollitt, 'The Role of Energy Policy in Energy Transitions: Lessons from the Energy Liberalisation Era' (2012) 50 Energy Policy 128.

[107] See eg European Commission, 'Why Is Competition Policy Important for Consumers?' <http://ec.europa.eu/competition/consumers/why_en.html> accessed 20 July 2020.

[108] Energy is a competence shared between the Union and its member states. This implies that both the EU and its member states may legislate in this area, as long as they respect the 'duty of sincere cooperation' flowing from Article 4(3) TEU. In short, each must refrain from acting against the interests of the other.

[109] For an overview, see AA Marhold, 'EU Regulatory Private Law in the Energy Community: The Synergy between the CEER and the ECRB in Facilitating Customer Protection' in M Cremona and HW Micklitz (eds), *Private Law in the External Relations of the EU* (OUP 2016) 249, 250–54.

integrated energy companies and introducing competition to the electricity and gas industries, where possible.[110] During the first phase of implementation of the IEM in the late 1980s, cross-border transit opened for both electricity and gas, meaning that EU member states could no longer oppose transnational flows of energy. In the early 2000s, the Second Energy Package introduced the legal unbundling of the gas and electricity sectors, requiring, as a minimum, that the production and sale of energy should be legally separated from energy transmission and distribution activities.[111]

By 2009, the Commission had adopted the Third Energy Package, which included the Electricity and Gas Directives 2009/72/EC and 2009/73/EC introducing a most stringent form of unbundling known as ownership unbundling (OU). This form of unbundling prescribed the complete separation of a company's electricity generation and sales activity from its transmission network activity, requiring the two activities to be operated by strictly independent entities.[112] Although all EU member states had to achieve full OU in both their electricity and gas sectors, it has proven difficult to realize in a timely manner in all member states, and milder forms of unbundling are still accepted (as is the case with the gas sector in Hungary, Croatia and Lithuania).[113]

The example of decentralization of the energy sector in the EU highlights how international trade law can both enable and constrain some of the processes related to these policies, which will be discussed in Chapters 5 and 7. These can be summarized as (1) the uneven global distribution of

---

[110] Pollitt (n 106) provides a historical overview of the 'liberalization era' and its effects. Liberalization is characterized by its attention to competition, and unbundling is one of the means used to that end. Privatization is often an effect of liberalization but not always. Liberalization remains incomplete partly because governments are afraid to lose control or the power to cross-subsidize.

[111] For electricity, Directive 2003/54/EC of the European Parliament and of the Council of 26 June 2003, concerning common rules for the internal market in electricity and repealing Directive 96/92/EC [2003] OJ L176/37; for gas, Directive 2003/55/EC of the European Parliament and of the Council of 26 June 2003, concerning common rules for the internal market in natural gas and repealing Directive 98/30/EC [2003] OJ L176/57.

[112] Directive 2009/72/EC of the European Parliament and of the Council of 13 July 2009 concerning common rules for the internal market in electricity and repealing Directive 2003/54/ EC [2009] OJ L211/69; Directive 2009/73/EC of the European Parliament and of the Council of 13 July 2009 concerning common rules for the internal market in natural gas and repealing Directive 2003/ 55 [2009] OJ L211/94. Ownership unbundling is dealt with in Article 9(1) and third-party access in Article 32 of the directives. See A Johnston and G Block, *EU Energy Law* (OUP 2012) 73; see also Case C-439/06 *Citiworks AG* (CJEU, 22 May 2008).

[113] See *EU – Energy Package*, panel report, paras 7.372–7.377.

fossil fuels and the import bias of current trade rules, including access to energy supplies; (2) challenges regarding market access and dissecting different parts of the industry; and (3) the accompanying issues of the entry of foreign players into the market and potential security concerns.

1.4.2 Decarbonization: Understanding the Shift from Fossil Fuels to Clean Energy

The emergence of decentralized markets is directly linked to the second major shift: the decarbonization of the energy sector. The complex but inevitable move towards decarbonizing energy markets is happening against the backdrop of climate change mitigation. Decarbonization can be described as shifting the markets away from CO_2 production and reducing emissions into the atmosphere. The grid must be physically and technologically able to absorb and transmit renewable and clean energy and one of the ways of achieving this is by decentralizing the system.[114] Renewable energy technologies began to enter the market in the 1970s, coinciding with the rise of global environmental movements.[115] During the following decade, the expression 'sustainable development', coined in the 1987 Brundtland report, entered policy debates.[116] In 1992, the Rio Declaration on Environment and Development proved to be a milestone in emphasizing the need to eliminate unsustainable patterns of production and establishing the notion of sustainable development.

There are two important dimensions to decarbonization of the energy sector. One is the scale-up of clean and renewable energy technologies into the grid. The second is the move away from subsidizing fossil fuels, a practice that is still prevalent in many, if not most, countries around the world, being connected to the vertical integration at the roots of the sector and to states' industrial policies.[117] There is a close link between decarbonizing the energy sector, climate change mitigation and

---

[114] Marhold (n 110) 66–67.

[115] Sørensen (n 5) 10.

[116] The most commonly used definition of sustainable development is that found in the Brundtland report: 'Sustainable development is development that meets the needs of the present without compromising the ability of future generations to meet their own needs'; Brundtland Commission, *Report of the World Commission on Environment and Development: Our Common Future* (OUP 1987).

[117] See the work of HB Asmelash, eg *Phasing Out Fossil Fuel Subsidies in the G20: Progress, Challenges, and Ways Forward* (ICTSD 2017).

sustainable development, as decarbonization is vital to climate change mitigation, which in turn is essential to achieving a sustainable future.

Today, there are two legal and policy frameworks crucial to decarbonization. First, there are the 2030 Sustainable Development Goals (UN SDGs),[118] several of which – such as Goals 7 (affordable and clean energy), 11 (sustainable cities and communities) and 13 (climate action) – are directly relevant to energy and sustainable development. Second, over recent decades, climate change mitigation efforts have been made, and the accompanying legal and policy instruments developed, under the United Nations Framework Convention on Climate Change Mitigation (UNFCCC). The parties to the 2015 Paris Agreement (197 in total) have to submit nationally determined contributions (NDCs), concrete action plans on how they intend to contribute to climate change mitigation.[119] Decarbonization of the energy sector plays a significant role here. For instance, the Paris Agreement requires parties to 'make finance flows consistent with a pathway towards low greenhouse gas emissions and climate-resilient development', which can be read as a shift away from fossil fuels.[120]

The requirement to decarbonize the energy sector poses several challenges for international trade rules, especially in the area of subsidies disciplines. Chapter 6 will examine what current trade rules can do to constrain harmful fossil fuel subsidies.

1.4.3   Changing Markets and the Eternal Quest for Energy Security

Societies have, to varying various degrees, been confronted with their energy interdependency for centuries. However, our reliance on energy systems becomes all the more complex in an increasingly globalized world and an era of great technological and digital advancement. It is therefore evident that energy security guaranteeing the proper and reliable operation of those systems is of vital importance to our economies (and arguably also to national security).

The term 'energy security' is often used both in the context of international relations and in international and national policy debates

---

[118] United Nations 2030 Sustainable Development Goals, <www.un.org/sustainabledevelop ment/sustainable-development-goals/> accessed 20 July 2020.

[119] United Nations Framework Convention on Climate Change (UNFCCC) UN Doc FCCC/CP/2015/L.9/Rev.1, Decision 1/CP.21 (adopted 12 December 2015) (COP21 Paris Agreement).

[120] ibid, art 2(c).

on a country's energy supply. However, its precise meaning is not always clear. Indeed, energy security has been described as a 'multifaceted and amorphous concept'.[121] Our inability to define energy security in detail, despite being familiar with it, is no coincidence. This is because in international relations literature and policy what exactly the term covers has for decades been the subject of debate.[122] Although many questions around the concept of energy security remain unanswered, we can conclude that it is commonly understood to refer to (1) a reliable supply that is (2) accessible and (3) affordable. Moreover, it is crucial to add that the supply should be sustainable in the long term (hence, sustainability is in this sense inseparable from energy security). It follows that, to guarantee energy security, energy markets must be resilient to shocks (such as, in the European context, the recurrent gas transit disputes between Russia and the Ukraine that took place in the 2000s and directly affected a great number of EU member states).[123]

In the context of international trade law, WTO panels and the Appellate Body have been confronted with the issue of energy security in several recent disputes and been required to consider its meaning.[124] In *India – Solar Cells*, the Appellate Body examined India's invocation of the Article XX(j) GATT exception (authorization of measures essential to the acquisition or distribution of products in general or local short supply) in the light of the overall objectives of energy security.[125] And in *EU – Energy Package*, the panel had to decide on energy security-related issues, first when considering Europe's 'gas diversification supply' criterion within the context of gas infrastructure incentives, and second when ruling on the EU's security of supply assessment carried out as part of the third-country certification process for pipeline transport services. Chapter 7 will return to these cases when discussing the interplay between international trade law and energy security.

---

[121] Johnston and Block (n 112) 233.
[122] See Chapter 7, Section 7.2.
[123] See generally AA Marhold, 'The Russo-Ukrainian Gas Disputes, the Energy Charter Treaty and the Kremlin Proposal: Is There Light at the End of the Gas Pipe?' (2011) 3 Oil, Gas & Energy Law Journal <www.ogel.org>.
[124] See A-A Marhold, 'Externalising Europe's Energy Policy in EU Free Trade Agreements: A Cognitive Dissonance between Promoting Sustainable Development and Ensuring Security of Supply?' (2019) 3 Europe and the World 1, 5–6.
[125] *India – Solar Cells*, AB report, para 34ff.

1.5 Conclusion

This introductory chapter has introduced the reader to the legal conceptualization of energy and relevant related concepts such as natural resources and raw materials. It distinguished between primary and secondary energy commodities, and sought to clarify the often-confused concepts of renewable and clean energy. It also described three international trade law regimes relevant to the regulation of cross-border energy trade – the World Trade Organization, the Energy Charter Treaty and preferential trade agreements – and provided an overview of the legal classification of energy products and services. In addition, it pondered the important question of when international trade rules become applicable to energy resources, and how this connects with the principle of sovereignty over natural resources. We can conclude that international trade rules start to apply to energy resources the moment they are extracted from the ground and made tradable for economic gain, though that starting point is not always clear-cut.

Last but not least, the chapter introduced three themes that will run throughout the book and demonstrate the challenges international trade rules pose to cross-border energy regulation. They are the move towards (1) decentralisation and (2) decarbonization of the energy market, and (3) the ongoing quest for energy security. The three are interlinked and cannot be viewed in isolation from one another. Under their influence, global energy markets have already undergone considerable transformations and will continue to transform for decades to come. The decentralization and opening-up of energy markets raises challenges of access to supplies and to energy markets. In addition, it causes industry unbundling, meaning that features of the industry's previous vertical integration (eg the often-complicated divide between goods and services) have to be fitted into categories not traditionally foreseen by international trade rules. Decarbonization of energy markets in the name of climate change mitigation and sustainable development is one of the greatest tasks that lies ahead for the energy sector. Yet the scale-up of renewable and clean energy in the grid is constrained by WTO subsidies disciplines, and the current legal toolkit does not provide enough incentives to curtail environmentally harmful fossil fuel subsidies. Energy security, finally, will remain an ever-growing concern amid increasingly connected markets and the digitization of the energy sector. This book will address questions relating to the provision made in international trade rules for realizing these objectives.

2

Energy's Place in International Trade Law History

2.1 Introduction

This chapter discusses the controversial status of energy in the multilateral trading forum from the initial years of GATT 1947 until today.[1] To better comprehend why energy continues to be a contentious topic in international trade law, one has to study its historical legal context. Through an investigation of crucial time periods, the chapter will highlight the significant shifts that have occurred with respect to the regulation of energy trade under GATT/WTO rules. By first examining commitments taken up in early GATT schedules, it will demonstrate that while energy was covered *de jure*, it was mostly dealt with outside the system. One thing is certain: the treatment of energy in the multilateral trading forum has been politically sensitive, uncertain and widely disputed since GATT's inception in 1947.[2] The chapter then analyses the factors – such as the oil crises in the 1970s and the emergence of new types of energy, as well as the inevitable climate change and sustainable development debate – that have attracted increased attention to energy in the multilateral trading system. The chapter will also cover developments following the establishment of the WTO in 1995, such as the accession of major energy producers and the inclusion of energy services as a negotiation topic in the Doha Round. Last but not least, it will touch upon the rising number of energy disputes before the WTO.

2.2 From GATT 1947 to the Tokyo Round: Energy In or Out?

2.2.1 GATT's Early Years: Energy on the Back Burner

In the run-up to GATT 1947, internationally traded energy was practically limited to the fossil fuels of coal, petroleum and gasoline. It is widely

---

[1] This chapter focuses solely on the GATT/WTO forum, as Chapter 4 covers the Energy Charter Treaty and relevant preferential trade arrangements.

[2] See UNCTAD, 'Trade Agreements, Petroleum and Energy Policies' (2000) UNCTAD/ITCD/TSB/9, 15 (UNCTAD report).

believed that trade in energy for a long time was, at least de facto, excluded from GATT/WTO coverage. The misunderstanding that the GATT/WTO legal framework would not apply to trade in energy can be traced back to the initial negotiations of GATT 1947. There seemed to be a generally accepted conviction that the founding members negotiated a gentlemen's agreement to keep petrol trade outside the scope of GATT.[3] This was the result of a combination of several factors:

1) First of all, the main petroleum producing and exporting countries, such as Saudi Arabia, the United Arab Emirates (UAE), Iran, Iraq, the Russian Federation and Venezuela, were not original parties to GATT 1947.[4] Although the original parties did include several significant energy producing countries, such as Indonesia, Kuwait and Nigeria, other leading energy trading countries were absent. Consequently, GATT did not regulate their trade with other nations, including their trade in energy.

2) During the early stages of GATT negotiations after the Second World War, the world's major petroleum fields were located in the Middle East, North America and South East Asia, and were controlled by a handful of transnational (often state-owned) corporations originating from the United States, the United Kingdom, the Netherlands and France.[5] Known as the Seven Sisters,[6] this reigning cartel dominated the petroleum industry from the 1940s until the 1970s and generally

---

[3] SL Sakmar, 'Bringing Energy Trade into the WTO: The Historical Context, Current Status, and Potential Implications for the Middle East Region' (2008) 18 Indiana International and Comparative Law Review 89. See also M Gibbs, 'Energy Services, Energy Policies and the Doha Agenda' in UNCTAD, *Energy and Environmental Services: Negotiating Objectives and Development Priorities* (2003) UNCTAD/DITC/TNCD/2003/3, 4: 'Issues related to petroleum and energy were not discussed in the GATT forum. It is said that a "gentleman's agreement" existed among the major trading countries not to discuss petroleum issues in the GATT, for fear that the strategic nature of petroleum trade and the importance of security concerns in respect of petroleum products would "politicize" the debate'; MG Desta, 'The Organization of Petroleum Exporting Countries, the World Trade Organization, and Regional Trade Agreements' (2003) 37 Journal of World Trade 523, 529: 'The role of the multilateral trading system on international trade in petroleum products has not always been clear. . . . However, there is not any GATT provision which exempts petroleum trade from its coverage. In principle, trade in petroleum products among GATT/WTO Members is governed by the rules of the trading system just like other products. But, de facto, there was a virtual exclusion of petroleum trade.'

[4] Some of these countries, such as Saudi Arabia and Venezuela, would later become members of the Organization of Petroleum Exporting Countries (OPEC).

[5] UNCTAD report (n 2) 14.

[6] The Seven Sisters were originally Royal Dutch Shell, Exxon, Gulf, Texaco, BP, Mobil and Standard Oil of California (now Chevron). For background on this, see D Yergin, *The*

preferred to settle its business outside the global trading system. For the greater part, it was composed of vertically integrated companies that dealt with everything from producing, shipping and refining petroleum products to marketing and selling them all over the world.[7] Trade in energy did occur, but mainly between public entities. The energy cartel eliminated competition on petrol, and energy trade liberalization was not a priority. Most petroleum fields were located in colonies or former colonies of Western states, which, given the sensitivity of control over natural resources, wanted to avoid creating political tensions.

3) As a strategic commodity, energy was a particularly sensitive topic in (post-colonial) international trade, which was clearly reflected in the history of the 1962 UNGA Resolution 'Permanent Sovereignty over Natural Resources'.[8] This resolution reiterated that it was up to resource-owning states to decide how to deplete their natural resources and at what rate. Resolution 1803 was adopted at a time when many resource-endowed states started renationalizing their energy resources, but it seems no less relevant today.[9] This also partially explains why it remains hard for some countries to fully open up their energy markets, if at all. There are undoubtedly advantages in governments allowing international competition and access to their natural resources and energy markets.[10] For instance, the importation of foreign technical expertise benefits financially from competition. Yet governments may have an interest in retaining control over their natural resources for security reasons, making them reluctant to liberalize trade in energy.[11]

4) Another reason for energy talks being on the back burner during GATT negotiations might have been that energy was considered

---

Prize: The Epic Quest for Oil, Money and Power (Free Press 2008) ch 21 ('The Postwar Petroleum Order').

[7] Sakmar (n 3) 91.

[8] UNGA Res 1803 (XVII) 'Permanent Sovereignty over Natural Resources' (18 December 1962). See Chapter 1, Section 1.3.3.

[9] On the international law principle of sovereignty over natural resources and the history of the UNGA resolution generally, see NJ Schrijver, 'Natural Resources, Permanent Sovereignty over' in R Wolfrum (ed), *Max Planck Encyclopedia of Public International Law* (OUP 2008) online edn; L Wernar, *Blood Oil: Tyrants, Violence and the Rules that Run the World* (OUP 2016) 194ff, explaining which countries have incorporated this resolution into their national constitutions. See also Chapter 5.

[10] See Chapter 5 on decentralization of the energy sector.

[11] Energy Charter Secretariat, *Trade in Energy: WTO Rules Applying under the Energy Charter Treaty* (ECS 2001) 12.

a scarce product not intended to be covered by GATT. This may be explained by GATT's traditional focus: trade rules were tailored to facilitate market access for producers (referred to as GATT's 'market access bias') and were focussed on manufactured products in unlimited supply, whereas fossil fuels are by definition a strategic finite commodity.[12] GATT's purpose was to restrain *import* barriers, whereas it is mostly *export* barriers that are of concern in energy trade.

With all this in mind, one can conclude that there was a state practice in place that caused energy issues to be largely ignored in the GATT forum for several decades. This led to the widespread perception that GATT/ WTO rules were not relevant for the regulation of cross-border energy trade.[13] Scholars and reports questioned the extent to which the rules applied to energy goods and services, if at all.[14] A 1998 background note by the WTO Secretariat strikingly concluded that 'energy goods have been treated for a long time as being outside the scope of the reach of GATT rules, by relying on the general exception relating to the conservation of exhaustible natural resources (Article XX(g) GATT) and on the national security exception (Article XXI GATT)'.[15]

It remains unclear, however, on what sources scholars were basing themselves when concluding that there was a gentlemen's agreement to keep petrol trade out of GATT.[16] The UNCTAD report on energy trade

---

[12] Y Selivanova, 'Managing the Patchwork of Agreements in Trade and Investment' in A Goldthau and JM Witte (eds), *Global Energy Governance: The New Rules of the Game* (Brookings Institution Press 2010) 53.

[13] See UNCTAD report (n 2) 15; authors and works cited in n 3.

[14] Desta, 'Organization' (n 3).

[15] WTO Council for Trade in Services, 'Energy Services: Background Note by the Secretariat' (9 September 1998) Doc S/C/W/52.

[16] See generally Sakmar (n 3); Gibbs (n 3); BA Garner, *Garner's Dictionary of Legal Usage* (OUP 2011) 389, under 'gentlemen's agreement'. The *Max Planck Encyclopedia of Public International Law* (n 9) classifies gentlemen's agreements under non-binding agreements: no legal rights and obligations can be derived from them. They are non-legally enforceable agreements, 'secured by the good faith and honour of the parties' (*Black's Law Dictionary*). By contrast, the *Encyclopedia of the United Nations and International Agreements* defines 'gentlemen's agreement' as an '[i]nternational term for an international agreement made orally rather than in writing, yet fully valid legally'; see EJ Osmańczyk, *Encyclopedia of the United Nations and International Agreements* (A Mango ed, 3rd edn, Routledge 2003) vol 2, 792. Lauterpacht points out that elementary textbooks on the law of contract explain that gentlemen's agreements are binding 'in honour only' and not intended to 'create legal obligations'; see E Lauterpacht 'Gentleman's Agreements' in W Flume (ed) *Internationales Recht und Wirtschaftsordnung: Festschrift für F. A. Mann zum 70. Geburtstag am 11. August 1977* (Beck 1977) 381.

and WTO rules issued in 2000 certainly stated that 'issues related to petroleum and energy were not discussed in the GATT forum',[17] and some even argue that there was an agreement 'to continue excluding issues relating to trade and price of crude oil from the GATT framework', but no proof of this seems to exist.[18] It is conceivable that, for the underlying reasons mentioned above, founding GATT parties were of the opinion that the energy sector was too volatile and politically sensitive for them to undertake hard legal commitments.[19] If anything, this was merely an expression of state practice already in place with respect to global petrol trade: energy importing countries used a zero per cent import tariff on petrol and did not have much room to negotiate on its price even if they so desired.

2.2.2   Tariffs on Petrol Taken Up in Members' Schedules since GATT 1947

While cross-border energy trade was mostly dealt with outside the multilateral trading system, nothing in the provisions of GATT 1947 or the WTO agreements stipulates that trade in energy is excluded from its scope. Quite to the contrary: tariffs on fossil fuels, such as crude oil, were in fact present in members' schedules of concessions (Article II(a) GATT 1947) from the start. Though to varying degrees, most founding members of GATT committed themselves in one way or another to trade in fossil fuels from 1947 onwards. On this basis, one can argue that the mere fact that categories of fossil fuels were taken up in members' schedules disproves the existence of an illusive gentlemen's agreement. Although, by their very nature, gentlemen's agreements do not necessarily have to be in writing, the fact that negotiated tariffs appeared in members' schedules in black and white from the start certainly helps to prove that energy was covered by GATT from its inception.

Prior to the establishment of GATT in 1947, members negotiated tariffs for their initial schedules of concessions. This resulted in the

---

[17] UNCTAD report (n 2) 4.

[18] W-C Shih, 'Energy Security, GATT/WTO, and Regional Agreements' (2009) 49 Natural Resources Law Journal 433, 439.

[19] Gautier mentions that gentlemen's agreements have been described in legal writings since the beginning of the twentieth century; see P Gautier, 'Non-Binding Agreements' in R Wolfrum (ed), *The Max Planck Encyclopedia of Public International Law* (OUP 2008) online edn. See also MG Desta, 'The GATT/WTO System and International Trade in Petroleum: An Overview' (2003) 21 Journal of Energy and Natural Resources Law 385.

1947 Geneva schedules, which were annexed to GATT 1947 and formed an integral part of the agreement.[20] The Geneva schedules predated the codifications of the HS Convention, as that convention entered into force only in 1988, after being transformed from the Customs Union Council. Therefore, members' products were based on their national classification schedules.

It is interesting to note that fossil fuel categories were included in parts I and II of many members' Geneva schedules from the beginning. Several founding members of GATT 1947 even committed themselves to binding tariffs on energy products and fossil fuels: France, for instance, had quite detailed schedules on (crude) petroleum and gasoline with related tariff bindings.[21] The country made even more detailed tariff bindings on behalf of all of its African protectorates (the French Union) at the time, grouped under French Equatorial Africa in the schedule.[22] Generally speaking, France's tariffs on petroleum ranged from 5 to 20 per cent in the Geneva schedules. Original GATT 1947 members Chile, Cuba and Canada also committed themselves to tariffs on crude petroleum: Chile set a tariff of 6.56 per cent for petroleum,[23] while Cuba bound its tariff to 0.31 per cent for petroleum and 0.96 per cent for gasoline.[24] Canada set its tariff on crude petroleum at 1 per cent.[25]

Subsequently, a second group of members decided to keep their petrol tariffs 'unbound', categorized as 'free' in their schedules, implying they could impose as high a tariff as they wished on fossil fuels. These were countries like the United States (hitherto kept unbound),

---

[20] The Geneva schedules contain the tariff bindings of the twenty-three founding members of GATT. They are recorded in the United Nations Treaty Series (UNTS) vols 56–61 (1950). For an overview of individual members' schedules, see (1950) 55 UNTS 306. See also A Hoda, *Tariff Negotiations and Renegotiations under the GATT and the WTO: Procedures and Practices* (CUP 2002) 111.

[21] France's fossil fuel commitments, as recorded in Schedule XI, sec A (metropolitan territory), pt I (MFN tariffs), were as follows: natural petroleum, crude, and assimilated products (French tariff item 332A) 18 per cent, petroleum gas (French tariff item 333) 3 per cent, gasoline (French tariff item 334A) 18 per cent, 59 UNTS 39–41 (1950).

[22] With respect to French Equatorial Africa, petroleum tariffs were usually around 10 per cent, see Gabon tariff item 146, 59 UNTS 217–19 (1950); French West Africa, refined and extra-refined petroleum (FWA tariff item 201) 10 per cent, 59 UNTS 220 (1950); French Somali Coast, petroleum (French Somali Coast tariff item ex 196) free (unbound), 59 UNTS 223 (1950).

[23] See Schedule VII, pt I, MFN tariffs, Chilean tariff item 43 I (petroleum: crude, for furnace or boilers, metric ton G), 58 UNTS 17 (1950).

[24] See Schedule IX, pt II, preferential tariffs, Cuban tariff 6-A and 7-A, 58 UNTS 49 (1950).

[25] See Schedule V, pt I MFN tariffs, Canadian tariff 267b, 57 UNTS 132 (1950).

Burma,[26] Brazil, the Benelux countries and Australia.[27] Yet, these GATT parties did acknowledge and classify the fossil fuel categories in their respective schedules. The 1930 US Tariff Act listed a category numbered 1733 comprising 'Oils, mineral: Petroleum, topped crude, fuel, or refined, and all distillates obtained from petroleum, including kerosene, benzine, naphtha, gasoline, paraffin, and paraffin oil.'[28]

Finally, a third group of GATT founding members completely omitted to categorize fossil fuels in their respective schedules. These were Great Britain and its former colonies, India, China (one of the original members of GATT), Ceylon and Czechoslovakia.

The 1947 Geneva schedules reveal several noteworthy facts. First, it can be inferred that, with respect to tariff bindings on fossil fuels, there were essentially three categories of GATT members:

a) those who scheduled fossil fuels and actually made tariff bindings on them;
b) those who scheduled fossil fuels in their protocols, but left the tariffs on these products free and unbound; and
c) those who did not recognize or include trade in fossil fuels in their schedules at all.

About half of the members who did include fossil fuels in their schedules of concessions left tariffs on these products unbound. The fact remains, however, that the majority of these members did include fossil fuels as a category in their schedules from the outset. This means that they did not altogether exclude trade in fossil fuels from GATT, since they acknowledged their significance in international trade and even listed them in their schedules in detail, potentially with a view to future developments in the field. More importantly, several members even made tariff bindings on fossil fuels.[29] These might have had more of a symbolic value, as a country's energy policy tends to be dominated by its energy needs, but they were nevertheless present.[30]

It is true that several prominent countries, including Great Britain, omitted the category of fossil fuels from their schedules altogether. This certainly suggests that for these GATT founding members energy trade

---

[26] Burma had a tariff of 25 per cent on 'all sorts of mineral oils'; see Schedule IV, pt I, MFN tariffs, Burma tariff item 158, 57 UNTS 92 (1950).

[27] See Schedule II, pt I, MFN tariffs, 56 UNTS 128–29 (1950).

[28] See Schedule XX, pt I, MFN tariffs, 61 UNTS 183 (1950).

[29] France, Canada, Cuba and Chile; see nn 21–25 and accompanying text.

[30] UNCTAD report (n 2) 5, 15.

indeed took place outside the GATT legal framework.[31] It may be assumed that Great Britain, home to two of the Seven Sisters (BP and the half-British Royal Dutch Shell), was not keen on making extensive commitments under GATT in the area of fossil fuel trade. Additionally, it can be seen from members' practices over the decades that no energy disputes reached dispute settlement under GATT, even though some prominent global conflicts concerning energy, including its trade-related aspects, did occur (the most striking example being the 1970s oil crises).[32] Generally, though, such disputes were solved in the political arena, outside the GATT framework.

In contrast to Great Britain, the United States and the Netherlands (as part of the Benelux countries), home to the other five of the Seven Sisters (Esso, Exxon, Gulf, Chevron and Texaco), did include the category of fossil fuels in their respective schedules, even though tariffs were left unbound. The fact that around half of the founding parties maintained unbound tariffs was a sign that the issue was too sensitive for them to make 'hard' commitments on energy, nor could it be assumed that other members requested any bindings on fossil fuels from those parties. Desta, for instance, argued that for decades the tariff schedules of GATT members hardly contained tariff reductions and binding commitments with regard to petroleum trade, because all members applied zero duties at the outset.[33] Applied tariffs on petroleum have generally remained low until now; countries may raise them to any level if they are unbound (which is the case, for instance, with the United States and Japan, which have kept their tariffs unbound). On the other hand, there is no denying that a substantial number of GATT founding parties did take up tariff bindings on fossil fuels.

---

[31] It should be mentioned, however, that WTO members nonetheless remained subject to the disciplines of Articles I, III and XI GATT; they could only avoid making tariff concessions.

[32] Yergin (n 6) ch 29 ('The Oil Weapon'). It may be noted that one of the early trade disputes under GATT did actually deal with an energy product, although not petrol. In 1954, the United States complained against Belgium, claiming that intensified quota restrictions on imported coal violated Article XI GATT ('General Elimination of Quantitative Restrictions'). However, the case was withdrawn before discussion and settled on the basis of increased quotas (SR 9/42 (4 March 1955)). Coal has been classified in GATT schedules since the beginning (1947) and is still the most used energy product today. See Belgian Import Restrictions on Coal, US, L/258 (26 October 1954), as mentioned in RE Hudec, *The GATT Legal System and World Trade Diplomacy* (2nd edn, Butterworth 1990) 285.

[33] Desta, 'Organization' (n 3) 531–32.

2.3 From Tokyo to Uruguay: Fuelling Concerns about Energy

In the decades following the conclusion of GATT, the global political and energy trading landscape changed significantly, and energy discussions entered the GATT forum. There are two possible explanations for this. First, from the Tokyo Round onwards, there was a growing awareness of emergent renewable energy entering the global market. Second, restrictive business practices by GATT parties in possession of strategic natural resources, which culminated in the 1970s oil crises, became an issue that the forum found increasingly hard to ignore. It seems that, over time, GATT parties acknowledged that some matters pertaining to energy, and fossil fuel trade in particular (such as dual-pricing practices), were too important and needed clarification.[34] It was during this period that the seeds of the WTO's challenges on energy regulation, which will be covered in Chapters 5, 6 and 7 (decentralization, decarbonization and energy security), were sown.

This section will address several factors that have contributed to the change in the debate and discuss the extent of their effects. Broadly speaking, these are:

- developments in the negotiation of tariffs on energy products and related services in the main rounds of trade negotiations;[35]
- selected members' concessions on energy in their GATT/WTO accession instruments;
- external factors fuelling the energy debate, such as the establishment of OPEC, oil producing and exporting countries joining GATT/WTO, the 1970s oil crisis and attendant dual-pricing practices and the climate change debate; and
- the establishment of the WTO in 1995, leading to new agreements relevant to energy regulation, including the GATS.

2.3.1 Tokyo Round (1973–79): OPEC and the Oil Crises

One possible way to understand the evolution of the energy debate in GATT is to take a closer look at tariff reductions and commitments in

---

[34] See generally Chapter 6; see also A-A Marhold, 'Fossil Fuel Subsidy Reform in the WTO: Options for Constraining Dual Pricing in the Multilateral Trading System' (2017) ICTSD Climate and Energy Issue Paper 2017-040.

[35] These are, in chronological order, conclusion of GATT 1947, the Kennedy Round (1964–67), the Tokyo Round (1973–79), the Uruguay Round (1986–94) and the Doha Round (2011–present) (the 'minor' rounds between the conclusion of the GATT and the Kennedy Round are not included in this list).

members' concessions during the negotiation rounds that followed GATT 1947. There was no clear evaluation of tariff reductions and other commitments during the first five GATT rounds of trade negotiations prior to the Tokyo Round (the Geneva Tariff Conference (1947), Annecy Tariff Conference (1949), Torquay Tariff Conference (1950–51), Geneva Tariff Conference (1956) and Dillion Round (Geneva II) (1960–61)).[36] The GATT Secretariat started to conduct studies on tariff lines only from the Kennedy Round (1964–67) onwards.[37] However, no significant new developments in the energy field occurred during the Kennedy Round. It was only during the Tokyo Round of multilateral Trade Negotiations (1973–79) that energy trade started to fuel concerns.[38]

With the Tokyo Round (1973–79) it was no longer possible for the GATT system to evade complex energy questions in the GATT system. In the 1960s, the major oil exporting countries had formed the Organization of Petroleum Exporting Countries (OPEC). Although OPEC was initially not very influential, by the 1970s most energy producing countries had assumed control over production of their natural resources and had nationalized their petroleum industries. Only with the momentous oil crises that followed did it become clear how powerful the OPEC cartel was and how vulnerable and dependent some countries were on the importation of natural resources from abroad.[39] Industrialized countries like the United States experienced a shortage of fossil fuels, causing petroleum issues – namely, export restrictions and export taxes – to be put on the agenda of the Tokyo Round.[40]

During the oil crisis, petrol producing and exporting countries either curtailed their exports or levied high export taxes on petrol sold abroad. The practice of taxing fossil fuel exports or selling them at high prices

---

[36] Hoda (n 20) 25, 70.

[37] The WTO Secretariat also conducted studies on the Tokyo Round (1973–79) and the Uruguay Round (1986–94); see Hoda (n 20) 70.

[38] T Cottier and others, 'Energy in WTO Law and Policy' in T Cottier and P Delimatsis (eds), *The Prospects of International Trade Regulation: From Fragmentation to Coherence* (CUP 2011) 212, 214; on the Tokyo Round, see UNCTAD report (n 2) 15.

[39] See eg GATT Committee on Trade and Development, 'The Impact of Higher Petroleum Prices on Developing Countries: Note by the Secretariat' (28 January 1974) COM.TD/W/ 208. More recently, however, we have seen a decline in OPEC's ability to influence world prices, as the discovery of shale gas in the United States has reduced the bargaining power of the Gulf countries.

[40] During the Tokyo Round, export restrictions were taken up in Group 3(b); see GATT doc MTN/3B/9; see also GATT Secretariat, Export Restrictions and Charges – Background Note by the Secretariat (8 August 1989) MTN.GNG/NG2/W/40.

while keeping domestic prices low is known as dual pricing (discussed in detail in Chapter 6).[41] Simply put, dual pricing means that natural resources, mainly oil and gas, are exported and sold on the world market for (much) higher prices than on the domestic market, where prices are kept artificially low.[42] In this way, governments incentivize their country's downstream petroleum industry and the economy at large. Article XI GATT prohibits export restrictions, but GATT does not regulate export taxes, so the issue of dual pricing has thus far remained unresolved and controversial.[43] It could be argued that dual pricing is a kind of inverted subsidy and thus contrary to Article 3 of the Agreement on Subsidies and Countervailing Measures (SCM Agreement). The unequal distribution of natural resources around the world has been criticized as a contributory cause of dual pricing.[44] Export taxes on energy products were considered an unfair method of competition under GATT, and some WTO members questioned whether they could legitimately form part of a country's economic policy.[45] During the Tokyo Round, the members who suffered most from the oil crisis and dual pricing, such as the United Sates, pushed for clear provisions on dual pricing to be included either in GATT or in a separate agreement.[46]

However, oil producing and exporting countries were opposed to binding commitments and no agreement on the subject was reached.[47] It was merely decided that there was a need to examine the adequacy of

---

[41] On energy dual pricing generally, see Y Selivanova, *Energy Dual Pricing in the WTO* (Cameron May 2008); V Pogoretskyy, 'Energy Dual Pricing in International Trade: Subsidies and Anti-Dumping Perspectives' in Y Selivanova (ed), *Regulation of Energy in International Trade Law: WTO, NAFTA and Energy Charter* (Wolters Kluwer 2011).

[42] Selinanova (n 41); Pogoretskyy (n 41). See also L Ehring and CF Chianale, 'Export Restrictions in the Field of Energy' in Selivanova (n 41) 112ff.

[43] But see PC Mavroidis, *The Regulation of International Trade*, vol 1 *GATT* (MIT Press 2015) 87, arguing that while export taxes escape the disciplines of Article XI, they must comply with Article I (MFN treatment) and could also potentially be caught by a non-violation complaint.

[44] UNCTAD report (n 2) 16.

[45] See the articles by the then United States trade representative: TR Graham, 'Results of the Tokyo Round' (1979) 6 Georgia Journal of International and Comparative Law 153, 161; 'Reforming the International Law Trading System: The Tokyo Round Trade Negotiations in the Final Stage' (1979) 12 Cornell International Law Journal 1, 20, 31.

[46] TR Graham, 'The Reorganization of Trade Policymaking: Prospects and Problems' (1980) 13 Cornell International Law Journal 221, 226ff; R Leal-Arcas, A Filis and ES Abu Gosh, *International Energy Governance: Selected Legal Issues* (Edward Elgar 2014) 123; GATT, Multilateral Trade Negotiations – Group on Non-Tariff Measures – Sub-Group on Subsidies and Countervailing Measures (31 May 1976) MTN/NTM/W/43/Add.6, 3.

[47] See Shih (n 18) 439.

GATT provisions dealing with export restrictions and taxes in the future.[48] The issue of export taxes and restrictions has so far not been clarified within the WTO. The dual-pricing debate therefore continues to resurface regularly, including, in recent years, in connection with the decarbonization of the energy sector and environmentally harmful fossil fuel subsidies.

It is interesting to observe in the schedules resulting from the Tokyo Round that Czechoslovakia, included the previously absent category of fossil fuels in its schedule under the label 'Petroleum oils and oils obtained from bituminous minerals, crude', but kept its tariffs unbound,[49] while other countries kept their fossil fuel tariffs unchanged.[50] Most of the newly acceded countries made commitments on fossil fuels by including them in their schedules, but left tariffs unbound. This was the case with New Zealand,[51] Norway,[52] Iceland,[53] Hungary,[54] Austria,[55] Japan[56] and Bulgaria.[57] The European Economic Community (EEC) committed to an import tariff of 16 per cent on gasoline.[58] There was no mention at all of fossil fuel categories in Argentina's schedule,[59] nor in those of Spain and Switzerland.[60]

2.3.2 Uruguay Round (1986–94): Natural Resource-Based Products and Important Energy Accessions

Though no pressing global energy-related issues were solved during the Tokyo Round, the oil crises made sure that energy found a place on the

---

[48] Graham, 'Results of the Tokyo Round' (n 46) 172.

[49] The situation prior to the Uruguay Round schedules can be found in GATT documents TAR/W/7 and TAR/W/85l; Schedule X, pt I, tariff item 27.09.00, Geneva (1979) Protocol to GATT (30 June 1979) Doc 156(I) (Tokyo Round Schedules, vol I) 460.

[50] Schedule V, tariff item 27101-1ff, Tokyo Round Schedules, vol I (n 49) 61.

[51] Schedule XIII, pt I, tariff item ex 34.03, Tokyo Round Schedules, vol I (n 49) 658.

[52] Schedule XIV, pt I, tariff items 27.09 and 27.10, Tokyo Round Schedules, vol I (n 49) 756.

[53] Schedule LXII, tariff items 27.10ff, Geneva (1979) Protocol to GATT (30 June 1979) Doc 156(IV) (Tokyo Round Schedules, vol IV) 2947.

[54] Schedule LXXI, tariff item 27.09-00, Tokyo Round Schedules, vol IV (n 53) 3088.

[55] Schedule XXXII, tariff items 2709ff ('Petroleum oils and oils obtained from bituminous minerals, crude', Geneva (1979) Protocol to GATT (30 June 1979) Doc 156(III) (Tokyo Round Schedules, vol III) 2029.

[56] Schedule XXXVIII, tariff items 27.10ff, Tokyo Round Schedules, vol III (n 55) 2321.

[57] Schedules of Tariff Concessions of Bulgaria, tariff items 2709ff, Tokyo Round Schedules 39–40.

[58] Schedule LXXII, Tokyo Round Schedules, vol IV (n 53) 3302.

[59] Schedule LXIV, Tokyo Round Schedules, vol IV (n 53) 3024.

[60] See these members' respective Tokyo Round Schedules.

agenda from then onwards. Prior to the launch of the Uruguay Round, the 1986 Ministerial Declaration of Punta del Este referred to natural resource-based products, thus including energy: 'Negotiations shall aim to achieve the fullest liberalization of trade in natural resource-based products, including in their processed and semi-processed forms. The negotiations shall aim to reduce or eliminate tariff and non-tariff measures, including tariff escalation.'[61]

The Uruguay Round of Trade Negotiations (1986–94), which led to the establishment of the World Trade Organization in 1995, was relevant to the energy debate in GATT for four reasons. First, members renegotiated tariffs in their schedules of concessions, resulting in tariff reductions on several fossil fuel products.[62] Second, a major achievement of the Uruguay Round was the negotiation of the General Agreement on Trade in Services (GATS),[63] whereupon some members made specific commitments on services relating to the energy sector in their services schedules, opening up the sector to services from abroad. Third, energy dual pricing resurfaced during discussions. Fourth, and lastly, this round of negotiations saw the two energy major oil producing and exporting countries accede to GATT: Venezuela and Mexico. The latter made explicit commitments and reservations with respect to restrictive practices in the energy sector in its accession protocol.[64]

On the whole, there were no reductions on import tariffs for crude petroleum in members' schedules of concessions resulting from the Uruguay Round (the EC was an exception).[65] Tariffs on other petroleum products under HS chapter 27 generally remained much higher than those for crude oil.[66] However, significant tariff reductions were achieved

---

[61] GATT, Punta del Este Ministerial Declaration (20 September 1986). See also SS Haghighi, *Energy Security: The External Legal Relations of the European Union with Major Oil and Gas Supplying Countries* (Hart 2007) 237.

[62] UNCTAD report (n 2) 27.

[63] Trade in services relevant to the energy sector was regulated only after the General Agreement on Trade in Services (GATS) was concluded in 1994. See Chapter 3.

[64] GATT, 'Protocol for the Accession of Mexico to the General Agreement on Tariffs and Trade' (Basic Instruments and Selected Documents Series, 33rd Supplement, 17 July 1986) para 5.

[65] UNCTAD report (n 2) 26: for the United States and Japan they remained unbound. See Table K, HS category 2709 ('Tariff Treatment for Crude Oil'). UNCTAD drew up comprehensive tables on fossil fuel tariff escalations pre- and post-Uruguay; see UNCTAD report (n 2) 138ff.

[66] See HS chapter 27 'Mineral fuels, mineral oils and products of their distillation; bituminous substances; mineral waxes'; see also UNCTAD report (n 2) 26, 141 (table L).

on hydrocarbons.[67] The 2000 UNCTAD report analysing the evolution of tariff lines during the Uruguay Round concluded that it did not impact tariffs for crude petroleum, but that there were noteworthy reductions with respect to other petrochemicals.[68] This report also pointed out that the limited tariff reductions on crude oil were likely linked to the small number of petroleum producing and exporting countries involved in the negotiations and predicted a change of practice if more of these countries were to join the WTO.

In 1989, the WTO set up a Negotiating Group on Natural Resource-Based Products, which attempted to revive discussions on dual pricing and export restrictions.[69] Together with the United States and the EC, the group argued that these practices distorted international trade and gave exporters a competitive advantage, and that they therefore constituted prohibited subsidies.[70] The parties proposed that they be dealt with at a general level under GATT.[71] As in the Tokyo Round, the United States and other fossil fuel importing parties were of the opinion that either a new code tailored to trade practices affecting natural resources should be drawn up or that provisions on restrictive practices in natural resources should be added to GATT articles.[72]

In short, these members proposed that these matters be dealt with under GATT through generally applicable rules.[73] They were met the intransigence of energy-endowed countries, which were opposed to the creation of binding rules on trade in natural resources.[74] Furthermore, these countries maintained that the group stick to its mandate, which

---

[67] See UNCTAD report (n 2) 144 (table M).

[68] ibid 26: '[T]here have been significant general tariff reductions across the tariff lines. MFN tariffs on petrochemicals in the developed markets were already bound before the Uruguay Round. Moreover, transparency has increased as the result of a shift away from numerous specific duties to *ad valorem* duties.'

[69] GATT, Multilateral Trade Negotiations – Negotiating Group on Natural Resources-Based Products – Note by the Secretariat (10 August 1989) MTN.GNG/NG3/11.

[70] UNCTAD report (n 2) 18. See the US submissions in MTN.GNG/NG3/W/2, MTN.GNG/NG3/W/13 and MTN.GNG/NG3/W/23, and the European Community's submission in MTN.GNG/NG3/W/37.

[71] UNCTAD report (n 2) 17.

[72] GATT, Negotiating Group on Natural Resources-Based Products – Note by the Secretariat (n 69) para 5. See also Y Selivanova, 'The WTO and Energy: WTO Rules and Agreements of Relevance to the Energy Sector' (2007) International Centre for Trade and Sustainable Development Issue Paper 1, 11.

[73] UNCTAD report (n 2) 17.

[74] See Multilateral Trade Negotiations – Group of Negotiations on Goods, Negotiating Group on Natural Resource-Based Products – Meeting of 11 February 1987 – Note by the Secretariat (26 February 1990) MTN.GNC/NG3/1, as cited in Selivanova, (n 12).

covered other exhaustible natural resources (such as forestry, fisheries, non-ferrous materials and metals) rather than fossil fuels.[75] Although agreement was reached within the group on the fact that energy 'is the single most important commodity, both in value and volume terms, traded internationally, accounting for nearly a third of world seaborne trade', translating that observation into concrete action seemed inconceivable.[76] Apart from the discussion and a report, these questions received no definitive answers, nor, yet again, was any agreement reached on how to include energy policies and products in GATT.[77]

By the end of the Uruguay Round two major petroleum producing and exporting countries had acceded to GATT: Mexico in 1986 and Venezuela in 1990. Interestingly, it was the petroleum discussions that deterred Mexico from joining earlier, in 1980.[78] Mexico was openly opposed to undertaking any commitments with respect to dual pricing. When it acceded in 1986, its accession protocol contained the following statement:

> Mexico will exercise its sovereignty over natural resources, in accordance with the Political Constitution of Mexico. Mexico may maintain certain export restrictions related to the conservation of natural resources, particularly in the energy sector, on the basis of its social and development needs if those export restrictions are made effective in conjunction with restrictions on domestic production or consumption.[79]

In conclusion, although no binding decisions were taken with respect to the dual-pricing debate, the Uruguay Round was nonetheless relevant for energy, notably through tariff reductions on several petrochemical products, the commitments made by members under GATS and the accessions of two substantial energy producing and exporting countries. And, last but not least, the raising of the controversial issue of energy dual pricing by the Negotiating Group on Natural Resource-Based Products showed that greater attention needed to be given to energy regulation in the multilateral trading forum.[80]

---

[75] UNCTAD report (n 2) 17.
[76] See Uruguay Round – Group of Negotiations on Goods – Negotiating Group on Natural Resource-Based Products – Energy Products – Note by the Secretariat (27 September 1988) MTN.GNG/NG3/W/16, 123, cited in Haghighi (n 61) 237.
[77] UNCTAD report (n 2) 18.
[78] ibid 20.
[79] Accession Protocol (n 64) para 5. Mexico's statement on export restrictions in the energy sector is very interesting in respect of the question of whether production quota could qualify as an export restriction within the meaning of Article XI:1 GATT. See also Pogoretskyy (n 41) 184.
[80] Haghighi (n 61) 238.

2.4   From Uruguay to Doha: Energy Accessions and Disputes Entering a New Era

2.4.1   Energy Issues after the Establishment of the WTO: Doha and Beyond

Not long after the close of the Uruguay Round and the establishment of the World Trade Organization in 1995, UNCTAD issued its comprehensive report on energy trade.[81] UNCTAD's members felt there was a need to clarify the status of energy within the WTO legal framework.[82] Additionally, there were (justified) expectations that an increasing number of OPEC countries would soon join the WTO. Indeed, it was resource-rich Arab countries that had requested the report after the Uruguay Round negotiations.[83] The report affirmed that there was no obvious reason why energy and petroleum products should *not* be covered by the GATT/WTO system.[84]

Various aspects of energy regulation have materialized in the ongoing, but stagnant, Doha Development Agenda negotiations (2001–). Former WTO director-general Pascal Lamy emphasized in a 2010 speech that 'through more open markets, greater competition, and the spread of clean technology, the Doha Round would help stabilize the international trade and investment landscape in the energy field'.[85] So far, however, no concrete steps have been taken within the WTO towards rule-making in the energy field, but, as will be described below, other developments have contributed to changes in the energy landscape within the multilateral trading system – notably, the inclusion of energy and environmental services as negotiation categories in GATS; references to energy in the accession protocols of major energy producing or transporting countries; and the rising number of energy disputes in the forum.

Most importantly, the Doha Round saw energy services being discussed for the first time as a specific services sector.[86] While this shows

---

[81] See UNCTAD report (n 2).

[82] Selivanova (n 12) 53.

[83] UNCTAD report (n 2) iv.

[84] ibid 118; Cottier (n 38) 212.

[85] See WTO, 'Lamy: "A stronger WTO rule book could benefit the energy sector"' <www.wto.org/english/news_e/sppl_e/sppl169_e.htm> accessed 20 July 2020.

[86] See WTO, 'Energy Services' <www.wto.org/english/tratop_e/serv_e/energy_e/energy_e.htm> accessed 20 July 2020. Energy services are identified by member in WTO, Council for Trade in Services – Special Session of the Council for the Trade in Services – Report by the Chairman to the Trade Negotiations Committee (28 November 2005) TN/S/23.

that energy regulation was being embraced at a more official level within the WTO, no conclusive list was agreed upon and the negotiations on the topic have remained dormant for a long time. The relevance of GATS to the energy sector will be discussed in greater detail in Chapter 3.

Though energy goods do not as yet appear on the negotiation agenda as a separate category,[87] mention should be made of two other related, sector-specific negotiations on the Doha agenda – namely, environmental goods[88] and environmental services. As is the case with energy services, negotiations on environmental goods and services are challenging and stalling.

The legitimacy of green subsidies under the SCM Agreement has been dominating the policy debate for several years.[89] Although green subsidies do not necessarily imply subsidies on energy, they can include subsidies on green energy products. On this basis, the Negotiating Group on Rules has repeatedly raised dual-pricing issues during the Doha Round and even proposed amendments to the SCM Agreement.[90] However, accomplishing this is proving to be very challenging, and efforts in this area have been mainly focused on solving issues related to the accession of individual energy producing and exporting countries such as Saudi Arabia and the Russian Federation.

2.4.2 Energy in Post-1995 WTO Accession Protocols (1996–2015)

Since the establishment of the WTO in 1995, 36 new countries have joined the organization, bringing the total number of WTO members to 164 in 2020.[91] Several of these countries, such as China, Ecuador, Kazakhstan, Oman, Saudi Arabia, Russia and Ukraine, are significant

---

[87] Instead, see negotiations on the Environmental Goods Agreement (EGA) <www.wto.org/english/tratop_e/envir_e/ega_e.htm> accessed 20 July 2020.

[88] Doha Ministerial Declaration (DMD) (adopted 20 November 2001) WT/MIN(01)/DEC/1, para 31(iii): there is no agreed list of environmental products; some members prefer to label them 'environmental projects'.

[89] Cottier (n 38) 213. See generally R Howse and BP van Bork, 'Options for Liberalising Trade in Environmental Goods in the Doha Round' (2006) International Centre for Trade and Sustainable Development Issue Paper 2.

[90] See WTO, Negotiating Group on Rules – New Draft Consolidated Chair Texts of the AD and SCM Agreements – Draft SCM Agreement (19 December 2008) TN/RL/W/326, arts 2.1(c) ('Specificity'), 14 ('Calculation of the Amount of Subsidy'); S Zarilli, 'The Doha Work Programme: Possible Impact on Energy Trade and on Domestic Policies in Energy-Producing Developing Countries' (2003) 21 Journal of Energy and Natural Resources Law 399.

[91] See WTO, 'Protocols of accession for new members since 1995, including commitments in goods and services' <www.wto.org/english/thewto_e/acc_e/completeacc_e.htm> accessed 8 January 2021.

energy and natural resources producing, exporting, importing and/or transporting countries and have undertaken commitments relevant to this sector. This section will highlight the most important of these commitments, taking each of these diverse countries in turn in chronological order of their accession to the WTO. They include several major fossil fuel producers: Ecuador, Oman, Saudi Arabia, Russia and Kazakhstan. Of this group, Ecuador and Saudi Arabia are respectively former and current OPEC members. China, on the other hand, which jointed the WTO in 2001, is the world's biggest solar panel producer and energy importer and possesses vast reserves of strategic commodities. Ukraine, which joined in 2008, is arguably the most controversial energy transit county in the world.

2.4.2.1   Ecuador (1996)

Ecuador is a significant petroleum producer and has been an OPEC member off and on. It was a part of OPEC from 1973 until 1992, and then again from 2007 until 2020.[92]Ecuador joined the WTO briefly after the organization's establishment in 1996.[93] As discussed previously, in the 1990s energy discussions were not yet centre-stage in the multilateral trading forum. Perhaps for this reason energy did not figure prominently in Ecuador's accession protocol. Energy (meaning oil and gas) was mentioned in connection with economic policies and state trading enterprises as the only sector where prices were controlled by the state,[94] but no stringent commitments were made in this sector. The country did, however, make some commitments in the energy services sector (namely, services incidental to mining).[95]

2.4.2.2   Oman (2000)

Although not a member of OPEC, Oman is a prominent oil producer and exporter. It acceded to the WTO in 2000. In contrast to Ecuador, energy

---

[92] OPEC, 'Member Countries' <www.opec.org> accessed 20 July 2020.

[93] Accession Protocol (22 August 1995) WT/ACC/ECU/6; Report of the Working Party on the Accession of Ecuador (21 January 1996) WT/L/77 + Corr.1 (Ecuador Report).

[94] Ecuador Report (n 93) paras 7 ('The only prices controlled by the State were internal prices of certain oil and gas products for domestic consumption, pharmaceuticals and electricity.'), 63 on state-owned enterprises ('Furthermore, there were no monopolies in Ecuador except in the case of natural gas and some petroleum products.'), 52 ('The price-setting policy Ecuador had established in the 1970s had been virtually dismantled. The exceptions to this trend were fuels and gas for household use, where prices were set by the Ministries of Finance and Energy and Mining; and medicaments.').

[95] UNCTAD, 'WTO Accession and Development Policies' (2001) UNCTAD/DITC/TNCD/11, 211.

issues played a more significant role in Oman's accession. For instance, Oman significantly liberalized its energy market in the run-up to accession.[96] Besides privatisation, it designated its national oil company, Petroleum Development Oman (PDO), a state trading enterprise within the meaning of the Article XVII GATT.[97] Oman also opened up its service sector unconditionally to the exploration of reserves and the distribution of electricity. Finally, it signed up to the optional plurilateral Agreement on Government Procurement.[98] As a consequence, when procuring energy products, the country has to abide by the rules contained in that agreement.

2.4.2.3   China (2001)

China joined the WTO in 2001.[99] Although not a major energy producer, it is the world's biggest importer of energy, as well as the leading manufacturer of solar panels worldwide. Moreover, China possesses vast reserves of strategic natural resources such as rare earths, to which restrictive practices have been applied in much the same way as to petroleum.[100] It is therefore relevant to discuss the country in this context. Because China's domestic market is so vast, during accession negotiations concerns were raised with over the price controls that the country maintains on various products.[101] Energy (meaning gas and electricity) was also subject to these price controls.[102] In its accession protocol, China agreed to apply its price controls in a manner consistent with the WTO, although it was permitted to maintain them.[103] It was also

---

[96] Accession Protocol (9 November 2000) WT/ACC/OMN/28; Report of the Working Party on the Accession of Oman (28 September 2000) WT/ACC/OMN/26, para 14 (Oman Report). See also *Oman: Energy Policy, Laws and Regulations Handbook*, vol 1 *Strategic Information and Basic Laws* (International Business Publications 2015) 114.

[97] Oman Report (n 96) paras 109–110; see also A Jiménez-Guerra, *The World Trade Organization and Oil* (Oxford Institute for Energy Studies SP 12, October 2001) 23.

[98] Oman Report (n 96) para 121.

[99] Accession Protocol (23 November 2001) WT/L/431; Report of the Working Party on the Accession of China (10 November 2001) WT/MIN(01)/3 (China Report).

[100] International Energy Agency, 'Solar PV' <www.iea.org/reports/tracking-power-2019/solar-pv> accessed 20 July 2020.

[101] P Milthorp and D Christy, 'Energy Issues in Selected WTO Accessions' in Selivanova, Regulation of Energy in International Trade Law (n 41) 314.

[102] China Report (n 99) annex 4.

[103] ibid, para 64 'In response, the representative of China confirmed that China would apply its current price controls and any other price controls upon accession in a WTO-consistent fashion, and would take account of the interests of exporting WTO Members as provided for in Article III:9 GATT 1994. He also confirmed that price controls would not have the effect of limiting or otherwise impairing China's

allowed to maintain import quotas on processed oil (a so-called WTO-minus commitment).[104]

With regard to state trading, China undertook WTO-minus commitments, as it retained the right to impose import and export state trading measures on crude and processed oil, but was required to do so in a fully transparent and WTO-compliant manner.[105] Last but not least, it is well known that, in its accession protocol, China agreed to bind its export duties on several raw materials and rare earths, and that it would eliminate other export restrictions (such as licensing). This matter was central to the *China – Raw Materials* and *China – Rare Earths* cases and relevant to the wider debate concerning restrictive behaviour with respect to raw materials and natural resources.[106]

2.4.2.4   Saudi Arabia (2005)

Saudi Arabia's accession to the WTO marked the entry of one of the world's biggest oil producers and the most prominent OPEC member. As mentioned throughout this book, energy dual pricing was a key issue in its accession.[107] After heated discussions, especially with the European Community, Saudi Arabia eventually committed not to sell its petroleum domestically below the world price:

> In response to a question from a Member of the Working Party, the representative of Saudi Arabia stated that all petroleum-based and natural gas-based products in Saudi Arabia were made available to all users regardless of whether the users were Saudi or foreign owned. He noted that currently domestic sales of heavy naphtha were not subject to any discount and were priced at the prevailing international price. Prices of exports of these products, he confirmed, were based entirely on international market conditions.[108]

It is questionable to what extent this constitutes a firm commitment to eliminate dual pricing, given the influence Saudi Arabia and OPEC have

---

market-access commitments on goods and services. The Working Party took note of these commitments.'

[104]   ibid, para 134, table 2.

[105]   ibid, annex 2A1 ('Products Subject to State Trading (Import)') items 50 (crude oil), 51–57 (processed oil), and annex 2A2 ('Products Subject to State Trading (Export)'), items 31–49 (coal, crude oil and processed oil).

[106]   See Appellate Body (AB) reports.

[107]   See also Milthorp and Christy (n 101) 306ff.

[108]   Accession Protocol (11 December 2005) WT/L/627; Report of the Working Party on the Accession of the Kingdom of Saudi Arabia (1 November 2005) WT/ACC/SAU/61, para 28 (Saudi Arabia Report).

on world prices through the production quota they apply to crude petroleum.[109] Additionally, Saudi Arabia's dual-pricing policies may be implemented in various ways, and not merely through low domestic petroleum prices (eg by making petroleum subject to export taxes which may not be included in the calculation of the world price).

In addition to petroleum, Saudi Arabia has significant reserves of natural gas, mostly in the form of liquefied natural gas (LNG) produced as a by-product of oil exploration. In its accession report, the country noted that natural gas was sold domestically at a regulated price, as this gas was not intended for export.[110]

As a matter closely tied to its petrochemical sector, state trading was another issue that attracted a lot of attention during Saudi Arabia's accession negotiations.[111] The State trading enterprises in the Saudi energy sector are the Saudi Arabian Basic Industries Corporation (SABIC), the Saudi Electricity Company (SEC) and the Saudi Arabian Oil Company (Aramco). Concerning the first, SABIC, the report stated that, although state-owned, the company did not enjoy any special or exclusive privileges and that there were no legal impediments to competition.[112] The same statement was made regarding SEC.[113] Aramco plays a prominent role in exploiting domestic energy resources and investment opportunities in the country's energy sector remain limited, although there has been some opening-up in recent years.[114] With regard to its procurement procedures, the Report stated that:

> Saudi Aramco's procurement procedures afforded full opportunity for all qualified suppliers of goods and services of WTO Member countries to compete for participation in competitive bidding. The company selects the most technically and financially qualified contractor whose bid represented the least overall cost to Saudi Aramco.[115]

---

[109] See Chapter 5, Section 5.2.

[110] But it emphasized that this price was available to all players on the domestic market, whether of domestic or foreign origin. See Saudi Arabia Report, para 29. This is deemed not to be contrary to Article III:9 GATT 'Saudi Arabia would apply its price regulations and profit controls in a WTO consistent fashion, taking into account the interests of exporting WTO Members as provided for in Article III:9 of the GATT 1994 and in Article VIII of the General Agreement on Trade in Services (GATS).' Saudi Arabia Report, para 37, referencing annex A, which includes an exhaustive list of goods that are subject to price controls.

[111] Milthorp and Christy (n 101) 311ff.

[112] Saudi Arabia Report, para 44(i).

[113] ibid, para 44(iii).

[114] Milthorp and Christy (n 101) 312.

[115] Saudi Arabia Report, para 44(vi).

In conclusion, energy issues took centre-stage in Saudi Arabia's accession negotiations. While not eliminating the problem of energy dual pricing, the country did undertake several noteworthy commitments in the energy sector.

2.4.2.5   Ukraine (2008)

Ukraine is a rather unique example in this list of newly acceded countries. Like China, it is not a significant energy producer. However, Ukraine is probably the most controversial energy transit state in the world. It is the gateway through which Russian and Central Asian gas passes to Europe, besides being itself highly dependent on gas imports from these countries. In the 2000s, Ukraine was at the centre of heated gas transit disputes with its neighbour, Russia, that left the European Union partially in the cold.[116] As these events occurred around the time of Ukraine's accession to the WTO, transit issues received special attention in its accession negotiations. Ukraine undertook comprehensive transit commitments with respect to both goods and services in the energy sector. Third-party access to pipelines was a topic of discussion in relation to Article V GATT.[117] Ukraine committed as follows:

> Ukraine would apply all its laws, regulations and other measures governing transit of goods (including energy), such as those governing charges for transportation of goods in transit, in conformity with the provisions of Article V of the GATT 1994 and other relevant provisions of the WTO Agreement.[118]

These commitments indicate that transit through fixed infrastructures such as pipelines is covered by Article V GATT for those countries that have made WTO-plus commitments in this area (see Kazakhstan below). In its services schedule, Ukraine moreover undertook commitments regarding '[s]ervices incidental to energy distribution' and '[p]ipeline transportations of fuels'.[119] In addition, Ukraine committed to:

---

[116] Chiefly in the winters of 2005/2006 and 2009/2010.

[117] Third-party access policy requires the owners of natural monopoly infrastructures, such as gas pipelines and electricity grids, to grant access to those facilities to parties other than their own customers – usually competitors in the provision of the relevant services and often from other countries – on commercial terms comparable to those that would apply in a competitive market.

[118] Accession Protocol (16 May 2008) WT/L/718; Report of the Working Party on the Accession of Ukraine (25 January 2008) WT/ACC/UKR/152 (Ukraine Report) para 367.

[119] Ukraine Report, Schedule of Specific Commitments in Services, WT/ACC/UKR/152/Add.2, 13 (Services incidental to energy distribution) (CPC 887), 33 (Pipeline Transport, (a) transportation of fuels (CPC 7131)). Both sections record no commitments for

provide full transparency in the formulation, adoption and application of measures affecting access to and trade in services of pipeline transportation.

Ukraine undertakes to ensure adherence to the principles of non-discriminatory treatment in access to and use of pipeline networks under its jurisdiction, within the technical capacities of these networks, with regard to the origin, destination or ownership of product transported, without imposing any unjustified delays, restrictions or charges, as well as without discriminatory pricing based on the differences in origin, destination or ownership.[120]

These commitments, especially in combination with Ukraine's state trading obligations, can be interpreted as a requirement for the country to give access to its gas transport network and operate it in a non-discriminatory (MFN) manner.[121]

Regarding state trading enterprises, three national energy and energy distribution companies, UkrGasEnergo, Naftogas and Energorynok, are listed as STEs in the report.[122] The language on STEs is very similar to that of Saudi Arabia's protocol, partly because it had to satisfy US trading demands.[123] Finally, although discussed in the report, Ukraine maintained price controls on energy, though no commitments were made in that regard.[124]

2.4.2.6   Russia (2012)

Russia's accession process was particularly lengthy and cumbersome, taking almost two decades.[125] While Russia did undertake some commitments with regard to energy, they were perhaps not as far-reaching as some negotiating parties would have wished (like the EU, which wanted Russia to commit to eliminate dual-pricing policies).[126] Additionally, some of the commitments Russia undertook were in the framework of

---

supply modes 1, 2 and 3, and unbound for supply mode 4, with respect to both market access (right to participate in the market) and national treatment (non-discrimination against non-nationals).

[120] ibid.

[121] Milthorp and Christy (n 101) 317ff.

[122] Ukraine Report, para 44.

[123] Milthorp and Christy (n 101) 318. The language agreed was sufficient for the US president to make the certification required by section 1106.

[124] ibid 317, referring to Ukraine Report, paras 63–67.

[125] Accession Protocol (22 August 2012) WT/L/839, WT/MIN(11)/27; Report of the Working Party on the Accession of the Russian Federation (17 November 2011) WT/ACC/RUS/70, WT/MIN(11)/2 (Russia Report).

[126] Milthorp and Christy (n 101) 324.

the Eurasian Economic Union (EAEU).[127] Overall, it seems that the nature of the commitments was not so much WTO-plus (ie going beyond those contained in the WTO agreements) but more a confirmation that Russia's energy sector had to comply with WTO rules.[128] Nevertheless, Russia did agree to bind some of its export duties on energy products and committed to phase out several of these duties over time.

With respect to export restrictions, Russia confirmed that these would not be justified under the WTO agreements.[129] While some parties expressed concern over licensing requirements for access to oil and gas pipelines, Russia stated that there were no such requirements with respect to oil and natural gas and that under the federal law on the licensing of specific activities there were no licensing requirements for the following activities either: (1) the operation of oil and gas production facilities; (2) the sale of oil, gas and oil/gas processing products; (3) the processing of oil, gas and oil/gas processing products; (4) the transportation of oil, gas and oil/gas processing products; (5) the storage of oil, gas and oil/gas processing products; and (6) the activity of operating gas networks.[130]

As noted above, Russia has made some binding commitments on export duties applied to energy goods, based on the HS chapter 27 classification.[131] Regarding export duties on crude oil, as well as some other oil products, Russia committed to a formula that calculates the duties on the basis of the world price of oil.[132]

Concerning state trading enterprises, Russia's state-owned (51 per cent) Gazprom group and other owners and operators of pipeline networks were much discussed in the course of the accession

---

[127] The Eurasian Economic Union was established in 2014 and comprises Russia, Kazakhstan, Belarus, Kyrgyzstan and Armenia; see <www.eaeunion.org/?lang=en> accessed 20 July 2020.

[128] Milthorp and Christy (n 101) 324. See generally TP Stewart and PJ McDonough, *Opportunities and Challenges from Russia's 2012 Accession to the WTO* (Stewart and Stewart 2011); Global Intelligence Alliance, 'Russia's Accession to the WTO and Its Impact on Her Energy and Commodities Industries' (March 2012) GIA Industry White Paper 1/2012.

[129] Milthorp and Christy (n 101) 324.

[130] Russia Report, para 270; Federal Law No 128-FZ on licensing of specific types of activity (8 August 2001, last amended 28 September 2010).

[131] See Russia's Schedule of Concessions and Commitments on Goods, Schedule CLXV, pt V, 853, 870; International Convention on the Harmonized Commodity Description and Coding System (adopted 14 June 1983) 1503 UNTS 167, ch 27 ('Mineral fuels, mineral oils and products of their distillation; bituminous substances; mineral waxes').

[132] Russia Report, annex 1.

process.[133] Russia stated that, upon accession, it would designate Gazprom as an STE in accordance with Article XVII GATT, adding that the Gazprom group was the only enterprise that enjoyed special or exclusive privileges with respect to the exportation of natural gas.

With regard to energy dual pricing, the EU (together with the US) insisted (unsuccessfully) on commitments from Russia's side.[134] Russia defended itself by arguing it was entitled to exercise sovereignty over its subsurface natural resources, including natural gas.[135] It further stressed that its practices did not differ much from those of many other members. With regard to subsidies, Russia additionally firmly stated that it did not believe that the governmental regulation of national monopoly prices constituted a subsidy within the meaning of the SCM Agreement.[136]

In relation to members' concerns over the disparity between the price of gas sold to industrial consumers in the Russian Federation and the world price of gas, the representative of the Russian Federation stated:

> that gas export prices were not regulated and were established on the basis of supply and demand in the importing country. He was of the view that there was no 'world market price' for gas, and noted that for gas shipped to Europe, costs of shipment and transport reflected a substantial part of the landed price.[137]

Hence, on dual pricing the negotiating parties did not obtain the full commitments sought. Russia did, however, confirm that producers and distributors of natural gas would operate on the basis of normal commercial considerations with respect to their supplies to industrial users.[138] It also stated its intention to increase its prices for natural gas by 2030. Under the guise of social policy, however, Russia would maintain dual-pricing policies with respect to domestic energy supplies to household and non-commercial users.[139]

Concerning price controls, Russia provided a list of goods and services and confirmed that they would be applied in a manner consistent with the WTO, especially with regard to Article III:9 GATT.[140] This list

---

[133] Milthorp and Christy (n 101) 294.
[134] Russia Report, paras 120–33.
[135] ibid, para 123.
[136] ibid, para 696; though other WTO members might of course see these as actionable or prohibited subsidies and may challenge them in dispute settlement.
[137] ibid, para 127.
[138] ibid, para 132.
[139] ibid.
[140] GATT art III:9; Russia Report, para 133.

included natural gas, gas transportation, nuclear fuel cycle products, electric power and heat generated by suppliers on the wholesale market, electric energy network transmission services and services for the transportation of crude oil and oil products through pipelines.[141]

Inevitably, the transit of energy was an important issue. In relation to its role as an energy transit country for Central Asian producers, Russia raised doubts as to whether Article V GATT would cover fixed infrastructures such as gas pipelines.[142] Its accession commitments on transit proved a partial turnaround on this issue. With respect to transit fees, the country confirmed that it would apply all its laws, regulations and other measures governing the transit of goods, including energy, in accordance with the obligations set out in Article V.[143] However, it made no commitments with regard to access to pipelines and pipeline transport services.[144] Moreover, Gazprom continued to be the sole exporter of natural gas as an STE,[145] and gas originating in Russia and exported to the EU Customs Union was the subject of an export monopoly.[146]

Last but not least, in its services schedule Russia made some commitments on market access in the energy sector in relation to mining, manufacturing and energy distribution,[147] but they were not particularly significant.

2.4.2.7   Kazakhstan (2015)

Kazakhstan is one of the WTO's newest members (it joined the organization in 2015).[148] It was the last in a string of significant energy producing countries to join the WTO. As with Russia, some of its energy commitments were made in the framework of the Eurasian Economic Union.

On transit, Kazakhstan's commitments went further than those of Russia, as it explicitly agreed that transit-related laws and regulations and other measures governing the transit of goods (including energy) would be regulated in accordance with Article V GATT.[149] Further, Kazakhstan

---

[141] Russia Report, 407–11, tables 7, 8.
[142] See Chapter 3.
[143] Russia Report, para 1161.
[144] ibid, para 136.
[145] ibid, para 271.
[146] ibid, para 1147, table 28.
[147] Mining under the UN Central Product Classification (CPC) 883, manufacturing under CPC 8845 and energy distribution under CPC 887.
[148] Accession Protocol (30 November 2015) WT/L/957; Report of the Working Party on the Accession of Kazakhstan (23 June 2015) WT/ACC/KAZ/93 (Kazakhstan Report).
[149] WTO, 'Overview of Kazakhstan's Commitments' <www.wto.org/english/news_e/news15_e/kazakhannex_e.pdf> accessed 8 January 2021.

made accession-specific commitments with respect to its government-regulated pipelines. Access to these pipelines was granted in a non-discriminatory manner to foreign investors producing crude oil and gas in Kazakhstan.[150] Additionally, when applying measures to transportation through pipelines, Kazakhstan committed not to discriminate with respect to the origin of crude oil and gas production and its destination, nor with respect to the application of tariffs vis-à-vis domestic and foreign investors.[151] Kazakhstan additionally made commitments regarding Trade-Related Investment Measures (TRIMs) in the energy sector and undertook to get rid of all WTO-inconsistent measures on local content requirements in oil and gas investments by 1 January 2021.[152]

What is striking when carefully studying the accession protocols discussed above is the gradual evolution in energy discussions and in the commitments made in countries' WTO accession protocols from 1995. While energy played only a minor role in Ecuador's accession, energy topics occupied an increasingly important place on the agenda of the working party reports from Oman's accession onwards. What is clear is that the WTO accession process inherently sheds light on countries' relevant sectors, energy included. Acceding countries have to make sure that, at a minimum, these sectors are WTO-compliant.

One trend is that energy transit issues are increasingly being discussed in the forum, at least in relation to acceding members. While there is some uncertainty as to whether Article V GATT applies to the fixed energy transmission structures of WTO members that joined the organization in 1995, it clearly does apply to those that have made specific energy commitments on it in their accession protocols (ie Ukraine, Russia and Kazakhstan). Though not always full-fledged, these commitments show that the WTO is a forum where energy transit issues are actively discussed and negotiated. Perhaps the WTO is complementing or even taking over from the Energy Charter Treaty in this respect, as energy trade discussions seem to have been inactive in that forum for quite a while now and the ECT is being renegotiated.[153]

Another trend is that acceding members are increasingly binding their export duties (eg China and Russia) and several members have bound

---

[150] Kazakhstan Report, paras 87, 162, 163.
[151] WTO, 'Overview' (n 149).
[152] Kazakhstan Report, para 897.
[153] The most recent draft of the Energy Charter Treaty's 'Transit Protocol' was dated 22 October 2010.

export duties specifically on energy goods (eg Russia). This shows that countries are shifting away from non-transparent pricing policies and realizing that export duties, like import duties, can be the subject of bargaining and that this may be to the negotiating country's advantage. Connected to this issue are commitments with regard to dual-pricing policies. While hard commitments and WTO-wide rules remain absent, the fact that export duties on energy goods featured prominently and were discussed in countries' accession negotiations is in itself a positive development. Both Saudi Arabia and Russia have partially committed to eliminating such practices, which may be a small victory, but better than no commitments at all in this sensitive area.

All in all, we can discern that as more major energy players accede to the WTO, these topics figure more prominently in accession negotiations, resulting in gradual clarification on important issues such as transit, export taxes and dual-pricing policies in WTO law.

2.4.3   Energy Disputes on the Rise

Apart from energy playing an increasingly important role in countries' WTO accession negotiations, there has been a steady increase in the number of energy disputes making their way into the WTO's dispute settlement system (DSS). These disputes will feature prominently throughout this book.

Interestingly enough, the first WTO dispute to make it to the Appellate Body was an energy-related dispute, the *Reformulated Gasoline* Case (1996).[154] This case considered to what extent the United States was allowed to derogate from Articles I (MFN treatment) and III:4 (national treatment) GATT and restrict imports of gasoline containing harmful pollutants by relying on the exception of protecting natural resources (in this case clean air) provided for in Article XX(g) GATT.[155] Although the number of energy disputes remained small in the immediately following years, since the 2010s disputes concerning both fossil fuels and renewables have been on the increase.

In the area of fossil fuels, *EU – Energy Package* (*Russian Federation v European Union*) was the first WTO case to deal with decentralization

---

[154] *US – Gasoline*, panel and AB reports. See also C Redgwell, 'International Regulation of Energy Activities' in MM Roggenkamp and others (eds), *Energy Law in Europe* (OUP 2007) 135–136. A GATT panel was seized of a case concerning energy in *US – Superfund* (1987).

[155] GATT, arts I, III:4, XX(g).

and energy security in the gas sector. In this landmark case, Russia accused the EU of discriminatory treatment of Russian gas service suppliers active on the EU market. The dispute concerned EU internal energy market legislation, including the Third Energy Package and its unbundling requirements.[156] Russia also brought an anti-dumping case against the EU over dual-pricing practices in connection with natural gas (*EU – Cost Adjustment Methodologies II*).[157]

Trade in alternative forms of energy – such as biofuels, solar panels, wind turbines and their related technologies – has become common and will doubtless increase in the future. Such trade poses challenges that need solutions under international trade law. For instance, biofuel subsidies raise questions over the balance to be struck between promoting the environmental policies of WTO members and consistency with WTO law.[158]

The growth in the number of WTO disputes concerning renewable energy during the last decade is striking. In 2010, Japan brought a case against Canada, the seminal dispute concerning the Ontario feed-in tariff programme and subsidies for renewable energy.[159] Local content requirements in WTO members' renewable energy schemes triggered tit-for-tat disputes between the US and India. In *India – Solar Cells*, the US successfully contested the Jawaharlal Nehru National Solar Mission local content requirements scheme. India then retaliated by contesting similar requirements in US states.[160] Since 2012, a number of anti-dumping disputes have also been lodged concerning solar panels and biodiesel.[161] In addition, there have been numerous dispute resolution consultations concerning various types of renewable energy that did not make it to the dispute settlement phase.[162]

---

[156] Panel report circulated 10 August 2018, appealed 21 September 2018, currently stalled. We will return to the case in greater depth in Chapters 5 and 7.

[157] *EU – Cost Adjustment Methodologies II (Second Complaint)* (7 May 2015); see also Marhold (n 34).

[158] See R Howse and AL Eliasion, 'Domestic and International Strategies to Address Climate Change: An Overview of the WTO Legal Issues' in T Cottier, O Nartova and SZ Bigdeli, *International Trade Regulation and the Mitigation of Climate Change: World Trade Forum* (CUP 2009) 80–90.

[159] *Canada – Renewable Energy / Canada – Feed-In Tariff Program*, panel and AB reports.

[160] *India – Solar Cells*, panel and AB reports; *US – Renewable Energy*, panel report.

[161] *US – Countervailing Measures (China)*; *EU – Biodiesel (Argentina)*; *EU – Biodiesel (Indonesia)*.

[162] See eg Request for Consultations by the United States, *China – Measures Concerning Wind Power Equipment* (6 January 2011) WT/DS419/1, G/L/950, G/SCM/D86/1; Request for Consultations by China, *European Union and Certain Member States –*

Chapter 3 includes a summary table of all disputes related to energy that have been brought to WTO dispute settlement so far.

2.5   Conclusion

In sum, trade in energy is, and has always been, covered by GATT/WTO disciplines, but in practice was long treated as mostly lying outside GATT. This chapter has demonstrated that the complex and indissociable relationship between energy trade and the GATT/WTO framework was formed at the inception of the multilateral trading system. Energy issues were in the background at the time of GATT 1947 and remained so for several decades due to the particularities of the fossil fuel trade, which reached full throttle only in the course of the twentieth century and seemed irreconcilable with the rationale of GATT. Cross-border energy trade was limited to fossil fuels and, moreover, was under the control of an oligopoly. Difficult questions concerning the relationship between energy and trade were consequently ducked in the GATT/WTO forum for a relatively long period of time. Also, at the time relatively few of the world's major energy producing, exporting and transporting countries were parties to GATT. Following widespread nationalization of oil production in the 1970s and the resulting emergent power of OPEC, leading to the global oil crises, energy issues began to find a place in GATT discussions from the Tokyo Round in 1973 onwards.

Although many contentious issues remain, it has today become accepted that energy lies fully within the ambit of WTO law. This is evidenced in the inclusion of energy services as a negotiation topic under GATS. Factors that have particularly contributed to energy playing an increasingly prominent role in the multilateral trading system include the growing number of energy producing and exporting countries that have acceded to the WTO ; the expansion of tradable energy beyond fossil fuels to include the burgeoning cross-border trade in clean energies (doubtless destined to outstrip fossil fuels in the future)[163]; and the growth in the number of energy disputes being settled in the WTO DSS as a result of these factors combined.[164] Although energy is fully covered

---

Certain Measures Affecting the Renewable Energy Generation Sector (7 November 2012) WT/DS452/1, G/L/1008, G/SCM/D95/1, G/TRIMS/D/34.

[163] See generally S Dale, 'The New Economics of Oil' (October 2015) Oxford Institute for Energy Studies.

[164] Y Selivanova, 'Energy Challenges for International Trade Rules' (2011) 8 Transnational Dispute Management 3, according to whom 'it is commonly accepted that the existing

by the WTO agreements, this does not mean that the legal framework is suitable to dealing with energy optimally. This book will demonstrate that there is still a long way to go. As former WTO secretary-general Lamy put it:

> When thinking about how the WTO can most effectively contribute to the energy goals of the international community, the question is not whether the WTO legal framework is relevant and applicable to trade in energy goods and services, for it clearly is. Instead, we need to ask ourselves how the WTO's contribution can be further improved, given rapid changes in the energy policy landscape and the international community's goals regarding energy.[165]

WTO Agreements, including fundamental principles of WTO – Most-Favoured-Nation Treatment (MFN) and National Treatment, apply equally to energy as to any other products'.

[165] P Lamy, 'Trade and Energy: The Case for a Greater WTO Role' in *The Geneva Consensus: Making Trade Work for All* (CUP 2013) 121.

The Current WTO Legal Framework Relevant to Energy

3.1 Introduction

Chapter 2 showed that, although fully covered by the WTO agreements, the regulation of cross-border energy trade has not always been self-evident. As energy was not at the heart of GATT/WTO negotiations, the result is a set of rules that are not specifically tailored to the needs of the energy sector. That said, Article XVI:4 of the Marrakech Agreement requires all members to ensure the conformity of their measures with the WTO agreements annexed to the Marrakech Agreement.[1]

One of the goals of this book is to demonstrate that this incoherency sometimes creates a mismatch between current WTO rules and an energy sector oriented towards decentralization, decarbonization and energy security.[2] With this in mind, we should recall the preamble to the Marrakech Agreement establishing the WTO, where parties agreed to 'allow optimal use of the world's resources in accordance with the objective of sustainable development'.[3]

This chapter will cover the rules of the WTO framework and disciplines relevant to energy, including several issues so far unresolved by case law, as well as provide a summary table of energy-related disputes to date. It will proceed methodically by following the current structure of WTO agreements on goods, services, intellectual property and plurilateral agreements.[4]

---

[1] Marrakesh Agreement Establishing the World Trade Organization (15 April 1994) 1867 UNTS 154 (1994) 33 ILM 1144 (WTO Agreement) art XVI:4.
[2] See, respectively, Chapters 5, 6 and 7.
[3] WTO Agreement (n 1) preamble.
[4] For a repertory of WTO legal texts, see <www.wto.org/english/docs_e/legal_e/legal_e.htm> accessed 20 July 2020.

3.2 Multilateral Agreements on Trade in Goods

3.2.1 General Agreement on Tariffs and Trade

The General Agreement on Tariffs and Trade (GATT) regulates international trade in goods. GATT applies to energy trade insofar as energy *goods* are involved. Virtually all goods that are globally traded are registered and classified in the HS Convention.[5] In the commodity description and coding system, products are classified as raw materials, semi-finished goods or finished products.

Non-discrimination is at the core of the multilateral trading system and is enshrined in GATT in several ways. The most-favoured-nation (MFN) clause (Article I) prescribes that the most favourable treatment accorded to a WTO member must be extended to all other WTO members.[6] The national treatment (NT) clause (Article III:2) guarantees that when goods enter the territory of another WTO member they cannot be treated less favourably than 'like' domestic goods.[7] WTO members are allowed to discriminate (on an MFN basis), but only by means of bound tariff rates (Article II).[8] Furthermore, the application of quantitative import and export restrictions (QRs) is prohibited in Article XI:1 GATT.[9] In addition to hampering trade, QRs are considered less transparent than bound tariffs.[10] If WTO members wish to deviate from their GATT obligations, they can have recourse to the exceptions in Articles XX ('General Exceptions') and XXI ('Security Exceptions').

3.2.1.1 Tariff Classifications: Article II GATT

Under GATT, import tariffs on foreign products are the only permitted form of protectionism.[11] Thus, tariffs are not illegal under WTO law, but

---

[5] International Convention on the Harmonized Commodity Description and Coding System (adopted 14 June 1983) 1503 UNTS 167 (HS Convention).

[6] General Agreement on Tariffs and Trade 1994, Marrakesh Agreement Establishing the World Trade Organization, Annex 1A (adopted 15 April 1994) 1867 UNTS 187 (1994) 33 ILM 1153 (GATT 1994) art I (most-favoured-nation treatment).

[7] GATT 1994, art III.2 (national treatment).

[8] Except in the case of government procurement (GATT 1994, art III:8).

[9] GATT 1994, art XI (elimination of quantitative restrictions).

[10] Economically speaking, free trade flows without barriers (based on the model of Ricardo's comparative advantage) is the optimal model. Tariffs hamper free trade, but are acceptable because they are negotiated and bound in a transparent manner. Quotas also hamper international trade flows but are less transparent. An outright trade ban is detrimental to free trade because it brings all trade flows to a standstill. See PC Mavroidis, *Trade in Goods* (OUP 2012) 57ff.

[11] On tariffs, the preamble to GATT 1947 stated, in relation to the parties' goal of promoting economic prosperity, '[b]eing desirous of contributing to these objectives by entering into

they are nevertheless considered a serious obstacle to trade, and it is therefore the long-term objective of the WTO to guarantee that tariffs are as low as possible or, preferably, to eliminate them altogether.[12] Article II GATT, entitled 'Schedules of Concessions' allows members to set tariffs, provided they are below the bounded rate.[13] Once a member has agreed to a particular tariff on a product, it must grant all other members the same tariff – that is, they have to be applied to the foreign 'like products' imported into the domestic market on a non-discriminatory basis.[14]

Import tariffs on energy products are generally low, though it depends on how different energy goods are classified. Due to their classification, some biofuels, for instance, are treated as agricultural products instead of conventional goods and fall within the disciplines of the Agreement on Agriculture.[15] As a result, they are subject to higher import tariffs than other energy products (such as petroleum, for which tariffs often remain unbound – see discussion in Chapter 2). Higher import tariffs apply to ethanol, for example, which is classified under chapter 22 of the HS Convention.[16]

Additionally, Article II:2 GATT allows a member to apply to the imported product 'a charge equivalent to an internal tax' imposed consistently with Article III:2 GATT in respect of the like domestic product. This provision is crucial to discussions on the so-called carbon tax on fossil fuels.[17] If a WTO member choses to apply a carbon tax, polluting products are taxed higher than non-polluting products at the border.[18]

---

reciprocal and mutually advantageous arrangements directed to the substantial reduction of tariffs and other barriers to trade and to the elimination of discriminatory treatment in international commerce'. See B Hoekman and PC Mavroidis, *The World Trade Organization: Law, Economics and Politics* (Routledge 2007) 15.

[12] ibid. See also L Ehring and CF Chianale, 'Export Restrictions in the Field of Energy' in Y Selivanova (ed), *Regulation of Energy in International Trade Law: WTO, NAFTA and Energy Charter* (Wolters Kluwer 2011) 109.

[13] GATT 1994, art II:1(a): 'Each contracting party shall accord to the commerce of the other contracting parties treatment no less favourable than that provided for in the appropriate Part of the appropriate Schedule annexed to this Agreement.'

[14] GATT 1994, art I (MFN treatment).

[15] See Section 3.2.2.

[16] A Yanovich, 'WTO Rules and the Energy Sector' in Selivanova (n 12) 27; HS Convention ch 22 ('Beverages, Spirits and Vinegar').

[17] eg the carbon tax proposed in the 2019 European Green Deal. See R Howse and A Eliason, 'Domestic and International Strategies to Address Climate Change: An Overview of the WTO Legal Issues' in: T Cottier, O Nartova and SZ Bigdeli (eds), *International Trade Regulation and the Mitigation of Climate Change* (CUP 2009).

[18] See generally K Holzer, *Carbon-Related Border Adjustment and WTO Law* (Edward Elgar 2014).

The risk of instituting a carbon tax might be that exporting countries would shift their production to countries where such a tax does not exist and where the imported fossil fuel or polluting product is not liable to be taxed.[19] Moreover, the institution of a carbon tax may meet with a lot of resistance from WTO members, as they may not be able to reach the standard set by another WTO member.

3.2.1.2 Non-discrimination and 'Like' Energy Goods: Articles I and III GATT

According to the MFN principle in Article I, 'like' energy goods cannot be discriminated against on the basis of their origin or destination.[20] Article III GATT (national treatment) provides that imported energy products cannot be treated differently from 'like' domestic products through taxes (Article III:2) or other regulations (Article III:4).[21]

In *EU – Energy Package*, the panel looked into non-discrimination in connection with the EU's TEN-E Regulation.[22] Under that regulation, the EU earmarked certain major energy infrastructure projects as 'projects of common interest' (PCIs), which allowed them to benefit from swifter permit procedures and a various financial incentives.[23] PCIs concern a range of energy projects and involve a number of third countries.[24] Russia, the dominant natural gas supplier to the EU, was of the opinion that it was treated less favourably than other countries benefiting from the TEN-E Regulation. It made an 'as such' claim in its challenge against the regulation, asserting that the measure resulted in Russian gas being afforded less favourable treatment under Article I:1 GATT.[25]

---

[19] Yanovich (n 16) 29.

[20] Y Selivanova, 'The WTO and Energy: WTO Rules and Agreements of Relevance to the Energy Sector' (2007) International Centre for Trade and Sustainable Development Issue Paper 1, 14.

[21] ibid.

[22] *EU – Energy Package*, panel report, para 7.1262.

[23] Regulation (EU) 347/2013 of the European Parliament and of the Council of 17 April 2013 on guidelines for trans-European energy infrastructure and repealing Decision 1364/2006/EC and amending Regulations (EC) 713/2009, (EC) 714/2009 and (EC) 715/2009 (TEN-E Regulation): *EU – Energy Package*, Russian Federation's request for the establishment of a panel (28 May 2015) WT/DS476/2 (Russia's panel request).

[24] Russia's panel request, 8.

[25] ibid. Russia claimed that:

> Natural gas originating in third-countries that is transported and placed on the EU market through pipelines or other infrastructure listed as PCIs is also accorded an advantage, favor, privilege or immunity that is not immediately and unconditionally accorded to natural gas originating in Russia,

One of reasons behind the TEN-E measure is the EU's wish to diversify the supply of natural gas.[26] In certain projects, the EU even stated its purpose was to 'end the isolation of the three Baltic States and Finland and their dependency on a single supplier' (meaning Russia).[27] The panel found the TEN-E measure to be discriminatory, as the incentives under the TEN-E Regulation were designed to prevent dependency on a single country for the supply of energy, thereby implicitly incentivizing all other supply sources and routes.[28] It considered that 'the TEN-E measure provides more favourable conditions for the transportation of natural gas of any origin other than Russian, including natural gas of domestic origin. Therefore, for these reasons, we conclude that the TEN-E measure negatively affects the competitive opportunities of Russian natural gas vis-à-vis domestic natural gas.'[29]

At the heart of non-discrimination disciplines in GATT is the concept of 'likeness'. Discrimination is illegal only if the two products are 'like'. Likeness is generally judged on the basis of: (1) the properties, nature and quality of the products; (2) the end-uses of the products; (3) consumers' tastes and habits; and (4) the tariff classification of the products (see eg *US – Poultry (China)*).[30] What constitutes a 'like' energy product is particularly relevant to the energy debate within the context of GATT. This question, too, was raised by Russia in *EU – Energy Package*. In its claim, Russia essentially argued that natural gas

> contrary to Article I:1 of GATT 1994. Such Russian-origin natural gas is also accorded less favorable treatment than domestic natural gas that is transported and placed on the market through pipelines or other infrastructure listed as PCIs, in a manner inconsistent with Article III:4 of GATT 1994.

[26] *EU – Energy Package*, panel report, para 7.1267; TEN-E Regulation, recital (5).

[27] *EU – Energy Package*, panel report, para 7.1268; TEN-E Regulation (Exhibit EU-4), annexes I.2(6), I.2(7), I.2(8).

[28] *EU – Energy Package*, panel report, paras 7.1298–7.1300, 7.1310–7.1312.

[29] ibid, para 7.1300.

[30] Yanovich (n 16) 34. This approach was first articulated by the 1970 Working Party on Border Tax Adjustments. It has been followed in a number of Appellate Body (AB) and panel reports. See eg *Japan – Alcoholic Beverages II*, AB report, para 22; *US – Poultry (China)*, panel report, paras 7.424–7.427, 7.429.

> The traditional approach for determining 'likeness' has, in the main, consisted of employing four general criteria: '(i) the properties, nature and quality of the products; (ii) the end-uses of the products; (iii) consumers' tastes and habits – more comprehensively termed consumers' perceptions and behaviour – in respect of the products; and (iv) the tariff classification of the products.

> *US – Poultry (China)*, panel report, para 7.425, citing inter alia *Japan – Alcoholic Beverages II*.

and liquefied natural gas (LNG) were 'like' products within the meaning of Article I:1 GATT.[31] It argued that, while transmission system operators (TSOs) for natural gas (ie gas pipeline operators) were required to legally and physically unbundle their sales and distribution activities under the Gas Directive 2009/73/EC of the EU's Third Energy Package, LNG system operators were not required to do so, thereby receiving an advantage.[32] Russia was of the opinion that, once regasified, LNG was 'like' natural gas, the only difference being the physical state of LNG upon transportation and importation into the EU.[33] The EU argued that these products were not 'like', as they were in different forms (one liquid, the other gaseous) and classified under different subheadings.[34] In addition, the EU pointed to the different end-uses of natural gas and LNG, especially the latter's use as transportation fuel.[35] Disputing this argument, Russia declared that both types of gas are used by consumers 'to heat their homes, for example, or cook their food'.[36] The panel sided with the EU and was not convinced by Russia's arguments that LNG and natural gas were 'like' products.[37]

While the panel's treatment of likeness regarding natural gas and LNG was informative in this particular case, it is hard to draw conclusions from this for the 'likeness' of energy goods under GATT in general. A case-by-case analysis on the likeness of various types remains essential. For instance, it remains unclear whether or not clean energy goods should be considered 'like' fossil fuels, despite the far-reaching environmental implications of distinguishing between the two. Here, the controversy over whether process and production methods that are not part of a product's physical characteristics ('unincorporated' PPMs) can be taken into account when analysing all tradable goods for 'likeness' comes into play. The question is, to what extent should PPMs be a determining factor? And can non–product-related criteria (ie elements that are not visible in the final product) be considered a product characteristic rendering 'same' products 'unlike' within the meaning of

---

[31] *EU – Energy Package*, panel report, s 7.7.2.1.
[32] ibid, paras 7.825–7.826.
[33] ibid, para 7.834.
[34] ibid, para 7.835.
[35] ibid, para 7.835.
[36] ibid, para 7.836.
[37] ibid, paras 7.843, 7.842 fn 1407 (referring to the different uses of LNG) 7.84 –7.855.

GATT?[38] Is a fossil fuel 'like' a biofuel? Is electricity generated by coal 'like' electricity generated by wind?[39]

In other words, can regulatory distinctions be made between products that are identical when in their final form, and can WTO members treat energy generated by clean(er) means differently under GATT from energy produced by traditional, more polluting means?[40] Based on existing WTO case law, this distinction is hard to make.[41] *US – Auto Taxes*, however, offered a more optimistic outlook when deciding that fuel-efficient cars are not 'like' other cars under Article III:2.[42] Similarly, in *Canada – Renewable Energy* the Appellate Body took the view that the market for electricity generated from renewable sources was not the same as the market for all electricity, thereby implying that it was possible to differentiate between the two.[43] While this bodes well for differentiating between clean and polluting energy products in the future, no conclusive

---

[38] See also G Marceau, 'The WTO in the Emerging Energy Governance Debate' in J Pauwelyn (ed), *Global Challenges at the Intersection of Trade, Energy and Environment* (Graduate Institute of International and Development Studies/Centre for Trade and Economic Integration 2010) 26–27; Selivanova (n 20) 14, on the *Asbestos* case:

> [T]he Appellate Body ruled that the criteria of likeness are 'neither a treaty-mandated nor a closed list of criteria'. In that case, it found that health risks associated with products can be taken into consideration as criteria related to physical properties and consumers' tastes and habits. If some goods present more risks for health than others, two products might be considered not like and treated differently.

See *EC – Asbestos*, AB report, para 122.

[39] There are arguments against this; see *Canada – Renewable Energy/ Feed-in Tariff Program* AB report, para 5.211, where it was determined that the market benchmark for renewable energy was not the same as for all electrical energy.

[40] Yanovich (n 16) 34; D Crosby, 'Energy Discrimination and International Rules in Hard Times: What's New This Time Around, and What Can Be Done' (2012) 5 Journal of World Energy Law and Business 325, 334.

[41] See *EU – Energy Package*, panel report, para 7.837, citing *EC – Asbestos*, AB report, paras 99, 101–102:

> We recall that the Appellate Body has found that a determination of whether the products at issue are like for the purposes of Article III:4 of the GATT 1994 involves an assessment, on a case-by-case basis, of the nature and extent of the competitive relationship between and among these products, taking into account all relevant evidence, including the following criteria: (a) the properties, nature and quality of the products; (b) the end-uses of the products; (c) consumers' tastes and habits in respect of the products; and (d) the tariff classification of the products.

[42] GATT Secretariat, *US – Taxes on Automobiles* (DS 31/R) (11 October 1994, panel report not adopted); Crosby (n 40) 333–36.

[43] *Canada – Renewable Energy/Canada – Feed-in Tariff Program*, AB report, para 5.211.

answers have been given to such questions. There are nonetheless other avenues also open to WTO members wishing to treat the import of clean energy products differently from polluting energy. Even when polluting and clean energy goods are deemed 'like', members may opt to invoke Article XX (on exceptions, and especially those provided for in paragraphs (b) and (g)) to pursue legitimate policy objectives and justify behaviour otherwise inconsistent with GATT.[44]

3.2.1.3 Transit of Energy: Article V GATT

Transit of energy, especially via fixed infrastructures, has been extensively covered by other scholars, and will therefore not be discussed in detail here.[45] Some important matters must nevertheless be mentioned. Of crucial relevance to trade in energy goods is Article V on freedom of transit (especially with regard to gas pipelines and electricity grids). This provision prohibits MFN and NT violations, in addition to unnecessary charges, delays and regulations for products transiting from one member's territory to the country of destination, possibly through the territory of one or more other WTO members. Article V:2 GATT states:

> There shall be freedom of transit through the territory of each contracting party, via the routes most convenient for international transit, for traffic in transit to or from the territory of other contracting parties. No distinction shall be made which is based on the flag of vessels, the place of origin, departure, entry, exit or destination, or on any circumstances relating to the ownership of goods, of vessels or of other means of transport.[46]

The description of freedom of transit of goods through the territory of one WTO member to that of another WTO member is rather broad, including by vessel and other means of transport.[47] What is covered by 'other means' is debatable. For a long time it was unclear whether 'fixed infrastructures' such as pipelines, used mainly to transport natural gas and petroleum, fall within the scope of Article V:1 GATT.[48] Whether or

---

[44] The AB report in *Brazil – Retreaded Tyres* (para 151) pointed to the considerable latitude that exists when invoking exceptions for health reasons; see the discussion of paragraphs (b) and (g) in Section 3.2.1.6.

[45] See esp V Pogoretskyy, *Freedom of Transit and Access to Gas Pipeline Networks under WTO Law* (CUP 2017); D Azaria, *Treaties on Transit of Energy via Pipelines and Countermeasures* (OUP 2015). But see Chapter 4 for interaction with Energy Charter Treaty rules on transit.

[46] GATT, art V:2.

[47] ibid.

[48] M Cossy, 'Energy Transport and Transit in the WTO' in Pauwelyn (n 38) 113. See also D Azaria, 'Energy Transit under the Energy Charter Treaty and the General Agreement

not fixed energy grids such as gas pipelines and electricity transmission networks are covered by Article V GATT can affect dispute settlement in the WTO: on that may depend whether an energy transit dispute (eg over the obstruction of gas flows) may be settled in the WTO forum.

Assuming that 'other means of transport' should be interpreted broadly, one has every reason to question why fixed energy grids should be excluded. The panel in *Colombia – Ports of Entry* provided an interpretation of the obligations under Article V:2, which it read as requiring parties to extend freedom of transit through the most convenient route.[49] Also, it can be inferred from the accession commitments of Ukraine, Russia and Kazakhstan that for these WTO members Article V unquestionably applied to gas pipelines.[50] Ukraine, for example, stated that as far as trade in fossil fuels was concerned, 'charges for transportation of goods in transit' would be bound by the disciplines of Article V GATT.[51]

The goods/services divide inevitably has a bearing on the transit of energy. Both GATT and GATS can apply to transit activities like the transportation of natural gas through gas pipelines or electricity through cross-border energy transmission networks. Assuming that Article V GATT indeed applies to fixed infrastructures such as gas pipeline networks, the energy goods in question (natural gas and electricity) are covered by that provision. However, the services connected to the transportation of energy would additionally be covered by GATS.[52] During the Uruguay Round and thereafter, several members made commitments

---

on Tariffs and Trade' (2009) 27 Journal of Energy and Natural Resources Law 559; Marceau (n 38) 87.

[49] *Colombia – Ports of Entry*, panel report, para 7.401.

[50] See Chapter 2, Section 2.4.2. Note that, before joining the WTO, Russia disputed that Article V applied to fixed infrastructures such as gas pipelines; see the audio recording of the presentation by Mr Medvedkov, director of the Department of Trade Negotiations in the Russian Ministry of Development, at the Workshop on the Role of Intergovernmental Agreements in Energy Policy (Geneva, 29 April 2013) Session 2 'Current Challenges for International Regulation of Trade in Energy: Transport and Transit' <www.wto.org/english/tratop_e/envir_e/wksp_envir_apr13_e/wksp_envir_apr13_e.htm> accessed 20 July 2020. However, in its accession report Russia partially committed to regulate its transit of energy in accordance with Article V GATT, namely with regard to transit fees (not with regard to access to pipelines). See Accession Protocol (22 August 2012) WT/L/839, WT/MIN(11)/27; Report of the Working Party on the Accession of the Russian Federation (17 November 2011) WT/ACC/RUS/70, WT/MIN(11)/2, para 1161.

[51] WTO, Report of the Working Party on the Accession of Ukraine(25 January 2008) WT/ACC/UKR/152 (Ukraine Report) para 367; see also PC Mavroidis, G Bermann, and M Wu, *The Law of the World Trade Organization* (West 2010) 97.

[52] See Section 3.3.2.

in their schedules concerning services incidental to energy distribution and the pipeline transportation of fuels.[53] In its service schedule, Ukraine made a specific commitment on pipeline transportation.[54]

3.2.1.4 Import and Export Restrictions on Energy: Article XI GATT

Import and export restrictions are prohibited by Article XI:1 GATT. In energy trading, export restrictions are usually a greater concern than import restrictions, as the need of energy consumers to access unevenly distributed energy supplies is generally greater than the need of energy producers for markets to export to. Because of the significance of export restrictions for cross-border energy trade, Chapter 5 will take a closer look at this issue and its interaction with Article XI GATT disciplines in the context of the decentralization of the energy sector.[55] One particularly controversial matter is whether or not domestic production quota on petroleum could qualify as an export restriction within the meaning of Article XI:1 GATT and therefore be considered to violate that provision.

In *EU – Energy Package*, restrictions on *imports* of natural gas were at issue. Russia objected to the 'infrastructure exemption measure' in Article 32 of the 2009 Gas Directive, which permits a lighter regime of ownership unbundling (OU) and lighter third-party access requirements.[56] The EU granted this exemption to 'major new gas infrastructure, i.e. interconnectors, LNG and storage facilities' under certain conditions, for instance when the major infrastructure in question contributes to 'significant increases of capacity in existing infrastructure and to modifications of such infrastructure which enable the development of new sources of gas supply'.[57] Simply put, Russia objected to the effects this measure had on the operation of the OPAL pipeline (connected to the Nord Stream gas pipeline and running from Germany to the Czech Republic), which is controlled by a Russian pipeline

---

[53] The I-TIP Services online platform contains information on what countries have committed to, under 11 Transport Services, 11.G Pipeline Transport <https://i-tip.wto.org/services/Search.aspx> accessed 20 July 2020.

[54] See Ukraine Report, Addendum: Schedule of Specific Commitments in Services, WT/ACC/UKR/152/Add.2, XI:7(a)(4). See also Section 2.4.2.5.

[55] See Chapter 5.

[56] Directive 2009/73/EC of the European Parliament and of the Council of 13 July 2009 concerning common rules for the internal market in natural gas and repealing Directive 2003/55/EC [2009] OJ L211/94 (Gas Directive) art 32. Ownership unbundling refers to EU-mandated breaking-up of exploration, sales and distribution activities in the energy sector.

[57] Gas Directive, art 36; Russia's panel request (n 23) 4–5.

transport service supplier.[58] This service supplier was granted a limited exemption only for capacities of gas passing through the pipeline and required that no more than 50 per cent of those capacities be allocated to 'dominant undertakings in the Czech gas market'.[59] Russia argued that this was a de facto restriction on the importation of Russian natural gas into Europe.[60] The panel sided with Russia and agreed that the cap was a violation of Article XI:1 GATT, as 'the challenged OPAL conditions effectively impose a limitation on the competitive opportunities for natural gas of Russian origin that may be imported (by Gazprom) into the European Union'.[61] The panel considered that 'the existence of, and requirements imposed by, this condition effectively operate so as to discourage certain importers of Russian natural gas, i.e. Gazprom and related companies, from exceeding the 50% capacity cap'.[62] It concluded that the measure had a limiting effect on the competitive opportunities for importation of Russian gas into the European Union.[63]

3.2.1.5 Energy Companies as State Trading Enterprises: Article XVII GATT

Article XVII GATT on state trading enterprises (STEs) requires STEs to act consistently with the general principles of non-discriminatory treatment when making purchases.[64] STEs must carry out sales and purchases solely in accordance with commercial considerations.[65]

However, it has not been clearly determined in WTO law, including case law, what entities qualify as STEs. The WTO website provides a definition agreed upon by WTO members: 'State trading enterprises are defined as governmental and non-governmental enterprises, including marketing boards, which deal with goods for export and/or import.'[66] It also provides information on STEs that have been notified to it and distinguishes between the following types of STEs: statutory marketing boards; export marketing boards; regulatory marketing boards; fiscal

---

[58] Russia's panel request 5.

[59] *EU – Energy Package*, panel report, para 7.983.

[60] Russia's panel request 4.

[61] *EU – Energy Package*, panel report, para 7.1000.

[62] ibid.

[63] ibid, also paras 7.1002–7.1003.

[64] GATT 1994, art XVII:1(a) (STEs).

[65] GATT 1994, art XVII:1(b).

[66] WTO, 'State Trading Enterprises' <www.wto.org/english/tratop_e/statra_e/statra_e.htm> accessed 20 July 2020; see also PC Mavroidis, *The Regulation of International Trade*, vol 1 *GATT* (MIT Press 2015) 401.

monopolies; canalizing agencies; foreign trade enterprises; and boards or corporations resulting from nationalized industries.[67]

Energy companies that continue to be vertically integrated and state-owned could fit into one of these categories of STEs. Controversial issues may arise when investigating whether such corporations act in accordance with 'commercial considerations', especially when it comes to energy dual-pricing practices.[68] It is possible that in such instances national energy monopolies control the energy market completely, preventing enterprises from other WTO members from competing for sales or purchases on an equal footing, which would be contrary to Article XVII GATT.[69] This is especially the case if energy prices are set by the government rather than through market forces,[70] which arguably would be contrary to the obligation to act 'solely in accordance with commercial considerations' set out in Article XVII(b).[71] Another potential difficulty relates to the transit of energy. Does the STE provision mean that energy companies that own distribution networks have to respect the rules of non-discrimination when it comes to third party access to pipelines?[72] This is relevant as Article XVII GATT applies to any enterprise that has been granted exclusive or special privileges, even if such a company is not owned by the state. Control over national energy infrastructures could be considered a special privilege, which implies that the enterprise in question would have to comply with Article XVII's non-discrimination .[73]

3.2.1.6   General Exceptions: Article XX GATT

If a WTO member wishes to deviate from its obligations under GATT to pursue legitimate policy objectives, it can seek to rely on the general exceptions in Article XX. If it is successful, the inconsistency of its behaviour with GATT will not be removed but merely justified.[74]

---

[67] WTO, 'Technical Information on State Trading Enterprises' <www.wto.org/english/tratop_e/statra_e/statra_info_e.htm> accessed 9 January 2021; Mavroidis (n 66) 402–403.

[68] See Chapter 2, Section 2.4.2, esp Saudi Arabia's accession protocol, and Chapter 6 on decarbonization and dual pricing.

[69] Marceau (n 38) 28.

[70] ibid.

[71] GATT 1994, art XVII:1(b); Mavroidis (n 66) 404–408, opposing the position espoused in case law that the 'commercial considerations' criterion is fulfilled where there has been no discrimination.

[72] Selivanova (n 20) 19.

[73] ibid.

[74] See Mavroidis, Bermann and Wu (n 51) ch 5 ('Deviating from WTO Obligations') 325ff.

Paragraphs (a) to (j) of Article XX provide an exhaustive list of measures covered by the exception. Note, however, that an Article XX invocation will not succeed if the WTO member does not comply with the chapeau, which requires that the measures 'are not applied in a manner which would constitute a means of arbitrary or unjustifiable discrimination between countries where the same conditions prevail, or a disguised restriction on international trade'.[75] In addition to guaranteeing non-discrimination, compliance with the chapeau is a means of preventing the exceptions from being misused for discriminatory purposes.[76]

Two paragraphs of Article XX are particularly relevant to trade in energy and will be discussed here (note that this excludes the applicability of other subparagraphs, too). They are: (b) measures 'necessary to protect human, animal, plant life or health' and (g) measures 'relating to the conservation of exhaustible natural resources'.[77] The broad interpretation in case law of what constitutes the protection of animal, plant life or health in Article XX(b) gives WTO members leeway to justify measures that may be inconsistent with GATT that have been put in place to further environmental policies. The Appellate Body in *Brazil – Retreaded Tyres* adopted a broad interpretation of what constitutes legitimate policy objectives in the context of the exceptions listed in Article XX GATT and of the extent to which a particular measure taken by a WTO member in this context has to fulfil the objective pursued by the exception in question.[78]

Paragraph (g) on measures relating to the conservation of exhaustible natural resources arguably also gives members considerable room to justify environmental policy objectives. The exhaustible natural resources referred to here range widely from minerals and raw materials to fish stocks and clean air.[79] Following confirmation by the Appellate Body in *US – Gasoline* that clean air is an exhaustible natural resource, one could maintain that measures inconsistent with GATT that promote clean air and curb CO_2 emissions may be justified under GATT.

To understand why the exception relating to the conservation of exhaustible natural resources under (g) was included in GATT, it is helpful

---

[75] GATT 1994, art XX, chapeau.
[76] See Mavroidis, Bermann and Wu (n 51) 359.
[77] GATT 1994, art XX(b), (g).
[78] *Brazil – Retreaded Tyres*, AB report, para 151.
[79] See Article XX negotiation history in ECOSOC, Preparatory Committee of the International Conference on Trade and Employment (13 November 1946) E/PC/T/C. II/50; see also case law developed by AB in *US – Shrimp* and *US – Gasoline*.

to look at the *travaux préparatoires* for Article XX(g) and the statements made by delegates negotiating on the matter back in 1947, which give us some insights into the provision's purpose. New Zealand's arguments show that one of the reasons for including this particular exception was that 'no member country should be compelled to export both manufactured and natural products which it wished to conserve for domestic purposes'.[80] This would suggest that the provision was drafted to give members the freedom to use their own resources for domestic use. India's representative added that 'he felt that his country might have to conserve for domestic use its exhaustible and scarce resources, even if such a measure was not "pursuant to international agreements", or was not "made effective in conjunction with restrictions on domestic production or consumption"'.[81]

In essence, it is plausible that the exception under (g) was drafted with commodities such as petrol and minerals in mind, although this is not spelled out as such anywhere in the *travaux préparatoires*.[82] It nevertheless seems that the negotiations on the exhaustible natural resources exception were oriented towards non-living organisms. Later, as case law developed, living organisms such as fish stocks were added to the definition.[83] Chapter 5 will analyse in greater depth the 'conservation of exhaustible natural resources' exception in relation to restrictive energy trade practices .

The recent cases *India – Solar Cells* and *EU – Energy Package* have pointed to the relevance to the energy sector also of Article XX(j) – measures 'essential to the acquisition or distribution of products in general or local short supply'.[84] Energy resources are susceptible to shortages and therefore potentially covered by this provision. In both cases India and the EU tried (unsuccessfully) to argue that solar cells and natural gas were in local short supply and argued that this had a bearing on energy security.[85]

3.2.1.7 Security Exceptions: Article XXI GATT

Article XXI GATT on security exceptions prescribes that nothing in GATT should be construed in such a way as to require 'any contracting

---

[80] ECOSOC (n 79) (New Zealand's representative).

[81] ibid 5.

[82] PC Mavroidis, *Trade in Goods* (2nd edn, OUP 2012) 345–46.

[83] ibid 346; *US – Shrimp*, AB report, paras 128, 130, 153, affirming that (g) is not limited to mineral resources.

[84] *India-Solar Cells*, panel and AB reports; *EU – Energy Package*, panel report, paras 7.1336–7.1353.

[85] See Chapter 7, Section 7.3.

party to furnish any information the disclosure of which it considers contrary to its essential security interests'.[86] Over the decades, states have relied on Article XXI to defend conduct inconsistent with GATT. The United States, for instance, has been said to have used the Article XXI security exception to justify its almost forty-year-long ban on the export of crude oil, which was lifted in 2015.[87] Article XXI was not litigated for decades, until it was invoked by Russia in the 2017 *Russia – Traffic in Transit* dispute.[88] The panel rejected that the view that the provision is completely 'self-judging', meaning that panels can, to some extent, look into the content of the measure.[89]

WTO members' energy policies are often tied to security policy (ie energy security). As a Pandora's box has now been opened with respect to litigation of this provision, it is conceivable that it will be invoked in future trade disputes concerning energy.

Finally, Article XXI(b)(i) is relevant to trade in nuclear materials insofar as it states that '[n]othing in this Agreement shall be construed ... to prevent any contracting party from taking any action which it considers necessary for the protection of its essential security interests relating to fissionable materials or the materials from which they are derived'.[90]

3.2.2   Agreement on Agriculture

The Agreement on Agriculture (AoA) was a result of the Uruguay Round and resulted in agricultural products being treated apart.[91] The rationale for treating farm trade differently in the GATT/WTO framework shows some parallels with the manner in which the multilateral trading system dealt with energy. Like energy, agriculture is a highly strategic sector, essential for human survival. After World War II, many countries chose

---

[86]   GATT 1994, art XXI ('Security Exceptions').

[87]   This ban was lifted in the autumn of 2015; see 'Lifting of America's 40-Year Oil Export Ban' *Financial Times* (17 December 2015). On the US crude oil ban, see also J Bordoff and T Houser, *Navigating the US Oil Export Debate* (January 2015) Columbia/SIPA Center on Global Energy Policy.

[88]   *Russia – Traffic in Transit*, panel report.

[89]   ibid, para 7.102.

[90]   GATT 1994, art XXI(b)(i): 'Nothing in this Agreement shall be construed to prevent any contracting party from taking any action which it considers necessary for the protection of its essential security interests relating to fissionable materials or the materials from which they are derived.'

[91]   Mavroidis, Bermann and Wu (n 51) 744.

to become self-sufficient in food production and introduced policies to that end.[92] This led to highly insulated and protectionist farm markets globally.[93] Europe, for instance, sought to achieve self-sufficiency through its common agricultural policy notorious for flexible levies and export subsidies.[94]

The ultimate goal of the AoA is to reduce and eliminate agricultural export subsidies and import tariffs completely, and to tame all domestic support.[95] Its main legal disciplines are (a) the requirement that non-tariff border measures be converted into tariffs (Article 42 AoA); (b) the curbing of domestic support through a system of 'boxes' (Articles 1(a), 6 and Annex 3)[96]; (c) product-specific reduction commitments on export subsidies for agricultural products (Articles 8–10); (d) *de minimis* provisions allowing subsidies up to 5 per cent (Article 6.4); and (e) other miscellaneous obligations such as transparency requirements.[97]

At first glance, the AoA seems to have little relevance to trade in energy, but this is deceptive. As mentioned in Section 3.2.1.2, some biofuels are treated as agricultural products and, as a consequence, are subject to high import tariffs, especially compared to traditional energy products. This is the case with ethanol, for instance.[98] Additionally, WTO rules on agricultural subsidies may affect biofuels and other subsidized fuels. Such rules may currently allow for domestic and export subsidies on such fuels, which should be kept in mind in relation to climate change mitigation.[99]

3.2.3 Agreement on Technical Barriers to Trade

Technical standards are important in the energy sector as, inter alia, they can encourage energy efficiency and sustainability. Technical regulations can restrict trade, but this is allowed insofar as the effects of the regulation do not restrict trade restrictive more than is necessary (Article 2.2 of the

---

[92] ibid 745.
[93] ibid.
[94] ibid 746.
[95] ibid 744.
[96] ibid 751, stating that support has to be reduced by 20 per cent: 'There are green, blue and yellow categories of "boxes", which escalate in their trade-distortedness. Members can place agricultural products in these boxes, as long as they respect the 20 per cent reduction.'
[97] ibid 751–52.
[98] Yanovich (n 16) 27; HS Convention, ch 22('Beverages, Spirits and Vinegar').
[99] Marceau (n 38) 28.

Agreement on Technical Barriers to Trade (TBT Agreement)) and are applied on an MFN basis (Article 2.1 TBT Agreement). Article 2.5 of the TBT Agreement further prescribes that when a regulation is based on an international standard, 'it shall be rebuttably presumed not to create an unnecessary obstacle to international trade'.[100] This is important to consider given the prevalence of standardization in the energy sector, with international standards on everything from solar energy to aviation fuels to pipeline transportation systems.[101]

3.2.4   Agreement on Trade-Related Investment Measures

The Agreement on Trade-Related Investment Measures (TRIMs) is a *lex specialis* to Articles III and XI GATT, as GATT prohibits export performance and local content requirements.[102] Article 2.1 of the TRIMs Agreement prohibits any investment measure that is inconsistent with Articles III or XI, and the annex to the agreement provides an illustrative (ie not necessarily conclusive) list of measures that are inconsistent with those articles.[103] They comprise: local content requirements; export performance requirements; trade balancing requirements; foreign exchange balancing restrictions; and restrictions on an enterprise's export of products or sale of products for export. If a challenged measure falls within the illustrative list, it is automatically deemed not to be consistent with WTO rules.[104]

For the energy sector, the TRIMs Agreement comes into play where cross-border energy investments or energy generation are concerned. In these instances, local content requirements are prohibited, except in the case of government procurement as set out in Article III:8 GATT. If a member maintains a feed-in tariff (FIT) for renewable energy (a popular form of subsidy to encourage the scale-up of clean energy) combined with a local content requirement, this is especially problematic and contrary to the TRIMs Agreement.

This was one of the issues at stake in the *Canada – Renewable Energy/ Canada – Feed-In Tariff Program* case. The province of Ontario

---

[100] TBT Agreement, art 2.5.

[101] For an overview of international standards in energy, see International Organization on Standardization, *ISO and Energy* (ISO 2018).

[102] See TRIMs Agreement; GATT 1994, arts III (national treatment), XI (prohibition of quantitative restrictions).

[103] See TRIMs Agreement, annex; Mavroidis, Bermann and Wu (n 51) 310.

[104] *India – Autos Measures*, AB report, para 7.157; Mavroidis, Bermann and Wu (n 51) 310.

maintained a feed-in tariff (FIT) programme, providing FIT and microFIT contracts to producers of renewable energy.[105] Only if these producers used locally produced wind energy generation equipment were they offered a contract and guaranteed preferential tariffs on the energy they produced.[106] The EU and Japan objected to this measure. The panel indeed was of the opinion that these programmes were designed in such a way as 'to encourage investment in the local production of equipment associated with renewable energy generation in the province of Ontario'.[107] Therefore, the panel decided (and the Appellate Body later confirmed) that the FIT programme and its contracts constituted a TRIM within the meaning of Article I of the TRIMs Agreement and were thus inconsistent with Articles III:4 and XI GATT.[108] Canada's defence that the FIT programme amounted to government procurement and therefore, pursuant to Article III:8, did not have to conform to the TRIMs Agreement, failed.[109] More recently, TRIMs were litigated in connection with domestic content requirements for renewable energy incentives schemes in *India – Solar Cells* and *US – Renewable Energy*.[110]

3.2.5 Anti-Dumping Agreement

The Anti-Dumping Agreement (ADA), which elaborates on Article VI GATT, provides detailed rules on the use of anti-dumping measures.[111] Dumping involves a foreign producer flooding the import market with a product below the home market price, thereby causing injury to the domestic industry producing the 'like' product.[112] Although the practice of dumping is not illegal per se, it is considered an unfair trade practice.[113] The rationale of the agreement therefore is that it protects WTO members against dumping by laying down anti-dumping rules and

---

[105] *Canada – Renewable Energy/Canada – Feed-in Tariff Program*, panel report, para 7.108.

[106] ibid, paras 2.1, 7.6, 7.9–7.68: 'Only projects that satisfy all of the specific eligibility requirements set out in the FIT and microFIT Rules, and that can be connected to the Ontario electricity system, will be offered a Contract, and thereby permitted to participate in the Programme.'

[107] ibid, paras 7.109–9.110.

[108] ibid, para 7.112.

[109] ibid, paras 7.152–7.154.

[110] *India – Solar Cells*, panel and AB reports; *US – Renewable Energy*, panel report. See Chapter 7, Section 7.3.

[111] P van den Bossche and W Zdouc, *The Law and Policy of the World Trade Organization* (4th edn, CUP 2017) 698ff.

[112] GATT 1994, art VI; Mavroidis, Bermann and Wu (n 51) 414.

[113] Mavroidis, Bermann and Wu (n 51) 415.

providing for countervailing duties.[114] The ADA allows WTO members that suffer 'material injury to an established industry' as a result of the dumping to levy anti-dumping duties to offset the effects of the dumping (Article VI:2 GATT). These duties cannot exceed the dumping margin on such product.[115]

The disciplines on anti-dumping become relevant (sometimes indirectly) to energy trade insofar as they are invoked in connection with energy goods and/or energy inputs into goods that are dumped on a foreign market. A company that exports a product at a lower price than it normally charges is said to be dumping the product on the foreign market.[116] For instance, the increasing trade in goods for renewable energy generation – the so-called solar panel trade wars triggered disputes between major producers of solar panels and photovoltaic cells.[117] While one of the cases mainly revolved around local content requirements and subsidies rather than dumping (*India – Solar Cells*), other cases such as *US – Countervailing Measures*, *EU – Biodiesel (Argentina)* and *EU – Biodiesel (Indonesia)*, concerned anti-dumping duties on renewable energy (ie solar panels and biofuels).

Anti-dumping also comes into play, indirectly, in connection with energy dual-pricing policies, as in *EU – Cost Adjustment Methodologies II (Russia)*.[118] Russia requested that a panel rule on the EU Council Regulation protecting against dumped imports and the use of cost adjustment administrative procedures.[119] The EU imposed

---

[114] ADA, art 18.1; Mavroidis, Bermann and Wu (n 51) 415.

[115] GATT 1994, art VI:2.

[116] See WTO, 'Technical Information on Anti-Dumping' <www.wto.org/english/tratop_e/adp_e/adp_info_e.htm#:~:text=Under%20Article%20VI%20of%20GATT%201994%2C%20and%20the,there%20is%20a%20causal%20link%20between%20the%20two> accessed 20 July 2020, explaining that dumping occurs when the price of the product sold abroad (a) is less than the comparable price, in the ordinary course of trade, for the like product when destined for consumption in the exporting country, or (b), in the absence of such domestic price, is less than either (i) the highest comparable price for the like product for export to any third country in the ordinary course of trade, or (ii) the cost of production of the product in the country of origin plus a reasonable addition for selling cost and profit.

[117] See eg K Bradsher, 'Solar Rises in Malaysia during Trade Wars over Panels' *New York Times* (11 December 2014) <www.nytimes.com/2014/12/12/business/energy-environment/solar-rises-in-malaysia-during-trade-wars-over-Panels.html?_r=0> accessed 20 July 2020.

[118] See Chapter 6.

[119] Council Regulation (EC) 1225/2009 of 30 November 2009 on protection against dumped imports from countries not members of the European Community; Russia's panel request (n 23) 1.

anti-dumping duties on ammonium nitrate and certain tubes, pipes and other goods originating in Russia.[120] The EU introduced these duties and cost adjustments to offset cheaper inputs, made possible through energy dual pricing, for the production of goods in Russia.[121] The EU justified these anti-dumping duties by arguing that Russia maintained cheaper inputs in its domestic industry because of the low domestic price of energy, and thus did not pay the actual cost of energy. As a consequence, Russia could dump certain products such as steel pipes on the European market.

3.2.6 Agreement on Subsidies and Countervailing Measures

The Agreement on Subsidies and Countervailing Measures (SCM Agreement), which elaborates on Articles XVI and VI GATT, sets out rules for WTO members concerning the use of subsidies. It prohibits the maintaining of export subsidies and local content requirements (Article 3.1(a) and (b)), and requires members to avoid producing adverse effects towards fellow members through other subsidies (Article 5). It also lays out rules for the imposition of countervailing duties, so that such subsidies can be offset (Articles 4 and 7).[122] Apart from the prohibited subsidies (subsidies on export and local content requirements), subsidies are not illegal per se, but WTO members can act against them if they cause harm to their domestic industries (so-called actionable subsidies).[123]

Whether based on fossil fuels or renewables, the energy sector is one of the most heavily subsidized sectors in the world.[124] This can be explained by the fact that it is often capital-intensive and closely connected to a state's industrial policy on fossil fuels or on the furtherance of alternative sources of energy. Because of the widespread presence of subsidies in the sector, WTO rules on subsidies automatically become relevant to energy. The rules of the SCM Agreement influence and bind the choices of governments with respect to their industrial and other policies.

Energy subsidies can be broadly divided into producer and consumer subsidies.[125] The former subsidize the producers of fuel products, coal,

---

[120] Russia's panel request 3.

[121] ibid, paras 5.1, 5.2.

[122] Mavroidis, Bermann and Wu (n 51) 520–21.

[123] SCM Agreement, art 5.

[124] HB Asmelash, 'Energy Subsidies and WTO Dispute Settlement: Why Only Renewable Energy Subsidies Are Challenged' (2015) 18 Journal of International Economic Law 261, 270.

[125] B Clements and others (eds), *Energy Subsidy Reform: Lessons and Implications* (IMF 2013) 1, 2.

natural gas and electricity.[126] Feed-in tariffs (FITs) to stimulate the scale-up of renewables in the energy mix are an example of producer subsidies. The latter cover intermediate consumers (firms) and final consumers (households). Examples are subsidies that result in cheaper inputs for energy intensive industries or lower energy bills for household consumers .

Overall, specificity is easier to locate in producer subsidies. Clean and renewable energy programmes (such as feed-in tariffs) generally take the form of regional or national programmes to stimulate the production of clean energy and are therefore more clearly defined as specific.[127] Fossil fuel subsidies, on the other hand, are often subsidies to consumers available across the entire economy, which makes it harder to qualify them as specific.[128]

In *Canada – Renewable Energy / Canada – Feed-In Tariff Program*, subsidies were a central issue. The question was whether, through its feed-in tariff (FIT) programme, the Canadian government conferred a benefit on local producers within the meaning of the SCM Agreement's Article 1.1(a)(1) (financial contribution and/or price support) and 1.1(b) (conferral of a benefit). While both the panel and the Appellate body were of the opinion that the measures of the Canadian government amounted to a financial contribution,[129] they disagreed over whether or not the measures conferred a benefit within the meaning of Article 1.1(b) of the SCM Agreement.[130] In the end, the Appellate Body

---

[126] ibid.

[127] Asmelash (n 124) 274 points out that the renewable energy market could already be regarded as specific compared to the energy market as a whole.

[128] ibid.

[129] *Canada – Renewable Energy/Canada – Feed-in Tariff Program*, panel report, paras 7.243–7.245 and AB report, para 5.121.

[130] *Canada – Renewable Energy/Canada – Feed-in Tariff Program* panel report, para 7.320: Unable to find the relevant market benchmark for electricity, the panel stated that 'the competitive wholesale electricity market that is at the centre of the complainants' main submissions cannot be the appropriate focus of the benefit analysis in these disputes'. Recalling that it had also rejected the complainants' alternative benchmarks, the panel concluded that '[t]here is therefore no basis to uphold the complainants' benefit arguments'. On appeal, the AB criticized certain aspects of the panel's reasoning, and it set out its own approach. Reversing the panel's findings, it took the view that a benefit was conferred, but could not complete its analysis ('we do not consider that there are sufficient factual findings by the Panel and uncontested evidence on the Panel record that would allow us to complete the legal analysis and conduct a benefit benchmark comparison between the prices of wind-generated electricity under the FIT Programme and the prices for wind-generated electricity under the RES initiative'). Thus, it could not determine whether the challenged measures conferred a benefit within the meaning of

was 'unable to complete the analysis' of whether the programme constituted a subsidy within the meaning of the SCM Agreement.[131] Scholars
accused both the panel and the Appellate Body of engaging in 'legal
acrobatics' to avoid categorizing the Ontario FIT programme.[132]
A plausible explanation for this is the dilemma adjudicators are faced
with, given that FIT programmes are omnipresent and generally seen as
furthering legitimate policy goals while being potentially incompatible
with current WTO disciplines on subsidies.

The *Canada – Renewable Energy / Canada – Feed-In Tariff Program*
example begs the question what the implications of the existing regime
are for clean energy subsidies under WTO rules as compared to fossil fuel
subsidies. Dual pricing, for instance – the practice whereby energy is sold
at a much lower price on the domestic market than abroad – could also be
seen as a subsidy and may be an actionable subsidy within the meaning of
Article 5 of the SCM Agreement. The problem, however, seems to be that
it is often difficult to characterize the subsidy (and therefore to qualify it
as an actionable subsidy).[133] It may nevertheless adversely affect another
WTO member, which finds itself having to pay much more for imported
energy inputs.[134]

The take-away is that subsidies on fossil fuels remain largely
untouched in the WTO, whereas subsidies on green energies seem
more problematic and have repeatedly been referred to dispute settlement. That this may lead to unfavourable policy outcomes is clear,
although it is also evident that a balance has to be struck to prevent
protectionism masquerading as the furtherance of policy goals (eg protection of the environment).[135] Government assistance (eg to update
existing facilities to meet new environmental requirements) was

---

Article 1.1(b) and whether they constituted prohibited subsidies inconsistent with the
SCM Agreement's Articles 3.1(b) and 3.2. *Canada – Renewable Energy/Canada – Feed-in
Tariff Program*, AB report, para 5.246.

[131] *Canada – Renewable Energy/Canada – Feed-in Tariff Program*, AB report, para 6.1
(b)(iii).

[132] See A Cosbey and PC Mavroidis, 'A Turquoise Mess: Green Subsidies, Blue Industrial
Policy and Renewable Energy: The Case for Redrafting the Subsidies Agreement of the
WTO' (2014) Robert Schuman Centre for Advanced Studies 2014/17, 82.

[133] Marceau (n 38) 27.

[134] Specificity is a requirement set out in Article 2 of the SCM Agreement to meet the
definition of a subsidy.

[135] See Chapter 6. On legal issues concerning renewable energy and WTO law, see Howse
and Eliason (n 17) 80–90; TL Meyer, 'Energy Subsidies and the World Trade
Organization' (2013) 17(22) ASIL Insights <www.asil.org/insights>.

sometimes deemed non-actionable under Article 8 of the SCM Agreement, but this provision remained unused and expired at the end of 1999.[136]

Disciplines on subsidies are of particular relevance to trade in energy and to the advancement of certain policy goals by governments and will be studied in more depth in Chapter 6 on energy dual pricing and harmful fossil fuel subsidies.

3.3   General Agreement on Trade in Services

3.3.1   The Goods/Services Divide in Energy

The architecture of GATT is such that its subject matter deals with trade in goods only. Trade in services is regulated by the General Agreement on Trade in Services (GATS). This divide creates a challenge for the energy sector in that it may at times be difficult to distinguish between the goods and the services aspects of energy trade and, consequently, to determine which of the agreements should apply. This also accounts for the Annex 1A agreements on trade in goods – covering agriculture, technical barriers to trade, trade-related investment measures, anti-dumping, etc. – which are presumed to apply to goods only and not to services.[137] Therefore, whether a certain energy-related economic activity is considered a good or a service can have far-reaching consequences as far as the WTO agreements potentially applicable to it are concerned. An additional reason why the classification of an energy commodity as a good or a service is important is that trade in services is generally considerably less liberalized than trade in goods.[138] It should be noted, however, that the panel in *EC – Bananas III* decided that

---

[136] SCM Agreement, art 8; Marceau (n 38) 27.

[137] See breakdown of WTO agreements at <www.wto.org/english/docs_e/legal_e/legal_e .htm> accessed 13 January 2021 (Annex 1A, Multilateral Trade in Goods; Annex 1B, General Agreement on Trade in Services; Annex 1C, Trade-Related Intellectual Property Rights). See also SCM Agreement, art 32.1 ('Other Final Provisions'): 'No specific action against a subsidy of another Member can be taken except in accordance with the provisions of GATT 1994, as interpreted by this Agreement.'

[138] Services are considerably less liberalized, due to the heavy domestic regulation on account of their far-reaching implications for national immigration and investment policies. See Mavroidis, Bermann and Wu (n 51) 757; B Hoekman and A Matoo, 'Liberalizing Trade in Services: Lessons from Regional and WTO Negotiations' (2013) 18 International Negotiation 131, 132ff.

GATT and GATS can overlap and be simultaneously applicable, although not with respect to the same measure.[139]

Much of the energy traded globally possesses elements of both goods and services.[140] The reason for this is that the manufacture of an energy good is sometimes hard to separate from the service or activity connected to its generation, extraction, or distribution.[141] Vertically integrated energy companies were traditionally, and often still are, in charge of all processes, from extracting to manufacturing to distributing the energy product in question.[142] These are often natural monopolies because of the high investment in infrastructure that energy extraction and distribution demands.[143] Consequently, the industry itself does not always clearly distinguish between the goods and services aspects of energy trade.[144]

The most straightforward way of identifying energy goods is by means of their codes in the HS Convention. Some energy products (eg petroleum, natural gas, LNG and coal) are easily identifiable as goods when in their final and tradable form after extraction.[145] However, it is not always clear whether, for example, the extraction of petroleum and petroleum products is a service or can also be qualified as the manufacturing of a good. Arguments could be made for both. Usually, services do not result in goods.[146] In those instances, one could regard the extraction process not as a service but as the manufacturing of a good. On the other hand, it is clear that the extraction process itself could be considered a service in certain circumstances, especially where foreign energy

---

[139] *EC – Bananas III*, panel report, para 7.283.

[140] Marceau (n 38) 25.

[141] Services can generally be distinguished from goods through their (a) intangibility, (b) non-storability, (c) differentiation (ie difficult to classify because tailored to the need of the customer) and (d) joint production (eg the customer often has to participate in the process); see Mavroidis, Bermann and Wu (n 51) 762.

[142] WTO, Council for Trade in Services, 'Energy Services: Background Note by the Secretariat' (9 September 1998) S/C/W/52 (WTO 1998 Background Note) states that most GATT contracting parties regard electricity as a good and some of them have also undertaken tariff bindings on it (para 8).

[143] JP Tomain, *Energy Law in a Nutshell* (2nd edn, West Academic 2011) 169ff.

[144] WTO 1998 Background Note 1; T Cottier and others, 'Energy in WTO Law and Policy' in T Cottier and P Delimatsis (eds), *The Prospects of International Trade Regulation: From Fragmentation to Coherence* (CUP 2011) 215.

[145] WTO, Council for Trade in Services, 'Energy Services: Background Note by the Secretariat' (12 January 2010) S/C/W/311 (WTO 2010 Background Note) 11, para 51. The note discusses in detail many forms of energy goods and services and insists on how difficult it is to make clear distinctions between them in a lot of cases.

[146] Mavroidis, Bermann and Wu (n 51) 762.

companies enter the territory of a WTO member to perform this some-times highly specialized and technically complex task.[147] Generally, energy services are perceived as a value added to energy goods which could not be dealt with separately (like the refining of crude petroleum).[148]

Cross-border electricity trade is a case in point. Under EU law, electri-city is considered a good, not a service.[149] In the WTO context, the HS Convention refers to 'electrical energy' (code 2716), but this may not always be identical to electricity. There may be service aspects to electri-city due to the vertical integration of the process from its generation (manufacture) to its transportation to households, often performed by one and the same company.[150] Like petroleum extraction, the generation of electricity is not classified as a separate service in the Central Product Classification (CPC), and it thus seems more logical to deem the gener-ation of electricity as the manufacturing of a good. By analogy with EU law, it seems a reasonable conclusion to consider electricity as a good in the WTO context. This would coincide with the findings in the *Canada – Renewable Energy/Canada – Feed-In Tariff Program* cases, where the Appellate Body confirmed the panel's finding that the government's purchase of electricity under the FIT programme constituted a government purchase of goods within the meaning of Article 1.1(a) (1)(iii) of the SCM Agreement.[151] The supply of electricity to a household, though, should be regarded as a service.[152]

The challenges the energy sector faces when trying to square its economic activity with the WTO legal framework's divide between goods and services was highlighted in *EU – Energy Package*. There, the panel was confronted with a complex set of complaints by Russia with regard to measures in the natural gas sector that had aspects related to both goods and services.[153] The panel was of the opinion that the challenged measures were 'accompanied by some argumentation

---

[147] There is no category 'extracting services'; the closest to this is 'services incidental to mining' (CPC 883 + 5115).

[148] Selivanova (n 20) 21.

[149] In Cases C-393/92 *Almelo v Energiebedrijf IJsselmij* [1994] ECR-I-1477, para 28, and C-158/94 *Commission v Italy* [1997] ECR I-5789, para 17, the European Court of Justice ruled that, despite its intangible character, electricity should be treated as a good.

[150] See L Macedo, 'Electrical Energy and the WTO Customs Valuations Agreement' <www .wto.org/english/res_e/publications_e/wtr10_2july10_e.htm> accessed 20 March 2021.

[151] *Canada – Renewable Energy/Canada – Feed-in Tariff Program*, AB report, para 5.128.

[152] Marceau (n 38) 25.

[153] *EU – Energy Package*, panel report, para 7.14.

seemingly blurring fundamental distinctions between the GATS and the GATT 1994. We note the important differences between Russia's claims under the GATS and the GATT 1994, the distinct scope and subject matter of the GATS and the GATT 1994, respectively, and the different nature of the specific obligations contained in each of these agreements.'[154] The panel was well aware of the realities of the energy sector and admitted that WTO rules were sometimes ill-suited to dealing with these issues;

> [W]e are cognizant that this dispute occurs in the context of certain highly complex factual realities of the natural gas industry, including particularities of the markets for natural gas and its transport. We are also aware that certain specificities of that industry, notably in terms of transport through fixed infrastructure, raise certain challenges in the application of WTO rules. However, we underline that our duty has been to assess Russia's claims within the confines of WTO law.[155]

In the context of the so-called TEN-E measure, the panel rejected the argument that, because the measure discriminated against natural gas (goods), it was discriminatory under GATS. The panel referred to its findings on discrimination under GATT 1994, but considered that those conclusions were not automatically transposable to GATS. The panel referred to the Appellate Body statement in *EC – Bananas* to the effect that GATT and GATS may apply concurrently to a measure, but pointed out that the focus of the two agreements was different – effect on services and service suppliers under GATS, but effect on goods under GATT.[156] Finding that Russia had not produced any arguments focused specifically on the effect of the TEN-E measure on services or service suppliers, the panel dismissed the complaint.[157]

It is finally worth mentioning that the WTO Secretariat issued two insightful background notes on the energy services negotiations, one in 1998 and the other in 2010.[158] Though no negotiations have been conducted under GATT on energy *goods* as a separate unified category, the 2010 background note, albeit primarily focused on energy services, does seem to imply that energy would benefit from being dealt with in

---

[154] ibid.
[155] ibid, para 7.15.
[156] ibid, para 7.1433, referring to *EC – Bananas* AB report, para 221.
[157] ibid, para 7.1434.
[158] See, respectively, nn 142 and 145.

a coherent manner in the WTO.[159] If a sectoral approach were taken to energy trade regulation, the cumbersome goods/services divide could be overcome, though this begs the question of what should happen to existing commitments. This is an idea also put forward by Cottier and colleagues, who even suggested that the WTO would be unable to deal properly with energy unless a separate framework agreement on energy were negotiated.[160] In this author's opinion, a separate or plurilateral agreement is just one possible way of more comprehensively incorporating international energy trade into the multilateral trading framework.[161]

3.3.2 GATS Coverage and Exceptions

The General Agreement on Trade in Services (GATS) contains rules for all measures connected to international trade in services. Under GATS, members are obliged to accord MFN treatment across the board to all 'like' services (Article II). This is one of the so-called horizontal commitments under GATS. However, granting market access (Article XVI) and non-discriminatory treatment (Article XVII) to foreign services and service suppliers is not a given. Members only have to do so if and to the extent that they have made commitments in their respective services schedules.[162] In such instances, members have to afford national treatment to the 'like' services in question and not impose the limitations on market access listed in Article XVI:2. Members make sector-specific commitments in their GATS schedules of specific commitments.[163]

In principle, GATS rules apply to all energy-related services. The list of services directly or indirectly connected to energy trade, such as generation, extraction, construction and distribution, is vast and potentially endless, covering pipeline transportation services, construction services, all kinds of technical services, installation services, maintenance services, mining services, distribution services, etc.[164]

---

[159] See 2010 Background Note, which discusses the following forms of energy: (1) oil and gas, (2) coal, (3) renewable energy, (4) nuclear and (5) electricity. In the Doha Round some members have expressed the view that nuclear energy should not be associated with energy trade in general; see 2010 Background Note 6.

[160] Cottier (n 144).

[161] See discussion in Chapter 8.

[162] See WTO online database of members' commitments relating to services <http://i-tip .wto.org/services/default.aspx> accessed 20 July 2020.

[163] Mavroidis, Bermann and Wu (n 51) 802–19.

[164] For an indication of potentially relevant services, see International Centre for Trade and Sustainable Development, 'Fostering Low Carbon Growth: The Case for a Sustainable

Additionally, GATS covers four modes of supply, all of which are relevant to the energy sector.[165] They are: mode 1, when neither the service supplier nor the service consumer has to move; mode 2, when the consumer moves to the country where the service is supplied; mode 3, when the service supplier establishes a commercial presence in the country of supply; and mode 4, when the service supplier is established in a different country.[166]

3.3.2.1 Market Access for Energy Services: Article XVI GATS

Market access (Article XVI) in the energy sector was at issue in *EU-Energy Package*. Russia objected to the European unbundling measures in the Third Energy Package legislation, which included the requirement to separate energy transmission and supply, claiming that it led to Russian service suppliers being treated less favourably in the natural gas sector in Hungary, Croatia and Lithuania.[167] As there was no EU-wide services schedule, Russia had to link its objections based on this article to the national schedules of the EU member states in which the EU requirements had been implemented.[168] Russia argued that the unbundling requirement restricted market access on the number of service suppliers (pipeline transportation services) in these countries in a manner that was inconsistent with Article XVI:2(a) GATS.[169] More interestingly, Russia also claimed that the unbundling measure in all three countries was contrary to Article XVI:2(e) GATS. Russia considered the unbundling requirement to be a measure that violated the market access obligation in these EU member states by ruling out specific types of legal entities or joint ventures (including vertically integrated, and thus not unbundled, undertakings like Russia's Gazprom) through which a service supplier could supply a service (in this case pipeline

---

Energy Trade Agreement' (ICTSD Global Platform on Climate Change, Trade and Sustainable Energy, November 2011) 52–55 . On pipeline transportation services, see *EU – Energy Package*, panel report, para 7.338.

[165] Mavroidis, Bermann and Wu (n 51) 810–11.

[166] See GATS, art I:2.

[167] *EU-Energy Package*, panel report, s 2.2.

[168] ibid, paras 7.585, 7.588.

[169] ibid, para 7.590. The panel was not convinced and stated that Russia 'has not demonstrated that the unbundling measure in the national implementing law of Croatia imposes an impermissible quantitative limitation on the number of service suppliers in the form of a monopoly or exclusive service suppliers within the meaning of Article XVI:2(a) of the GATS' (para 7.612). It argued likewise for Lithuania (para 7.622). See Chapter 5, Section 5.3.

transport services).[170] The panel again disagreed with Russia, stating that the EU's unbundling measure did not address the legal form of the entities concerned, but merely restricted the combination of services.[171] In other words, the panel argued, 'while a measure restricting the types of service that a service supplier is allowed to supply in the host Member may "affect trade in services", it is not, for that reason, a measure falling within the "carefully defined" scope of Article XVI:2(e)'.[172]

3.3.2.2 'Likeness' and Non-discrimination of Energy Services: Articles II and XVII GATS

WTO members must accord MFN treatment to all like services, but national treatment only to like services on which they have made commitments. As with goods, what constitutes a 'like' service is debatable. In *EU – Energy Package,* Russia objected to the European TEN-E measure that provided regulatory and financial incentives and benefits for certain selected gas infrastructure projects (projects of common interest (PCIs)).[173] According to Russia, the criteria to qualify for PCI designation were inherently biased against Russian services and service suppliers, as Russian gas projects were excluded from PCI eligibility.[174] Russia argued that its pipeline transport services and service suppliers were 'like' those of other third countries, including liquefied natural gas (LNG) services and service suppliers.[175] The EU did not object to the likeness of pipeline transport services and service suppliers, but disagreed about the likeness of LNG services and service suppliers under Article II:1 GATS. The panel applied the services likeness test as set out by the Appellate Body in *Argentina – Financial Services* to determine whether LNG services were like pipeline transport services[176] and came to the decision that Russia could not make a case for the likeness of these services. Regarding the nature of the services, the panel pointed out that LNG services included changing the physical state of the LNG

---

[170] GATS, art XVI:2(e); *EU – Energy Package,* panel report, para 7.623.

[171] ibid, para 7.663.

[172] ibid, para 7.664.

[173] ibid, para 7.1383; Regulation (EU) 347/2013 of the European Parliament and of the Council of 17 April 2013 on guidelines for trans-European energy infrastructure and repealing Decision No 1364/2006/EC and amending Regulations (EC) 713/2009, (EC) 714/2009 and (EC) 715/2009 [2013] OJ L115/39 (TEN-E Regulation). See also Section 3.2.1.

[174] *EU – Energy Package,* panel report, para 7.1383.

[175] ibid, para 7.1395.

[176] ibid, paras 7.1400ff.

(regasification), which was not the case of for natural gas.[177] The panel further noted, with respect to the end-uses of LNG services, that their function was to change the physical state of the product rather than simply distribute the gas through the pipeline system.[178] In addition, LNG services and pipeline transportation services were classified differently under the CPC.[179] Last but not least, the panel disagreed that these services were substitutable for each other, stating that 'pipeline transport services in relation to regasified LNG depend on, and therefore cannot substitute, LNG regasification services'.[180]

With regard to MFN treatment (Article II:1 GATS), Russia argued in *EU –Energy Package* that the TEN-E measure discriminated against energy infrastructure projects for Russian gas. The panel found that Russia had not demonstrated a sufficient link between such infrastructure projects and the services at issue. Given the absence of that link, the panel decided not to consider whether infrastructure projects for Russian gas received less favourable treatment under the TEN-E measure than infrastructure projects for gas from other countries.[181]

Russia also argued the EU's unbundling measure meant that Russian pipeline transport services and service suppliers were accorded less favourable treatment, as the measure allowed EU member states to opt for lighter unbundling models than the full OU required under the Third Energy Package in respect of transmission systems that belonged to a VIU.[182] Full OU requires a complete separation of the production, sales and distribution activities of energy companies, while the lighter ISO and ITO unbundling models (temporarily) allowed less strict separation of these activities of EU energy companies. The panel was not

---

[177] ibid, para 7.1404.
[178] ibid, para 7.1409.
[179] ibid, para 7.1413:

> We observe that, in CPC 2.1, the transportation of natural gas via pipelines is included in subclass 65131 ('Transport services via pipeline of petroleum and natural gas'). An explanatory note to this subclass provides that it does not include liquefaction and regasification services, which belong to subclass 67990 ('Other supporting transport services n.e.c.'). Thus, according to CPC 2.1, pipeline transport services and LNG services fall within different subclasses. They also belong to different broader groups of services, referred to in CPC 2.1 as 'divisions'. While pipeline transport services belong to division 65 ('Freight transport services'), LNG services are found in division 67 ('Supporting transport services').

[180] ibid, para 7.1415.
[181] ibid, paras 7.1422–7.1430.
[182] ibid, para 7.402.

convinced that this resulted de facto in less favourable treatment of Russian service suppliers:

> We do not believe that Russia has made a prima facie case that these regulatory distinctions result in de facto discrimination against Russian pipeline transport services and service suppliers. In other words, Russia has not demonstrated that the unbundling measure accords less favourable treatment to the group of Russian pipeline transport services and service suppliers than that accorded to the group of pipeline transport services and service suppliers from any other non-EU country.[183]

EU – Energy Package was also relevant regarding national treatment (Article XVII GATS) of energy services. The 'public body measure' challenged by Russia was a rule laid down in Article 9(6) of the Gas Directive, according to which the unbundling rules were deemed to be complied with where the production/supply and transmission functions were controlled by two different public bodies.[184] Russia argued that EU governments were thus effectively exempted from unbundling, while all foreign entities had to unbundle in order to be certified as TSOs in the EU.[185] While the panel found indeed that the public body measure created a different legal regime for service suppliers controlled by public bodies from the ownership unbundling obligation applicable to all other service suppliers, it disagreed with Russia that such differentiation amounted to discrimination within the meaning of Article XVII GATS. The panel stated that 'the mere fact that the public body measure … sets a legal regime that is different from the ownership unbundling requirement does not necessarily mean that this measure is an exemption from this requirement'.[186] After examining the design, structure and operation of the public body measure, the panel held that it required a separation of the function of production/supply of natural gas from the function of its transmission that was functionally equivalent to unbundling.[187] In that regard, the panel recalled Article XVII:3 GATS, which makes it clear that formally different treatment of domestic services/service suppliers and like foreign services/service suppliers does not in and of itself amount to a violation of Article XVII. It must result in worse conditions of

---

[183] ibid, paras 7.512–7.514.
[184] Gas Directive, art 9(6).
[185] *EU – Energy Package*, panel report, para 7.730.
[186] ibid, para 7.757.
[187] ibid, para 7.776.

competition for foreign services/service suppliers, which, in the panel's view, Russia failed to establish.[188]

3.3.2.3 Energy Monopolies and Exclusive Service Suppliers: Article VIII GATS

GATS also contains rules on monopolies and exclusive service suppliers in Article VIII.[189] This provision applies to those energy companies that are monopolies, which, given the prevalence of VIUs in the energy sector, is not uncommon. Article VIII GATS requires WTO members to ensure monopolies act in line with their specific commitments and in a manner that is not inconsistent with WTO rules.[190] In addition, a supplier that has a monopoly should not abuse its position when supplying services outside its monopoly that are the subject of a specific service commitment by a member.

3.3.2.4 Public Policy Exception and Energy Services: Article XVI(a) GATS

Last but not least, GATS includes in Article XIV(a) a public policy exception that is relevant to energy. This provision was invoked by the EU in *EU – Energy Package* in connection with measures pertaining to energy security and is discussed at greater length in Chapter 7, Section 7.3.

3.3.3 *Energy Services as a Separate Sector?*

Although energy services were not negotiated as a separate sector in GATS at the outset, several of the commitments made by members in their services schedules in other sectors were of relevance to the energy sector.[191] Examples are construction and related engineering services, distribution services, environmental services, financial services, transport services and other services not included elsewhere.[192] Members' commitments can be found in the WTO services database.[193] During the

---

[188] ibid, paras 7.784–7.785.

[189] GATS, art VIII (monopolies and exclusive suppliers).

[190] Marceau (n 38) 29.

[191] However, the WTO 1998 Background Note states on page 1 that 'the vast majority of the global energy services industry is not covered by GATS specific commitments'.

[192] See WTO, 'Services Sectoral Classifications List: Note by the Secretariat' (10 July 1991) MTN.GNS/W/120.

[193] See n 162.

Uruguay Round and thereafter, several members, for instance, made commitments in their schedules concerning services incidental to energy distribution and pipeline transportation of fuels.[194]

Negotiations specifically on energy services were initiated during the Doha Round. Besides meeting the needs of the energy industry, the rationale behind including energy services as a separate sector in the WTO was that allowing more competition in the energy sector would benefit members and contribute to their economic growth.[195] Negotiations were triggered by the gradual liberalization of the energy sector, with independent operators increasingly supplying energy services in fields such as energy transport, transmission and distribution.[196]

Proposals for negotiations on energy services include: (1) commitments based on the CPC for all activities in the energy services sector and across all modes of supply; and (2) commitments in the oil and gas sector (eg for exploration services; services incidental to mining, technical testing and analysis; and toll refining services).[197] However, as might be expected, ownership and sovereignty over natural resources are explicitly outside the scope of the negotiations.[198]

After the 2005 Hong Kong Ministerial Declaration, members identified twelve types of activities that could be classified as energy services within the three main sectors of business services, construction and distribution.[199] They include activities such as engineering, construction of pipelines and the wholesaling and retailing of energy products. While WTO panels understand the mixed nature of products and services, in the Doha negotiations trade in gas, for example, is marked as a service. In the sector of energy services forty-five members have made commitments on 'services incidental to mining',[200] twenty-seven on 'on-site

---

[194] The I-TIP Services online platform contains information on what countries have committed to <https://i-tip.wto.org/services/Search.aspx> accessed 20 July 2020.
[195] SS Haghighi, *Energy Security: The External Legal Relations of the European Union with Major Oil and Gas Supplying Countries* (Hart 2007) 295.
[196] WTO 1998 Background Note 1.
[197] See WTO, Council for Services, Special Session, Report by the Chairman to the Trade Negotiations Committee (28 November 2005) TN/S/23; see also M Cossy, 'Energy Services under the General Agreement on Trade in Services' in Selivanova (n 12) 169.
[198] Report to Trade Negotiations Committee (n 197).
[199] WTO, Doha Work Programme – Ministerial Declaration, Annex C – Services (adopted 18 December 2005) WT/MIN(05)/DEC. On energy services discussions in the Doha Round, see M Gibbs, 'Energy Services, Energy Policies and the Doha Agenda' in UNCTAD, 'Energy and Environmental Service: Negotiating Objectives and Development Priorities' (2003) UN Doc UNCTAD/DITC/TNCD/2003/.
[200] WTO 2010 Background Note.

preparation work for mining',[201] eighteen have made commitments 'incidental to energy distribution',[202] and twelve have undertaken specific commitments 'on pipeline transportation of fuels'.[203]

Negotiations on energy services also seek to address commitments on the four GATS modes of supply as set out in Article I:2 GATS, especially mode 3 – a foreign company setting up subsidiaries or branches to provide services in another country – which is the most far reaching and relevant to investment.[204] Unfortunately, not much progress has been made in energy services negotiations since the start of the Doha Round with no conclusions being reached on either the list of services or the negotiations themselves.

3.4 Trade-Related Aspects of Intellectual Property Rights

The Agreement on Trade-Related Aspects of Intellectual Property Rights (TRIPs Agreement) was the first WTO agreement to lay down positive regulatory obligations for WTO members.[205] It requires members to ensure a minimum level of protection and enforcement of intellectual property (IP) rights in their territories.[206] The preamble to the TRIPs Agreement explains its rationale as being:

> to reduce distortions and impediments to international trade ... taking into account the need to promote effective and adequate protection of intellectual property rights, and to ensure that measures and procedures to enforce intellectual property rights do not themselves become barriers to legitimate trade.[207]

Part I of the agreement contains general provisions and rules that apply to all IP rights covered by the agreement; Part II deals with all the different categories of IP protection (eight in total); and Part III sets out the obligations incumbent on WTO members with regard to the enforcement of these rights.[208] The rights covered by the agreement are: copyright and related rights (section 1); trademarks (section 2); geographical indications (section 3); industrial design (section 4); patents

---

[201] ibid (CPC 5115).
[202] ibid (CPC 887).
[203] ibid 14.
[204] WTO, 'Energy Services' <www.wto.org/english/tratop_e/serv_e/energy_e/energy_e.htm> accessed 20 July 2020. Mode 3 is particularly relevant to foreign investments; see GATS, art I:2.
[205] Van den Bossche and Zdouc (n 111) 994.
[206] ibid.
[207] TRIPs Agreement, preamble.
[208] Van den Bossche and Zdouc (n 111) 998–99.

(section 5); layout-designs of integrated circuits (section 6); and protection of undisclosed information (section 7).[209] The agreement strikes a balance giving members' governments the flexibility to comply with the agreement in a way that best suits the country's state of development and economic circumstances.[210]

One of the main objectives of the TRIPs Agreement (Article 7) is to foster technological innovation and the transfer and dissemination of technology.[211] The rules of the agreement come into play for cross-border trade in energy when it concerns the development of new technologies and access to technology.[212] This is clearly the case when it comes to climate change mitigation, as the design of clean energy technologies such as solar cells involves IP rights. Discussions relating to IP rights, trade in energy and climate change mitigation mainly revolve around whether the TRIPs Agreement provides enough flexibility to allow the necessary innovation and access to new technologies in a socially beneficial manner that protects the IP rights involved.[213]

3.5 Plurilateral Trade Agreements: Government Procurement

Plurilateral trade agreements within the WTO context are agreements of minority interest that not all WTO members want to join.[214] Only the Agreement on Government Procurement (GPA) is relevant to trade in energy.[215] The GPA elaborates on Article III:8 GATT relating to government procurement.[216] According to this provision, products purchased for governmental purposes 'not with a view of commercial resale or to use in the production of goods for commercial sale' do not have to comply with the national treatment obligations set out in Article III. The difference between this provision and the GPA lies in the fact that all

---

[209] ibid.

[210] Marceau (n 38) 37.

[211] TRIPs Agreement, art 7.

[212] Marceau (n 38) 37.

[213] WTO, *World Trade Report 2010: Trade in Natural Resources* (WTO 2010) 195.

[214] See WTO, 'Plurilaterals: Of Minority Interest' <www.wto.org/english/thewto_e/whatis_e/tif_e/agrm10_e.htm> accessed 20 July 2020.

[215] The other active plurilateral agreement is the Agreement on Trade in Civil Aircraft (bovine meat and dairy agreements were terminated in 1997).

[216] Article III:8 GATT and the GPA provide that products purchased for governmental purposes 'not with a view to commercial resale or to use in the production of goods for commercial sale' do not have to comply with the NT obligations set out in Article III. This covers energy products, as well.

GATT members have to respect the broad obligation set out in Article III:8, while only those WTO members that have adhered to the GPA have to abide by its more elaborate rules.

Governments can influence the trading conditions through their behaviour. It is for this reason that WTO members party to the GPA commit that certain governmental entities (as listed in their schedules of concessions) will buy products from other members on a non-discriminatory basis only (Article III:1(a)(national treatment) and III:1(b) (MFN)).[217] Each party is also required to make sure that the entities listed in its schedule of concessions do not treat domestic suppliers differently depending on the degree of foreign affiliation or ownership (Article III:2).[218] In addition, parties have to ensure that their entities do not discriminate against domestic suppliers when goods or services are produced in the territory of another member. The major difference between government procurement and STEs is that the GPA deals with purchases which are not destined for commercial resale.[219]

Given that energy is can be procured by governments for their own use, the GPA has a bearing on energy issues for those WTO members that have signed up to it. The entities that parties have listed in their schedules of concessions must procure energy on a non-discriminatory basis (NT and MFN). The GPA moreover allows parties, subject to certain conditions, to exempt measures from the scope of the agreement where necessary. Several parties (eg Canada, the EU and the United States) have done so with respect to items from the energy sector (eg fuels and nuclear reactors) or usable in the energy sector (eg electrical machinery, equipment and boilers).[220]

3.6 Summary Table of WTO Energy-Related Disputes

Table 3.1 provides an overview of all WTO disputes to date that are directly related to energy. Disputes that are only indirectly related to energy, such as those concerning anti-dumping measures connected to energy dual pricing (see Chapter 6) and several disputes concerning energy equipment, are omitted from the table.

---

[217] Mavroidis, Bermann and Wu (n 51) 798; *World Trade Report 2010* (n 213) 173: 'For instance, in respect of the procurement covered by the Agreement, parties are required to accord the products, services and suppliers of any other party to the Agreement treatment "no less favourable" than that given to their domestic products, services and suppliers (Article III:1(a)). Furthermore, parties may not discriminate among goods, services and suppliers of other parties (Article III:1(b)).'

[218] GPA, art III:2.

[219] Mavroidis, Bermann and Wu (n 51) 798.

[220] Marceau (n 38) 30.

Table 3.1 *Energy-related disputes in the World Trade Organization*[a]

DS number	Title[b]	Complainant	Legal provisions cited[c]	Energy product(s)/ service(s)	Initiation date[d]	Status as of 20 July 2020
DS593	European Union – Certain Measures Concerning Palm Oil and Oil Palm Crop-Based Biofuels	Indonesia	Arts I:1, III:2, III:4, X:3(a), XI:1 GATT 1994 Arts 1.1(a)(ii), 3.1(b), 5(c) SCM Agreement Arts 2.1, 2.2, 2.4, 2.5, 2.8, 2.9, 5.1.1, 5.1.2, 5.2, 5.6, 5.8, 12.1, 12.3 TBT Agreement	Palm crop-based biofuels	9 December 2019	Panel established 29 July 2020.
DS592	Indonesia – Measures Relating to Raw Materials	European Union	Arts X:1, XI:1 GATT 1994 Art 3.1(b) SCM Agreement	Certain coal and coke products	22 November 2019	Consultations
DS575	Colombia – Measures Concerning the Distribution of Liquid Fuels	Venezuela	Arts I:1, III:4, V, V:2, X:3, XI:1, XIII, XXIV:12 GATT 1994	Liquid fuels	9 January 2019	Consultations
DS572	Peru – Anti-Dumping and Countervailing Measures on Biodiesel from Argentina	Argentina	Arts 2.2, 2.2.1.1, 2.2.2(iii), 3.1, 3.4, 3.5, 5.2, 5.3, 5.8, 6.5, 9.3, 18.1, 18.4 ADA Arts 1.1(a), 1.1(a)(1)(iii), 1.1(b), 10, 12.4, 14(d), 15.1, 15.4, 15.5, 19.1, 19.4, 32.1, 32.5 SCM Agreement Arts VI:1, VI:2, VI:3, VI:5(a) GATT 1994 Art XVI:4 WTO Agreement	Biodiesel	29 November 2018	Consultations

DS	Title		Legal basis	Products	Date	Status
DS562	United States – Safeguard Measures on PV Products	China	Art XIX:1 GATT 1994 Arts 2.1, 3.1, 3.2, 4.2(b) Safeguards Agreement	Certain crystalline silicon photovoltaic cells	14 August 2018	Panel composed 24 October 2020. Panel process ongoing.
DS563	United States – Certain Measures Related to Renewable Energy	China	Art III:4 GATT 1994 Arts 2.1, 2.2 TRIMs Agreement Arts 3.1(b), 3.2 SCM Agreement	Renewable energy, electricity	14 August 2018	Consultations
DS545	United States – Safeguard Measures on PV Products	Korea	Arts 1, 3.1 Safeguards Agreement Art XIX:1 GATT 1994 Arts 2.1, 3.2, 4.1(c), 4.2, 4.1(a), 4.1(b), 4.2(a), 4.2(b), 4.2(c), 5.1, 7.4, 7.1, 8.1, 12.1, 12.2, 12.3 Safeguards Agreement Art II:1 GATT 1994	Certain crystalline silicon photovoltaic cells	14 May 2018	Panel established 26 September 2018, but not yet composed.
DS510	US – Renewable Energy	India	Arts 3.1(b), 3.2 SCM Agreement Art III:4 GATT 1994 Art 2.1 TRIMs Agreement Arts 25, 1.1 SCM Agreement Art 2.2 TRIMs Agreement	Renewable energy, electricity, power-generating equipment, ethanol, biodiesel	9 September 2016	Panel report under appeal since 15 August 2019.

Table 3.1 (*cont.*)

DS number	Title	Complainant	Legal provisions cited	Energy product(s)/ service(s)	Initiation date	Status as of 20 July 2020
DS480	EU – Biodiesel (Indonesia)	Indonesia	Art VI:1 GATT 1994 Art XVI:4 WTO Agreement Arts 2.2.1.1, 2.2.2(i), 18.4, 2.2.2, 2.2.2(iii), 2.4, 2.3, 9.3, 3.1, 3.4, 3.5, 6.5, 6.5.1, 7.1, 7.2, 9.2, 9.3, 1 ADA	Biodiesel	10 June 2014	Panel report adopted 28 February 2018 with the recommendation to bring the measures into conformity. Compliance measure notified by EU 8 November 2015, terminating the anti-dumping proceedings.
DS476	EU – Energy Package	Russia	Arts II:1, VI:1, VI:5(a), XVI:1, XVII GATS Arts I:1, III:4, X:3(a), XI:1, GATT 1994	Natural gas, LNG, natural gas pipeline transportation services.	30 April 2014	Panel report under appeal since 21 September 2018.
DS473	EU – Biodiesel	Argentina	Arts VI:1, VI:2 GATT 1994 Arts 1, 2.1, 2.2.1.1, 2.2.2(iii), 2.4, 3.1, 3.4, 3.5, 9.3, 18.4 ADA Art XVI:4 WTO Agreement	Biodiesel	19 December 2013	Appellate Body and panel reports adopted 26 October 2016. Compliance notified by EU 23 October 2017.

Case	Title	Complainant	Provisions	Product	Date	Status
DS459	European Union and Certain Member States – Certain Measures on the Importation and Marketing of Biodiesel and Measures Supporting the Biodiesel Industry	Argentina	Arts I:1, III, III:1, III:2, III:4, III:5 GATT 1994; Arts 2.1, 2.2, 5.1, 5.2 TBT Agreement; Art XVI:4 WTO Agreement; Arts 2.1, 2.2 TRIMs Agreement; Arts 3.1(b), 3.2, 5(b), 5(c), 2.3, 1.1, 6.3(a) SCM Agreement	Biodiesel	15 May 2013	Consultations
DS456	India – Solar Cells	United States	Art III:4 GATT 1994; Art 2 TRIMs Agreement	Solar cells and solar modules	6 February 2013	Compliance panel (art 21.5 DSU) established 28 February 2018. Compliance proceedings ongoing. Authorization to retaliate requested 12 January 2018. Arbitration ongoing.
DS452	European Union and Certain Member States – Certain Measures Affecting the Renewable Energy Generation Sector	China	Arts I, III:1, III:4, III:5 GATT 1994; Arts 1.1, 3.1(b), 3.2 SCM Agreement; Arts 2.1, 2.2 TRIMs Agreement	Renewable energy, electricity	5 November 2012	Consultations

Table 3.1 (*cont.*)

DS number	Title	Complainant	Legal provisions cited	Energy product(s)/ service(s)	Initiation date	Status as of 20 July 2020
DS443	European Union and a Member State – Certain Measures Concerning the Importation of Biodiesels	Argentina	Arts III:1, III:4, III:5 GATT 1994 Arts 2.1, 2.2 TRIMs Agreement Art XVI:4 WTO Agreement	Biodiesel	17 August 2012	Establishment of panel requested by Argentina 6 December 2012, deferred by DSB 17 December 2012.
DS426	Canada – Feed-In Tariff Program	EU	Arts 3.1(b), 3.2, 1.1 SCM Agreement Art III:4 GATT 1994 Art 2.1 TRIMs Agreement	Certain electricity generation equipment in the renewable energy sector and the electricity generated by such equipment	11 August 2011	AB and panel reports adopted 24 May 2013. Implementation notified by Canada 5 June 2014.
DS419	China – Measures Concerning Wind Power Equipment	United States	Art XVI:1 GATT 1994 Arts 3, 25.1, 25.2, 25.3, 25.4 SCM Agreement Pt I, para 1.2 Accession Protocol	Wind power equipment	22 December 2010	Consultations
DS412	Canada – Renewable Energy	Japan	Art XXIII:1 GATT 1994 Arts 1.1, 3.1(b), 3.2 SCM Agreement Art III:4 GATT 1994 Art 2.1 TRIMs Agreement	Certain electricity generation equipment in the renewable energy sector and the electricity generated by such equipment	13 September 2010	AB and panel reports adopted 24 May 2013. Implementation notified by Canada 5 June 2014.

DS	Short title	Complainant	Provisions	Product	Date	Status
DS398	China – Raw Materials	Mexico	Arts VIII:1, VIII:4, X:1, X:3, XI:1 GATT 1994 Pt I, paras 1.2, 5.1, 5.2, 8.2 Accession Protocol	Coke	21 August 2009	Panel and AB reports adopted 22 February 2012. Implementation notified by China 28 January 2013.
DS395	China – Raw Materials	European Communities	Pt I, paras 1.2, 5.1, 5.2, 8.2 Accession Protocol Arts VIII:1, VIII:4, X:1, X:3, XI:1 GATT 1994	Coke	23 June 2009	Panel and AB reports adopted 22 February 2012. Implementation notified by China 28 January 2013.
DS394	China – Raw Materials	United States	Arts VIII:1, VIII:4, X:1, X:3, XI:1 GATT 1994 Pt I, paras 1.2, 5.1, 5.2, 8.2 Accession Protocol	Coke	23 June 2009	Panel and AB reports adopted 22 February 2012. Implementation notified by China 28 January 2013.
DS4	US – Gasoline	Brazil	Art I, III GATT 1994 Art 2 TBT Agreement	Gasoline	10 April 1995	Panel and AB reports adopted 20 May 1996. Implementation notified by US 25 September 1997.

Table 3.1 (*cont.*)

DS number	Title	Complainant	Legal provisions cited	Energy product(s)/ service(s)	Initiation date	Status as of 20 July 2020
DS2	US – Gasoline	Venezuela	Art I, III GATT 1994 Art 2 TBT Agreement	Gasoline	24 January 1995	Panel and AB reports adopted 20 May 1996. Implementation notified by US 25 September 1997.

[a] Based on the information available on the WTO website <www.wto.org/english/tratop_e/dispu_e/dispu_status_e.htm> accessed 20 July 2020.
[b] Short title where available (normally when the dispute has progressed beyond the consultations stage. In all other cases – long title.
[c] If the dispute has not progressed beyond the consultations stage – as cited by the complainant in the request for consultations. In all other cases – as cited by the complainant in the panel request.
[d] Date of request for consultations.

3.7 Conclusion

This chapter has provided an overview of the issues in WTO agreements that are of particular relevance to international trade in energy. It exposed several incoherencies between the current international trade rules and certain peculiarities and common practices in the energy sector. It covered the agreements on multilateral trade in goods; the General Agreement on Trade in Services; trade-related intellectual property rights; and the plurilateral Agreement on Government Procurement. We can conclude that, although WTO rules may not always reflect the needs of the energy sector, there is an abundance of relevant provisions in WTO law, as well as a host of unresolved issues related to the regulation of cross-border energy trade in the multilateral trading system.

Beyond the WTO: The Energy Charter Treaty and Preferential Trade Agreements

4.1 Introduction

The previous chapters examined energy regulation in the GATT/WTO context. This chapter sheds light on energy trade regulation beyond the WTO in the Energy Charter Treaty (ECT) and in preferential trade agreements (PTAs). The chapter first clarifies the complex legal and institutional relationship between the WTO and the ECT, including overlaps and tension concerning subject matter, procedure and membership. This is especially relevant in view of the evolution of both the WTO and the ECT during their twenty-five year existence. The chapter will then discuss the energy-specific provisions in a selection of PTAs, which now increasingly include sections specifically regulating the energy sector.[1] The negotiation and conclusion of such instruments is part of an emerging trend which was spearheaded by the conclusion of the North-American Free Trade Agreement (NAFTA) in 1994, and to which the EU Common Commercial Policy gave an added boost from the 2010s onwards. The chapter will analyse several instruments containing commitments relevant to the energy sector – namely, the NAFTA and its successor, the US-Mexico-Canada Agreement (USMCA), as well as the FTAs concluded by the EU with Singapore, Ukraine and Mexico.

4.2 The Nexus between the WTO and the Energy Charter Treaty

4.2.1 Overview

As discussed in Chapter 2, energy products have been covered *de jure* in the GATT/WTO system since 1947, and energy services were added after the

---

[1] Possible under the General Agreement on Tariffs and Trade, Marrakesh Agreement Establishing the World Trade Organization, Annex 1A (signed 15 April 1994) 1867 UNTS 187 (1994) 33 ILM 1153 (GATT 1994), art XXIV ('Territorial Application – Frontier Traffic – Customs Unions and Free Trade Areas').

establishment of the WTO. However, as the rules of the multilateral trading system were not tailored to energy, this continues to pose challenges for the WTO legal framework today.[2] The 1998 Energy Charter Treaty (ECT), on the other hand, was specifically conceived to regulate economic activity (trade and investment) in the energy sector. ECT negotiations were conducted separately from multilateral trade negotiations, but it would be a mistake to view the ECT as a treaty regime hermetically closed off from the WTO. The purpose of including trade provisions in the ECT seems to have been to introduce GATT-type standards in the energy sector to former communist countries that had not yet ratified GATT.[3] They were intended to promote reform towards GATT compatibility and, consequently, help with GATT/WTO accessions.[4] Thus, although a separate treaty on paper, there was a clear intention to introduce the multilateral trading system to countries that had not yet joined the WTO. This can be seen from the way in which ECT trade rules are formulated: the ECT incorporates WTO rules on trade in goods (not services) *by reference* in Article 4.[5]

The relationship between the ECT and the WTO is asymmetrical: while the ECT clearly refers to WTO rules and determines which rules should take precedence in given situations, describing itself as a 'stepping stone' to WTO accession for ECT parties,[6] the WTO merely mentions the

---

[2] See generally AA Marhold, 'Fragmentation and the Nexus between the WTO and the ECT in Global Energy Governance: A Legal-Institutional Analysis Twenty Years Later' (2015) 16(3) Journal of World Investment and Trade 389. For a brief overview of challenges with respect to energy regulation in the WTO, see AA Marhold, 'The World Trade Organization and Energy: Fuel for Debate' (2013) 2(8) ESIL Reflections.

[3] I Frasl, 'The Trade Rules of the GATT and Related Instruments and the Energy Charter Treaty' in TW Wälde (ed), *The Energy Charter Treaty: An East-West Gateway for Investment and Trade* (Kluwer Law International 1996) 460–61.

[4] ibid.

[5] Energy Charter Treaty (adopted 17 December 1994, entered into force 16 April 1998) 2080 UNTS 100 (ECT), art 4 ('Non-Derogation from WTO Agreement'), also art 29 ('Interim Provisions on Trade-Related Matters').

[6] See International Energy Charter, 'Frequently Asked Questions about the Energy Charter Process' <www.energycharter.org/process/frequently-asked-questions/> accessed 20 July 2020 (in answer to the question 'If a country becomes a member of the WTO, what is the added benefit of being part of the Energy Charter?'):

> The Energy Charter shares core principles with the World Trade Organisation, in particular the principles of transparency and non-discrimination. The rules of the Treaty are fully compatible with those of the international trading system, and in practice the Energy Charter Treaty has been a valuable stepping stone for some member states on their way towards accession to the WTO.

See also Energy Charter Secretariat, *The Energy Charter Treaty and Related Documents: A Legal Framework for International Energy Cooperation* (ECS 2004) 15.

ECT as an 'intergovernmental organization working with the WTO Secretariat'.[7] Russia's failure to ratify the ECT and the withdrawal of its provisional application in 2009 was a major setback for the treaty, whose effectiveness has been questioned many times since then.[8] Nevertheless, the ECT has so far survived the test of time, not least because of its contribution to investment protection and dispute settlement. Additionally, it serves as one of the few fora where stakeholders actively discuss international energy transit issues.[9] The Energy Charter Secretariat (ECS), the administrative body overseeing the ECT, has taken account of the tension and overlap between the WTO and the ECT by providing extensive guidelines on incorporating WTO rules into the treaty.[10] This so-called coordination *ex ante* was seen as a means of preventing conflicts,[11] However, gaps, uncertainties and even conflicts remain. Since 2018, the ECT has been undergoing a process of modernization and renegotiation, though it is chiefly focused on the existing investment protection disciplines.[12]

---

[7] See WTO, 'Intergovernmental Organizations working with the WTO Secretariat' <www.wto.org/english/thewto_e/coher_e/igo_divisions_e.htm> accessed 20 July 2020.

[8] See International Energy Charter, 'Members and Observers' <www.energycharter.org/who-we-are/members-observers/countries/russian-federation/> accessed 20 July 2020:

> On 20 August 2009 the Russian Federation has officially informed the Depository that it did not intend to become a Contracting Party to the Energy Charter Treaty and the Protocol on Energy Efficiency and Related Environmental Aspects. In accordance with Article 45(3(a)) of the Energy Charter Treaty, such notification results in Russia's termination of its provisional application of the ECT and the PEEREA upon expiration of 60 calendar days from the date on which the notification is received by the Depository.

> See T Voon, 'Modernizing the Energy Charter Treaty: What about Termination?' (*Investment Treaty News*, 2 October 2009) <https://cf.iisd.net/itn/2019/10/02/modernizing-the-energy-charter-treaty-what-about-termination-tania-voon/> accessed 20 July 2020.

[9] The ECT maintains a 'Trade and Transit Group', which facilitates transit talks between ECT parties.

[10] GATT and several WTO agreements are incorporated into the ECT by reference through Article 4 ECT, but important exceptions exist. See Energy Charter Secretariat, *Applicable Trade Provisions of the Energy Charter Treaty* (ECS 2003); Energy Charter Secretariat, *Trade in Energy: WTO Rules Applying under the Energy Charter Treaty* (ECS 2001).

[11] J Pauwelyn, *Conflict of Norms in Public International Law: How WTO Law Relates to Other Rules of International Law* (CUP 2003) 327ff.

[12] See Energy Charter Secretariat, 'Modernisation of the Energy Charter Treaty' (Decision of the Energy Charter Conference, 27 November 2018) CCDEC 2018 18 STR.

With respect to their subject matter, the WTO and the ECT partly overlap with each other. The WTO regulates trade in goods and services, of which energy goods and services are a subcategory,[13] while the ECT regulates trade and investment in energy materials and products and related services.[14]

Geographically, neither treaty is confined to a specific region. There is extensive overlap in their membership, which, moreover, has changed significantly since the regimes of the two treaties were established.[15]

There is also some overlap between the WTO's and the ECT's jurisdiction over disputes. The WTO aspires to be a self-contained regime with its own built-in dispute settlement mechanism, the Dispute Settlement Body (DSB).[16] Article 23.2 DSU states that (energy-)trading disputes between WTO members must be settled solely by the DSB.[17] The ECT provides a rather 'informal' mechanism to resolve trade disputes through diplomatic means, and additionally has a mechanism specifically for investor-state and state-state dispute settlement.[18] Thus, there is overlap between the WTO and ECT regimes with respect to both substantive (ie energy goods, related services and the membership of both organizations) and procedural (settlement of disputes relating to both trade and investment) matters, which will be covered successively below.

---

[13] See Chapter 3, Section 3.3.1.

[14] ECT, annex EM ('Energy Materials and Products').

[15] See Tables 4.1 and 4.2.

[16] On self-contained regimes in international law generally, see B Simma and D Pulkowski, 'Of Planets and the Universe: Self-Contained Regimes in International Law' (2006) 17 European Journal of International Law 483. There are two diverging views on this matter with respect to WTO law. Pauwelyn argues that WTO law cannot operate as a 'closed legal circuit', Pauwelyn, *Conflict of Norms* (n 11) 35. Others, notably Mavroidis and Trachtman, are of the opinion that even though general international law may be used to interpret WTO law, this does not mean that non-WTO law is directly applicable as law in the WTO. They point to the risks of expecting trade delegates 'to move outside the (illusory) comfort of the covered agreements in order to adjudicate disputes'. PC Mavroidis, 'No Outsourcing of Law? WTO Law as Practiced by WTO Courts' (2008) 102 American Journal of International Law 421, 474; J Trachtman, Review of *Conflict of Norms in Public International Law: How WTO Law Relates to Other Rules of International Law* by J Pauwelyn (2004) 98 American Journal of International Law 855, 857.

[17] See WTO, Understanding on Rules and Procedures Governing the Settlement of Disputes, Marrakesh Agreement Establishing the World Trade Organization, Annex 2 (signed 15 April 1994) 1869 UNTS 401 (1994) 33 ILM 1226 (DSU).

[18] ECT, annex D ('Interim Provisions for Trade Dispute Settlement'), arts 26 ('Settlement of Disputes between an Investor and a Contracting Party'), 27 ('Settlement of Disputes between Contracting Parties').

4.2.2   WTO and ECT: Overlaps and Changes in Membership

4.2.2.1   WTO

When established in 1995, the organization had 113 members and 61 observers.[19] A total of 14 countries were neither members nor observers, and 12 continue to function outside the multilateral trading system today.[20] By 2020, WTO membership had greatly expanded, numbering 164 after the General Council's approval of the accession of Afghanistan and Liberia in 2016. Current members include major fossil fuel producing, exporting and transporting countries such as Angola, Bahrain, Brazil, Canada, China, Ecuador, Indonesia, Kuwait, Nigeria, Oman, Qatar, Russia, Saudi Arabia, Ukraine, the United Arab Emirates, the United States and Venezuela, many of which joined the WTO subsequent to its establishment in 1995.[21] Other major players in the energy field such as Algeria, Azerbaijan, Iran, Iraq, Libya and Sudan are in the process of negotiating accession. Eight of the thirteen members of the Organization of Oil Exporting Countries (OPEC) are already in the WTO.[22] It can thus be seen that major stakeholders in the global energy landscape are full-fledged participants in the multilateral trade system.

4.2.2.2   ECT

The WTO's wide-ranging membership contrasts starkly with the membership of the ECT. When the ECT entered into force in 1998, it had forty parties.[23] Eight signatories chose to apply the treaty provisionally pending ratification, while twenty-nine countries were observers.[24] Although those numbers had changed by 2020, the ECT's membership is still far less wide-ranging than that of the WTO, with only 51 countries having

---

[19] Observers must start accession negotiations within five years of becoming observers; see WTO, 'Members and Observers' <www.wto.org/english/thewto_e/whatis_e/tif_e/org6_e.htm#observer> accessed 20 July 2020.

[20] See Tables 4.1 and 4.2.

[21] The major energy producing, exporting and/or transporting states that joined the WTO after 1995 were Angola (1996), China (2001), Ecuador (1996), Oman (2000), Qatar (1996), Russia (2012), Saudi Arabia (2005), Ukraine (2008) and the United Arab Emirates (1996).

[22] See OPEC, 'Member Countries' <www.opec.org/opec_web/en/about_us/25.htm> accessed 20 July 2020. OPEC membership has fluctuated over time; see Chapter 5, Section 5.2.2.

[23] As shown in Table 4.1. See International Energy Charter (IEC), 'Members and Observers to the International Energy Conference' <www.energycharter.org/who-we-are/members-observers/> accessed 20 July 2020.

[24] See Table 4.1; IEC (n 23).

ratified the ECT.[25] Four ECT signatories continue to apply the treaty provisionally and forty-four countries have observer status at the Energy Charter Conference (many of which have acquired that status during the last decade).[26] In a notorious move touched on in Section 4.2.1, Russia stepped back from the agreement in 2009, after having applied it provisionally since signing it in 1994.[27] In 2016, Italy withdrew as well and became an observer only.[28] A total of 102 countries are neither parties nor observers. Major energy producing and exporting countries like Algeria, Canada, China, Indonesia, Kuwait, Nigeria, Oman, Qatar, Saudi Arabia, the United Arab Emirates, the United States and Venezuela have observer status only.[29]

4.2.3 WTO and ECT Membership: Changes and Overlaps 1998–2020

As Tables 4.1 and 4.2 below show, substantial changes have taken place in the membership of both the WTO and the ECT between their early days and some two decades later. The biggest development is certainly the huge number of former WTO observers that have acceded to the WTO, bringing the number of observers down from fifty in 1998 to twenty-four in 2020. They include such prominent non-ECT countries as China, Oman, Russia and Saudi Arabia.

Overlapping membership between the two treaty regimes became a reality with the entry into force of the ECT in 1998. This de facto resulted in two tiers of ECT members: (1) countries that were simultaneously WTO members and parties to the ECT (so-called WTO/ECT members);

---

[25] See Table 4.1; IEC (n 23).

[26] As shown in Table 4.2. Russia ceased provisional application of the ECT in 2009, but investments made during the period of provisional application (1998–2009) are protected until 29 October 2029.

[27] This move was made in the context of the controversial Yukos arbitration cases *Hulley Enterprises Limited v Russian Federation* (PCA Case No AA226), *Yukos Universal Limited v the Russian Federation* (PCA Case No AA227) and *Veteran Petroleum Limited v the Russian Federation* (PCA Case No AA228), Final Awards (18 July 2014). See also, in the same cases, Interim Awards on Jurisdiction and Admissibility (30 November 2009) para 395: 'Accordingly, the Tribunal has concluded that the ECT in its entirety applied provisionally in the Russian Federation until 19 October 2009, and that Parts III and V of the Treaty (including Article 26 thereof) remain in force until 19 October 2029 for any investments made prior to 19 October 2009.'

[28] Pursuant Article 47 ECT, Italy's withdrawal took effect a year after notification, thus in January 2016.

[29] ECT (n 23).

Table 4.1 *WTO/ECT membership status and overlaps (1998)*
Total: 198 (including EC and Palestine)

	WTO members (including EC, former EU) (134)	WTO observers (50)	Non-WTO members (14)
ECT members (including EC, former EU) (40)	: Austria, Belgium, Bulgaria, Cyprus, Czech Republic, Denmark, EC, Finland, France, Greece, Hungary, Ireland, Italy, Kyrgyzstan, Liechtenstein, Luxemburg, Netherlands, Portugal, Romania, Slovakia, Slovenia, Spain, Sweden, Switzerland, United Kingdom **(25)**	Albania, Armenia, Azerbaijan, Croatia, Estonia, Georgia, Kazakhstan, Latvia, Lithuania, Moldova, FYROM (Macedonia), Ukraine, Uzbekistan, Tajikistan **(14)**	Turkmenistan **(1)**
ECT signatories[a] (provisional application) (8)	Australia, Iceland, Malta, Norway, Poland, Turkey **(6)**	Belarus, Russian Federation **(2)**	–
ECT observers (29)	Bahrain, Canada, Egypt, Indonesia, Japan, Korea, Kuwait, Mauritania, Mongolia, Morocco, Nigeria, Pakistan, Qatar, Tunisia, United Arab Emirates, USA, Venezuela **(17)**	Afghanistan, Algeria, Bosnia and Herzegovina, Iran, Jordan, Montenegro, Oman, Saudi Arabia, Serbia, Syria, Yemen **(11)**	Palestine National Authority **(1)**
Non-ECT members (121)	Angola, Antigua and Barbuda, Argentina, Bangladesh, Barbados, Belize, Benin, Bolivia, Botswana, Brazil, Brunei, Burkina Faso, Burundi, Cameroon, Central African Republic, Chad, Chile, Chinese Taipei, Colombia, Congo Republic, Costa Rica, Côte	Andorra, Bahamas, Bhutan, Cabo Verde, Cambodia, China, Comoros, Equatorial Guinea, Ethiopia, Holy See, Iraq, Laos, Lebanon, Liberia, Libya, Nepal, Samoa, Sao	Eritrea, Kiribati, Marshall Islands, Micronesia, Monaco, Nauru, North Korea, Palau, San Marino, Somalia, Timor Leste, Tuvalu **(12)**

d'Ivoire, Cuba, Djibouti, Dominica, Dominican Republic, DR Congo, Ecuador, Egypt, El Salvador, Fiji, Gabon, Gambia, Ghana, Grenada, Guatemala, Guinea, Guinea-Bissau, Guyana, Haiti, Honduras, Hong Kong, India, Israel, Jamaica, Kenya, Lesotho, Macao, Madagascar, Malawi, Malaysia, Maldives, Mali, Mauritius, Mexico, Mozambique, Myanmar, Namibia, New Zealand, Nicaragua, Niger, Panama, Papua New Guinea, Paraguay, Peru, Philippines, Rwanda, Saint Kitts and Nevis, Saint Lucia, Saint Vincent and the Grenadines, Senegal, Sierra Leone, Singapore, Solomon Island, South Africa, Sri Lanka, Suriname, Swaziland, Tanzania, Thailand, Togo, Trinidad and Tobago, Uganda, Uruguay, Zambia, Zimbabwe (**86**)

Tomé and Principe, Seychelles, Sudan, Tonga, Vanuatu, Vietnam (**23**)

[a] All ECT signatories apply part VII of the treaty provisionally; only Belarus applies the entire ECT provisionally.

Table 4.2 *WTO/ECT membership status and overlaps (2020)*
Total: 200 (including EU and Palestine)

	WTO members (164, including EU)	WTO observers (24)	Non-WTO members (12)
ECT members (50, including EU)	Afghanistan, Albania, Armenia, Austria, Belgium, Bulgaria, Croatia, Cyprus, Czech Republic, Denmark, Estonia, EU, Finland, France, Georgia, Greece, Hungary, Iceland, Ireland, Japan, Jordan, Kazakhstan, Kyrgyzstan, Latvia, Liechtenstein, Lithuania, Luxemburg, Malta, Moldova, Mongolia, Montenegro, Netherlands, Poland, Portugal, Romania, Slovakia, Slovenia, Spain, Sweden, Switzerland, Tajikistan, North Macedonia, Turkey, Ukraine, United Kingdom, Yemen **(46)**	Azerbaijan, Bosnia and Herzegovina, Uzbekistan, Turkmenistan **(4)**	–
ECT signatories (provisional application)[a] (4)	Australia, Norway, Russian Federation[b] **(3)**	Belarus **(1)**	–
ECT observers (44)	Bahrain, Bangladesh, Benin, Burkina Faso, Burundi, Cambodia, Canada, Chad, Chile, China, Colombia, Egypt, Gambia, Indonesia, Italy,[c] Kenya, Korea, Kuwait, Mali, Mauritania,	Algeria, Iran, Serbia, Syria **(4)**	Palestine National Authority **(1)**

	Morocco, Niger, Nigeria, Oman, Pakistan, Panama, Qatar, Rwanda, Saudi Arabia, Senegal, Sierra Leone, Swaziland, Tanzania, Tunisia, Uganda, United Arab Emirates, USA, Venezuela, Vietnam (39)	Andorra, Bahamas, Bhutan, Comoros, Curaçao, Equatorial Guinea, Ethiopia, Holy See, Iraq, Lebanon, Libya, Sao Tomé and Principe, Sudan, South Sudan, Timor Leste (15)	Eritrea, Kiribati, Marshall Islands, Micronesia, Monaco, Nauru, North Korea, Palau, San Marino, Somalia, Tuvalu (11)
Non-ECT members (102)	Angola, Antigua and Barbuda, Argentina, Barbados, Belize, Bolivia, Botswana, Brazil, Brunei, Cabo Verde, Cameroon, Central African Republic, Chinese Taipei, Congo Republic, Costa Rica, Cote d'Ivoire, Cuba, Djibouti, Dominica, Dominican Republic, DR Congo, Ecuador, Egypt, El Salvador, Fiji, Gabon, Ghana, Grenada, Guatemala, Guinea, Guinea-Bissau, Guyana, Haiti, Honduras, Hong Kong, India, Israel, Jamaica, Laos, Lesotho, Liberia, Macao, Madagascar, Malawi, Malaysia, Maldives, Mauritius, Mexico, Mozambique, Myanmar, Namibia, Nepal, New Zealand, Nicaragua, Papua New Guinea, Paraguay, Peru, Philippines, Saint Kitts and Nevis, Saint Lucia, Saint Vincent and the Grenadines, Samoa, Seychelles, Singapore,		

Table 4.2 (*cont.*)

WTO members (164, including EU)	WTO observers (24)	Non-WTO members (12)
Solomon Island, South Africa, Sri Lanka, Suriname, Thailand, Togo, Tonga, Trinidad and Tobago, Uruguay, Vanuatu, Zambia, Zimbabwe (**76**)		

Sources <www.energycharter.org/who-we-are/members-observers/>, <www.wto.org/english/thewto_e/whatis_e/tif_e/org6_e.htm> accessed 20 July 2020

[a] All ECT signatories apply part VII of the treaty provisionally; only Belarus applies the entire ECT provisionally.
[b] The Russian Federation signed the ECT and applied it provisionally up to and including 18 October 2009, before completely withdrawing in 2018.
[c] Italy withdrew from the ECT in 2016.

and (2) ECT parties that had not (yet) acceded to the WTO (so-called non-WTO ECT parties). Therefore, there are three possible modes of membership interaction within the legal framework of the ECT: (1) among ECT/WTO members; (2) between ECT/WTO members and non-WTO ECT parties; and (3) among non-WTO ECT parties. The two tiers of ECT membership and the three possible modes of interaction among them will be continuously referred to in this chapter.

In 1998, twenty-five WTO members were simultaneously parties to the ECT. By 2020, the number of simultaneous ECT/WTO members had risen to forty-six. This increase shows that a substantial number of countries that were only parties to the ECT in 1998 went on to accede to the WTO during the following twenty years, hence realizing the ECT's aspiration to function as a stepping-stone to WTO accession. Russia, the major Eurasian energy producing and exporting country, was a case apart as the only country to effectively swap (provisional) ECT membership for WTO accession, while minimizing unwanted commitments on energy along the way.[30]

4.2.4 Subject-Matter Overlaps between the WTO and the ECT

4.2.4.1 Trade in Energy

As already mentioned, the WTO and the ECT partially overlap with respect to their subject matter, as both instruments are relevant to trade in energy products and related services. Consequently, common to both is the objective of promoting free(er) trade.[31] The WTO deals with trade in goods and services, of which energy goods and services are a subcategory.

The ECT deals with trade only in energy goods and related economic activity (ie services),[32] but covers investments in energy, in addition to trade.[33] Energy under the ECT is to be understood broadly as relating to trade in energy, energy products and energy-related equipment, as

---

[30] WTO, Report of the Working Party on the Accession of the Russian Federation to the World Trade Organization (17 November 2011) WT/ACC/RUS/70, WT/MIN(11)/2. See also Chapter 2, Section 2.4.2.

[31] See MG Desta, 'The Organization of Petroleum Exporting Countries, the World Trade Organization, and Regional Trade Agreements' (2003) 37 Journal of World Trade 523, 539.

[32] ECT, arts 4–6, 29.

[33] A Konoplaynik and T Wälde, 'Energy Charter Treaty and its Role in International Energy' (2006) 24 Journal of Energy and Natural Resources Law 523, 529. For more information on the background and legal provisions of the ECT, see generally Wälde (n 3).

detailed in the treaty's Annex EM. The ECT generally focuses on five broad areas:

1. protection and promotion of foreign energy investments based on most-favoured-nation treatment or national treatment, depending on whichever is more favourable, set out in Article 10(3) ECT;
2. free trade in energy materials, products and energy-related equipment based on WTO rules, in Articles 4, 5, 6, and 29 ECT; [34]
3. freedom of energy transit through pipelines and grids based on Article V GATT (transit) in Article 7, which is much more precise than GATT 1994 about what energy transit exactly entails (eg gas pipelines are clearly a means of transit); [35]
4. reducing the negative environmental impact of the energy cycle through improvements in energy efficiency, set out in Article 19 ECT and the Protocol on Energy Efficiency and Related Environmental Aspects (PEEREA); and
5. mechanisms for resolving disputes of various kinds, such as trade-related disputes, state-to-state and/or investor-to-state disputes in Articles 26–32 ECT, and transit disputes in Article 7 ECT.

The Energy Charter Secretariat (ECS) intentionally based ECT trade rules on GATT/WTO rules. The ECT has incorporated GATT in its trade part by means of Article 4 ECT. [36] The trade provisions of each treaty regime therefore overlap where the trade provisions of the WTO (GATT) meet the energy trade provisions of the ECT (Articles 4, 5, 6, 7 and 29). To elucidate this overlap between GATT and the ECT, the ECS provided a cross-referencing tool in two detailed guides issued in 2001 and 2003. [37] It also formalized the interplay between the WTO and the ECT in the area of trade in the 2010 Amendment to the Trade-Related Provisions of the Energy Charter Treaty ('Trade Amendment'). At the

---

[34] ECT, art 29 ('Interim Provisions on Trade-Related Matters') sets out temporary trade rules for ECT parties in the process of WTO accession.

[35] See ECT, art 7(10)(ii)(b): '"Energy Transport Facilities" consist of high-pressure gas transmission pipelines, high-voltage electricity transmission grids and lines, crude oil transmission pipelines, coal slurry pipelines, oil product pipelines, and other fixed facilities specifically for handling Energy Materials and Products.' A 'Transit Protocol' intended to elaborate on Article 7 ECT and the ECT as a whole is still under negotiation.

[36] ECT, art 4: 'Nothing in this Treaty shall derogate, as between particular Contracting Parties which are parties to the GATT, from the provisions of the GATT and Related Instruments as they are applied between those Contracting Parties.'

[37] ECS, *Applicable Trade Provisions* ; ECS, *Trade in Energy* (n 10).

heart of this incorporation of GATT rules by reference in the ECT are the following fundamentals:[38]

1. Trade in energy materials and products (ie goods) between ECT parties that are also WTO members are regulated by the trade provisions of the WTO *and* the ECT. However, by virtue of Article 4 ECT, the provisions of the latter should not be interpreted as derogating from the provisions of the former.
2. Trade between ECT members, at least one of which is not a WTO member, is (subject to some exceptions) governed by WTO rules incorporated into the ECT through Article 29(2)(a) ECT, in addition to those of the ECT. In that case, Article 4 ECT does not apply.[39]
3. The ECT uses negative referencing, meaning that it incorporates all WTO provisions unless they appear in Annex W(A) listing the provisions of the WTO Agreement that are not applicable under Article 29 (2)(a) ECT.

There are several exceptions to the incorporation of WTO rules in the ECT. For instance, bindings on customs duties as set out in Article II GATT are not automatically incorporated. Instead, they are replaced by a softer, 'best endeavours' commitment discouraging ECT parties from increasing customs duties or importation and exportation charges of any kind.[40]

Article 7 ECT on transit goes further than Article V GATT and explicitly includes gas pipelines as a means of transport.[41] It thereby creates additional obligations for ECT parties that are also WTO members. This in essence means that Article 7 ECT, to the extent that its provisions are broader than those of GATT, imposes additional disciplines to those of Article V GATT, which bind all ECT parties (the

---

[38] ECS, *Applicable Trade Provisions* (n 10) viii.

[39] The exceptions are listed partly in Annex W to the Trade Amendment and partly in Article 29(2)(b) ECT. The most important concerns the WTO Dispute Settlement System (DSS), which cannot be used by non-WTO members and is replaced in Annex D by a panel-based dispute resolution mechanism inspired by the DSU but less heavy (no standing appellate body is foreseen). Note however, that Japan and Turkey did not ratify the ECT Trade Amendment, and some other countries apply it only provisionally. See ECS, *Energy Charter Treaty and Related Documents* (n 6) 223–25. The ECT refers only to GATT; it was the Trade Amendment that introduced a reference to the WTO and the commitment to protect intellectual property rights.

[40] ECT, art 29(3)–(5).

[41] On transit generally, see D Azaria, 'Energy Transit under the Energy Charter Treaty and the General Agreement on Tariffs and Trade' (2009) 27 Journal of Energy and Natural Resources Law 559.

so-called WTO-plus effect of the ECT).[42] It is also worth mentioning that since 1999 negotiations have been taking place (although they are currently at a standstill) on an ECT Protocol on Transit that would pursue similar WTO-plus ambitions, complementing the ECT while conforming to Article 7 ECT.[43]

GATS,[44] TRIPs[45] and TRIMs[46] have not been taken up in the ECT, though each has a corresponding provision in the ECT: services are covered by the overarching label 'Economic Activity in the Energy Sector';[47] a commitment to protect intellectual property rights is taken up in the final act of the international conference;[48] and Article 5 ECT incorporates trade-related investment measures.[49] It should be mentioned that here the conflict between the two treaties caused by simultaneously applicable provisions is not solved. Additionally, the WTO provisions on special and differential treatment do not apply in the ECT, except for paragraphs 1–4 of the Enabling Clause.[50]

Relevant WTO remedial agreements, such as those on technical barriers to trade, anti-dumping subsidies and safeguards, are incorporated into the ECT, as are the market-access agreements on import licensing, rules of origin, customs valuation and pre-shipment inspection.[51]

Plurilaterals which are not binding on all WTO members have not been taken over into the ECT. Likewise, WTO multilateral agreements,

---

[42] Frasl (n 3) 484.

[43] See the most recent informal text of the 'Transit Protocol' (22 October 2010) TT87 22/01/ 2010. Article 7 ECT is a complex provision. On the non-discrimination requirement under Article 7(3), see N Nychay and D Shemelin, 'Interpretation of Article 7(3) of the Energy Charter Treaty' (2012) Graduate Institute of International and Development Studies/Centre for Trade and Economic Integration, Trade and Investment Law Clinic Paper.

[44] ECT, annex W (A)(b).

[45] ECT, annex W (A)(c).

[46] ECT, annex W (A)(iv). See also S Defilla, 'Energy Trade under the ECT and Accession to the WTO' (2003) 21 Journal of Energy and Natural Resources Law 428.

[47] ECT, art 1(5): '"Economic Activity in the Energy Sector" means an economic activity concerning the exploration, extraction, refining, production, storage, land transport, transmission, distribution, trade, marketing, or sale of Energy Materials and Products except those included in Annex NI, or concerning the distribution of heat to multiple premises.'

[48] See Joint Declaration on Trade-Related Intellectual Property Rights, Final Act of the International Conference and Decision by the Energy Charter Conference in Respect of the Amendment to the Trade-Related Provisions of the Energy Charter Treaty.

[49] Article 5 is linked to Annex D and Article 26 ECT.

[50] WTO Enabling Clause (through ECT, annex W(A), para 2(a)).

[51] See ECS, *Trade in Energy* (n 10) 66–82.

which are largely irrelevant to the subject matter of the ECT, such as those on sanitary and phytosanitary measures, textiles and agriculture, do not apply either.[52] Nor does the ECT incorporate the accession protocols of new WTO members.[53]

While it is possible for WTO members to negotiate plurilateral agreements (PTAs) under the GATT (Article XXIV), the ECT, interestingly enough, does not provide for such a possibility.[54] The reason for this may be that the ECT was seen as a sectoral/plurilateral type of agreement of sorts, and PTAs within the ECT would therefore have been superfluous and cumbersome.

One can conclude that, with regard to provisions on trade in goods, the ECS considered the risks stemming from the substantive overlap and tension between the ECT and the WTO and pre-emptively set out conflict rules to reconcile both treaties. Conflicts not (directly) solved in the ECT concern TRIMs, TRIPs and GATS.

4.2.4.2   Investments in Energy

Another important area where a conflict between WTO and ECT rules remains unresolved concerns investment protection under the WTO (through GATS Mode 3)[55] and the protection of investments in energy services under the ECT (part III ECT). The ECT covers trade in services through Article 1(5), but it does not incorporate GATS as such.[56] This leads to concurrent applicability of WTO rules and ECT rules concerning the protection of energy investments as described in the following paragraph.

The ECT protects investments in the energy sector directly by granting them national treatment (NT) and most-favoured-nation (MFN) treatment in Article 10(3) ECT. Investment in the energy

---

[52] Note, however, that the Agreement of Agriculture is of relevance with regard to the energy sector as it incorporates tariffs on biofuels; see Chapter 3, Section 3.2.2. See also A Yanovich, 'Chapter 1: WTO Rules and the Energy Sector' in Y Selivanova (ed), *Regulation of Energy in International Trade Law: WTO, NAFTA and Energy Charter* (Wolters Kluwer 2011) 27; Convention on the Harmonized Commodity Description and Coding System (adopted 14 June 1983) 1503 UNTS 167, ch 22 ('Beverages, Spirits and Vinegar').

[53] See Agreement Establishing the World Trade Organization (signed 15 April 1994) 1867 UNTS 154 (1994) 33 ILM 1144, art XII:1; ECT, annex W(A)(1).

[54] GATT, art XXIV ('Territorial Application – Frontier Traffic – Customs Unions and Free Trade Areas). This is one of the issues on the ECT modernization agenda.

[55] General Agreement on Trade in Services, Marrakesh Agreement Establishing the World Trade Organization, Annex 1B (signed 15 April 1994) 1869 UNTS 183 (1994) 33 ILM 1167 (GATS), art 1.2(c).

[56] ECT, annex W(A)(b).

sector should be understood in the context of the ECT as referring to any investment associated with what it calls 'Economic Activity in the Energy Sector' (ie concerning the exploration, extraction, refining, production, storage, land transport, transmission, distribution, trade, marketing or sale of energy materials and products covered in the ECT).[57] Under WTO law, on the other hand, investment is covered via the modes of supply of services defined in GATS. WTO members make sector-specific commitments in their GATS schedules of specific commitments, where they agree on particular market access commitments with regard to trade in services in a similar manner to their GATT schedules.[58] Horizontal commitments apply generally, whereas sector-specific commitments apply only to the sector they concern, and possibly also only to one or more of the four modes of supply defined in GATS: Mode 1, when neither the service supplier nor the service consumer has to move; Mode 2, when the consumer moves to the country where the service is supplied; Mode 3, when the service supplier establishes a commercial presence in the country where the service is supplied; and Mode 4, when the service supplier is established in a different country.[59]

WTO members must grant MFN treatment to all foreign services and NT to GATS commitments made in their services schedules.[60] Investments in services, and particularly investments in energy services, can be covered by Article I:2(c) (Mode 3) GATS when the service supplier establishes a commercial presence in the country where the service is supplied (ie a foreign company sets up subsidiaries or branches to provide services in another country).[61]

In principle, GATS rules apply to all energy-related services.[62] Some sectors in which members made commitments in their services schedules

---

[57] See definitions of 'Economic Activity in the Energy Sector' and 'Investment' in ECT, arts 1 (5), (6) respectively.

[58] PC Mavroidis, G Bermann and M Wu, *The Law of the World Trade Organization* (West 2010) 802–19. See Chapter 3, Section 3.3.2.

[59] GATS, art I:2.

[60] GATS, arts II, XVII. See Chapter 3, Section 3.3.2.

[61] On this issue in particular, see PC Mavroidis, 'Regulation of Investment in the Trade Regime' in Z Drabek and PC Mavroidis (eds), *Regulation of Foreign Investment: Challenges to International Harmonization* (2013) World Scientific Studies in International Economics, vol 21; see also generally M Molinuevo, *Protecting Investment in Services: Investor State Arbitration versus WTO Dispute Settlement* (Wolters Kluwer 2011).

[62] See Chapter 3, Section 3.2.2. see also G Marceau, 'The WTO in the Emerging Energy Governance Debate' in J Pauwelyn (ed), *Global Challenges at the Intersection of Trade,*

are more relevant to energy than others.[63] They include construction and related engineering services, distribution services, environmental services, financial services, transport services and other services not included elsewhere.[64]

The ECT's rules of conflict of the ECT have not taken sufficient account of this, presumably because the complete exclusion of the GATS from the ECT left the possibility of an ECT/WTO overlap in relation to energy investments unforeseen. In this regard, it should be noted that, unlike Articles II and XVI GATS, the ECT does not set forth any pre-establishment or market access obligations, so the conflict between the ECT and GATS is likely to arise in the post-establishment phase only.[65] This results in fragmentation, however, as both treaties can apply to the protection of investments in the energy sector. The overlap can also extend to procedural aspects of the two treaties, with the resolution of energy investment disputes, for example, being potentially subject to the procedures provided in both instruments.

4.2.5   Procedural Overlaps: Dispute Settlement in the WTO vs the ECT

The concurrent competence of the WTO and the ECT relates to both trade and investment disputes. The ECT's conflict rules address the former but not the latter.[66] This section will briefly discuss both.

4.2.5.1   Settlement of Trade Disputes

Article 3.2 DSU describes the dispute settlement mechanism as central to ensuring the security and predictability of the multilateral trading

---

Energy and the Environment (Graduate Institute of International and Development Studies/Centre for Trade and Economic Integration 2011) 26.

[63] However, see WTO, Council for Trade in Services, 'Energy Services: Background Note by the Secretariat' (9 September 1998) Doc S/C/W/52, 1 ('the vast majority of the global energy services industry is not covered by GATS specific commitments').

[64] See Chapter 3, Section 3.3.3. See also energy services identified by members in WTO, Council for Trade in Services, Special Session of the Council for the Trade in Services, Report by the Chairman to the Trade Negotiations Committee (28 November 2005) TN/S/23; GATT Secretariat, Services Sectoral Classifications List – Note by the Secretariat (10 July 1991) MTN.GNS/W/120; Central Product Classification (CPC) 883, 5115, 887.

[65] See eg R Dolzer and C Schreuer, *Principles of International Investment Law* (OUP 2008) 80. Note that Russia wanted to incorporate pre-investment protection and thereby mutual consistency with GATS. This was expressed during initial ECT negotiations; see the chairman's statement at the adoption session (17 December 1994).

[66] See Table 4.3.

system.[67] WTO members are required to settle any (energy) trade disputes in this forum alone. In practice, this means that WTO members are in effect precluded from settling their trade disputes elsewhere – the rationale for this being that members are provided with a single multilateral forum for the settlement of their disputes and at the same time are prevented from unilaterally seeking rulings on WTO law outside the forum.[68]

The ECT, by contrast, provides mechanisms for settling both energy trade and investment disputes – namely, in the form of state-state,[69] investor-state,[70] transit,[71] energy trade[72] and environment and competition[73] dispute settlement procedures. The ECT has addressed the overlap in WTO/ECT competence with respect to energy trade dispute settlement by providing for several conflict resolution measures designed to avoid parallelism and forum shopping.[74] According to Article 4 ECT, the DSU applies to the resolution of energy trade disputes between ECT parties that are also WTO members.[75] Since the DSU is not available to non-WTO members, it is replaced by a dispute resolution mechanism for trade disputes between an ECT/WTO member and a non-WTO ECT party and disputes between non-WTO ECT parties.[76] This special mechanism closely follows the WTO dispute settlement model, but is more informal in nature, meaning less detailed and legalistic. For instance, unlike the DSU, it does not provide for the right to appeal.[77] Nor does it provide for the automatic adoption of panel reports, which instead must be adopted by the Energy Charter Conference with no less than a three-quarters majority.[78]

Transit disputes are subject to different conflict rules from those applicable to 'regular' trade disputes.[79] In the ECT, the resolution of

---

[67] DSU, art 3.2.

[68] In US – Section 301 Trade Act, the panel held that Article 23.1 DSU imposes 'a general duty of a dual nature'.

[69] ECT, art 27 ('Settlement of Disputes between Contracting Parties'). This article does not explicitly apply to energy trade disputes; see ECT, art 28.

[70] ECT, art 26 ('Settlement of Disputes between an Investor and a Contracting Party').

[71] ECT, art 7.7.

[72] ECT, art 29 ('Interim Provisions on Trade-Related Matters'), annex D ('Interim Provisions for Trade Dispute Settlement').

[73] ECT, arts 6 ('Competition'), 19 ('Environmental Aspects').

[74] Frasl (n 3) 478.

[75] ECT, art 4; ECS, Applicable Trade Provisions (n 10) viii.

[76] ECT, annex D, art 29(7).

[77] DSU, arts 17, 20. See also Frasl (n 3) 479.

[78] ECT, annex D(2)(c), 4(c).

[79] See generally Azaria (n 41).

transit disputes is addressed in Article 7(7),[80] which requires ECT parties to exhaust any other relevant contractual remedies they may have agreed upon before having recourse to the mechanism provided in Article 7 (7).[81] That mechanism is conciliatory in nature, largely conducted through diplomatic channels, with the ECT secretary general appointing a conciliator, who 'shall seek the agreement of the parties to the dispute.'[82]

There is no apparent conflict between Article V GATT and the procedure set out in Article 7(7) ECT, since requirement set out in Article 7 (7) stems from the WTO-plus nature of the ECT[83] in that it offers a means of settling transit disputes that is not provided by Article V GATT.[84] As a result, the rights and obligations established in Article 7 (7) ECT go beyond WTO commitments for simultaneous WTO/ECT members. Article 7(8) ECT further emphasizes that nothing in Article 7 ECT shall derogate from a party's rights and obligations under international law, including customary international law and existing bilateral or multilateral agreements (ergo including Article V GATT).[85] Article 7 ECT, including its dispute resolution mechanism, therefore elaborates on the obligations laid down in Article V GATT, which should be regarded as setting a minimum standard.[86] For energy transit disputes involving ECT members whatever their relationship with the WTO (ie disputes between ECT/WTO members, between an ECT/WTO member and a

---

[80] ECT, art 7(7).

[81] ibid; Frasl (n 3) 495; ECS, *Trade in Energy* (n 10) 37, Azaria (n 41).

[82] ECT art 7(7)(b); ECT, art 7(7)(c):

> Only If within 90 days of his appointment he has failed to secure such agreement, he shall recommend a resolution to the dispute or a procedure to achieve such resolution and shall decide the interim tariffs and other terms and conditions to be observed for Transit from a date which he shall specify until the dispute is resolved.

[83] It seems that this was the intention of the ECT *travaux préparatoires*; see 'Legal Sub-Group's Report on Inter-relationship of the Charter Treaty with the GATT' (European Energy Charter, Conference Secretariat, Room Document 1, Plenary Session, 14–18 December 1993) 1; But see ECT, art 7(7):

> The following provisions shall apply to a dispute described in paragraph (6), but only following the exhaustion of all relevant contractual or other dispute resolution remedies previously agreed between the Contracting Parties party to the dispute or between any entity referred to in paragraph (6) and an entity of another Contracting Party party to the dispute.

[84] GATT, art V ('Freedom of Transit').

[85] ECT, art 7(8); Azaria (n 41) 589.

[86] Azaria (n 41) 591, referring to ECT *travaux préparatoires*.

non-WTO ECT party or between non-WTO ECT parties), the obligations in Article 7 thus seem to go further than those in Article V GATT
for disputes of the same kind.

4.2.5.2   Settlement of Investment Disputes

The overlap between the ECT and WTO in the field of energy investment
disputes can also be found in certain procedures for their settlement.

Article 26 ECT provides for investor-state dispute settlement, while
Article 27 covers state to-state disputes (non-trade issues only).[87] The
unresolved conflict between energy investment dispute resolution under
each system flows from overlap between ECT energy investment protection and the possible protection of such investments also through GATS
Mode 3, but only in the case of state-to-state dispute resolution as set out
in Article 27 ECT .[88] In other words, there may be overlap and conflict
between the dispute settlement mechanisms if they are available to the
same parties (ie states that are simultaneously ECT and WTO members).
While Article 27 ECT offers a means of resolving such disputes for ECT
members, for WTO members the DSU arguably also applies to disputes
over energy investment protection stemming from a violation of GATS
Mode 3, theoretically opening the way to forum shopping for WTO/ECT
members where energy investment disputes are concerned.

Mention should be made, however, of Article 16 ECT with regard to
ECT investment protection and its relationship with other agreements,.[89]
This article comes closest to being a conflict prevention/coordination
provision and is aimed at situations where one or more contracting
parties enter or have entered into other international agreements relating
to the subject matter of parts III (investment) or V (dispute settlement)
ECT. In essence, the article – albeit in a somewhat cumbersome manner –
gives precedence to those provisions of either the ECT or the other
agreement which are more favourable to the investor or the investment.[90]

There is no overlap or conflict (in the private international law sense)
between the WTO and the ECT when it comes to GATS Mode 3 dispute
resolution under the WTO (state-to-state) and investor-state dispute
settlement under Article 26 ECT. Here, the two dispute settlement
mechanisms work in parallel rather than in conflict with each other,
since they do not involve the same parties or the same applicable law,

---

[87] ECT, arts 26, 27 ECT.
[88] See Section 4.2.4.
[89] ECT, art 16 ('Relation to Other Agreements').
[90] ibid.

even though the disputes may stem from the same circumstances.[91] In this case there is a fruitful complementarity between the ECT and the WTO dispute resolution mechanisms, with each – the WTO for states and the ECT for investors – providing a potential forum for redress in the field of energy investment protection.

4.2.6 The WTO-ECT Relationship Twenty-Five Years On: Unresolved Issues and ECT Modernization

4.2.6.1 Unresolved Issues

A particularly noteworthy observation that emerges from an analysis of the membership situation is that the ECT provisions on trade in energy appears to be diminishing. As pointed out in Section 4.2.4.1, the ECT's provisions on trade apply only between non-WTO members that are parties to the ECT. Because of the large number of accessions to the WTO in recent years, these trade rules are now applicable to only a handful of ECT parties – namely, Azerbaijan, Bosnia and Herzegovina, Uzbekistan and Turkmenistan (ie far fewer than in 1998).[92] These countries are all WTO observers aspiring to join the WTO. Between ECT parties that already are WTO members, and even between such ECT/WTO members and non-WTO ECT parties, the applicable rules are those of GATT, subject to the exceptions mentioned earlier in this chapter.

This begs the fundamental question of what will happen to the trade provisions of the ECT once all WTO observers that are currently ECT parties have acceded to the organization? Will such provisions become obsolete (with the exception of those of a WTO-plus nature, such as Article 7 on transit, which is especially relevant for natural gas). Will they still have a legitimate purpose?

The main risk of overlap between the WTO and the ECT clearly lies in their concurrent applicability to substantive or procedural issues in the absence of a clear hierarchy between them. Although the inclusion of conflict rules in the ECT from the outset has helped to avert tension between the WTO's and the ECT's main trade provisions, some conflicts

---

[91] As an interesting analogy to the WTO/ECT conflict with respect to dispute settlement, see the discussion on conflicting judicial decisions and res judicata in investment law and diplomatic protection in M Paparinskis, 'Investment Arbitration and the Law of Countermeasures' (2008) 79 BYIL 264, 297–98.

[92] Compare Table 4.2 with Table 4.1. Countries that apply the ECT provisionally or have applied it provisionally in the past have been left out (Australia, Belarus, Iceland, Norway and Russia).

remain unresolved even two decades later. This makes the energy governance system inefficient, which is a problem and potentially harmful given the importance of a well-functioning trade framework capable of responding to modern energy and sustainable development needs.

An illustration can be found in the TRIMs, TRIPs and GATS provisions on trade in energy under the WTO and the corresponding provisions in the ECT (Article 5 on trade-related investment measures; the commitment to protect IP rights in the Joint Declaration on Trade-Related Intellectual Property Rights; and Article 1(5) defining 'Economic Activity in the Energy Sector').[93] The tension here has not been solved: TRIMs, TRIPs and GATS provisions cover energy goods and services insofar as they fall within the scope of the WTO, while the wording of the ECT shows that it, too, provides protection for the energy sector in these areas.

Although these norms do not explicitly contradict each other, and although both the WTO and the ECT are here pursuing a common goal of providing rules on trade-related investment measures, intellectual property and trade in services, the fact that the two sets of rules are not identical means that they could lead to significantly divergent results in practice.[94] Rather than a conflict of norms, the problem here is one of primacy. Which of the norms should take precedence? It appears there is no straightforward answer. The ECT does not explicitly regulate conflicts with TRIMs, TRIPs and GATS provisions, which are deemed of equal applicability. As Pauwelyn suggests, this can be deemed a *non liquet*.[95] That said, the TRIMs, TRIPs and GATS provisions related to are drafted with greater clarity and precision than the corresponding ECT rules and may be litigated more successfully under the DSU. Yet the fact remains that no hierarchy has been established in law between the two regimes with respect to their application.

Another area where conflicts caused by the concurrent applicability of WTO and ECT rules on both substance and procedure concerns the protection of energy investments and the settlement of energy investment disputes. This overlap is not peculiar to the WTO and the ECT, but part of the broader friction between trade and investment law in general.

While the substantive overlap between GATS Mode 3 investment protection and part III of the ECT raises issues similar to those discussed

---

[93] See Table 4.3.

[94] It goes without saying that TRIMs, TRIPs and GATS rules are significantly more detailed than the ECT rules on these topics.

[95] Pauwelyn, *Conflict of Norms* (n 11) 418.

above in relation to the TRIMs, TRIPs and GATS provisions, the procedural overlap poses a practical problem for countries that are simultaneously WTO members and parties to the ECT. Investments by one WTO
member in the energy sector of another WTO member are arguably
protected by GATS rules under GATS Mode 3. At the same time, energy
investments by an ECT party or an investor from an ECT Party are
protected through the rules set out in part III of the ECT.[96] It would
therefore seem possible for states (not investors) that are WTO/ECT
members to have recourse to both the DSU and Article 27 for the purpose
of settling disputes.[97] If both regimes have competence over energy
investment disputes, which dispute settlement forum should take precedence? One could argue either way, but there is no conclusive legal
answer to the question.

On the one hand, one could claim that a dispute in the energy sector
between WTO members arising from a violation of GATS Mode 3
(commercial presence) should be litigated first and foremost before a
WTO panel. A strong argument in support of such a claim is that the
WTO offers a dispute resolution forum reserved for its members, and
they are precluded from going elsewhere. Furthermore, GATS Mode 3 is
clearly part of the WTO agreements (namely, GATS) and consequently
falls within the jurisdiction of WTO panels.[98] That said, GATS Mode 3
has been at issue in only one WTO dispute so far – namely, *China –
Electronic Payment Services*, a dispute which moreover did not concern
energy investment protection.[99]

On the other hand, there is a case to be made for giving Article 27
ECT precedence over the WTO where state-to-state energy investment
disputes are concerned. The ECT offers a specialized regime for the
settlement of energy investment disputes. That the more specialized
regime should prevail in this case would be consistent with the rules of
conflict resolution. What is more, the ECT has indeed already been
frequently used for such disputes, unlike the WTO.[100] It should be
said, however, that, in contrast to the WTO, the ECT does not

---

[96] ECT, pt III ('Investment Promotion and Protection').
[97] Note, however, that in the case of Article 26 ECT the litigating party would be the
investor, whereas under the DSU it would be a state – namely, a WTO member.
[98] Pauwelyn, *Conflict of Norms* (n 11) 443; DSU, art 1.1.
[99] *China – Electronic Payment Services*, panel report.
[100] ibid; cf International Energy Charter, 'Investor Dispute Settlement Cases'accessed 20 July 2020.

expressly require energy investment disputes to be settled under the ECT.[101]

Another possible solution in such circumstances would be to rely on Article 16 ECT and determine which provision in which regime (WTO or ECT) is more favourable to the case at hand. Here too, however, no legal hierarchy has been established between the two fora, which once again creates a risk of forum shopping and of the procedure being fragmented between the WTO and the ECT. If nothing else, the availability of a parallel route for settling energy investment disputes (ie through the ECT) certainly throws the perceived exclusivity of the WTO dispute settlement system into question.

From the above, it is obvious that the parallel applicability of their rules causes tension between the WTO and ECT. But how can these institutions best manage the unresolved conflicts stemming from their substantive and procedural overlaps? The answer is difficult to predict and largely depends on the direction taken by each treaty regime in the future.

In the absence of clear rules prescribing how to manage the problems of overlap and the resulting tension between the legal regimes of the WTO and ECT, it is nonetheless worth considering by analogy the pragmatic suggestions made in the related field of international environmental law.[102] Wolfrum and Matz propose an approach that sees closer cooperation and coordination between overlapping regimes and institutions as a means of overcoming such tension.[103] Both concepts – cooperation and coordination – are understood broadly and imply voluntary and coordinated action between stakeholders in both institutions.[104] For coordination and cooperation to be successful, both institutions need to share a common objective. As far as the WTO and the ECT are concerned, this could be a (more) optimal regime for the regulation of economic activity in the energy sector. Fruitful cooperation presupposes

---

[101] If parties fail to settle a dispute amicably, Article 26(2)ECT gives the investor three options for submitting the dispute for resolution: '(a) to the courts or administrative tribunals of the Contracting Party to the dispute; (b) in accordance with any applicable, previously agreed dispute settlement procedure; or (c) in accordance with the following paragraphs of this Article'.

[102] J Pauwelyn, 'Fragmentation in International Law' in R Wolfrum (ed), *The Max Planck Encyclopedia of Public International Law* (OUP 2008) online edn, para 25, citing R Wolfrum and N Matz, *Conflicts in International Environmental Law* (Springer 2003) 159–63.

[103] Wolfrum and Matz (n 102) 159–63. For a more detailed discussion on the various scenarios, see Chapter 8, Section 8.3 blow.

[104] Wolfrum and Matz (n 102) 161.

not only active involvement on the part of the institutions, but also the involvement of states in the work of international institutions and interaction between different institutions.[105] It can certainly be expected that increased coordination and closer cooperation between the WTO and the ECT would help to resolve more efficiently the problems caused by overlapping and conflicting areas of competence.[106] It should not be one-off, but rather part of a continuing process.[107] A step in that direction was taken in the early 2000s, with the Energy Charter Secretariat providing rules of coordination for WTO and the ECT, but this did not suffice. As this chapter has shown, gaps and overlaps continue to exist. Moreover, resolving conflicts between the WTO and the ECT on the basis of the ECS guidelines seems to be proving rather a complex matter, and perhaps unnecessarily so.[108] Table 4.3 attempts to present a highly simplified picture of the overlap between the two treaties and the extent to which conflicts have or have not been resolved. Perhaps it is not unthinkable that coordination between the two treaty regimes could happen in a simpler manner in the future.

4.2.6.2   ECT Modernization

In 2015, the ECS issued a political declaration on global cooperation in the field of energy, the International Energy Charter.[109] While this declaration has the status of soft law and therefore has no legal validity, the fact that ECT members, signatories and non-signatories gathered to discuss the global energy challenges that lay ahead was a positive sign. Through the International Energy Charter, the ECS sought to update the founding document of the ECT, the European Energy Charter, concluded in 1991. The concept of such an instrument was aimed at 'enhancing international cooperation in order to meet common challenges related to energy at national, regional and international levels, including the evolution of global energy architecture'.[110] Additionally, the document alludes to increased cooperation and coordination between multilateral agreements in the field of energy. Its signatories have agreed to foster synergies among energy-related multilateral fora and indicated

---

[105] ibid.

[106] ibid 162.

[107] ibid 159.

[108] See ECS, *Applicable Trade Provisions*; ECS, *Trade in Energy* (n 10).

[109] 'Agreed Text for Adoption in The Hague at the Ministerial Conference on the International Energy Charter on 20 May 2015'.

[110] 2015 International Energy Charter, preamble.

Table 4.3 *Resolution of conflicts, issue-areas and procedural overlaps – A comparison between the WTO and the ECT*

	WTO	ECT	WTO rules in ECT: resolution of conflict
Trade in Energy Goods	- GATT - TBT - TRIMs - TRIPs - Trade remedy agreements: (Anti-Dumping, Subsidies and Safeguards) - Market access agreements (Import Licensing, Rules of Origin, Customs Valuation and Preshipment Inspection)	- Trade provisions ECT (arts 4, 5, 6, 29 ECT[a]) - Article 5 ECT ('Trade-Related Investment Measures') - Article 7 ECT ('Transit') (ECT Transit Protocol to elaborate on ECT and this article) - Transit Protocol (under negotiation – Most recent	**GATT 1994 incorporation into ECT by reference (art 4 ECT):** - GATT 1994 Applies: a) Among ECT/WTO members (art 4 ECT) b) Between ECT/WTO members and non-WTO ECT parties (art 29(2)(a) ECT)[a] - Trade provisions ECT (arts 4, 5, 6 and 29 ECT) apply among non-WTO ECT parties only (art 29(1) ECT)[a] - Article 7 ECT creates additional obligations for ECT/WTO members (ie Article 7 prevails over Article V GATT (the so-called WTO-plus effect of ECT) – same would account for an ECT Transit Protocol (draft art 3 Transit Protocol) **Main exception to GATT incorporation by reference (art 4 ECT):**

Not directly relevant for trade in energy goods:
- SPS
- Other WTO agreements: (Agriculture, Textiles)
- Plurilaterals, not binding on all WTO members (GSP, Government Procurement, Civil Aircraft)

informal text available: TT87 22/01/2010)
NB The aim of the Transit Protocol is to complement the ECT while being in accordance with Art 7 ECT (Draft Art 3 Transit Protocol)

- Schedules of concessions Article II GATT are not incorporated into ECT, but ECT has 'best-endeavours' clause (art 29(3), (4), (5) ECT[a])

WTO agreements excluded from incorporation into ECT:
a) Plurilaterals, not binding on all members (annex W ECT), eg Government Procurement, Civil Aircraft
b) WTO agreements, not directly relevant for ECT (annex W ECT), eg Agriculture, SPS, Textiles
c) WTO special and differential treatment provisions do not apply in ECT, except for paras 1–4 of Enabling Clause (through annex W, s A, para 2(a) ECT)

Conflict not solved:
- TRIMs not incorporated in ECT (annex W(A)(iv) ECT), but similar provision in Article 5 ECT ('Trade Related Investment Measures')

Table 4.3 (cont.)

	WTO	ECT	WTO rules in ECT: resolution of conflict
			- TRIPs not incorporated in ECT (annex W (A)(c) ECT), but commitment to provide protection of intellectual property rights (Joint Declaration on Trade-Related Intellectual Property Rights, Final Act of the International Conference and Decision by the Energy Charter Conference in Respect of the Amendment to the Trade-Related Provisions of the Energy Charter Treaty)
Trade in energy services	- GATS	- 'Economic Activity in the Energy Sector' (art 1(5) ECT) - Transit Protocol (under negotiation – most recent informal text available: TT87 22/01/2010)	- Article 11 ECT ('Key Personnel') takes up issues treated as specific commitments under GATS (the so-called WTO-plus effect of ECT) **Conflict not solved:** GATS not incorporated in ECT (annex W (A)(b) ECT), but energy services nevertheless covered in ECT as 'Economic Activity in the Energy Sector'

Resolution energy trade disputes	- DSU	- Annex D ('Interim Provisions for Trade Dispute Settlement') - Article 7(7) ECT for transit disputes	- DSU applies: among ECT/WTO members (art 4 ECT) - Annex D applies: a) between ECT/WTO members and non-WTO ECT parties (art 29(7) ECT[a]) b) among non-WTO ECT parties (art 29(7) ECT[a]) - Article 7(7) ECT creates additional obligations for ECT/WTO members (the so-called WTO-plus effect of ECT)
Energy investment protection	- GATS Mode 3 (commercial presence)	- Part III ECT ('Investment Promotion and Protection')	**Conflict not solved:** Overlap/tension where GATS Mode 3 investment protection coincides with Part III ECT (because GATS not incorporated in ECT)
Resolution energy investment disputes	- DSU for GATS Mode 3 disputes	- Part V ECT ('Dispute Settlement'): a) Investor-state (art 26 ECT) b) State-state (art 27 ECT, non-trade matters only)	**Conflict not solved:** (Stems from substantive conflict) Overlap/tension where GATS Mode 3 investment protection disputes coincide with Part III ECT, state-state disputes (art 27 ECT (post-establishment). However, see Article 16 ECT ('Relation to Other

Table 4.3 (*cont.*)

	WTO	ECT	WTO rules in ECT: resolution of conflict
			Agreements') regarding Parts III and V ECT. WTO/ECT complementarity regarding investor-state disputes (art 26 ECT)
Environmental protection	- Possible through Article XX GATT **NB** See also WTO Decision on Trade and Environment	- Article 19 ECT ('Environmental Aspects') - Article 24 ECT ('Exceptions') Environmental Protocol (PEEREA)	- Article 19 ECT and the Environmental Protocol (PEEREA) create additional obligations for ECT/WTO members (the so-called WTO-plus effect of ECT)

[a] Article 29 ECT sets out transitional arrangements and ceases to exist for an ECT party when it joins the WTO. The application of Article 29 ECT will end only when all ECT parties are WTO members.

Sources: (1) The Energy Charter Treaty & Related Documents; ECT Draft Transit Protocol (Preliminary Draft TTG87, 22/01/2010); WTO Agreements. (2) Energy Charter Secretariat, *Trade in Energy: WTO Rules Applying under the Energy Charter Treaty* (ECS 2001); Energy Charter Secretariat, *Applicable Trade Provisions of the Energy Charter Treaty* (ECS 2003); I Frasl, 'The Trade Rules of GATT and Related Instruments and the Energy Charter Treaty' and MM Roggenkamp, 'Transit of Network-Bound Energy: The European Experience' in TW Wälde (ed), *The Energy Charter Treaty: An East-West Gateway to Investment and Trade* (Kluwer Law 1996).

their willingness to take full advantage of the expertise of existing inter-national organizations in the energy field.[111] More importantly for cooperation between the ECT and WTO, the signatories to the 2015 charter commit to ensuring that the development of trade in energy is consistent 'with major multilateral agreements such as the WTO Agreement and its related instruments'.[112] This goal should be achieved by means of, for instance, guaranteeing an open and competitive market for energy products, materials, equipment and services, access to energy resources and access to national, regional and international markets.[113]

The ECS initiated the official process of modernizing the ECT in 2018.[114] However, the underlying trigger for this, in the words of the ECS secretary general Urban Rusnák, was the withdrawal of the Russian Federation in 2009, which led to the 2010 'Roadmap for the Modernisation of the Energy Charter Treaty Process'.[115] In 2018, the parties approved a list of twenty-five topics as a starting point for the renegotiation of the treaty.[116] As mentioned in Section 4.2.1, these mostly concern the investment provisions of the ECT. However, some topics are also directly relevant to the trade disciplines in the ECT, such as the definition of transit, access to infrastructure (including denial of access and available capacities), the definitions and principles of tariff-setting and regional economic integration organizations (REIO).[117] In its draft negotiating directives issued in 2019, the EU laid emphasis on sustainable development, climate change and the clean energy transition.[118]

4.3 Energy in Selected Preferential Trade Agreements

Apart from multilateral instruments such as the Energy Charter Treaty, there is a growing tendency to include energy-specific chapters in prefer-ential trade agreements (PTAs).[119] Such chapters attempt to address the

---

[111] ibid.

[112] ibid, title I ('Objectives') para 1.

[113] ibid.

[114] See Decision of the Energy Charter Conference (n 12).

[115] U Rusnák, 'Modernisation of the Energy Charter: The Long Story Told Short' (*Kluwer Arbitration Blog*, 21 July 2020).

[116] See Decision of the Energy Charter Conference (n 12)

[117] ibid.

[118] Council of the EU, 'Negotiating Directives for the Modernisation of the Energy Charter Treaty – Adoption' (2 July 2019) 10745/19 Add 1, 4.

[119] The energy security dimension of several PTAs is addressed in Chapter 7, Section 7.2.4. See also AA Marhold, 'Externalising Europe's Energy Policy in EU Free Trade

specific needs of the energy sector, while also taking account of the particular situations and interests of the contracting parties involved. This section will discuss two types of such chapters from agreements on both sides of the Atlantic. The North American Free Trade Agreement (NAFTA, no longer in force) was arguably the first PTA to include a trade-related energy chapter and therefore deserves to be discussed.[120] Its successor, the United States-Mexico-Canada Agreement (USMCA), will also be briefly touched on in this context. On the other side of the Atlantic, the EU has more recently been including energy chapters in its free trade agreements with third countries. The new free trade agreements concluded with Mexico, Singapore and Ukraine offer good examples of modern-day PTAs that provide for progressive energy and environmental regulation. These chapters in PTAs are proof of the fact that, even if the WTO is currently at a standstill, countries nonetheless wish to push the agenda on specific trade topics and continue to conclude agreements on them.[121]

4.3.1   NAFTA and USMCA

4.3.1.1   North American Free Trade Agreement (NAFTA)

The 1994 NAFTA (as of July 2020 no longer in force) was one of the first PTAs that included a separate chapter on trade in energy (chapter 6, entitled 'Energy and Basic Petrochemicals').[122] As indicated in Article 602, the chapter covered trade and investment in energy goods *and* services.[123] The chapter's function was threefold: (1) it confirmed NAFTA's applicability to trade and investment in energy goods and

---

Agreements: A Cognitive Dissonance between Promoting Sustainable Development and Ensuring Security of Supply?' (2019) 3 Europe and the World 1.

[120] North American Free Trade Agreement (entered into force 1 January 1994) 1867 UNTS 14 (NAFTA).

[121] Free Trade Agreement between the European Union and the Republic of (entered into force 21 November 2019) [2019] OJ L294/3 (EU-Singapore FTA); EU-Ukraine Deep and Comprehensive Free Trade Agreement (EU-Ukraine DCFTA), part of the Association Agreement between the European Union and Its Member States, of the one part, and Ukraine, of the other part (signed 21 March 2014, entered into force 1 September 2017) [2014] OJ L161/3 (provisionally in force): EU-Mexico Free Trade Agreement: 'The Agreement in Principle' (26 April 2018, updated May 2020) (EU-Mexico FTA) (not yet in force).

[122] NAFTA, ch 6 ('Energy and Basic Petrochemicals'). Substancewise, the chapter was based on the energy chapter in the preceding US-Canada PTA.

[123] NAFTA, art 602: 'This Chapter applies to measures relating to energy and basic petrochemical goods originating in the territories of the Parties and to measures relating to

services; (2) it explicitly stated that domestic measures regulating energy had to comply with national treatment and promote a stable commercial environment; and (3) it reduced some of the exceptions to import and export restrictions on energy beyond what was provided in the WTO agreements.[124]

It was above all the United States that pushed for the inclusion of an energy chapter in NAFTA, as it wished to secure its energy supply and gain as much access as possible not only to Canadian but also particularly to Mexican energy reserves.[125] Mexico did open up its energy sector somewhat, but it did make extensive reservations to the chapter as well.[126] For example, it refused to make any concessions on sovereignty over its natural resources or its Pemex oil exploration and production monopoly.[127] It did, however, agree to increase US and Canadian access to markets for the transport of electricity, petrochemicals and natural gas.[128] With regard to government procurement, Mexico also agreed to foreign participation in procurement contracts with Pemex and the State Electricity Commission.[129] Some NAFTA provisions were stricter than those of GATT, or added to them.[130] This, for instance, was the case with Article 603(2) on import and export restrictions, which read:

> The Parties understand that the provisions of the GATT incorporated in paragraph 1 prohibit, in any circumstances in which any other form of quantitative restriction is prohibited, minimum or maximum export-price requirements and, except as permitted in enforcement of countervailing and antidumping orders and undertakings, minimum or maximum import-price requirements.

This provision is of a GATT-plus nature in that it adds to GATT Article XI:1 GATT ('General Elimination of Quantitative Restrictions'): Article 603(2) NAFTA prohibits minimum or maximum import- and

---

investment and to the cross-border trade in services associated with such goods, as set forth in this Chapter.'
[124] KJ Benes, *Considerations for the Treatment of Energy in the US-EU Transatlantic Trade and Investment Partnership* (September 2015) Columbia/SIPA Center on Global Energy Policy, 11.
[125] Benes (n 124) 11–12.
[126] ibid.
[127] ibid.
[128] ibid 12–13.
[129] ibid 13.
[130] R Rios Herrán and P Poreti, 'Energy Trade and Investment under the North American Free Trade Agreement' in Y Selivanova (ed), *Regulation of Energy in International Trade Law: WTO, NAFTA and Energy Charter* (Wolters Kluwer 2011) 383.

export-price requirements, which are permitted under GATT.[131] It thus de facto prevents parties from segmenting markets and engaging in energy dual-pricing practices.[132]

Article 604 NAFTA on export taxes is another important GATT-plus provision in that it limits export taxes on energy goods:

> No Party may adopt or maintain any duty, tax or other charge on the export of any energy or basic petrochemical good to the territory of another Party, unless such duty, tax or charge is adopted or maintained on:
>
> a) exports of any such good to the territory of all other Parties; and
> b) any such good when destined for domestic consumption.

GATT does not prohibit export taxes.[133] Under NAFTA, they were allowed only when two conditions were met: they had to be applied (1) on an MFN basis and (2) only to goods that were intended for domestic consumption.[134] Moreover, there were no exceptions to this provision.

The underlying rationale of Article 605 NAFTA on other export measures was to ensure security of supply and price stabilization in the NAFTA region.[135] It subjected parties to more stringent conditions when invoking GATT exceptions with respect to energy goods.[136] Though NAFTA parties could still avail themselves of such exceptions, their freedom to do so was limited by the three conditions listed in paragraphs (a), (b) and (c) of Article 605, all of which had to be met. First of all, restrictions imposed on energy goods must not result in a relative reduction in exports.[137] Second, an export restriction must not result in higher export prices for the energy good due to taxes, fees, licences and minimum price requirements.[138] This was a de facto equal access clause for supplies (in other words, a supply commitment), because it required NAFTA parties to sell energy on the domestic market at the same price as

---

[131] Herrán and Poreti (n 130) 383.
[132] ibid 400. However, as Herrán and Poreti note: 'Under Annex 603.6 Mexico reserved the right to conduct foreign trade in certain goods through the monopolist Pemex. Mexico's reservations listed in Annex 603.6 are rather comprehensive in scope and include virtually all refined petroleum products plus bitumen, oil shale, tar sand and liquefied petroleum gas (LPG).'
[133] See Chapter 5, Section 5.2.
[134] Herrán and Poreti (n 130) 399.
[135] ibid 401ff.
[136] NAFTA, art 605 ('Other Export Measures'); GATT, arts XI:2(a), XX(g)(i)(j).
[137] NAFTA, art 605(a).
[138] NAFTA, art 605(b).

abroad.[139] Thirdly, restrictions must not disrupt normal channels of supply.[140] This was a rather progressive provision, as it prevented NAFTA parties from completely shutting down production on the pretext of critical shortages or the conservation of natural resources. Mexico made a reservation in respect of this clause in its entirety, which meant that in practice it applied only between Canada and the United States.

Last but not least, Article 607 on national security measures allowed parties to restrict imports or exports on grounds of national security, although in more stringent ways than under Article XXI GATT. Mexico again made a reservation in respect of this article, and it therefore applied only between Canada and the United States. Article 607 NAFTA in fact excluded the application of Article XXI GATT on energy goods and petrochemicals unless the restrictions were needed (a) to supply a military establishment of a party or enable fulfilment of a critical defence contract of a party; (b) to respond to a situation of armed conflict involving the party taking the measure; (c) to implement national policies or international agreements relating to the non-proliferation of nuclear weapons or other nuclear explosive devices; or (d) to respond to direct threats of disruption in the supply of nuclear materials for defence purposes.

4.3.1.2   The US-Mexico-Canada Free Trade Agreement (USMCA)

Much has changed since the conclusion of NAFTA. Not least, the United States has become a net energy exporter due to the discoveries of large amounts of shale gas in the mid-2000s. This may well explain why the follow-up agreement to NAFTA – the US-Mexico-Canada Free Trade Agreement (USMCA, which entered into force in July 2020), does not contain an energy-specific chapter.[141] As already noted, it was the United States, at the time in need of greater access to energy supplies, that pushed for an energy chapter in NAFTA. Today, the United States may be less dependent on energy supplies from abroad or agreements guaranteeing access to such supplies. Apparently, an energy chapter was negotiated but dropped at the request of Mexico at the last moment.[142] Instead, the

---

[139] Herrán and Poreti (n 130) 401.

[140] NAFTA, art 605(c).

[141] Agreement between the United States of America, the United Mexican States and Canada (signed 30 November 2018) (USMCA).

[142] JM Weekes and others, 'NAFTA 2.0 Drilling Down: The Impact of the CUSMA/USMCA on Canadian Energy Stakeholders' (2019) 7(1) Energy Regulation Quarterly <www.energyregulationquarterly.ca> accessed 20 July 2020, para 5, fn 35.

United States and Canada issued a side letter,[143] which functions as a de facto energy trade-related agreement between them, but applies only to regulatory measures at central government level (Article 2).[144] The side letter also calls for the establishment of independent energy regulators and imposes transparency requirements in relation to the energy sector (Article 4). Additionally, access to energy infrastructure must not be 'unduly discriminatory or unduly preferential' (Article 5.1). In essence, the purpose of this bilateral side agreement was to ensure that the United States and Canada would not be made worse off by the regulation of their energy relations than under NAFTA.[145]

In chapter 8 of the USMCA (consisting of a single provision, Article 8.1) Mexico nevertheless ensured that, much as under NAFTA, its ownership of hydrocarbons would be respected:

> Mexico has the direct, inalienable, and imprescriptible ownership of all hydrocarbons in the subsoil of the national territory, including the continental shelf and the exclusive economic zone located outside the territorial sea and adjacent thereto, in strata or deposits, regardless of their physical conditions pursuant to Mexico's Constitution (*Constitución Política de los Estados Unidos Mexicanos*).[146]

4.3.2   EU Free Trade Agreements: Singapore, Ukraine and Mexico

4.3.2.1   EU-Singapore FTA

The EU-Singapore Free Trade Agreement entered into force on 21 November 2019.[147] Singapore is the biggest trade partner of the EU in the region of the Association of the Southeast Asian Nations (ASEAN). Chapter 7 is called 'Non-Tariff Barriers to Trade and Investment in Renewable Energy Generation'. The chapter is quite progressive as it covers not just energy but precisely renewable energy, with a focus on sustainable development and climate change mitigation. Moreover, it adopts a comprehensive perspective on renewable energy encompassing both trade and investment, rather than viewing these two elements separately. The chapter's preamble addresses the need to move away from fossil sources:

---

[143] See also Chapter 7, Section 7.2.
[144] See Weekes (n 142).
[145] ibid.
[146] USMCA, art 8.1.2(b).
[147] See European Commission, 'Countries and Regions: Singapore' <https://ec.europa.eu/trade/policy/countries-and-regions/countries/singapore/> accessed 20 July 2020.

In line with global efforts to reduce greenhouse gas emissions, the Parties share the objective of promoting, developing and increasing the generation of energy from renewable and sustainable non-fossil sources, particularly through facilitating trade and investment. To this effect, the Parties shall cooperate towards removing or reducing tariffs as well as non-tariff barriers and fostering regulatory convergence with or towards regional and international standards.[148]

The chapter consists of seven articles, most of which contain commitments on trade and investment in renewable energy of a GATT-plus nature. The obligations set out in the chapter apply to all measures that may affect trade and investment between the parties related to the generation of energy from renewable and sustainable non-fossil sources (eg wind; solar, aerothermal, geothermal, hydrothermal and ocean energy; hydropower; biomass; landfill gas, sewage treatment plant gas and biogases), but not to the products from which energy is generated (Article 7.3(1)). To prevent potential conflict with other parts of the agreement, the FTA states in Article 7.3(3) that the other provisions of the agreement shall prevail.

The chapter sets out five main principles that the parties are required to observe. They must:

a) refrain from adopting measures imposing local content requirements;
b) refrain from adopting measures requiring the formation of local partnerships;
c) ensure that procedures concerning authorization, certification and licensing are applied in a non-discriminatory, objective and transparent manner;
d) ensure that any administrative charges in connection with the importation of goods and provision of services comply with other provisions of the agreement; and
e) ensure that the terms, conditions and procedures for connection and access to electricity transmission grids are transparent and non-discriminatory.[149]

Article 7.5 sets out rules on non-tariff barriers for the parties' trade in energy products generated from renewable and sustainable non-fossil

---

[148] EU-Singapore FTA, ch 7 ('Non-Tariff Barriers to Trade and Investment in Renewable Energy Generation') preamble.
[149] EU-Singapore FTA, art 7.4 ('Principles').

sources.[150] It requires the EU and Singapore to use international standards as a basis for their technical regulations relating to trade in such
products.[151] The parties are, moreover, encouraged to integrate environmental performance into their technical regulations.[152]

Finally, Article 7.6 of the Agreement allows parties to invoke general
exceptions provided for at various places in the agreement (eg Articles
2.14 and 8.62), and which cannot override those provided for in the WTO
agreements.[153]

All in all, we can conclude that, although the obligations it imposes are
somewhat modest and not very far-reaching, the chapter in the EU-
Singapore FTA sets the current standard for the regulation of renewable
energy in PTAs. Not only does it firmly commit to eliminating greenhouse gas emissions, but it also approaches (clean) energy holistically.

4.3.2.2   EU-Ukraine DCFTA

The Deep and Comprehensive Free Trade Agreement (DCFTA) is part of
the larger Association Agreement that the EU concluded with Ukraine. It
entered into force on 1 September 2017. Chapter 11 DCFTA, entitled
'Trade-Related Energy', is another example of an advanced PTA as far as
energy is concerned. It focuses less on renewable energy than the EU-
Singapore FTA, but it does go a long way in clarifying some outstanding
issues in the traditional fields of fossil fuels and electrical energy. This
more thorough regulation of energy between the EU and Ukraine can be
explained through Ukraine's being a party to the Energy Community
Treaty, which extends the EU internal energy acquis to third countries.[154]
Fundamentally, the chapter's underlying rationale was clearly to enhance
security of supply for the EU.

The chapter consists of twelve articles centring on issues of dual
pricing, transit, transport and quantitative restrictions. It opens with
clear and unambiguous definitions of terms that otherwise often cause
confusion. 'Energy goods' refers to natural gas, electricity and crude oil,

---

[150] EU-Singapore FTA, art 7.5(1).
[151] The International Organization for Standardization (ISO) and the International
Electrotechnical Commission (IEC) are considered to be relevant international standards whose use is particularly encouraged.
[152] EU-Singapore FTA, art 7.5(2).
[153] Article 2.14 EU-Singapore FTA lists exceptions for trade in goods and Article 8.62
likewise for trade in services.
[154] Treaty Establishing the Energy Community (signed 25 October 2005, entered into force
1 July 2006) [2006] OJ L198/18.

which are accompanied by their respective HS codes.[155] The definition of 'fixed infrastructure', which covers gas storage facilities and gas and electricity grids, incorporates the definition provided in the 2003 EU gas and electricity directives.[156] Last but not least, 'transit' and 'transport' of energy is refer to the transit and transportation of energy goods though fixed infrastructures and pipelines, including those used to convey oil.[157]

Articles 269–71 of chapter 11, which constitute its centre of gravity, explicitly prohibit any form of dual pricing and related discriminatory measures when trading in energy. Article 269(1) requires the price of gas and electricity supplies to be determined on the basis of supply and demand only, although parties are allowed to regulate prices 'in the general economic interest'.[158] In that case, however, they must ensure that the method of calculating the regulated price is published prior to its entry into force.[159]

Article 270 prohibits dual pricing altogether. This GATT-plus requirement takes a very clear stance on the practice and is in line with the EU stance on dual-pricing policies during recent decades. Although the prohibition does not explicitly link dual pricing with subsidization, as is often the case in WTO debates, it does so implicitly by referring to all measures that may result in dual pricing:

> '[N]either Party, or a regulatory authority thereof, shall adopt or maintain a measure resulting in a higher price for exports of energy goods to the other Party than the price charged for such goods when intended for domestic consumption.[160]

The same goes for customs duties and quantitative restrictions, which are prohibited unless justified on grounds of public policy or public security, the protection of human, animal or plant life or health, or the protection of industrial and commercial property.[161] It goes without saying that any

---

[155] EU-Ukraine DCFTA, art 268(1)

[156] EU-Ukraine DCFTA, art 268(2); Directive 2003/54/EC of the European Parliament and of the Council of 26 June 2003 concerning common rules for the internal market in electricity and repealing Directive 96/92/EC [2003] OJ L176/37; Directive 2003/55/EC of the European Parliament and of the Council of 26 June 2003 concerning common rules for the internal market in natural gas and repealing Directive 98/30/EC [2003] OJ L176/57.

[157] EU-Ukraine DCFTA, art 268(3), (4).

[158] ibid, art 269(2).

[159] ibid, art 269(3).

[160] ibid, art 270(1).

[161] ibid, art 270(2).

such restrictions or measures must not amount to arbitrary discrimination or constitute a disguised restriction on trade between the parties.

Given that Ukraine lies in a geopolitically sensitive position, especially as far as the transit of energy is concerned, Chapter 11 could not leave out rules on energy transit and the transportation of energy.[162] To avoid any ambiguity, the drafters of Article 272 on transit clearly wanted to make its coverage as broad as possible. For that reason, the principle of freedom of transit enshrined in the rules of both GATT and the ECT was comprehensively taken up:[163]

> The Parties shall take the necessary measures to facilitate transit, consistent with the principle of freedom of transit, and in accordance with Article V.2, V.4 and V.5 of GATT 1994 and Articles 7.1 and 7.3 of the Energy Charter Treaty of 1994, which are incorporated into and made part of this Agreement.[164]

The result is that, without a doubt, this article goes beyond any commitment we have seen in the past, setting a new and higher standard on energy transit. Most importantly, it combines the relevant transit provision of both GATT and the ECT, incorporating Article V GATT[165] plus Article 7 ECT, which imposes obligations that beyond those of GATT. In so doing, the article removes any uncertainty over the extent of coverage of energy transit in the EU-Ukraine DCFTA. That being said, as both the EU and Ukraine are parties to the WTO and the ECT, the article in fact merely reiterates their existing commitments. Nevertheless, it is novel to see them combined in the same article.

Related to the above, Article 275 obliges parties to take all measures to prevent the unauthorized taking of energy goods, while Article 276 deals with interruptions in transit, notably prohibiting the interruption of existing transport or transit of energy goods in any circumstances:

> A Party through whose territory energy goods transit or are transported shall not, in the event of a dispute over any matter involving the Parties or one or more entities subject to the control or jurisdiction of one of the Parties, interrupt or reduce, permit any entity subject to its control or jurisdiction, including a state trading enterprise, to interrupt or reduce, or

---

[162] As is well known, Ukraine was the subject of many gas transit issues in the 2000s; see AA Marhold, 'The Russo-Ukrainian Gas Disputes, the Energy Charter Treaty and the Kremlin Proposal: Is There Light at the End of the Gas Pipe?' [2011] 3 Oil, Gas and Energy Law Journal <www.ogel.org>.

[163] See Section 4.2.2.

[164] EU-Ukraine DCFTA, art 272 ('Transit').

[165] GATT, art V ('Freedom of Transit').

require any entity subject to its jurisdiction to interrupt or reduce the existing transport or transit of energy goods, except where this is specifically provided for in a contract or other agreement governing such transit or transport, prior to the conclusion of a dispute resolution procedure under the relevant contract.[166]

Article 276 does, however, admits that

> a Party shall not be held liable for an interruption or reduction pursuant to this Article where that Party is in an impossibility to supply, transit or transport energy goods as a result of actions attributable to a third country or an entity under the control or jurisdiction of a third country.[167]

It is obvious that Articles 275 and 276 were included with a view to avoiding, with hindsight, a repeat of the unreliable energy supply and transit situation caused by the gas disputes between Russia and Ukraine in the 2000s.

Article 273 on energy transport focuses mainly on third-party access to the grid. Parties must ensure that the tariffs, capacity allocation procedures and all other conditions are objective, reasonable and transparent and do not discriminate on the basis of the origin, ownership or destination of the electricity or gas. Here, explicit reference is made to the Energy Community Treaty. The relationship with the Energy Community Treaty is also taken up in Articles 277 and 278 – the latter in connection with regulatory authorities for electricity and gas, to which the Energy Community's unbundling legislation applies.[168]

Lastly, the chapter incorporates a provision (Article 279) on access to and the conduct of activities of prospection, exploration and production of hydrocarbons. It emphasizes the parties' rights under international law, including the United Nations Convention on the Law of the Sea of 1982.[169] Each party retains full sovereignty over hydrocarbon resources located in its territory and in its archipelagic and territorial waters, as well as sovereign rights for the purposes of exploring and exploiting hydrocarbon resources located in its exclusive economic zone and continental shelf.[170]

---

[166] EU-Ukraine DCFTA, art 276(2).

[167] ibid, art 276(3).

[168] EU-Ukraine DCFTA, arts 277 ('Regulatory Authority for Electricity and Gas'), 278 ('Relationship with the Energy Community').

[169] United Nations Convention on the Law of the Sea (adopted 10 December 1982, entered into force 14 November 1994) 1833 UNTS 379 (UNCLOS).

[170] EU-Ukraine DCFTA, art 279(1).

Although very different from the EU-Singapore FTA, the EU-Ukraine FTA's chapter on trade-related energy managed to comprehensively address many contentious and outstanding energy issues. The parties here undertook bilateral energy trade commitments, most of which have so far proven impossible to achieve on a global scale. It is a prime example of the extent to which energy rules can be developed in PTAs, defying the failures at the multilateral level. A valuable takeaway from the chapter is that it provides a lesson on how to deal more holistically and comprehensively with matters such as dual pricing and transit in the future.

4.3.2.3   EU-Mexico FTA (not yet in force)

In May 2020, the European Commission published the text 'in principle' of the new EU-Mexico FTA. The agreement has not yet entered into force and is undergoing linguistic revision.[171] Chapter X of the FTA regulates energy and raw materials.[172] Like NAFTA and the USMCA, it affirms the parties' sovereignty over natural resources in Article 1.1. The chapter is tailored to goods, not services, and this is the first energy-specific chapter in an EU FTA to contain detailed definitions of energy goods, raw materials and renewable energy, including their HS classifications.[173] Article 3 prohibits parties from maintaining import or export monopolies on energy. As will be discussed in Chapters 5 and 6, export taxes are not regulated in the WTO, and energy exporting countries often use export taxes to obtain maximum revenue from sales of their fossil fuels abroad. Article 4, however, has followed the progressive approach taken in Article 270(1) of the EU-Ukraine DCFTA by curbing this practice: 'A Party shall not adopt or maintain a higher price for exports of energy goods or raw materials to the other Party than the price charged for such goods when destined for the domestic market, *by means of any measure.*[174] According to Article 5, domestic pricing should remain unregulated, except where a party imposes a public service obligation.[175] Article 6 allows the procedure for authorizing energy exploration and production to be lightened under certain conditions. Article 7 requires that third parties be granted non-discriminatory access to gas and electricity infrastructure, subject to

---

[171] European Commission, 'Countries and Regions: Mexico' <https://ec.europa.eu/trade/policy/countries-and-regions/countries/mexico/> accessed 20 July 2020. See also Chapter 7, Section 7.2.4.
[172] EU-Mexico FTA, ch X ('Energy and Raw Materials').
[173] ibid, art 2; see also Chapter 1, Section 1.3.2.
[174] EU-Mexico FTA, art 4 ('Export pricing') (emphasis added).
[175] ibid, art 5 ('Domestic pricing').

possible derogations for legitimate policy purposes. More importantly, Article 10 requires the parties to promote cooperation on standards and technical regulations in the area of energy efficiency and 'sustainable' renewable energy,[176] while Article 11 imposes on the parties an obligation of cooperation in the area of energy and raw materials.

4.3.3   Trends in Preferential Trade Agreement Energy Chapters

As is clear from the discussion above, we are witnessing significantly more progress in detailed and technical negotiations on trade-related energy in PTAs, outside the multilateral WTO context. Given that the Doha Round is at a standstill, countries are independently pushing for progress on outstanding issues, including energy, by concluding PTAs. Consequently, much more far-reaching energy commitments are being made in PTAs than in WTO accession protocols. NAFTA's inclusion of a comprehensive chapter on energy was a pioneering example of this. The EU has gradually taken over where NAFTA left off by including increasingly sophisticated energy chapters in its FTAs with third countries.

The new rules emanating from these chapters across various PTAs point towards certain trends. First, countries are negotiating with energy security in mind.[177] They seek to achieve greater energy security by including the following types of requirements in their PTAs:

a) facilitating access to energy supplies (NAFTA, EU-Mexico FTA);
b) prohibiting energy dual-pricing policies (NAFTA, EU-Ukraine DCFTA, EU-Mexico FTA);
c) limiting export taxes on energy (NAFTA, EU-Ukraine DCFTA, EU-Mexico FTA);
d) limiting the scope of energy import and export restrictions (NAFTA, EU-Ukraine DCFTA and EU-Mexico FTA).
e) limiting recourse to exceptions that permit energy export restrictions (NAFTA); and
f) undertaking broad and far-reaching commitments on energy transit and transport, including granting third-party access to infrastructure (EU-Ukraine DCFTA and EU-Mexico FTA).

---

[176] This is a deft way of distinguishing between different kinds of renewable energy according to their sustainability (cf the discussion on renewable energy in Chapter 1, Section 1.2.3). This may imply the exclusion of certain types of renewable energy (possibly nuclear and biofuels) which are renewable but not necessarily sustainable.
[177] See Chapter 7.

Another trend we can observe is the negotiation of PTAs that take a more holistic approach to energy by including services and environmental aspects. This finds expression in the following types of commitments:

a) widening the scope of energy-specific chapters to cover goods and services (NAFTA, USMCA side letter, EU-Singapore FTA);
b) widening the scope of energy-specific chapters to cover trade and investment in energy (EU-Singapore FTA);
c) including rules that take an all-encompassing approach covering energy, the environment, sustainable development, and climate change mitigation and standardization (EU-Singapore FTA, EU-Mexico FTA);
d) setting standards to serve as a benchmark for a global energy governance framework (EU-Mexico FTA).

4.4   Conclusion

The goal of this chapter was twofold: to examine the nexus between two major treaty-based regimes relevant to governance in the energy sector (those of the WTO and the ECT), and to explore energy-specific chapters in selected preferential trade agreements.

While the WTO, established in 1995, governs global trade in general, the ECT, which came into force in 1998, offers a specialized regime for the regulation of the energy sector. Both treaties intersect and overlap in several places. This chapter looked into the origins of the overlaps and the resulting tension and concurrent applicability occurs. It offered a synthetic overview of areas of overlap in order to show where solutions have been found or, on the contrary, where conflicts remain unresolved.

There is a risk of fragmentation due to the parallel applicability of the WTO and the ECT in the fields of TRIMs, TRIPs and GATS. Another challenge is the tension between energy investment protection and state-to-state dispute resolution in the ECT on the one hand, and the protection offered to such investments under Mode 3 of GATS on the other. One obvious way of preventing and overcoming conflict in these areas of the WTO and the ECT is through increased cooperation and coordination between institutions, as proposed by Wolfrum and Matz.[178] In the course of roughly two decades, significant changes have taken place in the membership of the two organizations (in particular concerning WTO

---

[178] Wolfrum and Matz (n 102).

accessions), with far-reaching consequences for both regimes. Once all ECT parties that are currently WTO observers have acceded to the WTO, the future of the ECT trade will become particularly unclear. Nevertheless, with an eye on future energy governance, both treaty regimes would arguably benefit greatly from increased cooperation, coordination and perhaps even integration.

The chapter also considered the emergence of new rules in energy governance by looking at the commitments that have been made in a selection of PTAs. The PTAs discussed contain more comprehensive and far-reaching provisions in their energy chapters than we have seen at WTO level. Rules are beginning to crystallize that enhance energy security and take a more holistic approach to energy, for instance by bridging the trade/services divide in the sector and embracing environmental issues and energy efficiency. Recourse to PTAs for the negotiation of more detailed rules on energy is likely to form a growing trend, as it allows smaller groups of countries to be more innovative and rigorous in their rule-making – a feat that has so far proved much harder to achieve at the multilateral level.

PART II

International Trade Law and Changing Energy
Markets: Decentralization, Decarbonization and
Energy Security

5

Decentralizing Energy Markets in the Light of International Trade Law: OPEC and the EU Internal Energy Market

5.1 Introduction

Part I of this book covered the concepts, history and regulation of energy in international trade law. Part II continues by elaborating on the three themes introduced in Chapter 1 which affect changing energy markets today: decentralization, decarbonization and energy security. Chapters 6 and 7 will in turn discuss aspects of decarbonization and energy security relevant to the regulation of energy in international trade law. The present chapter will focus on the decentralization of the energy sector,[1] which here refers to the breaking-up of the energy sector and its vertically integrated enterprises and/or global cartels by separating out the various constituent activities (extraction, transmission and sale), thereby allowing for increased competition on the market. This is important for several reasons. First and foremost, decentralizing the energy sector is advantageous for the consumer, who will benefit from a wider choice of energy sources and lower prices. It is also pivotal for the scale-up of renewable energy in our energy systems, whose break-up is a prerequisite for the entry of new, clean forms of energy. Last but not least, decentralizing a particular (eg regional) energy sector (always tied to, and dependent on, its geographical location) is vital for energy security, especially as it avoids over-dependence on a single form of energy or a limited number of energy suppliers.[2] It becomes clear that decentralization is not an isolated concept, but is always connected to the decarbonization of the energy sector and to energy security. For this reason, these concepts are often referred to together as the 'trilemma' of today's changing energy markets.[3]

---

[1] See Chapter 1, Section 1.4.1.
[2] See Chapter 7.
[3] eg World Energy Council, 'World Energy Trilemma Index' <www.worldenergy.org/transi tion-toolkit/world-energy-trilemma-index> accessed 20 July 2020.

We will use two case studies to analyse the manner in which international trade law can either aid or impede the decentralization process in the energy sector and its still largely integrated markets. First, in Section 5.2, we look at energy cartels on the global, transnational level by studying the Organization of Petroleum Exporting States (OPEC). We show how challenging it is to deal comprehensively with such cartels in international trade law, and discuss the available options. We then turn to regional energy decentralization policies by focusing on the case of the EU internal energy market in Section 5.3. We demonstrate that it is the EU's intention to create a decentralized energy market, and that while some aspects of international trade law enable this, others may be less conducive to that end. Although there have been no WTO disputes on OPEC measures to date, the EU internal energy market was the subject of an intense dispute between Russia and the EU, *EU – Energy Package*.[4] The chapter will conclude with a recap of our findings, summarizing in what respects international trade law helps or hinders the decentralization of energy markets.

5.2   Global Energy Cartels: OPEC's Restrictive Practices in the Context of WTO Law

5.2.1   GATT Rationale, Restrictive Practices and Quotas

5.2.1.1   Terms of Trade Theory

It is no secret that, at its core, WTO law is biased towards imports. Its focus is on access to markets, and the elimination of import barriers is central to the system.[5] This can be explained by the fact that the original focus of GATT 1947 was trade liberalization. Consumers will generally want access to globally unevenly distributed (ie scarce) energy supplies, which shifts the power balance towards energy producers. This distinguishes energy in the form of fossil fuels from most other manufactured goods traded internationally. There are three reasons for this singularity, which were highlighted in Chapter 1, Sections 1.2.1 (in connection with

---

[4] This dispute is discussed in various parts of this book, notably Chapters 3 and 7.

[5] Most GATT provisions focus on eliminating import barriers and very few check barriers on exports. This can be seen in the asymmetry between the treatment of import tariffs (Article II GATT) and export tariffs (no GATT provision). Although export tariffs are increasingly being negotiated, they remain much less frequent; see K Bagwell, RW Staiger and AO Sykes, 'Border Instruments' in H Horn and PC Mavroidis (eds), *Legal and Economic Principles of World Trade Law* (CUP 2015) 129.

natural resources) and 1.4.1: (1) energy is essential for human life and development, and fossil fuels are still the main source of energy the world relies on; (2) fossils fuels are unevenly distributed around the world, with a relatively small number of countries possessing large quantities of them; and (3) the combination of the first two reasons results in fossil-fuel-rich countries having market power over these resources,[6] as explained below.

Cornerstone GATT provisions can be viewed through the prism of various possible economic theories of trade.[7] From the perspective of one such theory, terms of trade, core WTO disciplines essentially seek to promote free trade and lower trade barriers for the organization's members in order to secure a long-term gain of greater economic welfare.[8] Lower trade barriers and improved terms of trade (the price of countries' exports relative to their imports) lead to increased trade and bigger gains.[9] This also explains why it is in a country's interest to join a multilateral trade agreement.

In a nutshell, by cooperating through the conclusion of binding trade agreements and reciprocal lowering of trade barriers, countries overcome the risk of an inefficient Nash equilibrium, which would be the case if countries were able to unilaterally set their trade policies.[10] According to this theory, a small country that cannot influence the terms of trade will maximize its income by unilaterally opting for free trade.[11]

Bagwell and Staiger have discussed core WTO disciplines in light of the terms of trade theory and concluded that non-discrimination and reciprocity (two important features of GATT) are essential to striking efficient trade agreements.[12] By entering into cooperative trade

---

[6] A Sykes, PC Mavroidis and DA Irwin, *The Genesis of the GATT* (CUP 2008) 179.

[7] ibid, ch 3 ('Rationales for the GATT').

[8] ibid 177.

[9] ibid.

[10] Sykes, Mavroidis and Irwin (n 6) 178. In game theory, the Nash equilibrium is a solution concept in a non-cooperative game involving two or more players, where each player is assumed to know the equilibrium strategies of the other players and no player has anything to gain by changing only their own strategy; see eg MJ Osborne and A Rubinstein, *A Course in Game Theory* (MIT 1994).

[11] Sykes, Mavroidis and Irwin (n 6) 177.

[12] See generally K Bagwell and RW Staiger, *The Economics of the World Trading System* (MIT Press 2002); Sykes, Mavroidis and Irwin (n 6) 178; K Bagwell and RW Staiger, 'An Economic Theory of the GATT' (1999) 89 American Economic Review 215. See also S Charnovitz, 'Triangulating the World Trade Organization' (2002) 96 American Journal of International Law 28, 34, arguing that the WTO pushes economies towards greater efficiency.

agreements such as GATT, countries collectively lower trade barriers and overcome disadvantageous externalities resulting from unilateral tariff settings.[13] GATT provisions are consequently designed to promote market access and curtail import barriers, for instance by prohibiting quantitative restrictions (QRs) in Article XI, and by binding import tariffs (to be applied on an MFN basis as per Article I GATT) as the only discriminatory measure permitted with respect to imported goods in Article II.[14]

The dilemma here is that the terms of trade theory as developed by Bagwell and Staiger does not account for export-restricting trade practices based on market power. One criticism that can be made of this theory is of particular importance here: GATT does not constrain the use of export taxes, which can therefore be used to manipulate the terms of trade as some countries can exercise market power over their exported goods.[15] Although import tariffs are normally a significantly stronger means of influencing the terms of trade, for certain products like petroleum export taxes prove to be a much more compelling tool.[16] GATT does almost nothing to constrain export-related measures; its regulatory thrust is the free flow of imports.[17] However, export taxes can be a powerful means of manipulation for governments that have market power over certain goods, and they are frequently resorted to when it comes to energy. Thus, in the global energy trade – in contrast to GATT's goal of reducing import barriers between nations to facilitate market access – we are often confronted with export taxes and export

---

[13] Sykes, Mavroidis and Irwin (n 6) 178.

[14] General Agreement on Tariffs and Trade, Marrakesh Agreement Establishing the World Trade Organization, Annex 1A (signed 15 April 1994) 1867 UNTS 187 (1994) 33 ILM 1153 (GATT 1994), arts I ('General Most-Favoured-Nation Treatment'), II ('Schedules of Concessions').

[15] Sykes, Mavroidis and Irwin (n 6) 179, esp fns 4ff: 'For example, it is often the case that a country has the market power to influence the terms of trade via its exports, e.g. the OPEC and oil, Chile and Copper, Morocco and phosphates, Russia and South Africa and gold and diamonds.' Note, however, that export duties are increasingly becoming a subject of negotiation, though very few countries have bound export duties in their national schedules of concessions. For instance, Russia consented to bind and reduce some of its export duties (ie on lumber, fish, crabs and leather), but reserved its right to continue applying export taxes on raw mineral materials and fuels; see Accession Protocol (22 August 2012) WT/L/839, WT/MIN(11)/27; Report of the Working Party on the Accession of the Russian Federation (17 November 2011) WT/ACC/RUS/70, WT/MIN (11)/2.

[16] Sykes, Mavroidis and Irwin (n 6) 180.

[17] ibid 179. For an economic analysis of this critique, see WJ Ethier, 'Political Externalities, Nondiscrimination, and a Multilateral World' (2004) 12 Review of International Economics 303.

restrictions, with the result that free trade ends up distorting energy trade practices.

It follows that countries in possession of strategic natural resources can – to a certain extent – unilaterally influence the terms of trade.[18] This conflict stems from the difference between natural resources and manufactured goods. In most trade disputes involving manufactured goods, the importing country seeks to restrict foreign imports to favour domestic producers.[19] By contrast, most importing countries want access to energy from foreign suppliers. Exporting countries, on the other hand, may be reluctant to allow their resources to flow freely to other nations and might apply restrictions on fossil fuel production and exports in order to increase their income.

5.2.1.2   Absence of Competition Rules in the WTO

Another issue is that, as an organization promoting freer trade, the WTO does not regulate competition, whose effect is to contain market power. Competition rules are designed to protect consumers and prevent firms (eg in the energy sector) from abusing their dominant position. While competition and antitrust rules exist at national (eg US antitrust law) and regional (eg EU competition law) levels, there are no such rules in the WTO.[20] Consequently, abusive practices by global public monopolies – for instance, those administered by a state or a group of states – are likely to go uncaught as being outside the scope of national and regional antitrust laws and passed over internationally in WTO law.[21]

The result is that cartels (notably active in the energy sector) can exercise their market power on a global scale. The Organization of Petroleum Exporting States (OPEC) is the most famous public cartel in

---

[18] Sykes, Mavroidis and Irwin (n 6) 179.

[19] WTO, *World Trade Report 2010: Trade in Natural Resources* (WTO 2010) 48.

[20] Discussions on competition, although a topic taken up by the WTO, were abandoned in the Doha context; see WTO, 'Interaction between Trade and Competition Policy' <www .wto.org/english/tratop_e/comp_e/comp_e.htm> accessed 20 July 2020. Some argue that the issue should be revisited; see P van den Bossche and W Zdouc, *Law and Policy of the World Trade: Texts, Cases and Materials* (3rd edn, CUP 2013) 1019. Note, however, that it may in some cases be possible to apply anti-dumping duties against anti-competitive behaviour by states, as suggested by B Hoekman and M Kostecki, *The Political Economy of the World Trading System: From GATT to WTO* (3rd edn, OUP 2009) 258. It should also be noted that there were rules on competition in the predecessor to GATT 1947, the International Trade Organization (ITO), which never came into being. Nevertheless, Article XXIX GATT ('The Relation of this Agreement to the Havana Charter') keeps the link to the ITO through a best endeavours provision.

[21] Not all countries have full-fledged anti-trust and competition policies in place.

the field of energy.[22] The organization effectively amounts to an international agreement among oil producing countries. Although times are changing because of the steep decline in world oil prices, OPEC managed to push world oil prices above competitive levels for several decades.[23] OPEC behaves in an anti-competitive way and exercises its market power by restricting its members' petroleum exports through quotas imposed on their production of crude oil.

5.2.1.3   The Link between Export Restrictions and Production Quotas

The absence of competition rules in the WTO makes it very difficult for the organization to deal comprehensively with restrictive export practices pursued by public cartels such as OPEC.[24] It does, however, have other relevant rules, such as Article XI GATT prohibiting quantitative restrictions.[25]

The prohibition on quotas in international trade can be apprehended from the perspective of the severity of barriers posed to international trade by cross-border measures. The optimal model in terms of efficiency in international trade flows between nations would be full-fledged free trade without any protectionism. If countries cannot commit to that, tariffs are an acceptable (albeit undesirable) barrier to trade because they are quantifiable and can be negotiated in a transparent and binding manner. A level up from tariffs in terms of trade restrictiveness are quotas, which are dismissed as the most inefficient barriers to trade (short of an outright ban on imports/exports). Tariffs are in fact similar to quotas in terms of their economic effect on international trade, with the crucial above-mentioned difference that tariffs are more easily

---

[22] Public monopolies are maintained by states, whereas private monopolies are maintained by private entities.

[23] Most recently in the 2020 Russia-Saudi Arabia oil price war. See RS Pindyck and DL Rubinfeld, *Microeconomics* (8th edn, Pearson 2013) 478ff. However, many factors influence the price of oil and OPEC is not omnipotent. It is clear that we are at a watershed, as prices of oil are at an all-time low; see eg V Yermakov and J Henderson, 'The New Deal for Oil Markets: Implications for Russia's Short-Term Tactics and Long-Term Strategy' (2020) Oxford Institute for Energy Studies Energy Insight 67.

[24] Although WTO members may dishonour their obligations under GATT if the they maintain restrictive business practices directly attributable to them; see *Japan – Film*, panel report.

[25] GATT 1994, art XI ('Elimination of Quantitative Restrictions').

quantifiable.[26] Therefore, although considered inefficient when it comes to promoting open trade flows, tariffs are nonetheless allowed, whereas quotas and import/export restrictions are prohibited in GATT.

The economic rationale underlying the prohibition of QRs in any form Article XI:1 GATT is that both import and export quotas acts as barriers to freer trade flows.[27] One of the reasons that caused the drafters of GATT to prohibit export as well as import restrictions in Article XI:1 must have been a shared concern that upstream industries (eg natural resources such as fossil fuels or raw materials) would receive an unfair advantage if the countries that could exercise market power in those sectors were allowed to maintain export quotas.[28] That said, an exception to this prohibition designed to protect exhaustible natural resources is allowed under Article XX(g), though recourse to QRs for this purpose is justified only 'if such measures are made effective in conjunction with restrictions on domestic production or consumption' and meet the chapeau of Article XX.

This reference to domestic production and consumption in relation to export restrictions raises the question of the difference between a production quota and an export quota. It is clear that 'made effective in conjunction with restrictions on domestic production or consumption' is a prerequisite for a party availing itself of the Article XX(g) exception for the measures it wishes to take to conserve exhaustible natural resources. The question, then, is when does a production quota coincide with an export restriction in terms of their economic effect.

When it comes to geographically unevenly distributed natural resources, domestic measures (eg concerning production and extraction) are very similar to trade measures. It follows that governments have greater leeway to influence trade in natural resources through the use of domestic measures than they do to influence trade in other

---

[26] Bagwell, Staiger and Sykes (n 5) 93ff. On the economics of quantitative restrictions, see PC Mavroidis, *The Regulation of International Trade*, vol 1 *The GATT* (MIT Press 2015) ch 2.

[27] Mavroidis (n 26).

[28] In practice, domestic policies like production quotas lead to the same result. On export restrictions, see Bagwell, Staiger and Sykes (n 5) 145:

> It is worth underscoring that Article XI applies to export QRs as well (but not to export taxes). A common practice that would fall under Article XI, for example, would be a prohibition on the exportation of an unprocessed product, perhaps enacted for the purpose of lowering the price of the unprocessed product to the local processing industry.

products.[29] In this respect, economically speaking, the effect of a production quota can sometimes be the same as that of an export quota, especially in cases where there is no domestic consumption (ie where the entire resources are destined for export).[30]

Like export restrictions, production quotas imposed in the country of export will reduce the supply of a product on the international market, and thus cause its price to rise.[31] If a production quota applies also to domestic consumption, the effect may still be restrictive, but not necessarily discriminatory in GATT terms. However, let us say that there is some domestic consumption and thus that the production quota is not an outright export quota. In this case, one could imagine that domestic demand would perhaps be served first (at least if we are talking about oil) and the rest of the production exported. Here, therefore, the quota would apply only to the residual output after domestic consumption has been satisfied, and thus become a de facto export quota.

5.2.2   Understanding the OPEC Cartel and Its Anti-Competitive Effects

5.2.2.1   OPEC Policies and Economic Rationale: An Overview

OPEC was founded in the 1960s to coordinate the petroleum policies of its members.[32] Its original purpose was strongly tied to the struggle of former colonies to regain control over their oil resources and the

---

[29] *World Trade Report 2010* (n 19) 147; see generally K Bagwell and RW Staiger, 'Domestic Policies, National Sovereignty and International Economic Institutions' (2001) 116 Quarterly Journal of Economics 519.

[30] Likewise, an export tax applied to resources has the same effect as a consumption subsidy; see *World Trade Report 2010* (n 19) 185. See M Ruta and AJ Venables, 'International Trade in Natural Resources' (March 2012) WTO Staff Working Paper ERDS-2012-07, 24:

> [I]n natural resource sectors, a number of trade and domestic instruments can be close substitutes: a production quota is equivalent to an export quota for countries that export the quasi-totality of their resource production, and a tax at the border has the same effect as a domestic tax where countries importing the resource do not produce it. In these cases, regulating only one of the equivalent measures is insufficient to achieve undistorted trade in natural resources.

[31] *World Trade Report 2010* (n 19) 185.

[32] See generally AA Marhold, 'WTO Law and Economics and Restrictive Practices in Energy Trade: The Case of the OPEC Cartel' (2016) 9 Journal of World Energy Law and Business 475; D Yergin, *The Prize: The Epic Quest for Oil, Money and Power* (Free Press 2009) chs 26 ('9(6)'), 31 ('OPEC's Imperium'). OPEC was formed at a meeting between Iran, Iraq, Kuwait, Saudi Arabia and Venezuela held in Baghdad on 14 September 14, 1960. It was registered with the United Nations Secretariat on 6 November 1962 (UN Res 6363) <www.opec.org/opec_web/en/index.htm> accessed 20 July 2020.

emergence of the UN principle of permanent sovereignty over natural resources.[33] OPEC thus started out as a consortium of producers forming an oligopoly. At the outset it was not actively involved in imposing quotas on the production of oil (by means of which it exercises market power globally). It began consciously to influence the price of petroleum only later, during the oil crisis of the 1970s.[34] Since 1987, it has been administering a flagrant production quota system.[35] The organization's self-proclaimed mission is to coordinate and unify the petroleum policies of its members and secure an efficient, economic and regular supply of petroleum to consumers, a steady income to producers and a fair return on investments.[36]

The OPEC Statute functions as its founding document. OPEC has the status of an intergovernmental organization (IGO) and is headquartered in Vienna.[37] It currently comprises thirteen members: Algeria, Angola, Congo, Equatorial Guinea, Gabon, Iran, Iraq, Kuwait, Libya, Nigeria, Saudi Arabia, the United Arab Emirates and Venezuela.[38] Its membership fluctuates, however, depending, inter alia, on whether the country in question is a net-exporter of petroleum.[39] The organization also has associate members, which produce substantial amounts of petrol and are entitled to attend OPEC meetings.[40] OPEC members hold the bulk of the world's oil reserves (about 80 per cent) and produce around 40 per cent of the crude oil traded on the global market.[41] Saudi Arabia, Venezuela and Iran alone own over half of the reserves held by OPEC members.[42]

In contrast to the earlier years of its existence, since the late 1980s OPEC has been actively managing its supply of oil, thereby influencing the price on the world market to the maximum of its abilities. OPEC does

---

[33] Yergin (n 32) ch 31; UNGA Res 1803 (XVII) (18 December 1962) 'Permanent Sovereignty over Natural Resources'. See also Chapter 1, Section 1.3.3.

[34] See Chapter 2, Section 2.3.

[35] F Chalabi, *Oil Policies, Oil Myths: Analysis and Memoir of an OPEC 'Insider'* (IB Tauris 2010) 215.

[36] Statute of the Organization of Petroleum Exporting Countries (1 May 1965) 443 UNTS 427 (1965) 4 ILM 1175 (OPEC Statute) art 2 ('Our Mission').

[37] OPEC Statute, art 5.

[38] See OPEC, 'Member Countries' <www.opec.org/opec_web/en/about_us/25.htm> accessed 20 July 2020.

[39] ibid.

[40] OPEC Statute, arts 11.D, 7.D.

[41] See OPEC, 'OPEC Share of World Crude Oil Reserves, 2018' <www.opec.org/opec_web/en/data_graphs/330.htm> accessed 20 July 2020.

[42] ibid.

this by setting a quota for the production of crude petroleum by its members:[43] It decides when and how much oil they can extract from the ground. It regularly reassesses and adjusts the ceiling at its biannual ministerial conference, where its members' oil, mining and energy ministers meet and decide on the organization's output level. Adjustments are based on current and anticipated market developments. Generally speaking, when the quota is increased, the world price drops and vice versa. The price of crude oil is famously volatile; it is at a record low at present, due to the 2020 Russia-Saudi Arabia oil price war.

OPEC has to strike a fine balance to safeguard its interest. It seeks to derive maximum revenue from its crude oil exports without causing consumers to look elsewhere for cheaper (and perhaps even cleaner) energy sources.[44] This strategy is connected to the price elasticity of demand.[45] To obtain maximum revenue from its crude oil, it must also ensure that the price is not too low. Behaving as a monopolist, OPEC therefore aims to achieve a balance between supply and demand that serves its economic interest. OPEC's practices lack transparency, as neither the quotas it sets nor their distribution among its members are publicized, so remain a matter of speculation.[46]

---

[43] Although not the only energy cartel in the world, OPEC is without doubt the most well-known public energy cartel. The Gas Exporting Countries Forum (GECF) (<www.gecf.org> accessed 20 July 2020) is similar to OPEC and comprises the world's leading gas producers (Algeria, Bolivia, Egypt, Equatorial Guinea, Iran, Libya, Nigeria, Qatar, Russia, Trinidad and Tobago and Venezuela), so its membership partly overlaps with that of OPEC. See Section 5.3 for more on the major gas monopolist Gazprom, Russia's state-owned energy company.

[44] WTO, 'Oil Price Volatility: Origins and Effects' <www.wto.org/english/res_e/reser_e/ersd201002_e.htm> accessed 20 July 2020.

[45] Price elasticity of demand (PED or Ed) is a measure used in economics to show the responsiveness, or elasticity, of the quantity demanded consequent upon a change in its price. More precisely, it gives the percentage change in quantity demanded corresponding to a 1 per cent change in price (keeping all the other determinants of demand, such as income, constant). The price elasticity of demand for oil remains relatively low – around −0.4 – as there are few direct substitutes.

[46] The internal politics behind OPEC production quotas are generally influenced by the economic needs of its members. It is said that several members have pushed for reductions in production quotas to increase the price of oil and thus their own revenues. However, this conflicts with Saudi Arabia's stated long-term strategy of partnering with the world's economic powers to ensure a steady flow of oil, reflecting a fear that expensive oil or supply uncertainty would encourage developed nations to conserve and develop alternative fuels. See NA Owen, OR Inderwildi and DA King, 'The Status of Conventional World Oil Reserves: Hype or Cause for Concern?' (2010) 38 Energy Policy 4743; P Waldman, 'Saudi Arabia's Plan to Extend the Age of Oil' (*Bloomberg News*,

In economics, a cartel is usually defined as an international group of producers that collude and agree to cooperate on output levels and prices.[47] Not all producers of the cartelized product have to join for the cartel to be successful. The cartel's effectiveness depends on two main conditions: first, enough producers must join the cartel and adhere to what has been agreed; and second, market demand for the product (here petroleum) must be sufficiently inelastic for there to be a potential monopoly of power.[48]

OPEC satisfies both of these conditions and therefore is a relatively 'well-functioning' cartel. OPEC is a state-led cartel – what we call a 'public monopoly' – in contrast to cartels maintained by private companies.[49] While OPEC does not have complete control over world oil production completely, its role and influence are considerable as its members unite to avoid competition between themselves.[50] Major energy producers that do not belong to OPEC may support the cartel's policies as they can offer to undercut OPEC's oil price by a fixed margin.

OPEC members trade in a vital good for which the market demand is quite inelastic and predicted to last for a long time (unless other, cleaner forms of energy outcompete crude petroleum – something that OPEC

---

12 April 2015) <www.bloomberg.com/news/articles/2015–04-12/saudi-arabia-s-plan-to-extend-the-age-of-oil> accessed 20 July 2020.

[47] Pindyck and Rubinfeld (n 23) 477ff. The Oxford English Dictionary defines a cartel as 'an agreement or association between two or more business houses for regulating output, fixing prices, etc.' <www.oed.com> accessed 28 January 2021. However, some argue that OPEC's behaviour is much less collusive than a full cartel; see eg Ruta and Venables (n 30) 21.

[48] Pindyck and Rubinfeld (n 23) 477–78. See also *World Trade Report 2010* (n 19) 104 (citations omitted):

> Higher oil prices do not stimulate global production in the near future because the short-run price elasticity of oil supply is near zero (i.e. oil supply is not very responsive to price changes in the short-run). At the same time, in the case of oil, there is no evidence to suggest that, on the supply side, the Organization of the Petroleum-Exporting Countries (OPEC) attempted to act as a cartel and hold back production from 2004 to 2008.

[49] A distinction is drawn between public and private cartels. In the case of public cartels, governments may establish and enforce rules relating to such matters as prices and output. While the private /public monopoly divide may be insignificant to economists, it is important to lawyers as it determines what type of laws apply: public cartels are often 'allowed', meaning that there are no laws constraining them, whereas private cartels are viewed as contrary to anti-trust laws in most jurisdictions.

[50] T Carey, 'Cartel Price Controls vs. Free Trade: A Study of Proposals to Challenge OPEC's Influence in the Oil Market through WTO Dispute Settlement' (2009) 24 American University International Law Review 786, 789.

tries to delay through its policies). Fossil fuel cartels such as OPEC have a greater chance of remaining successful, as they generally have little fear of losing market power quickly. They also occupy a dominant position as the strategic resources they possess cannot be harnessed elsewhere.[51]

It should be mentioned that energy is not the only sector in which global monopolies and restrictive practices exist.[52] Other examples are raw materials (at issue in the *China – Raw Materials* and *China – Rare Earths* disputes), natural resources and commodities such as copper and diamonds, discussed in Chapter 1, Section 1.2.1.[53] Generally speaking, natural resources for which there is a high demand tend to be the subject of restrictive practices and corresponding market power.[54] This is undoubtedly explained by their uneven distribution and the fact that the states in which they are situated have full control over their extraction from the ground. It is precisely in relation to these natural resources that the import bias of the WTO is most acutely felt.[55]

5.2.2.2   OPEC Production Quota: Definition and Economic Effect

In economics, a production quota represents a goal for the production of a good: it fixes the quantity of that good that can be produced. A company, government or organization (as an IGO, OPEC is a combination of the last two) may set a production quota, which they in turn may apply to a certain industry, company or worker.

Quotas can be set high to encourage production, or they can be set low to control and restrict the supply of goods for the purpose of maintaining a certain price level (as is the case with OPEC). To force up the price of a product, the quota will often be below the market clearing level, which means below market demand for the good in question.[56] Of course, every manufactured product is subject to a production quota in one way or

---

[51] However, demand may shift to other products, as illustrated by the shale gas discoveries in the United States.

[52] See KJ Dogaheh, 'Integrating Energy into the World Trading System: Law and Policy' (PhD thesis, University of Warwick 2007) 73.

[53] One could think of the CIPEC copper cartel (Chile, Peru, Zambia and Congo), diamonds (Angola and Congo, de Beers), international shipping conferences <https://stats.oecd.org /glossary/detail.asp?ID=3311> accessed 20 July 2020, to name a few. See Ruta and Venables (n 30).

[54] See WTO's Quantitative Restrictions Database for export restrictions on natural resources.

[55] Ruta and Venables (n 30).

[56] Pindyck and Rubinfeld (n 23) 333–34.

another, as there is no such thing as a manufacturing process with unlimited output. Ideally, though, the quota of production and supply of a good should be determined by market demand.

Pindyck and Rubinfeld explain that maintaining a production quota will always be accompanied by dead-weight losses as compared to a free trade equilibrium.[57] Having a production quota in place will inevitably imply extra costs and therefore losses for a government and, indirectly, for consumers, too.[58] Arguably, a production quota that is applied with the goal of raising the price of a product is in theory contrary to the notion of free trade, because it can restrict imports or exports.

It is clear from OPEC's intervention in the petroleum market that the market forces of free trade are not alone in determining global supply and demand for crude oil. As reflected in Article 2 of its statute, the organization's objective is not free trade for mutual benefit, but rather price increases in the interests of its members achieved by restricting production and trade in petroleum. Accordingly, OPEC uses its market power to fix production quotas and thereby influence the world price of oil to its advantage. The organization does not hide this intention; its policies are openly and explicitly tailored to controlling the production and thereby demand for and the price of crude oil. Consequently, there is no denying that it functions in an anti-competitive manner, and its policies are therefore not in line with the competition pillar of free trade policy.

5.2.3   OPEC in the WTO Context

5.2.3.1   OPEC's Status in the WTO

It is possible to distinguish two kinds of interaction between IGOs and the WTO. First of all, there are those (numerous) organizations that 'work with' the WTO – a term that here has a broad meaning ranging from mere informal contacts and information sharing to collaboration on joint projects and programmes.[59] The second form of interaction lies in more intense cooperation realized through the IGO acquiring official observer status (OS) with the WTO. The purpose of this status is to enable these organizations to follow discussions within the WTO on

---

[57] ibid 334.
[58] ibid 335.
[59] WTO, 'Intergovernmental Organizations Working with the WTO Secretariat' <www .wto.org/english/thewto_e/coher_e/igo_divisions_e.htm> accessed 20 July 2020.

matters of direct interest to them.[60] The basis for the attribution of OS to IGOs is Article V of the WTO Agreement, which states that 'the General Council shall make appropriate arrangements for effective cooperation with other intergovernmental organizations that have responsibilities related to those of the WTO'.[61]

OPEC is listed as an IGO that 'works with' the WTO, but only in the context of the Committee on Trade and Environment.[62]

OPEC has sought more solid forms of cooperation and, since the late 1990s, has repeatedly requested OS with the WTO's Committee on Trade and Development.[63] The request was often made in conjunction with that of the League of Arab States. However, two WTO members (the United States and Israel) have hitherto been strongly opposed to OPEC

---

[60] WTO 'International Intergovernmental Organizations Granted Observer Status to WTO Bodies' <www.wto.org/english/thewto_e/igo_obs_e.htm> accessed 20 July 2020; WTO, Rules of Procedure for Sessions of the Ministerial Conference (25 July 1996) WT/L/161, annex 3 (guidelines on observer status for international organizations) para 1.

[61] Marrakesh Agreement Establishing the Establishing the World Trade Organization (signed 15 April 1994) 1867 UNTS 154 (1994) 33 ILM 1144 (WTO Agreement) art V:1.

[62] This is interesting because it shows that observer status was (obviously) strongly supported by individual OPEC states, see statements made by representatives on the Committee on Trade and Development, reported in WT/COMTD/M/29 (14 November 2000) paras 16 and 18 (reporting respectively on statements made by Nigeria's and Venezuela's representatives):

> He said that OPEC had also applied to the Committee on Trade and Environment (CTE), and that by applying to both the CTD and the CTE, it wished to correct the impression that it was only concerned with price and quota fixing, which were the most visible parts of its activities. He said that OPEC was also seriously concerned with the environmental impact of oil resources, as well as the equilibrium between oil producers and oil exporters. OPEC therefore sought ad hoc Observer Status with the CTD and the CTE, in order to benefit from the work of the Committees in these areas. He said that the Nigerian delegation strongly supported the application by OPEC for ad hoc Observer Status, and called on members to give the application favourable consideration.
>
> The representative of Venezuela put on record his country's support of the request made for ad hoc Observer Status made by OPEC. He said that OPEC could become an instrument in helping Members analyse the new dimensions of development which the WTO was reviewing. He said that OPEC was in fact reviewing its own role, and he believed that granting ad hoc Observer Status to the OPEC would enhance debates on questions related to development in the WTO.

[63] See eg WT/COMTD/M/29 (n 62) paras 8, 16–23; WT/GC/M/69 (October 2001) para 18; WT/COMTD/M/82 (19 October 2011).

becoming an official observer IGO within the WTO, as the documents relating to the negotiation history show.[64]

5.2.3.2   Membership and Accession of Individual OPEC Members to the WTO

The fact that a country is a member of OPEC in no way prevents it from being a member of the WTO, too.[65] On the contrary, eight of the thirteen current OPEC members are also members of the WTO (Angola, Congo, Gabon, Kuwait, Nigeria, Saudi Arabia, the United Arab Emirates and Venezuela).[66] Algeria, Equatorial Guinea, Iran, Iraq and Libya are WTO observers currently in the process of negotiating WTO accession. Gabon, Kuwait, Nigeria and Venezuela acceded to the WTO in 1995; Angola, Ecuador and the UAE in 1996; Congo in 1997; and Saudi Arabia in 2005.[67] Although there has never been a WTO dispute challenging the restrictive practices of OPEC members, the divergent statuses of OPEC countries within the WTO would have consequences for a WTO dispute settlement situation, were it to arise. If a dispute over OPEC-related behaviour were to arise between a WTO member and any of the OPEC members, dispute settlement proceedings could be initiated only against dual OPEC/WTO members individually, not against OPEC as a whole. The Dispute Settlement System (DSS) only allows for disputes brought by states against states (but not against other entities such as IGOs).[68] This effectively means

---

[64] eg WT/COMTD/M/29 (n 62) para 21:

> The representative of the United States said that her delegation had examined the material provided by OPEC which explained that organisation's interest in the CTD and its interest in trade. She said that unlike the submission made by the League of Arab States, her delegation was unable to go along with granting ad hoc Observer Status to the OPEC, but hoped to be in position to do so at the time of the next meeting, provided further material was provided which could substantiate both the interest of the OPEC in the CTD and its trade function.

[65] P Milthorp and D Christy, 'Energy Issues in Selected WTO Accessions' in Y Selivanova (ed), *Regulation of Energy in International Trade Law: WTO, NAFTA and Energy Charter* (Wolters Kluwer 2011).

[66] See OPEC, 'Member Countries' <www.opec.org/opec_web/en/about_us/25.htm> accessed 20 July 2020.

[67] See WTO, 'Members and Observers' <www.wto.org/english/thewto_e/whatis_e/tif_e/org6_e.htm> accessed 28 January 2021.

[68] Understanding on Rules and Procedures Governing the Settlement of Disputes, Marrakesh Agreement Establishing the World Trade Organization, Annex 2, 1869 UNTS 401 (1994) 33 ILM 1226 (DSU) art 1.1.

that only eight of the thirteen OPEC countries that are in the WTO could be challenged in WTO dispute settlement proceedings.

5.2.4   Avenues for Tackling OPEC Production Quotas under WTO Law

Having discussed above the ethos of GATT, the workings of the OPEC cartel and some economic aspects of production quotas, we now move on to a legal analysis. As mentioned in Section 5.2.1, Article XI:1's prohibition of QRs that, inter alia, limit the import and export of goods is one of the cornerstones of the GATT.[69] Article XI:1 GATT reads as follows:

> No prohibitions or restrictions other than duties, taxes or other charges, whether made effective through quotas, import or export licences or other measures, shall be instituted or maintained by any contracting party on the importation of any product of the territory of any other contracting party or on the exportation or sale for export of any product destined for the territory of any other contracting party.

We saw in Section 5.2.1 that, from an economic perspective, production quotas may have a similar effect to export restrictions. The effect actually becomes the same if nearly all the production of a certain good is destined for export and not for domestic consumption.[70] Let us assess OPEC's practice of maintaining production quotas on crude oil in the light of the Article XI:1 prohibiting QRs.

As discussed in Chapter 1, the WTO is not primarily concerned with the ownership of and sovereignty over natural resources situated within the territory of a state.[71] WTO rules are designed to regulate access to markets for producers, but not necessarily to facilitate access to supplies for consumers.[72] WTO rules are widely considered to kick in after the natural resources in question have been extracted and are tradable for economic gain.[73] In line with this, supporters of OPEC policies argue that production quotas escape GATT disciplines, because petroleum becomes subject to the

---

[69] Together with most-favoured-nation and national treatment.
[70] *World Trade Report 2010* (n 19).
[71] ibid 177.
[72] See Section 5.2.1.
[73] The issue arose in connection with another natural resource – fish stock – *Canada – Herring*, GATT panel report, paras 3.31–3.32. In that case, there was apparent agreement that GATT rules do not apply to any measures restricting fish catch (ie upstream measures) but only to measures restricting the export of fish after they have been caught.

rules only after extraction from the ground.[74] Some additionally argue that the principle of sovereignty over natural resources affords states unrestrained discretion to deal with their natural resources as they please.[75] As no precise legal basis has been put forward to support this proposition, we must wait for a dispute in the WTO to provide clarity on the matter.

The fact remains that, for the moment, there is no black letter WTO rule determining at what point trade in natural resources becomes subject to WTO law. Moreover, there are exceptions to the generally accepted view described in the preceding paragraph, as when the Appellate Body (AB) in *US – Softwood Lumber IV* held that trees are a tradable good before they are harvested.[76] In that case it was decided that there were no grounds for excluding 'tangible items – such as standing, unfelled trees – that are not both tradable as such and subject to tariff classification' from the scope of the term 'goods' in Article I:1 GATT.[77]

As things currently stand, we are left with two ways of interpreting Article XI:1 with respect to OPEC production quotas – either narrowly, by excluding them from its scope, or broadly, by bringing production quotas within the ambit of Article XI:1. The crucial point in this discussion is thus whether and to what extent the definition of restrictions in Article XI:1 covers restrictions in the form of domestic quotas.

Note that while Article X:1 prohibits both import and export quotas on goods, it does not rule out duties, taxes and other charges. Furthermore, it applies to import and export restrictions made effective through state-trading enterprises.[78]

Article XI:1 provides for several exceptions to the principle of prohibition. They include export prohibitions or restrictions temporarily applied to prevent or relieve critical shortages of foodstuffs and other products essential to the exporting contracting party (Article XI:2(a) GATT), and import restrictions on agricultural and fisheries products (Article XI:1(c) GATT). OPEC would have difficulty relying on the

---

[74] *World Trade Report 2010* (n 19) 162.

[75] See generally D Crosby, 'Energy Discrimination and International Rules in Hard Times: What's New This Time Around, and What Can Be Done' (2012) 5 Journal of World Energy Law and Business 325.

[76] See *US – Softwood Lumber IV*, AB report, para 57.

[77] ibid.

[78] The prohibition in Article XI GATT and the non-discrimination obligation in Article XIII GATT apply to import and export restrictions made effective through state-trading operations (see notes on Articles XI, XII, XIII, XIV and XVIII GATT). Therefore, state-trading enterprises of energy exporting WTO members, such as the Saudi energy company Aramco, must respect Article XI:1 GATT.

critical shortages argument of Article XI:2(a), not least because this exception is conditional upon the restrictive measure being applied temporarily. This can hardly be said of OPEC, which has been maintaining production quotas for decades.[79]

5.2.4.1   Article XI:1 and OPEC Production Quotas: The Narrow Interpretation

A narrow interpretation of Article XI:1 GATT is based on the premise that if the negotiators had wanted the term 'quota' as used in the article to cover domestic production quotas in addition to those on imports and exports, they could have explicitly referred to them in the wording of the article.[80] In the light of their analysis of the negotiation history of Article XI, Irwin, Mavroidis and Sykes conclude that 'it is obvious that domestic quotas were not meant to be covered by the disciplines on QRs, although it was on the table in prior International Trade Organization (ITO) negotiations to remove internal quantitative regulations not expressly approved by the ITO'.[81]

This view stems from the observation that the WTO does not regulate ownership over the natural resources of states, but simply provides rules on non-discrimination. Even if some OPEC WTO members export the near totality of their oil production, causing the production quota to have the same economic effect as an export quota, there are arguments against considering production quotas as a prohibited restriction. One such argument is that domestic production quotas are deemed to be consistent with GATT. This is because only quotas directly tied to imports and exports are prohibited.[82] Domestic quotas on production do not

---

[79] An exception also exists under Article XI:2(b) for import and export prohibitions or restrictions necessary to the application of standards or regulations for international commodity agreements. It is highly questionable whether the OPEC Agreement would qualify as a commodity agreement for GATT purposes. First of all, the OPEC Agreement has never been registered as such with the WTO. Moreover, it is commonly understood that commodity agreements are concluded between exporting and importing countries, whereas the OPEC Agreement is between exporting countries only. See *World Trade Report 2010* (n 19) 179; PC Mavroidis, *Trade in Goods* (2nd edn, OUP 2012) 351.

[80] Mavroidis (n 79) 62.

[81] Sykes, Mavroidis and Irwin (n 6) 152.

[82] ibid; L Ehring and CF Chianale, 'Export Restrictions in the Field of Energy' in Selivanova (n 65) 163:

> However, the restriction remains a production restraint rather than an export restraint, even if all additionally produced quantities would be exported. There still remains a significant difference because additionally

discriminate between domestic and foreign markets. As they therefore do not necessarily favour the domestic market, they are not caught by a narrow reading of Article XI:1.[83]

When the export of a certain product is restricted, there is more of that product available on the domestic market. This was the situation in the *China – Raw Materials* and *China – Rare Earths* cases.[84] China restricted the export of strategic raw materials and rare earths, enabling the domestic industry to have cheaper inputs. With production quotas, however, one could say that as they apply to both domestic and export markets alike, exports are not more restricted than domestic sales.[85] It could thus be argued that production measures in the form of quotas are unlikely to be border measures and therefore fall outside the scope of Article XI:1.

WTO members could moreover argue that if production quotas were covered by Article XI:1, this would encroach upon their national sovereignty, since it would effectively require them to grant access to energy/natural resources supplies. While international trade rules may require states to respect their WTO obligations regarding non-discrimination and import and export quotas, a state can hardly be compelled to explore its natural resources and trade in them. After all, under the established international law principle of permanent sovereignty over natural resources, it is a state's prerogative to decide which of its natural resources it wants to deplete and at what rate.[86]

5.2.4.2   Article XI:1 and OPEC Production Quota: The Broad Interpretation

No matter how convincing the narrow view may seem, the arguments for a wider understanding of Article XI:1 GATT need to be considered. After all, it would offer one of the few avenues for constraining OPEC's behaviour and avoiding the adverse economic effects of its restrictive policies discussed in the preceding sections.

> produced quantities would in theory be available also for the domestic market and would have an impact on the price level there.

In support of this, see also Article XI:2 GATT, listing a minimum set of exemptions, but all related to import and export. Bagwell, Staiger and Sykes (n 5) 144 ('To fall under Article XI, a measure must be maintained "on importation or exportation". It is not enough that a measure merely has some effect on imports or exports. Thus, purely domestic restrictions are not covered.'); *World Trade Report 2010* (n 19) 185.

[83] Mavroidis (n 79) 57; see generally Ehring and Chianale (n 82).
[84] *China – Raw Materials*, panel and AB reports; *China – Rare Earths*, panel and AB reports.
[85] Ehring and Chianale (n 82).
[86] UNGA Res 1803 (n 33).

Our starting point in this analysis will be to disentangle the economic effect of production quotas from its interpretation in the context of relevant WTO rules. As explained earlier, the text itself does not make clear when Article XI:1 starts applying to trade in natural resources. One could maintain that if standing trees in a forest can be considered a tradable good under GATT, then so too could other natural resources in their natural state like petroleum.[87] It is moreover perfectly conceivable that petroleum needs less treatment than trees in a forest to become a tradable good for economic gain. If one takes this view, there is no compelling reason why petroleum, even when in the ground, should not be subject to the disciplines of Article XI:1.

The economic rationale behind the QR prohibition in Article XI:1 is the prevention of disruptions to trade flows. As already explained, production quotas are accompanied by dead-weight losses, which is the kind of inefficiency that indeed disrupts trade flows. In this respect, it is not unthinkable that OPEC production quotas could be considered QRs falling within the scope of Article XI:1, and therefore, contrary to GATT.

As far as their economic effect is concerned, the production quotas set by the cartel clearly have the effect of restricting international trade. There may be some OPEC WTO members that export the near totality of their oil production and have next to no domestic production. When applied by those OPEC WTO members, production quotas have the same economic effect as export quotas.

Moreover, OPEC's policy of restricting the quantities of oil on the market falls squarely within the plain meaning of 'production quota' in the sense of 'restricting' the 'quantities' of oil on the market. Even when the setting of production quotas is solely a domestic policy, in practice such quotas nonetheless affect the terms of international trade. Production quotas may escape the disciplines of WTO law, but their economic effect in the end is clearly to favour the domestic market. OPEC members gain revenues from applying a production quota, and even openly admit that this is their purpose – namely, to influence the price of oil and thus terms of trade to their advantage. Through a variety of other means, such as dual-pricing policies, they may additionally ensure that their domestic industries benefit from cheaper inputs.[88]

Support for the broad reading of an export restriction can also be found in case law. In *Japan – Semiconductors*, for instance, Japan and the

---

[87] *US – Softwood Lumber IV*, AB report.
[88] Ehring and Chianale (n 82) 165. See also discussion in Chapter 6.

United States made an arrangement consisting of a range of monitoring measures that resulted in restricting the trade in semiconductors from Japan.[89] Japan's measures did not include a production quota on semiconductors, but rather a restriction on exports and sales, the effect of which was to influence the price of semiconductors.[90] In its defence, Japan maintained that the measures it instituted were not legally binding.[91] However, the panel was of the opinion that the wording 'restrictions or prohibitions' in Article XI:1 should be interpreted broadly to include:[92] '*all measures* instituted or maintained by a contracting party prohibiting or *restricting* the importation, *exportation*, or sale for export of products other than measures that take the form of duties, taxes or other charges'.[93] Addressing Japan's contention that the measures complained of were not restrictions within the meaning of Article XI:1 because they were not legally binding or mandatory, the panel continued:

> Article XI:1, unlike other provisions of the General Agreement, did not refer to laws or regulations *but more broadly to measures. This wording indicated clearly that any measure instituted or maintained by a contracting party which restricted the exportation or sale for export of products was covered by this provision, irrespective of the legal status of the measure.*[94]

As the panel found that 'all measures' restricting importation, exportation or sale for export lie within the scope of the article, production quotas, which in essence restrict exportation, could arguably be included here. Admittedly, semiconductors as a manufactured product are different from scarce natural resources such as petroleum.

---

[89] *Japan – Semiconductors*, GATT panel report, paras 104–109; see Mavroidis (n 26) 82.

[90] *Japan – Semiconductors*, GATT panel report, paras 104–109.

[91] ibid.

[92] ibid, para 106 (finding that Article XI unequivocally forbids any measures instituted or maintained by a party to GATT that restricts the exportation or sale for export of products, regardless of whether the measures are legally binding on those affected).

[93] ibid, para 104 (emphasis added).

[94] ibid, para 106 (emphasis added) – view endorsed in *India – Autos*, panel report, para 7.269:

> The question of whether this form of measure can appropriately be described as a restriction on importation turns on the issue of whether Article XI can be considered to cover situations where products are technically allowed into the market without an express formal quantitative restriction, but are only allowed under certain conditions which make the importation more onerous than if the condition had not existed, thus generating a disincentive to import.

Another case that adopted a similarly broad view of QRs was *Argentina – Hides and Leather*, in which all de facto restrictive measures were deemed to be quantitative restrictions as described in Article XI:1.[95] There was also the case of *India – Quantitative Restrictions*,[96] where the panel used the expression 'limiting condition' in defining the scope of the term 'restriction' used in Article XI. The panel considered a 'limiting condition' to be not only one placed on imports, but any condition that has a limiting effect.[97] Again, it would not seem unreasonable to consider a production quota for petroleum intended for trading on the international market as a measure that is de facto restrictive and thus has a limiting effect.[98] Although panels and the Appellate Body can be seen to have opted for a broad interpretation of a QR, there is a risk of confusion between the economic effect of an export quota and its legal characterization under Article XI:1.[99]

The arguments above make a strong case for qualifying production quota maintained by OPEC WTO members as falling within the scope of Article XI:1. However, it also becomes clear that the law does not provide any definitive answer on this issue, leading to the conclusion that the current situation favours OPEC.[100] For the purpose of completeness, however, we must enquire into whether OPEC members would be able to rely on the Article XX(g) exception as a defence in the event that an OPEC production quota were to be qualified as a prohibited QR.

5.2.5   Production Quotas as Quantitative Restrictions: Article XX(g) GATT Defences?

Should production quotas constitute prohibited QRs under Article XI:1, could OPEC Members successfully invoke the Article XX(g) exception in GATT? Article XX(g) reads as follows:

---

[95] *Argentina – Hides and Leather*, panel report, para 11.17.

[96] *India – Quantitative Restrictions*, panel report, para 5.119.

[97] ibid.

[98] See *Argentina – Hides and Leather*, panel report, para 11.17 on de facto restrictions; *India – Quantitative Restrictions*, panel report, para 5.129. In the latter instance, the panel used the expression 'limiting condition' to define the scope of the term 'restriction', which it regarded as not just a condition placed on importation, but any condition that has a limiting effect.

[99] As argued by PD Farah and E Cima, 'Energy Trade and the WTO: Implications for Renewable Energy and the OPEC Cartel' (2013) 16 Journal of International Economic Law 707, 736.

[100] Carey (n 50) 797.

> Subject to the requirement that such measures are not applied in a manner which would constitute a means of arbitrary or unjustifiable discrimination between countries where the same conditions prevail, or a disguised restriction on international trade, nothing in this Agreement shall be construed to prevent the adoption or enforcement by any contracting party of measures:
>
> (g) relating to the conservation of exhaustible natural resources if such measures are made effective in conjunction with restrictions on domestic production or consumption; . . .

For an Article XX(g) defence to be successful, the OPEC WTO member invoking it would have to demonstrate not only that it complies with the conditions set out in paragraph (g), but also satisfies the chapeau of Article XX. In other words, they would have to show that the measures they have introduced in pursuing their objectives are not more restrictive than necessary and do not arbitrarily or unjustifiably discriminate between countries or amount to a disguised restriction on trade. In the *EU – Seals* case, the Appellate Body considered that one important way of determining whether a measure is applied in an arbitrary or discriminatory manner is to look at whether the discrimination is rationally related to the purpose of the measure under any of the Article XX exceptions.[101]

The examination of a measure under paragraph (g) (leaving aside the conditions laid down in the Article XX chapeau) consists in a two-step enquiry into:[102]

1. whether the measure in question relates to the conservation of exhaustible natural resources; and
2. whether it is made effective in conjunction with restrictions on domestic production or consumption.

5.2.5.1 'Relating to the conservation of exhaustible natural resources'

It goes without saying that, as a non-renewable commodity, petroleum is an exhaustible natural resource as referred to in paragraph (g). However, there the question remains of what is meant by the words 'relating to the conservation of' such resources.[103] In *US – Shrimp*, the Appellate Body

---

[101] See *EC – Seal Products*, AB report, paras 5.296–5.306.
[102] Mavroidis (n 86) 348.
[103] The panel in *US – Gasoline* held that the US measure at issue could not be justified in the light of Article XX(g) as a measure 'relating to the conservation of exhaustible natural

stated that 'relating to' implies a rational connection between a measure and the conservation of exhaustible natural resources, but no more than that.[104] This was confirmed in the *EC – Seals* case. According to this broad reading, even measures that are not primarily aimed at the conservation of the resource could be justified under Article XX(g), provided they are not inappropriately used for another purpose – which was the criterion applied by the AB prior to *US – Gasoline*.[105] In *EC – Asbestos*, the AB added that the importance of the objective also has to be taken into account.[106] In addition, the measure in question has to be the least restrictive measure that it is reasonable to apply in pursuing that objective.[107]

When investigating the meaning of 'relating to the conservation of' exhaustible natural resources, several sub-questions arise as far as OPEC is concerned. Does the setting of production quotas qualify as a measure rationally related to the conservation of petroleum? What is the policy objective behind the conservation of petroleum? And is a production quota the least restrictive measure it can reasonably take to achieve its objective?

The *China – Raw Materials* case may offer some more clarity on this. The United States brought a complaint against China's export restraints on various raw materials (mainly used in high-tech equipment such as smartphones) that benefited the domestic industry.[108] China sought recourse to Article XX to justify the export restraints on these raw materials, arguing, inter alia, that the motive for restricting the export of raw materials was to pursue a 'conservation programme' for exhaustible natural resources.[109] Its argument was dismissed, however, with the

resources' (panel report, para 6.40). The AB reversed the panel's finding and held that the US measure was justified under Article XX(g), although it ultimately found that the measure was inconsistent with the chapeau of Article XX. The AB held that the panel was in error in searching for a link between the discriminatory aspect of the US measure (rather than the measure itself) and the policy goal embodied in Article XX(g) (AB report, para 16).

104 Mavroidis (n 79) 349.
105 ibid; *US – Gasoline*, AB report, para 1336.
106 Mavroidis (n 79) 332; *EC – Asbestos*, AB report, para 102.
107 Mavroidis (n 79) 349.
108 See SE Rolland, '*China–Raw Materials*: WTO Rules on Chinese Natural Resources Export Dispute' (2012) (21) ASIL Insights <www.asil.org/insights>.
109 *China – Raw Materials*, panel report, paras 7.426–7.428. In its first written submission, China argued that it had adopted a 'comprehensive set of measures relating to the conservation of fluorspar' and a 'comprehensive set of measures relating to the conservation of bauxite'. However, the panel noted that a 'policy document' mentioned by

panel concluding – and the AB subsequently confirming – that China could not invoke GATT exceptions to commitments made in its accession protocol.[110] Continuing its analysis, the panel explored, arguendo, whether there might be any circumstances in which China could have successfully invoked the Article XX(g) exception.

The panel took the view that 'conservation' in Article XX(g) meant an act of preserving and maintaining the existing state of something – in this case natural resources, including the raw materials in question.[111] The panel doubted, however, that the challenged export restrictions were 'related to' a conservation programme.[112] It then went on to scrutinize the relationship between the export duties and the China's purported aim of conserving the raw materials in question.[113]

The panel was of the opinion that there should be a close and genuine relationship between the end and the means – that is, between the goal of conserving refractory-grade bauxite and fluorspar (the raw materials in question) and the means embodied in the applicable export duty and export quota.[114] In order to determine whether the challenged export restriction could be regarded as 'relating to' conservation, one had to look at the text, design, architecture and context of the measure.[115] In this instance, the panel concluded that the measure 'does not refer to the goal of conservation' and 'does not refer to the relationship between the export quota and the goal of the conservation'.[116]

As part of its Article XX(g) defence, China also asserted that nothing should interfere with the principle of sovereignty over natural resources.[117] It stated that Article XX(g) 'protects its sovereign right to adopt a comprehensive and sustainable mineral conservation policy, taking into account China's social and economic development

---

China 'refers for the most part to the economic and development gains that China can make through the exploitation of its mineral resources'. The panel could not find any 'measures relating to the conservation of' refractory-grade bauxite and fluorspar in the evidence China submitted relating to what it terms its "mineral policy"' (panel report, para 7.419).

[110] Accession Protocol (23 November 2001) WT/L/431; Report of the Working Party on the Accession of China (10 November 2001) WT/MIN(01)/3.

[111] *China – Raw Materials*, panel report, para 7.372.

[112] ibid, paras 7.369, 7.416.

[113] ibid, paras 7.370–7.371.

[114] ibid, para 7.416.

[115] ibid, para 7.418.

[116] ibid.

[117] ibid, paras 7.377–7.380.

needs'.[118] While conceding that, when interpreting the exception in paragraph (g), it was required by Article 31(3)(c) of the Vienna Convention of the Law of Treaties to take into account 'principles of general international law as applicable to WTO Members',[119] the panel found that the sovereignty principle did not clash with WTO obligations, but rather operated in harmony with them.[120] It acknowledged that the principle 'affords Members the opportunity to use their natural resources to promote their own development while regulating the use of these resources to ensure sustainable development,'[121] but concluded that 'Members must exercise their sovereignty over natural resources consistently with their WTO obligations' and that Article XX(g) was to be interpreted and applied in this way.[122] It added that resource-rich countries are entitled to manage the supply and use of their resources through conservation-related measures that foster the sustainable development of their domestic economies, provided this is done consistently with general international law and WTO law.[123]

In short, the panel affirmed that Article XX(g) 'cannot be invoked for GATT-inconsistent measures whose goals or effect is to insulate domestic producers from foreign competition in the name of conservation' (which would be discriminatory).[124] It should be noted that, after the case was closed, China reportedly – and unsurprisingly – decided to set production quotas for the raw materials instead of maintaining export restrictions.[125]

What can we take from this analysis that is relevant to OPEC? Would the measure of setting a production quota relate to the conservation of exhaustible natural resources? And assuming OPEC's production quotas concern an exhaustible natural resource within the meaning of Article XX(g), would the other requirements of Article XX be satisfied? Especially problematic would be the 'relating to the conservation' condition of paragraph (g). Given the panel's arguendo finding on the matter, we must ask what policy objective lay behind the conservation ensured

[118] ibid, para 7.363.
[119] ibid, paras 7.377–7.380; Vienna Convention on the Law of Treaties (adopted 23 May 1969, entered into force 27 January 1980, 1155 UNTS 331 (VCLT) art 31(3)(c).
[120] *China – Raw Materials*, panel report, paras 7.381–7.383.
[121] ibid.
[122] ibid.
[123] ibid para 7.404.
[124] ibid, para 7.408.
[125] See Y Shen, R Moomy and RG Eggert, 'China's Public Policies toward Rare Earths, 1975–2018' (2019) 33 Mineral Economics 127, 139–142.

through a production quota on petroleum and whether there was a close and genuine relationship between that objective and the measure. In addressing this question, it is necessary to have regard to the text, design, architecture and context of the measure in question.[126]

Clearly, it is questionable whether OPEC's production quota are primarily aimed at conserving oil as an exhaustible natural resource.[127] In *China – Raw Materials*, conservation was defined as 'the action of keeping from harm, decay, loss or waste; careful preservation'.[128] It is very unlikely that OPEC's primary purpose is to protect the petroleum from 'harm, decay, loss or waste'. After all, OPEC extracts petroleum for the purpose of trading it.

OPEC might argue that it keeps petroleum in the ground in order to mitigate its exhaustibility and/or protect the environment. Although a slower extraction rate could have positive externalities for the environment, this argument is not convincing. Rather, OPEC members conserve petroleum to influence its international price to their advantage and are quite open about it. Hence, as far as the design and context of the measure is concerned, we can conclude that the measure is ultimately designed to influence the price of oil rather than conserve or protect the petroleum as a vulnerable resource.

It is highly doubtful whether conserving petrol to influence the world price of oil in OPEC's interest qualifies as a legitimate objective satisfying the conditions of paragraph (g). It would be entirely logical to maintain that OPEC is using its production quota inappropriately for another purpose – namely, deriving the maximum benefit possible through the exercise of its market power, a practice clearly at variance with free trade policy.

The analysis above shows that the production quota maintained by OPEC would likely fail to meet the requirement of subparagraph (g). However, as case law currently stands (*US – Shrimp*), it seems that measures that are not primarily aimed at conserving petroleum could still be justified under Article XX(g).[129]

---

[126] *China – Raw Materials*, panel report, para 7.418.
[127] Ibid, para 7.372: 'The dictionary definition of the noun "conservation" is "the action of keeping from harm, decay, loss or waste; careful preservation. The preservation of existing conditions . . . The preservation of the environment, esp. of natural resources".'
[128] *China – Raw Materials*, panel report, para 7.372.
[129] *US – Shrimp*, AB report, para 133:

> We do not pass upon the question of whether there is an implied jurisdictional limitation in Article XX(g), and if so, the nature or extent of that

5.2.5.2   'Made effective in conjunction with restrictions on domestic production or consumption'

Generally, OPEC production quota apply to both domestic and foreign markets alike (unless the country exports its entire production), and therefore do not necessarily discriminate against the latter. In *China – Raw Materials*, while affirming that the Member must make sure its measures apply in conjunction with restrictions on domestic production or consumption, the AB did not specify to what extent they have to be equal to the import/export restrictions.[130] The panel stated that Article XX(g) 'does not oblige resource-endowed countries to ensure that the economic development of other user-countries benefits identically from the exploitation of the resources of the endowed countries'.[131] In other words, while it is clear that there must be matching domestic restrictions, the extent to which they have to be effective remains unclear.[132] Consequently, OPEC would arguably satisfy the paragraph (g) requirement of even-handedness with respect to domestic production or consumption, even if the domestic restrictions are not equal to the export restrictions on oil.

5.2.5.3   The Article XX Chapeau

Even if an OPEC defence satisfies the conditions of paragraph (g), it is likely to have difficulty meeting the requirements of the chapeau of Article XX, which must be satisfied in addition to the conditions set out in the individual paragraphs of the article. Here, however, it is not the substantive conformity of a measure with the chapeau that has to be assessed.[133] In *US – Gasoline*, the AB clarified that when moving to the chapeau, the only question to answer is whether the measure at hand is applied in a GATT-consistent manner.[134] This seems somewhat contradictory, since the function of the chapeau remains 'the prevention of the

---

limitation. We note only that in the specific circumstances of the case before us, there is a sufficient nexus between the migratory and endangered marine populations involved and the United States for purposes of Article XX(g).

[130] Mavroidis (n 79) 350; *China – Raw Materials*, AB report, paras 360–361, panel report, para 7.408: In short, the panel in fact concluded that the Article XX(g) defence can be successfully invoked if the measures 'are primarily aimed at rendering effective parallel domestic restrictions operating for the conservation of natural resources'.

[131] *China – Raw Materials*, panel report, paras 7.403–7.404.

[132] ibid, paras 7.387–7.410; see also Mavroidis (n 79) 350.

[133] *US – Gasoline*, panel report, para 22; Mavroidis (n 79) 355.

[134] *US – Gasoline*, panel report, para 22.

abuse of exceptions' and will arguably in some cases demand that the substantive conformity of a measure be addressed.[135] There are three cumulative conditions that have to be met in order for a measure to conform to the chapeau: (1) there must be no 'arbitrary' discrimination between countries where the same conditions prevail; (2) there must be no 'unjustifiable' discrimination between countries where the same conditions prevail; and (3) there must be no 'disguised restriction on international trade'.[136]

While OPEC production quota do not seem to be contrary to the first two conditions, they may not be compliant with the third. The GATT panel report on *US – Canadian Tuna* explained that '"disguised restriction", whatever else it covers, may properly be read as embracing restrictions amounting to arbitrary or unjustifiable discrimination in international trade taken under the guise of a measure formally within the terms of an exception listed in Article XX'.[137] Mavroidis, in his treatment of the issue, rightly points out that this is very similar to the French doctrine of *abus de droit*.[138] More importantly, in *EC – Asbestos* it was subsequently stated that the 'disguised restriction' question should be understood as prohibiting interventions which, while purporting to protect an interest listed in Article XX(a)–(j), actually seek to promote other interests.[139] The panel added:

> [W]e consider that the key to understanding what is covered by 'disguised restriction on international trade' is not so much the word 'restriction', inasmuch as, in essence, any measure falling within Article XX is a restriction on international trade, but the word 'disguised'. In accordance with the approach defined in Article 31 of the Vienna Convention, we note that, as ordinarily understood, the verb 'to disguise' implies an *intention*. Thus, 'to disguise' (*déguiser*) means, in particular, 'conceal beneath deceptive appearances, counterfeit', 'alter so as to deceive', 'misrepresent', 'dissimulate'. *Accordingly, a restriction which formally meets the requirements of Article XX(b) will constitute an abuse if such compliance is in fact only a disguise to conceal the pursuit of trade-restrictive objectives.*[140]

In Section 5.2.2, we have clearly established that the restrictive practices OPEC engages in through its production quota are contrary to the

---

[135] Mavroidis (n 79) 355.
[136] *US – Shrimp*, AB report, para 118; Mavroidis (n 79) 255–56.
[137] *US – Tuna*, GATT panel report, 25.
[138] Mavroidis (n 79) 359.
[139] *EC – Asbestos*, panel report, para 8.236; Mavroidis (n 79) 359.
[140] *EC – Asbestos*, panel report, para 8.236 (emphasis added in final sentence).

notion of free trade. It could thus be argued that OPEC in fact pursues trade-restrictive objectives – influencing the world oil price in such a way as to maximize the benefit for the cartel. For these reasons, it is highly likely that, even if OPEC could satisfy the conditions under paragraph (g), its measures would not be consistent with the Article XX chapeau, as they would ultimately constitute a 'disguised restriction on trade'. It is therefore doubtful that OPEC would be successful in invoking the Article XX(g) defence.

5.3   Decentralizing the European Internal Energy Market in the Light of WTO Law

Having examined in detail whether and how WTO law can comprehensively deal with global energy cartels such as OPEC, we now turn to our case study of the EU internal energy market (IEM). We will take the example of the EU internal market for gas, the Third Energy Package (TEP) and the Gas Directive as litigated between Russia and the EU in *EU – Energy Package*.[141] This will allow us to determine where WTO law enables the decentralization of energy markets and where multilateral trade rules are liable to constrain certain policy objectives. We begin by discussing some of the cornerstones of the IEM and the TEP, before moving on to the case and its implications.

5.3.1   Rationale of EU Unbundling and the Third Energy Package

5.3.1.1   The EU Internal Energy Market for Gas

As discussed in Chapter 1, Section 1.4.1, the IEM is the outcome of gradually introducing more coherent EU-wide energy legislation and policy from the 1980s onwards, with the ultimate objective of creating a fully interconnected, liberalized and decarbonized EU energy market that can also guarantee the security of the energy supply. In addition, a parallel move to break up and decentralize the EU's energy sector was

---

[141] *EU – Energy Package*, panel report. The Third Energy Package (TEP) is a comprehensive package of EU energy legislation, including Directive 2009/72/EC of the European Parliament and of the Council of 13 July 2009 concerning common rules for the internal market in electricity and repealing Directive 2003/54/EC [2009] OJ L211/55 (Electricity Directive); Directive 2009/73/EC of the European Parliament and of the Council of 13 July 2009 concerning common rules for the internal market in natural gas and repealing Directive 2003/55/EC [2009] OJ L211/94 (Gas Directive).

aimed at extending to the energy market Union competition policies that were already in place in other sectors of the internal market.[142]

Historically, the energy markets of EU member states were rather insular, closely tied to national security and industrial policy, and often vertically integrated, resulting in limited cross-border flows of energy between member states . During the first phase of implementing the IEM in the late 1980s, cross-border transit opened for both electricity and gas, meaning that member states could no longer oppose transnational flows of energy from another Member State. In the early 2000s, the Second Energy Package introduced the legal unbundling of the gas and electricity sectors, laying down as a minimum requirement that the production and sale of energy should be legally separate from energy transmission and distribution activities.[143]

5.3.1.2 The Third Energy Package

In 2009, the Commission adopted the Third Energy Package (TEP), applicable to both the electricity and natural gas sectors. As our case study relates to natural gas, we will focus below on the legislation related to the gas sector.

The TEP continues the efforts to introduce more competition in the natural gas market which the EU had initiated with the two previous packages. The first energy package, adopted in 1998, introduced the requirement of third-party accesses (TPA) to pipelines. Member states could either establish conditions under which the owners of pipelines would grant access to other parties (regulated TPA), or allow the owners of pipelines to grant TPA on the basis of the contracts they negotiate with third parties (negotiated TPA). The first energy package did not contain any provisions on interconnectors between member states, and excluded upstream pipelines from the limited access conditions applying to onshore pipelines. This changed with the introduction in 2003 of the second energy package, which extended the harmonization of access

---

[142] AA Marhold, 'The Interplay between Liberalisation and Decarbonisation in the European Internal Energy Market for Electricity' in K Mathis and BR Huber (eds), *Energy Law and Economics* (Springer 2018) 59, 63–64.

[143] For an overview of the first and second energy packages, see TM Dralle, *Ownership Unbundling and Related Measures in the EU Energy Sector* (Springer 2018) 21ff; K Talus, *Introduction to EU Energy Law* (OUP 2016) 15. On the completion of the EU internal market for gas, see V Pogoretskyy and K Talus, 'The WTO Panel Report in EU–Energy Package and Its Implications for the EU's Gas market and Energy Security' (2019) World Trade Review 1, 2–6.

regulation, provided for exemptions from mandatory TPA and regulated interconnection tariffs.[144]

The third energy package takes EU energy market liberalization reforms a step further by introducing the requirement of ownership unbundling and rules on Commission certification of entities owning and operating gas infrastructures (so-called transmission system operators (TSOs)). It further cemented the TPA requirements and the possibility of infrastructure exemptions. Below we discuss the key rules of the TEP, as set out in the Gas Directive, a pivotal legal instrument in the EU IEM.

5.3.1.3 Unbundling

Article 9 of the Gas Directive contains the unbundling obligation aimed achieving a clear separation between natural gas extraction/supply activities and the activity of natural gas transmission. Although Article 9 may appear to impose a single, general requirement to unbundle, unbundling can in fact be achieved in three different ways under the directive.[145] There are also special rules that apply to government-controlled entities.[146]

A vertically integrated undertaking (VIU) in the energy sector could thus comply with the directive's unbundling obligation (a) by implementing full ownership unbundling; (b) by designating an independent system operator (ISO); or (c) by establishing an independent transmission operator (ITO).[147] The VIU is free to choose whichever model it prefers to use for unbundling. The choice is not unlimited, however, as it depends on which unbundling models have been implemented in the member states where the entity engaged in natural gas transmission is to operate.

---

[144] L Hancher and AA Marhold, 'A Common EU Framework Regulating Import Pipelines for Gas? Exploring the Commission's Proposal to Amend the 2009 Gas Directive' (2019) 37 Journal of Energy and Natural Resources Law 289, 291. See also L Hancher and FM Salerno, 'Energy Policy after Lisbon' in A Biondi, P Eeckhout and S Ripley (eds), *EU Law after Lisbon* (OUP 2012).

[145] Gas Directive, art 9(1), (8).

[146] Gas Directive, art 9(6).

[147] Gas Directive, art 9(1), (8). Article 2(20) defines a VIU as:

> a natural gas undertaking or a group of natural gas undertakings where the same person or the same persons are entitled, directly or indirectly, to exercise control, and where the undertaking or group of undertakings perform at least one of the functions of transmission, distribution, LNG or storage, and at least one of the functions of production or supply of natural gas.

Ownership unbundling is the strictest form of unbundling. The key characteristic of this model is that the transmission infrastructure belongs to the entity responsible for its operation – a TSO.[148] Any ownership interest in a transmission infrastructure held by a VIU had to be transferred to a TSO by 3 March 2012. This requirement was intended to make TSOs fully and solely responsible for maintenance of the infrastructure and for complying with the obligations imposed by the Gas Directive (eg granting TPA). It was accompanied by a set of additional requirements consolidating the separation between the former VIU parent and the TSO. A VIU is thus no longer allowed to exercise direct or indirect control over both the production/supply of natural gas and its transmission. Control here includes the holding of a majority share in a company involved in either side of the business and the ability to appoint members of the supervisory board, the administrative board or bodies legally representing such a company.[149]

Article 9(8) allows EU member states not to implement the ownership unbundling model in cases where the transmission system belonged to a VIU on 3 September 2009 and instead to apply the lighter regime of either the ISO or the ITO model. Under these two models, a VIU is not required to divest itself of its interest in the transmission business, but is obliged to comply with the additional and other requirements.

Under the ISO model, the entity responsible for the operation of the transmission infrastructure (the ISO) must be independent of the VIU, just as a TSO must be independent of a VIU under the ownership unbundling model; in other words, a VIU may not exercise direct or indirect control over it.[150] In addition, the ISO must have sufficient financial, technical, physical and human resources to carry out its tasks as an operator of transmission infrastructure, as listed in Article 13 of the Gas Directive; must comply with a ten-year network development plan monitored by the regulatory authority; must be enabled to perform its tasks by the owner of the transmission infrastructure, including any necessary financing arrangements and the coverage of liability relating to the network assets; and must have demonstrated its ability to comply with its obligations under Regulation (EC) 715/2009, including the cooperation of transmission system operators at European and regional level.[151]

---

[148] Gas Directive, art 9(1)(a). See also Dralle (n 143) 26ff.
[149] Gas Directive, art 9(1)–(2).
[150] Gas Directive, art 14(2)(a).
[151] Gas Directive, art 14(2); Regulation (EC) 715/2009 of the European Parliament and of the Council of 13 July 2009 on conditions for access to the natural gas transmission networks and repealing Regulation (EC) 1775/2005[2009] OJ L211/36.

The rules of the ITO model are set out in chapter IV of the Gas Directive. Unlike the ISO model, this model does not require a complete separation of the entity responsible for the operation of the transmission infrastructure (the ITO). Article 18 of the Gas Directive contains two key guarantees of independence under this model: the TSO must have (a) effective decision-making rights, independent of the VIU, with respect to assets necessary to operate, maintain or develop the transmission system; and (b) the power to raise money on the capital market, in particular through borrowing and capital increase. Other requirements include the independence of the TSO's staff and management, and the establishment of a supervisory body in charge of taking decisions that may have a significant impact on the value of shareholders' assets within the TSO, in particular those concerning approval of annual and longer-term financial plans, the level of indebtedness of the TSO and the amount of the dividends distributed to shareholders.[152]

As noted above, special unbundling rules apply to government-controlled entities. Pursuant to Article 9(6) of the Gas Directive, in case of such entities, the unbundling obligation is deemed to be fulfilled in respect of such entities where there are two separate public bodies, one of which exercises control over the transmission of natural gas and the other control over the production/supply of natural gas. Moreover, the operators of some types of infrastructure are not subject to the unbundling obligation. This is the case with the operators of upstream pipelines, for example, whose activity lies essentially in bringing unprocessed natural gas from the extraction source to a point of transmission. As Article 9 of the Gas Directive makes it clear that the unbundling obligation applies to transmission systems and transmission system operators,[153] and the directive's definition of transmission explicitly excludes upstream pipelines,[154] operators of upstream pipelines are not subject to this obligation.

---

[152] Gas Directive, arts 19–20.

[153] The article is entitled 'Unbundling of transmission systems and transmission operators'.

[154] Article 2(3) of the Gas Directive defines 'transmission' as:

> the transport of natural gas through a network, which mainly contains high-pressure pipelines, *other than an upstream pipeline network* and other than the part of high-pressure pipelines primarily used in the context of local distribution of natural gas, with a view to its delivery to customers, but not including supply [emphasis added].

5.3.1.4   Third-Party Access

Article 32 of the Gas Directive requires EU member states to implement a system of third-party access (TPA) to the transmission system, based on published tariffs, applicable to all eligible customers, including supply undertakings, and applied objectively and without discrimination between system users.[155] The obligation to grant TPA does not prevent the conclusion of long-term contracts, provided they comply with EU competition rules.[156]

The TPA obligation in respect of upstream pipelines is found in Article 34 of the directive, which requires EU member states to ensure TPA to upstream pipeline networks, except those parts of such networks and facilities that are used for local production operations at the site of a field where the gas is produced.[157] Article 34(2) allows EU member states to determine the manner of TPA to upstream pipelines, in accordance with 'the objectives of fair and open access, achieving a competitive market in natural gas and avoiding any abuse of a dominant position, taking into account security and regularity of supplies, capacity which is or can reasonably be made available, and environmental protection'.[158] Article 35(1) allows the infrastructure operator to refuse access to the system in certain cases. The grounds for refusal include lack of capacity, incompatibility with the Article 3(2) public service obligations assigned to it, and serious economic and financial difficulties with take-or-pay contracts.[159]

---

[155] Gas Directive, art 32(1).

[156] Gas Directive, art 32(3). For a detailed discussion of TPA under WTO law in connection with pipeline gas transit, see V Pogoretskyy, *Freedom of Transit and Access to Gas Pipeline Networks under WTO Law* (CUP 2017) ch 4.

[157] Gas Directive, art 34(1).

[158] Gas Directive, art 34(2).

[159] Article 3(2) of the Gas Directive reads as follows:

> Having full regard to the relevant provisions of the Treaty, in particular Article 86 thereof, Member States may impose on undertakings operating in the gas sector, in the general economic interest, public service obligations which may relate to security, including security of supply, regularity, quality and price of supplies, and environmental protection, including energy efficiency, energy from renewable sources and climate protection. Such obligations shall be clearly defined, transparent, non-discriminatory, verifiable and shall guarantee equality of access for natural gas undertakings of the Community to national consumers. In relation to security of supply, energy efficiency/demand-side management and for the fulfilment of environmental goals and goals for energy from renewable sources, as referred to in this paragraph, Member States may introduce the

5.3.1.5   Tariff Regulation

Article 41 of the Gas Directive empowers the regulatory authorities of EU member states to fix or approve transmission tariffs or their methodologies.[160] Specifically, regulatory authorities are responsible for fixing or approving at least the methodologies used to calculate or establish the terms and conditions for (a) connection and access to national networks, including transmission tariffs; (b) the provision of balancing services, which shall be performed in the most economic manner and provide appropriate incentives for network users to balance their input and off-takes; and (c) access to cross-border infrastructures, including procedures for the allocation of capacity and congestion management.[161] Moreover, regulatory authorities are authorized to require transmission system operators, if necessary, to modify the terms and conditions, including tariffs and methodologies, to ensure that they are proportionate and applied in a non-discriminatory manner.[162]

5.3.1.6   Infrastructure Exemptions

Article 36 of the Gas Directive allows for new gas infrastructure projects to be exempted from the unbundling and TPA obligations and the regulated tariff requirements. The exemptions granted under the previous directive remain valid. In order to qualify for exemption, an investment must meet the conditions specified in Article 36(1): (a) it must enhance both competition in gas supply and security of supply; (b) the level of risk attached to the investment must be such that the investment would be made without the exemption; (c) the infrastructure must be owned by a natural or legal person that is separate, at least in terms of its legal form, from the system operators in whose systems the infrastructure will be built; (d) charges must be levied on users of that infrastructure; and (e) the exemption must not be detrimental to competition in the relevant markets likely to be affected by the investment, nor to the effective functioning of the internal market in natural gas, the efficient functioning of the regulated systems concerned or security of supply of natural gas in the EU.[163]

---

       implementation of long-term planning, taking into account the possibility
       of third parties seeking access to the system.
[160] Gas Directive, art 41(1)(a).
[161] Gas Directive, art 41(6).
[162] Gas Directive, art 41(10).
[163] Gas Directive, art 36(1).

5.3.1.7   Certification of TSOs

In order to ensure compliance with the applicable obligations, the Gas Directive created a certification mechanism for TSOs. National regulatory authorities are responsible for the certification of domestic TSOs.[164] Where certification is requested by a transmission system owner or a transmission system operator that is controlled by a person or persons from one or more third countries, the regulatory authority, before taking its decision, must request an opinion from the Commission on whether the entity concerned satisfies the unbundling obligation and whether the security of the supply of energy to the EU would be put at risk if certification were granted.[165]

5.3.2   EU – Energy Package: *Russia Challenging EU Decentralization Policies*

From the foregoing discussion, it can be seen that the EU's TEP rules were aimed at bringing about the decentralization of energy VIUs active in the European internal energy market by separating their production and supply activities from their energy transmission activities and ownership of TSOs. The principal means of achieving this is through unbundling, third-party access and regulated tariffs following rules laid down in the TEP directives and implemented by EU member states.

Russia has long voiced its discontent with the Union's TEP policies and their implications for the activities of its state-owned VIU energy company Gazprom, which is active in broad swathes of the EU market and the dominant energy supplier in some EU member states.[166] Russia claimed that the EU should not make the involvement of foreign partners in the Union's energy sector conditional on their satisfying requirements concerning how the participant entities should be organized. After unsuccessful bilateral negotiations on the topic, it announced that it would take its dispute to the WTO.[167]

---

[164] Gas Directive, art 10.

[165] Gas Directive, art 11(5). On security of supply, see Chapter 7, Section 7.3.

[166] Information about Gazprom's shareholders is available at <www.gazprom.com/invest ors/stock/> accessed 20 July 2020.

[167] See eg B van Vooren and RA Wessel, *EU External Relations Law: Text, Cases and Materials* (CUP 2014) 452, fn 44.

In 2015, Russia indeed challenged various aspects of the TEP under the WTO DSU.[168] In *EU – Energy Package*, it contested several of the EU rules relating to the natural gas market, claiming inter alia that the unbundling rules, including those concerning public bodies and the different treatment of upstream pipelines and LNG operators, disadvantaged Gazprom entities present in the EU.[169] It further contended that the implementation of the unbundling models by EU member states resulted in discrimination against Russia and impermissible market access restrictions on the supply of services.[170]

Russia also took issue with the conditions attached to the infrastructure exemption decision on the OPAL pipeline – the EU inland extension of the Nord Stream 1 gas pipeline running from Russia to Germany via the Baltic Sea. Russia's objection was particularly targeted at the capacity cap on the amount of gas that could be transported through the OPAL pipeline, which, it argued, amounted to an import restriction.[171]

Two other aspects of the EU energy rules were also covered by Russia's claims. First, Russia regarded the third-country certification mechanism contained in Article 11 of the Gas Directive (and as transposed in the national laws of EU member states) as discriminatory towards foreign TSOs (including those from Russia).[172] Second, Russia argued that the EU's framework of incentives for new energy projects resulted in less favourable treatment for Russian natural gas and natural gas suppliers compared to the gas and gas suppliers from EU member states and other countries.[173]

Briefly, the panel in *EU – Energy Package* found that the EU unbundling rules and their implementation in EU member states did not violate WTO law.[174] It did, however, find that the OPAL capacity cap was an import restriction on Russian gas contrary to Article XI GATT, and that the EU's framework of incentives for new energy projects unfavourably

---

[168] WTO, *European Union and Its Member States – Certain Measures Relating to the Energy Sector*, 'Request for the Establishment of a Panel by the Russian Federation' (28 May 2015) WT/DS476/2.

[169] ibid.

[170] *EU – Energy Package*, panel report, paras 7.379, 7.402, 7.515, 7.594, 7.623, 7.702, 7.730, 7.825, 7.1000–7.1004.

[171] ibid, paras 7.976–7.977. See also K-O Lang and K Westphal, 'Nord Stream 2: A Political and Economic Contextualization' (2017) SWP Research Paper 3/2017, 17–18.

[172] *EU – Energy Package*, panel report, para 7.1116.

[173] ibid, paras 7.1261, 7.1263, 7.1383.

[174] ibid, paras 8.1(a)–(c), 8.1(d)(i)–(ii).

impacted on Russia as a source to diversify away from.[175] This resulted in a violation of Articles I and III:4 GATT. The panel was not convinced by the EU's attempted justification of the capacity cap under Article XX(j) GATT ('goods in general or local or short supply').[176] Lastly, the panel considered that the EU's third-country certification mechanism was discriminatory towards non-EU natural gas suppliers (which the EU itself acknowledged in so many words) and, further, was not justified under the public order exception of Article XIV(a) GATS.[177]

The panel report in *EU – Energy Package* was issued on 10 August 2018. Both parties appealed against it. Currently, the WTO Appellate Body does not have a sufficient number of adjudicators to consider appeals, so it is unclear when this case will be finally resolved.[178]

At the panel stage, the *EU – Energy Package* has resulted in a split outcome. On the one hand, the EU finds its position vindicated insofar as the panel cleared unbundling, the TEP's core competition component, as WTO-compliant. On the other hand, the EU can be disappointed with the OPAL capacity cap outcome and the failed justification of third-country certification, as well as by the panel's assessment of the framework of incentives for new energy projects as being discriminatory against Russia. Despite winning on the OPAL capacity cap, third-country certification and new energy projects, Russia too might feel aggrieved that its attack on unbundling per se (which is likely to affect Gazprom's position in the EU market most) did not yield the desired result. Russia may also find it difficult to accept that its arguments about certain specific aspects of unbundling – such as different rules for public bodies, upstream pipelines and LNG operators – seemingly fell on deaf ears.

After this brief overview of the case, we will now discuss its findings from the perspective of WTO rules that either facilitate or impede the implementation of EU policies aimed at decentralizing the European internal market for gas. As a forewarning, it is worth pointing out that WTO rules sometimes approve to be blunt instruments in cases related to this technically complex and political sector, as illustrated in *EU – Energy Package*. They constitute general rules on market access and non-discrimination for goods and services and may not incorporate the

---

[175] ibid, paras 7.1003, 7.1301, 7.1313, 8.1(d)(iii).

[176] ibid, paras 7.1382, 8.1(g)(i). See also Chapter 7, Section 7.3.

[177] *EU – Energy Package*, panel report, paras 7.1134, 7.1254, 8.1(f)(ii).

[178] For the current status of the dispute, see <www.wto.org/english/tratop_e/dispu_e/cases_e/ds476_e.htm> accessed 20 July 2020.

necessary energy sector know-how. As reflected in some of the case outcomes, certain rules may consequently suffer from an inflexibility that constrains decentralization policies.

5.3.3 WTO Rules Facilitating EU Energy Market Decentralization Policies

In the light of the panel findings in *EU – Energy Package*, we first discuss how WTO rules can facilitate certain decentralization policies that the EU is pursuing in the energy sector through the TEP. We cover, in turn, unbundling and exemptions allowed for certain types of infrastructure.

5.3.3.1   Unbundling and Related Measures

Russia challenged the unbundling regime itself as set forth in the Gas Directive, as well as the application of the regime in EU member states Hungary, Croatia and Lithuania.[179] It claimed that unbundling violated both GATT and GATS by forcing non-EU VIUs to restructure their activities to be able to operate on the EU market.[180]

First, Russia argued that its pipeline transport services and service suppliers were afforded less favourable treatment than service suppliers from other non-EU countries, and that this violated Article II:1 GATS (MFN treatment). It asserted that the directive was discriminatory by allowing EU member states to opt for the lighter ISO/ITO models alongside the OU model.[181] In essence, Russia claimed that in the EU market the stricter OU regime applied more often to its VIU Gazprom than to other non-EU service suppliers. While Russia did not dispute the measure *de jure*, it sought to demonstrate that Russian pipeline transport services and service suppliers were de facto accorded less favourable treatment.[182] The panel thus had to examine two issues:

> (a) whether Russia has demonstrated that pipeline transport services and service suppliers are accorded less favourable treatment under the OU model in comparison with that accorded to pipeline transport services and service suppliers under the ISO and/or the ITO models; and

---

[179] *EU – Energy Package*, panel report, ss 2.2.2.1, 2.2.2.2.

[180] ibid, paras 7.372–7.377; General Agreement on Trade in Services, Marrakesh Agreement Establishing the World Trade Organization, Annex 1B (signed 15 April 1994) 1869 UNTS 183 (1994) 33 ILM 1167 (GATS), art II:1; GATT 1994, arts I:1, III:4.

[181] *EU – Energy Package*, panel report, paras 7.402–7.403.

[182] ibid, paras 7.481–7.482.

(b) if so, whether Russia has demonstrated that the unbundling measure in the Directive accords less favourable treatment to Russian pipeline
transport services and service suppliers than that accorded to pipeline
transport services and service suppliers of any other non-EU country by
'enabling' EU member States to choose between implementing only the
OU model or implementing the ISO and/or the ITO models in addition to
the OU model in respect of transmission systems that belonged to a VIU
on 3 September 2009.[183]

While agreeing that the OU model afforded less favourable treatment
than the ITO model, the panel found that Russia had failed to demonstrate that the Russian VIU had less access to the ITO model than other
non-EU countries.[184] It stated that even if Gazprom had to cease supplying pipeline transport services through TSOs it owned before the directive was in force, it was nonetheless still supplying services through the
commercial presence of ITOs.[185] Therefore, the panel concluded, the
unbundling measure in the directive was not discriminatory.[186]

Russia also asserted that via the unbundling measure, its natural gas
was treated less favourably than that of entities that were subject to lighter
unbundling regimes, which violated Articles III:4 and I:1 GATT.[187] First,
Russia submitted that, by requiring it to unbundle its VIU, resulting in
loss of control over previously owned TSOs, the unbundling caused it to
miss out on transport fees and investment control. On this basis, it
contended that natural gas imported from Russia was treated less favourably than domestic EU gas transmitted by entities operating under the
ITO and ISO models, in violation of Article III:4.[188] The panel found
Russia's argument that it was missing out on certain revenues under the
OU model to be insufficient and insisted that Russia 'must demonstrate
that such sources of revenue translate into a competitive advantage for
the natural gas produced or supplied by the VIU', which, according to the
panel, it had failed to do.[189] In other words, Russia could not prove that
the severing of ties between a VIU and its formerly owned TSOs due to
unbundling was negatively affecting the treatment of its natural gas.
According to the panel's findings under Article III:4, Russia had
not demonstrated that the unbundling models operated differently for

[183] ibid, para 7.427.
[184] ibid, paras 7.450–7.480.
[185] ibid, para 7.494.
[186] ibid, paras 7.511–7.514.
[187] ibid, paras 7.372–7.377.
[188] ibid, para 7.540.
[189] ibid, para 7.556.

non-EU countries and Russia and had therefore failed to make a prima facie case that this measure violated Article I:1 GATT.[190]

Russia also brought a claim under Article XVI:2(a), (e) and (f) GATS (limitations on market access), arguing that, as transposed in Croatia, Lithuania and Hungary, the directive had the effect of limiting the number of services suppliers, the types of entity through which a service may be supplied and the participation of foreign capital, thereby violating paragraphs (a), (e) and (f) respectively.[191] In the case of Croatia, the panel found that there was nothing in the 'provisions indicating that the unbundling requirement is of such a nature that it limits to one, or a small number, the number of service suppliers'.[192] With regard to Lithuania's laws, the panel found that Russia failed to explain why 'other suppliers of pipeline transport services cannot supply pipeline transport services in Lithuania' or 'how the OU model is of such a nature that it limits to one, or a small number, the number of authorized TSOs in Lithuania'.[193] Nor was the panel convinced by Russia's argument that the prohibition of both domestic and foreign majority ownership in the laws of those three EU members states has the effect of limiting the participation of foreign capital as described in Article XVI:2(f).[194]

Perhaps Russia's strongest argument was based on subparagraph (e) of Article XVI:2 GATS, namely that unbundling requires or restricts specific types of legal entities through which pipeline transport services may be supplied.[195] The panel, however, was of the opinion that 'the mere fact that an entity may (or may not) own or control another entity is not sufficient to make the former entity (or the latter) a "specific type of legal entity" within the meaning of Article XVI:2(e) because ownership or control *per se* does not speak to the legal form of either entity'.[196]

Another issue, related to the unbundling measure, was the public body measure set out in Article 9(6) of the Gas Directive. This provision allows distinct public entities in EU member states to own and operate energy infrastructure (eg two different ministries). It states that, for the purposes of the directive, 'separate public bodies exercising control over a transmission system operator or over a transmission system on the

---

[190] ibid, para 7.584.
[191] See also Chapter 3, Sections 3.3.1 and 3.3.2.
[192] *EU – Energy Package*, panel report, para 7.609.
[193] ibid, paras 7.602–7.622, 7.728.
[194] ibid, paras 7.725–7.726.
[195] ibid, paras 7.623–7.625. See also Chapter 3, Section 3.3.2.
[196] *EU – Energy Package*, panel report, para 7.663.

one hand, and over an undertaking performing any of the functions of production or supply on the other, shall be deemed not to be the same person or persons'. Russia challenged the measure under Article XVII GATS ('National Treatment'). Here, the panel again disagreed with Russia. It held that, as implemented by the EU member states in question, the public body measure was origin-neutral and could be read as covering service suppliers controlled by domestic public bodies as well as service suppliers controlled by foreign public bodies.[197] The panel also found that while the public body measure provides that service suppliers controlled by public bodies are subject to different rules from those applicable to all other service suppliers under the unbundling measure, both sets of rules were functionally equivalent in ensuring a separation of the function of natural gas transmission from that of natural gas production and/or supply.[198]

Russia also challenged the so-called liquefied natural gas (LNG) measure in Article 2(11) of the Gas Directive,[199] claiming that pipeline operators were treated unfairly compared to LNG terminals, as the former were required to unbundle, but not the latter. Russia argued that its gas, which is supplied via pipelines, was consequently treated less favourably than LNG supplied by other non-EU countries and that this constituted a violation of Article I:1 GATT given that LNG and natural gas were like products.[200] The panel disagreed, observing that they were separate products as not all imported LNG was re-gasified and that Russia had failed to demonstrate their likeness. Hence, the panel considered it unnecessary to further examine the consistency of the LNG measure with Article I:1 GATT.[201]

Lastly, Russia argued that that the exclusion of upstream pipelines (ie those pipelines that bring 'raw' natural gas to a point of transmission) from the directive's unbundling requirement was contrary to Articles III:4 and I:1 GATT. It argued that their exclusion gave an advantage to third-country gas imported into the EU via upstream pipelines.[202] The panel disagreed, stating that 'Russia has not demonstrated that the legal regime of the operators of upstream pipeline networks creates more

---

[197] ibid, paras 7.822–7.823.
[198] ibid, para 7.786.
[199] See Chapter 3, Section 3.2.1.
[200] *EU – Energy Package*, panel report, para 7.834.
[201] ibid, paras 7.855–7.856.
[202] ibid, para 7.1007.

favourable conditions for the transportation of natural gas via upstream pipelines than via transmission pipelines'.[203]

5.3.3.2   Infrastructure Exemption Measure

In Article 36 of the Gas Directive the EU provided that, upon request and subject to their fulfilling certain conditions, infrastructures could be exempted from some of the directive's core rules, such as those on unbundling, TEP and regulated tariffs, in two cases: (1) if they were new infrastructures or (2) if there was a significant increase in the capacity of an existing infrastructure or an existing infrastructure was modified to enable the development of new sources of gas supply. Russia claimed that the measure set out in Article 36 was contrary to Article X:3 (a) GATT, because it was not applied in a uniform, impartial and reasonable manner as required by the article. According to Russia, the Commissions' exemption decisions concerning pipelines not connected to Russian import pipelines, such as Gazelle, the Trans-Adriatic Pipeline (TAP), Nabucco and Poseidon, meant that they were treated more favourably than the OPAL pipeline connected to Nord Stream 1, which brings Russian gas to Germany.[204] Disagreeing, the panel took the view that Russia's issues were concerned with the content of the criteria set out in Article 36, rather than their application.[205] It therefore dismissed Russia's claim in this respect.

5.3.3.3   WTO Rules Facilitating Decentralization Policies: The Take-Away

The overall take-away from this case study of the EU internal energy market and the decision of the panel in *EU – Energy Package* is that WTO rules in GATT and GATS to a large extent allow the EU to order the break-up of its internal energy market by compelling VIUs active in its market to separate their production and sales activities from their transmission activities. The fact that unbundling can be accomplished by means of different models and that the production/supply of energy and its transmission can be handled by two public bodies should not be

---

[203] ibid, para 7.1043.

[204] ibid, paras 7.868–7.869. Gazelle is a pipeline in the Czech Republic operated by Net4Gas; the TAP runs from Greece to Italy via Albania and is operated by TAP AG; the Nabucco pipeline runs from Turkey to Austria and is operated by Nabucco Gaspipeline International GmbH; and the Poseidon pipeline runs from Turkey to Italy via Greece and is operated by IGI Poseidon SA.

[205] ibid, para 7.950.

regarded as obstacles. The break-up should always take place in a non-discriminatory and origin-neutral manner and concern a 'like product' or 'like service', which in this case did not always prove to be a straightforward matter. Russia did not make a strong enough case for LNG and natural gas to be considered 'like' products, meaning that the EU can differentiate between the treatment of these goods by regulating LNG and pipeline infrastructures differently in respect of each good. The GATT and GATS rules also allow members to implement decentralization differently where different types of pipelines are concerned. For instance, the regulation of upstream pipelines, where arguably less competition exists, can differ from that of transmission pipelines. The panel appears to have taken a restrictive approach to infrastructure exemptions when investigating whether the EU applied the criteria in Article 36 of the Gas Directive in a 'uniform, impartial and reasonable manner', which would leave the EU with considerable leeway when deciding whether particular pipelines meet the criteria for infrastructure exemptions. In sum, where the core competition aspects of unbundling are concerned, WTO rules can be said to enable rather than hamper such policies. However, as the discussion below will demonstrate, where political aspects of regional energy policy are concerned, WTO rules prove to be less flexible.

5.3.4   WTO Rules Constraining EU Energy Market Decentralization Policies

EU – Energy Package has shown that WTO law is conducive to the core of decentralization policies pursued through unbundling. However, there are other aspects of the EU's energy decentralization policy where WTO law can have a constraining effect. These aspects are third-country certification, the OPAL capacity cap and projects of common interest, each of which will be discussed in turn below.[206]

5.3.4.1   Third-Country Certification

An important feature of the EU unbundling regime is Certification in relation to third countries dealt with in Article 11 of the Gas Directive. Article 9 of the directive requires the unbundling of TSOs. If a non-EU entity wishes to own a TSO in the EU internal market, it must not only comply with the rules of Article 9 but also be certified in accordance with

---

[206] On third-country certification in relation to energy security, see Chapter 7, Section 7.3.

Article 11. In other words, the regulatory authority of the member state concerned must refer the case to the Commission, which will issue an opinion on whether or not ownership of the TSO would put security of supply within Europe at risk.[207] The Commission must take into account the specific facts of the case and the third country or countries concerned, as well as the European Community's rights and obligations vis-à-vis that third country or countries under international law, including any agreement concluded with one or more third countries to which the EC is a party and which addresses issues of security of supply.[208]

In its current form, Article 11 seems to give the European Commission wide discretion to determine which TSOs from which third countries pose a risk to security of supply, and thus to determine whether a given country should be granted or denied certification. Russia objected to this article and the manner in which it was transposed in the laws of Croatia, Hungary and Lithuania, claiming that it was contrary to the principles of MFN and national treatment in Articles II:1 and XVII GATS in respect of Russian pipeline services and service suppliers (Mode 3 commercial presence).[209] Russia contended that the measure resulted in less favourable treatment, as it applied a 'double standard' or 'differential treatment accorded by the Commission and the Member States in implementing the third-country certification measure'.[210] The panel did not share Russia's position that other non-EU service suppliers were afforded less favourable treatment on the basis of this article. However, it observed that 'the requirement of security of energy supply assessment is an additional condition imposed on all third-country pipeline transport service suppliers before they are allowed to supply pipeline transport services through the commercial presence of TSOs', while '[d]omestic service suppliers are generally not subject to the same requirement'.[211] This implied that third-country service suppliers were subject to modified conditions of competition compared to domestic services suppliers.[212] The panel therefore decided that the third-country certification measure was inconsistent with Article XVII GATS.[213]

---

[207] Gas Directive, art 11(1), (5)(b).
[208] Gas Directive, art 11(7)(a), (b).
[209] *EU – Energy Package*, panel report, paras 7.1056–7.1060.
[210] ibid, para 7.1075.
[211] ibid, paras 7.1128–7.1129.
[212] ibid.
[213] ibid.

The EU attempted to avail itself of the public order defence in Article XIV(a) GATS in connection with security of supply, but was not successful as the panel decided that the requirements set out in the article's chapeau were not met.[214] The connection between decentralization and energy security will be discussed in greater depth in Chapter 7, Section 7.3. In essence, the panel's decision on this matter constrains the decentralization policy of the EU and its member states.

The EU's wish to safeguard energy security by carefully choosing which non-EU entities can operate on its internal market and which cannot was a step too far for the panel. The question is whether, in a strategic and political sector such as energy, the standard rules of the WTO suffice. A thought worth exploring is that discrimination with regard to a member's security supply should be acceptable under certain conditions, such as where a WTO member wants to diversify its energy supplies away from one dominant supplier. Under current WTO rules, this is not straightforward.

5.3.4.2   OPAL Capacity Cap

Another aspect of the infrastructure exemption measure where the EU's policies were frustrated was the so-called OPAL capacity cap and gas release programme. The OPAL interconnector pipeline, which was linked to the Nord Stream 1 pipeline and brought gas from Germany to the Czech Republic, benefited from an exemption from the European Commission on the basis of Article 36 of the Gas Directive.[215] The pipeline is operated by two German companies, Wingas and Wintershall, the former being a subsidiary of Gazprom.[216] Because of the exemption, the OPAL gas pipeline did not have to unbundle, but the Commission attached several conditions to the exemption. They concerned a capacity cap on the amount of gas Gazprom could import via the pipeline and a gas release programme.[217]

---

[214] ibid, para 7.1254. See Chapter 7, Section 7.3.

[215] See *EU – Energy Package*, panel report, paras 7.976–7.977; Lang and Westphal (n 171) 17–18. Russia did not challenge the rules in Article 36 of the directive per se, but rather their application in the light of Article X:3(a) GATT. See K Yafimava, *The OPAL Exemption Decision: Past, Present and Future* (Oxford Institute for Energy Studies Paper NG 117, 2017).

[216] See <www.wingas.com/en/index.html> accessed 20 July 2020.

[217] Bundesnetsagentur, Decision in the administrative proceedings concerning non-compliance with the OPAL exemption decision of 25 February 2009 as amended by the decision of 7 July 2009 (BK7-08–009-E2) (in German).

According to the conditions, no more than 50 per cent of the OPAL pipeline's capacity could be taken up by gas from Russia's VIU.[218] The likely reason for the EU's imposing this cap was to limit Gazprom's activity on the EU internal gas market and prevent it from dominating the market. Regardless of the EU's motives, the panel quite straightforwardly decided that the capacity cap on Russian natural gas effectively limited the competitive opportunities for Russian natural gas imported into the EU by Gazprom to be transported through the OPAL pipeline upon its arrival Nord Stream pipeline's termination point at Greifswald, Germany.[219] Therefore, the EU's measure was inconsistent with Article XI:1 GATT.[220]

While the decision of the panel is wholly understandable and just from the perspective of international trade law disciplines as applied to the realities of the energy sector, the implications are far-reaching. In essence, the rules frustrate the EU's efforts to limit imports by a dominant energy supplier, with a view to diversifying its energy sources and becoming less dependent on one supplier so as to enhance energy security. In other words, WTO law offers little to members seeking protection from a dominant energy supplier on its markets. As a member cannot change its geographical location, these are circumstances that are hard to overcome. In this respect, WTO law will act as a constraining force on members' attempts to restrict certain energy imports when pursuing decentralization objectives. Recourse to exceptions may be the only possibility for WTO members wishing to introduce such restrictions, but they tend to be interpreted strictly.

5.3.4.3   Projects of Common Interest

The final measure in the EU's decentralization policy that it was unsuccessful in defending was the Trans-European Networks for Energy (TEN-E) measure. Under the TEN-E Regulation, the EU earmarked certain infrastructure projects as projects of common interest (PCIs).[221] These PCIs (which included transmission pipelines for gas)

---

[218] *EU – Energy Package*, panel report, para 7.983.
[219] *EU – Energy Package*, panel report, para 7.1000.
[220] *EU – Energy Package*, panel report, para 7.1002.
[221] Regulation (EU) 347/2013 of the European Parliament and of the Council of 17 April 2013 on guidelines for trans-European energy infrastructure and repealing Decision 1364/2006/EC and amending Regulations (EC) 713/2009, (EC) 714/2009 and (EC) 715/2009 [2013] OJ L115/39 (TEN-E Regulation). For a discussion on the Article XX(j) GATT exception invoked by the EU, see Chapter 7, Section 7.3.

benefit, inter alia, from lighter authorization procedures and financial incentives. To qualify, gas projects have to contribute to EU internal energy market integration, security of supply, competition and sustainability.[222] Russia challenged this measure under Articles I:1 and III:4 GATT. Its main argument was that the criteria used to selected certain projects as PCIs were discriminatory towards Russian gas.[223] Russia considered that the TEN-Regulation, specifically the criteria of 'diversification of gas supply' and 'end[ing] the isolation of the three Baltic States and Finland and their dependency on a single supplier,' were designed to reduce the supply and transmission of imported Russian natural gas into and within the European Union.[224] The panel first examined the claim based on Article III:4. It noted that while 'diversification of gas supply' appeared to be a crucial concept in the TEN-E Regulation, no definition was provided. Based on the available information, the panel concluded that 'introducing or increasing variety in the countries supplying natural gas' was the EU's goal here.[225] And where there was only one dominant supplier, this meant ensuring that there was at least one more supplier.[226] In favouring certain infrastructure projects, the EU was clearly wanting to further this goal. In other words, some projects were designated as PCIs in order to develop pipeline infrastructures to transport gas of non-Russian origin.[227] Based on these findings, the panel held that 'the TEN-E measure provides more favourable conditions for the transportation of natural gas of any origin other than Russian, including natural gas of domestic origin'.[228] The measure was thus inconsistent with Article III:4 GATT. With regard to Article I:1 GATT, the panel found that 'the TEN-E measure is thus designed to increase the availability of new projects developing pipeline infrastructure to transport natural gas of non-Russian origin and decrease the availability of new projects developing pipeline infrastructure to transport natural gas of Russian origin'.[229] The consequence of this was that imported

---

[222] TEN-E Regulation, art 4(2)(b)(i)–(iv).
[223] *EU – Energy Package*, panel report, paras 7.1261–7.1265.
[224] ibid; TEN-Regulation, annex I(4).
[225] *EU – Energy Package* panel report, para 7.1273.
[226] ibid.
[227] ibid.
[228] ibid, para 7.1300.
[229] ibid.

natural gas of any origin other than Russian benefited from more favourable conditions of transportation and, as a result, from more favourable competitive opportunities.[230] Therefore, the TEN-E measure was deemed inconsistent with Article I:1 GATT.

The EU tried – unsuccessfully – to invoke the Article XX(j) GATT defence (products in general or local short supply).[231] It argued that, as natural gas was a product in general or local short supply, there was a risk of supply disruptions and it was therefore necessary to develop additional gas infrastructure.[232] However, referring to the analysis of the Appellate Body in *India – Solar Cells,* the panel was not convinced that the alleged existence of genuine and serious risks of disruption of supply was sufficient to establish that natural gas is a product in short supply.[233] In other words, the fact that natural gas could risk being in short supply in the future did not mean that it was in short supply at present.

Last but not least, Russia claimed that the TEN-E measure was inherently biased against Russian services and services suppliers in violation of Article II:1 GATS (MFN treatment).[234] In the panel's opinion, however, Russia did not manage to establish a close enough connection between the infrastructure projects falling under the TEN-E Regulation and the alleged discriminatory treatment of Russian services and service suppliers, and therefore failed to demonstrate that the measure was inconsistent with Article II:1 GATS.[235]

The take-away from the above is again, however, that the rules of the WTO have a constraining influence on decentralization policies where a WTO member wishes to diversify away from one dominant supplier by favouring energy infrastructure projects involving other suppliers. This is understandable, as the rules of the multilateral trading system were designed to favour producers. However, due to the unmoveable geographical location of countries and the degree to which their energy sectors are intertwined, WTO law offers little protection for those Members that do not wish to become overly dependent on a single dominant supplier.

---

[230] ibid, para 7.1312.
[231] See Chapter 7, Section 7.3.
[232] *EU – Energy Package,* panel report, para 7.1326.
[233] *India – Solar Cells,* AB report, para 5.71; *EU – Energy Package,* panel report, paras 7.1345–7.1353.
[234] *EU – Energy Package,* panel report, paras 7.1383–7.1388.
[235] ibid, paras 7.1430–7.1438.

5.3.4.4   WTO Rules Constraining Decentralization Policies: The Take-Away

While decentralization policies such as unbundling and the infrastructure exemption measure do not seem to pose problems in their current forms for WTO members wishing to open up their energy markets, other policies are certainly more problematic. Based on the *EU – Energy Package* case, measures problematic under WTO law are those that touch on the more political field of national and regional energy policy-making. A case in point is the liberty to decide, on grounds of energy security, which foreign transmission system operators from which countries can operate in the market and which cannot, as this discriminates against foreign TSOs. Neither is it easy under WTO law to restrict the quantities of natural gas imports from a dominant supplier into the market with a view to diversifying energy resources. While countries generally wish to have access to fossil fuel supplies, for strategic and energy security reasons they may also want to have enough flexibility to protect themselves against the influence of one dominant fossil fuel supplier in their market. This proves difficult under current WTO rules, and members may have to resort to exceptions in order to carry through such policies. The same applies to decentralization and diversification policies, which aim to favour infrastructure projects that allow connections with other third-countries suppliers rather than restricting quantities of natural gas imports into their markets. Again, while such outcomes can be explained by the rationale underlying WTO rules, it is worth exploring whether they are a corollary of the political and strategic realities of the energy sector, which is highly dependent on the volatility of the market, its geographical rootedness and relationships with supplier countries.

5.4   Conclusion

Through a study of two major players in the global and regional energy markets, this chapter has discussed decentralization policies in the energy sector in the light of international trade rules. In Section 5.2, the chapter explored to what extent OPEC's production quota on petroleum could be caught by existing WTO rules, specifically Article XI:1 GATT. It investigated the economic rationale behind that provision and the prohibition of quotas in the WTO, and tried to assess whether production quotas as maintained by OPEC could be squared with the WTO position. We saw that, on the basis of a narrow interpretation of the provision, it would be difficult equate production quotas with quantitative export restrictions. Although perhaps inconsistent with the economic rationale of GATT, the status quo is in OPEC's favour, making it difficult to deal comprehensively with a global energy cartel under WTO law.

In Section 5.3, the chapter discussed the example of the EU internal energy market for gas, in the light of the decisions reached by the panel in *EU – Energy Package*. It concluded that while WTO rules foster decentralization policies in the energy market, such as the break-up of VIUs, some multilateral trading rules may constrain such policies, especially where they concern the more political aspects of decentralization policies, such as limiting energy imports by a dominant suppliers in the market or favouring energy infrastructure projects with a view to diversifying energy sources away from a dominant supplier.

6

Decarbonizing Energy Markets: Constraining Dual Pricing and Options for Fossil Fuel Subsidy Reform in the WTO

6.1 Introduction

The decarbonization of energy markets can be realized in various ways. This chapter will study a particularly pertinent challenge in international trade law in this regard: energy dual pricing. This is a practice whereby resource-endowed states (eg through monopolistic STEs) sell their energy resources on the domestic market at lower prices significantly than on the export market or than the prevailing global market price for the commodity in question.[1] It is in effect a multi-tier pricing system, through which domestic prices are kept artificially low compared to export prices for the same commodity. Dual-pricing policies are most commonly applied by resource-rich states in possession of large quantities of geographically unevenly distributed energy commodities for which overall demand is high and constant. It is the combination of these factors that gives states the market power allowing them to engage in such practices .[2] Prime examples of resources subject to dual pricing are coal, natural gas and petroleum, though it is known to have been

---

[1] See generally AA Marhold, 'Fossil Fuel Subsidy Reform in the WTO: Options for Constraining Dual Pricing in the Multilateral Trading System' (E15 Initiative Issue Paper, International Centre for Trade and Sustainable Development and World Economic Forum, December 2017); WTO, *World Trade Report 2010: Trade in Natural Resources* (WTO 2010) 173–74. On dual pricing, see V Pogoretskyy, 'Energy Dual Pricing in International Trade: Subsidies and Anti-Dumping Perspectives' in Y Selivanova (ed), *Regulation of Energy in International Trade Law: WTO, NAFTA and Energy Charter* (Wolters Kluwer 2011) 213ff; Y Selivanova, *Energy Dual Pricing in the WTO: Analysis and Prospects in the Context of Russia's Accession to the World Trade Organization* (Cameron Ma 2008); D Behn, 'The Potential Problem with Dual Gas Pricing Practices at the WTO' (17 December 2007) <https://ssrn.com/abstract=1151553> accessed 18 February 2021; S Ripinsky, 'The System of Gas Dual Pricing in Russia: Compatibility with WTO rules' (2004) 3 World Trade Review 463.

[2] UNCTAD, 'Trade Agreements, Petroleum and Energy Policies' (2000) UNCTAD/ITCD/TSB/9 (UNCTAD report) 16; B Fliess and T Mård, 'Taking Stock of the Measures

applied to other (raw) materials as well.[3] The principal motive for states maintaining dual-pricing policies is to provide their energy-intensive industries with cheap fuel inputs and thereby give them an advantage over competitors. Such policies have been applied by Russia, Ukraine and OPEC countries, notably Saudi Arabia.[4] For instance, dual-pricing schemes have led to capital-intensive investments in the Saudi petrochemical sector.[5] In essence, the practice amounts to a kind of inverted subsidy: the higher price charged for the commodity on the export market allows the price to be kept artificially low on the domestic market. It can consequently be argued that this results in an unfair advantage for domestic industries, which are able to purchase the commodity at a price below the global market rate.

Dual-pricing policies reveal the asymmetries and diverging interests between WTO members that are net energy exporters and those that are net energy importers. Apart from the trade-distorting effects such policies have, they are also a cause of substantial negative environmental externalities. They lead to over-consumption of fossil fuels by encouraging energy-intensive industries to profit from the availability of cheap fossil energy inputs, and they ignore the importance of innovation and energy efficiency by discouraging investments in cleaner forms of energy.[6]

Restricting the Export of Raw Materials: Analysis of OECD Inventory Data' (2012) OECD Trade Policy Paper 140, 24.

[3] They include leather and soybean oil (eg WTO dispute *Australia – Automotive Leather II*; GATT dispute *Spain – Soybean Oil* (panel report not adopted)), and log and lumber (eg the softwood lumber saga between the United States and Canada concerning log export bans to offset tariff escalation by Japan aimed at forcing export of logs, not lumber, to Japan; see *US – Softwood Lumber IV*, *US – Softwood Lumber V* and *US – Softwood Lumber VI*). Note that electricity dual pricing also exists but is a somewhat separate issue (see Pogoretskyy (n 1) 213–14) and will not be discussed here as this chapter focuses on the curbing of fossil fuel subsidies.

[4] See V Pogoretskyy, 'The System of Energy Dual Pricing in Russia and Ukraine: The Consistency of the Energy Dual Pricing System with the WTO Agreement on Anti-Dumping' (2009) 4 Global Trade and Customs Journal 313; D Tarr and PD Thomson, 'The Merits of Dual Pricing of Russian Natural Gas' (2004) 27 World Economy 1173; V Pogoretskyy and S Melnyk, 'Russian Energy and the WTO: Overview of the Accession Negotiations of the Russian Federation and Final Commitments' [2018] 1 Oil, Gas and Energy Law Journal <www.ogel.org>; Selivanova (n 1); Ripinsky (n 1).

[5] OPEC members (notably Saudi-Arabia) and Russia are notorious for implementing energy dual-pricing policies; see R Quick, 'Dual Pricing' in J Pauwelyn (ed), *Global Challenges at the Intersection of Trade, Energy and Environment* (Graduate Institute of International and Development Studies/Centre for Trade and Economic Integration 2010) 194–95.

[6] Pogoretskyy (n 1) 215.

Placing the discussion on dual pricing within the wider context of combating climate change and the need to reform environmentally harmful fossil fuel subsidies, this chapter will look beyond the trade-distortive effects of dual pricing towards options for disciplining these practices in the WTO system in view of their negative environmental impact. After a background introduction, the chapter will explore two main avenues for dealing with dual pricing, discussing, first, what possibilities exist under current WTO rules and, second, what action the WTO can take beyond the current legal toolkit in the wider context of reforming fossil fuel subsidies. The key argument is that the WTO can be a crucial actor in eliminating dual-pricing policies and can facilitate and significantly contribute to fossil fuel subsidy reform.

6.2   Dual Pricing as an Environmentally Harmful Fossil Fuel Subsidy

Considering their negative environmental impact and the manner in which they are applied, dual-pricing practices belong within the broader category of environmentally harmful fossil fuel subsidies (FFS). FFS is an overarching term used to refer to government aids for the production and consumption of energy from fossil fuels.[7] They concern not only the energy industry but also those industries that use energy as an immediate input (eg steel, glass, cement, petrochemical and other heavy industries).[8] Coal, petroleum and natural gas are heavily subsidized worldwide.[9]

There are various forms of FFS, ranging from direct cash transfers for producers and consumers to more covert practices such as indirect support mechanisms, tax exemptions, rebates, price controls, trade restrictions, limitations on market access and energy conservation subsidies. Overall, FFS can be divided into two categories: consumer subsidies, which are targeted at reducing the price for domestic consumers; and producer subsidies, aimed at increasing domestic supplies.[10] FFS can be

---

[7] International Institute for Sustainable Development Global Subsidies Initiative <www.iisd.org/gsi>; International Energy Agency (IEA), 'Energy Subsidies: Tracking the Impact of Fossil-Fuel Subsidies' <www.iea.org/topics/energy-subsidies> both accessed 20 July 2020.

[8] R Steenblik, 'Subsidies in the Traditional Energy Sector' in Pauwelyn (n 5) 187.

[9] See IEA (n 7); International Monetary Fund, *Energy Subsidy Reform: Lessons and Implications* (IMF 2013) app I ('Estimating Pre-tax and Post-tax Global Energy Subsidies').

[10] Steenblik (n 8) 186; HB Asmelash, 'Energy Subsidies and WTO Dispute Settlement: Why Only Renewable Energy Subsidies Are Challenged' (2015) 18 Journal of International Economic Law 261, 267; IMF, *Energy Subsidy Reform* (n 9) 5–7.

further divided into pre-tax and post-tax subsidies.[11] The first type implies that the price paid by a household or firm is below the actual cost of distribution and supply, while the latter means that the taxes paid are below the level of tax-efficiency. FFS are wasteful and have a negative impact on the environment; indeed, research has shown that FFS displace cleaner alternatives and keep the fossil fuel industry artificially afloat.[12] Despite their trade-distortive, wasteful and environmentally harmful effects, many countries opt to maintain FFS on the grounds of security of supply, industrial policy, protectionism, economic benefits, protection of labour-intensive industries (employment) and/or access to energy.[13]

Dual-pricing practices can be categorized according to both criteria (consumer/producer, pre/post-tax). For instance, energy consumers may benefit from artificially low prices for energy (pre-tax consumer subsidies), as may energy producers (pre-tax producer subsidies). Or producers may receive tax breaks on their industrial energy bill (post-tax producer subsidy). Such subsidies are compensated for by selling the fossil fuel at a higher price on the export market, thereby allowing the domestic price of energy to be kept artificially low. Such a policy acts as a disincentive to curbing CO_2 emissions, as it encourages countries to continue burning cheap fossil fuels, available at below-market prices, rather than switch to cleaner forms of energy. Moreover, not only does it result in wasteful consumption of fossil fuels and increased CO_2 emissions in the atmosphere but also undermines the competitiveness of renewable energy. For these reasons, curbing dual-pricing practices is of the essence in the bigger challenge of reducing and reforming FFS.

According to the International Energy Agency (IEA), phasing out fossil fuel subsidies is one of four policies essential to keeping the world on track to meet the two-degree global warming target at no net economic cost.[14] Even a partial phase-out by 2020 would reduce greenhouse gas (GHG) emissions by 360 million tonnes, which corresponds to 12 per cent of the reduction in GHGs needed to prevent the temperature rise from exceeding 2°C.[15] Hence, there is a pressing case for fossil fuel

---

[11] IMF, *Energy Subsidy Reform* (n 9) 7.

[12] OECD and World Bank, 'The Scope of Fossil-Fuel Subsidies in 2009 and a Roadmap for Phasing out Fossil Fuel Subsidies' (Joint Report for G-20 Summit Seoul, 11–12 November 2010) 11.

[13] Pogoretskyy (n 1) 247: 'Indeed, it leads to inefficient and artificially stimulated consumption of energy resources, especially, with respect to coal and coal-based electricity.'

[14] See IEA (n 7).

[15] S Hayer, *Fossil Fuel Subsidies* (Directorate-General for Internal Policies in-depth analysis PE 595.372, European Parliament 2017) 5.

reform. Unfortunately, however, there is a lack of clear standards in reporting and curbing FFS, even among leading proponents of reform within the G20.[16] Consequently, many states continue to heavily subsidize their fossil fuel industries.

A major obstacle to curbing FFS is the lack of transparency over the ways in which they are instituted in practice, due in no small measure to the absence of an international standardized system allowing them to be comprehensively monitored.[17] The situation is such that even in data-rich countries substantial disagreement exists over the degree of subsidization of the energy sector and the method by which this is calculated, but it is estimated to represent a vast sum.[18] In many instances, the existence of FFS may be difficult to detect in the first place. Sometimes, the only available means of measuring their existence is to examine energy prices within a national jurisdiction (eg strikingly low energy prices for consumers, below their international market price).[19]

That said, some important first steps towards monitoring and eliminating FFS have nonetheless been made. Back in 2009, the G20 committed to phasing out FFS, viewing them as wasteful and inefficient.[20] However, its actions have so far concentrated mainly on voluntary self-reporting and voluntary peer-reviews on FFS.[21] The G7 also vowed to eliminate FFS by the year 2025 in the 2016 Ise-Shima Leaders' Declaration.[22]

While this a good start, obstacles to further progress are still manifold, notably the lack of a standardized, clear and mutually agreed upon terminology. Indeed, there continues to be considerable disagreement over terminology among G20 members .[23] Improved monitoring and data would greatly contribute to establishing the legal definitions relevant to FFS reform. And last but certainly not least, it is also necessary to

---

[16] For a clear explanation of the challenges this poses, see HB Asmelash, *Phasing Out Fossil Fuel Subsidies in the G20: Progress, Challenges and Ways Forward* (ICTSD Gene 2017) 6–9.

[17] IMF, *Energy Subsidy Reform* (n 9) 5; Steenblik (n 8) 184.

[18] IMF, *Energy Subsidy Reform* (n 9) 8–13. In the United States, for instance, they amounted to around $600 billion in 2011.

[19] Steenblik (n 8) 184.

[20] G20 Leaders' Statement, Pittsburgh Summit (24–25 September 2009) <www.g20.org /Documents/pittsburgh_summit_leaders_statement_250909.pdf> accessed 20 July 2020.

[21] Asmelash (n 16) 7–8.

[22] G7 Leaders' Declaration (Ise-Shima Summit (26–27 May 2016) <www.mofa.go.jp/files/ 000160266.pdf> 28.

[23] Asmelash (n 16) points out that Saudi Arabia defines fossil fuel subsidies in such a way that it excludes the bulk of the subsidies it provides for fossil fuel consumers by setting domestic oil prices below international rates.

develop a workable means of ensuring that the G20 honours its promises on the phasing-out of FFS. For efforts in this direction to be successful, it is vital to have an enforcement mechanism with firm deadlines that countries must adhere to in phasing out their FFS.

Aside from the efforts being made outside the WTO to reform FFS, the multilateral trading system itself can make a significant contribution in curbing FFS. One step in the right direction would be to address environmentally harmful dual-pricing policies in the forum. The WTO has the capacity to make this happen, by virtue of both its broad membership and its substantive mandate. Although the WTO is primarily an organization tasked with issues pertaining to international trade, there is an undisputed consensus among its members on the need to combat climate change. Most WTO members have undertaken to curb their CO_2 emissions as part of their commitment to the UN Sustainable Development Goals (SDGs).[24] These commitments are in addition to those made by the G20 and Friends of FFS Reform. Below, after a brief overview of dual pricing in the GATT/WTO context, we will ponder how the WTO and its membership could play an active role in curbing dual pricing.

6.3   Understanding Dual Pricing in the GATT/WTO Context

Dual pricing is by no means a new topic in the multilateral trading forum; it has been a recurring issue in GATT/WTO negotiations for decades. Moreover, both academics and policy-makers have written extensively on the subject, albeit mainly from the perspective of its trade-distorting aspects rather than its adverse impact on the environment.[25] That said, combating the two may very well go hand in hand, although the negative environmental impacts of dual pricing likely outweigh its trade-distorting effects. Anyway, the emphasis in this chapter will be especially on the need to tackle dual pricing for its negative impacts on the environment and combating climate change.

Discussions on dual pricing first entered the multilateral trading forum during the oil crises of the 1970s in connection with the restrictions placed on trade in natural resources and the diverging interests this revealed between net exporting and net importing countries.[26] Talks on

---

[24] <www.un.org/sustainabledevelopment/sustainable-development-goals/> accessed 20 July 2020.

[25] For a selection of authors, see n 1. An exception is Pogoretskyy (n 1) 214–16, addressing the negative environmental impacts of dual pricing. See also Chapter 2.

[26] Pogoretskyy (n 1) 313.

export restrictions and export taxes were included on the agenda of the Tokyo Round.[27] The debate was fuelled mostly by the concerns of the United States and the European Union.[28] The former was chiefly worried about cheaper inputs for domestic industries in members operating dual-pricing policies, which it considered an unfair trade practice. The EU (or EC as it was then) expressed concerns about the higher price of Russian gas exported to the EU due to dual-pricing policies. It should be mentioned, however, that the United States behaved inconsistently over dual pricing in 1980 when challenged by the EC for imposing price controls on natural gas while maintaining export bans in the Committee on Subsidies and Countervailing Measures. The United States replied that this was not a subsidy because it was distributed throughout the whole economy – foreshadowing what would become Article 2 of the SCM Agreement fifteen years later.

Despite this instance of inconsistency in the 1980s, the United States has generally pushed for including clear provisions on dual pricing either in GATT or in a separate agreement.[29] However, there was strong resistance to binding commitments from oil producing and exporting countries and no agreement was reached on the subject.[30] The topic returned to the agenda during the Uruguay Round with the establishment in 1989 of a Negotiating Group on Natural Resource-Based Products, whose mandate covered not only energy commodities but also forestry, fisheries, non-ferrous materials and metals.[31] GATT members opposed to dual pricing attempted to re-address the issue and proposed the development

---

[27] During the Tokyo Round, export restrictions were discussed in Group 3(b); see GATT doc MTN/3B/9. See also GATT, Export Restrictions and Charges – Background Note by the Secretariat (8 August 1989) MTN.GNG/NG2/W/40.

[28] eg GATT, Committee on Trade and Development – The Impact of Higher Petroleum Prices on Developing Countries – Note by the Secretariat (28 January 1974) COM.TD/W/208.

[29] See the articles by the then US trade representative TR Graham, 'Results of the Tokyo Round' (1979) 6 Georgia Journal of International and Comparative Law 153, 161; 'Reforming the International Law Trading System: The Tokyo Round Trade Negotiations in the Final Stage' (1979) 12 Cornell International Law Journal 1, 20, 31; 'The Reorganization of Trade Policymaking: Prospects and Problems' (1980) 13 Cornell International Law Journal 221, 226ff; R Leal-Arcas, A Filis and ES Abu Gosh, *International Energy Governance: Selected Legal Issues* (Edward Elgar 2014) 123.

[30] See W-C Shih, 'Energy Security, GATT/WTO, and Regional Agreements' (2009) 49 Natural Resources Law Journal 433,439; Chapter 2.

[31] UNCTAD report (n 2) 18. See US submissions MTN.GNG/NG3/W/2, MTN.GNG/NG3/W/13, MTN.GNG/NG3/W/23; EC submission MTN.GNG/NG3/W/37.

of a new code.[32] However, energy-endowed states yet again resisted the introduction of binding rules on trade in natural resources.[33] During the Uruguay Round, an attempt was also made to include in the draft SCM Agreement a specific provision on dual pricing of government-supplied inputs, unfortunately without success. The issue of dual pricing re-emerged in the Doha Round negotiations with the United States and the EU proposing to expand the category of prohibited subsidies under Article 3 of the SCM Agreement, but to no effect.[34] The EU was of the opinion that Article 3.1 should also cover 'the provision, by the virtue of government action, of goods to domestic production on terms and conditions more favourable than those generally available for such goods when destined for export'.[35] Alas, however, the proposal failed to gain traction among WTO members.

The dual-pricing debate within the multilateral trading forum can broadly be summarized as follows. On the one hand, WTO members opposed to dual pricing have historically argued that states administering dual-pricing policies are indirectly subsidizing their energy-intensive industries by providing them with cheaper inputs. Members that maintain dual-pricing policies, on the other hand, believe they are merely exploiting their comparative advantage, using dual pricing as a development tool to diversify their economies. As a result, the issue remains unsettled in the WTO.

---

[32] See GATT, Multilateral Trade Negotiations – Negotiating Group on Natural Resources-Based Products – Note by the Secretariat (10 August 1989) MTN.GNG/NG3/11, para 5; UNCTAD report (n 2) 17; Y Selivanova, 'The WTO and Energy: WTO Rules and Agreements of Relevance to the Energy Sector' (2007) International Centre for Trade and Sustainable Development Issue Paper 1, 11.

[33] See GATT, Multilateral Trade Negotiations, Group of Negotiations on Goods, Negotiating Group on Natural Resource-Based Products – Meeting of 11 February 1987 – Note by the Secretariat (26 February 1990) MTN.GNC/NG3/1, as cited in Y Selivanova, 'Managing the Patchwork of Agreements in Trade and Investment' in A Goldthau and JM Witte (eds), Global Energy Governance: The New Rules of the Game (Brookings Institution Press 2010).

[34] World Trade Report 2010 (n 1) 174, citing C Canuto and TC Fienberg 'Natural Resource-Based Products' in TP Stewart (ed), The GATT Uruguay Round: A Negotiating History (1986–1992) (Volume Ia: Commentary), (Kluwer Law and Taxation 2003) vol 1a, 459–522; I Espa and SE Rolland, 'Subsidies, Clean Energy and Climate Change' (E15 Initiative Think Piece, International Centre for Trade and Sustainable Development and World Economic Forum February 2015) 6, citing 'Expanding the Prohibited "Red Light" Subsidy Category, United States Proposal' (16 January 2006) WTO/RL/GEN/94; WTO, Negotiating Group on Rules – Subsidies – Submission of the European Communities (24 April 2006) TN/RL/GEN/135.

[35] Espa and Rolland (n 34).

Although the attempts to establish some binding rules on dual pricing proved unsuccessful, some progress has nonetheless been made in recent years, especially in the context of negotiations on the accession of new members. Dual pricing was discussed, for instance, in connection with the accession of Saudi Arabia in 2005.[36] The Russian Federation went even a step further on the occasion of its accession in 2011, making commitments on dual pricing when binding and undertaking to phase out some of its export duties on energy products.[37] For non-petroleum gases, for instance, the export duty was to decrease to zero during the four-year period of implementation of the accession protocol.[38] These commitments are, however, tailored narrowly to natural gas. For crude oil and some other oil products, Russia committed to a formula that calculated export duties on the basis of world oil prices.[39] However, the question of whether and to what extent Saudi Arabia and Russia have honoured their accession commitments on energy remains unanswered.

While these developments show that dual pricing remains a widely used practice among WTO members, they are also a positive sign that acceding members are willing to make binding commitments on the issue, which demonstrates that it is open to negotiation. Negotiating binding commitments on dual pricing could thus offer a partial solution to the problem, at least with respect to nations that are in the process of acceding to the WTO (of which a fair share, including Algeria, Azerbaijan, Iran, Iraq, Libya and Sudan, are major fossil fuel energy producing and exporting countries). If, in addition to this, a move is made to increase awareness of the negative environmental impacts of dual pricing, acceding countries may be encouraged to make binding commitments on the issue. A prime motivator here would be the fact that curbing dual pricing could

---

[36] Accession Protocol (11 December 2005) WT/L/627; Report of the Working Party on the Accession of the Kingdom of Saudi Arabia (1 November 2005) WT/ACC/SAU/61, para 28. See Chapter 2, Section 2.4.2.4.

[37] See Russia's Schedule of Concessions and Commitments on Goods, Schedule CLXV, pt V, 853, 870; Convention on the Harmonized Commodity Description and Coding System (adopted 14 June 1983) 1503 UNTS 167, ch 27 ('Mineral fuels, mineral oils and products of their distillation; bituminous substances; mineral waxes').

[38] Russia's Schedule of Concessions (n 37). On Russia's final commitments, see generally Pogoretskyy and Melnyk (n 4).

[39] Accession Protocol (22 August 2012) WT/L/839, WT/MIN(11)/27; Report of the Working Party on the Accession of the Russian Federation (17 November 2011) WT/ACC/RUS/70, WT/MIN(11)/2, annex 1. See also Chapter 3.

significantly help countries to meet their commitments to reduce CO_2 emissions made under the Paris Agreement.[40] Of course, obtaining binding commitments on dual pricing would be only a partial solution to the problem and would not address dual-pricing practices maintained by existing WTO members. In this regard, it is important to realize that we are now looking at dual pricing through a different lens than previously. Historically, the objective behind tackling dual pricing in the GATT/WTO setting was to ensure that exports would become cheaper.[41] Today, in the context of curbing CO_2 emissions, the goal should be the opposite – namely, to make domestic consumption of fossil fuels more expensive, including outputs from downstream industry in the countries that apply dual-pricing policies. The next section will explore how the WTO can address dual pricing through current rules.

6.4 Options for Constraining Dual Pricing in the WTO under Existing Rules

As we have seen, there are two dimensions to dual pricing: the purely trade distortive aspect of the practice, and the negative environmental impact of dual pricing in the context of curbing harmful FFS. Section 6.1 showed that there are convincing arguments for considering dual-pricing practices as violating current WTO rules, especially under GATT and the SCM Agreement and the ADA.[42] Although the WTO is a forum primarily set up to deal with matters that affect cross-border trade, it can, and should, contribute positively to eliminating dual pricing and thereby its negative impacts on the environment. This section explores options for tackling dual pricing under existing rules with a view to addressing its environmental impact and FFS reform. In counteracting the trade-distorting and negative environmental effects of dual pricing, WTO members can resort to either individual remedies or plurilateral and multilateral action.

When considering what action can be taken against dual pricing and/ or FFS in the multilateral trading forum, an important lacuna is that none of these issues have as yet been dealt with and clarified through WTO

---

[40] United Nations Framework Convention on Climate Change (UNFCCC), UN Doc FCCC/ CP/2015/L.9/Rev.1, Decision 1/CP.21 (adopted 12 December 2015).

[41] See Chapter 2, Section 2.3.

[42] It should be mentioned that avenues for constraining dual-pricing polices under the SCM Agreement and the ADA are solely applicable to trade in goods, not in services.

dispute settlement.[43] One explanation for this may be the fact that energy did not feature prominently in the forum until relatively recently.[44] Another reason may be that curbing a problem so omnipresent as FFS requires collective action and WTO members may have been reluctant to raise the issue in the Dispute Settlement System for fear of causing what might be perceived as self-inflicted harm. However, this is a misperception, as leaving FFS reform unaddressed is significantly more harmful. It is therefore of utmost importance to raise awareness of the negative environmental impacts of FFS among WTO members.

Disputes concerning dual pricing or FFS are most likely to arise in the WTO in situations where these practices negatively affect trade with and the national industry of another WTO member. For instance, a case could be brought if a domestic industry of a WTO member suffers significantly from the dual-pricing policies applied by another WTO Member that result in cheap energy inputs for competing industries. While such action would not be strictly motivated by environmental concerns, if it resulted in restrictions on such policies it could have a positive knock-on effect for the environment. The discussion below on GATT will concentrate exclusively on Articles XI ('General Elimination of Quantitative Restrictions') and XVII ('State Trading Enterprises') as these are of particular relevance to dual pricing. Note that when considering the arguments below, Article XX GATT defences should always be kept in mind, as members operating dual pricing policies may argue that the practice serves certain legitimate and social objectives, especially in the face of global market volatility.

6.4.1   General Agreement on Tariffs and Trade (GATT): Articles XI and XVII

6.4.1.1   Article XI ('General Elimination of Quantitative Restrictions')

If administered in a way that restricts quantitative exports of an energy resource, a dual-pricing measure (other than duties, taxes or other charges), may fall foul of Article XI: GATT, which prohibits quantitative import and export restrictions on goods. Members may be applying

---

[43] On why this should be so, see Asmelash (n 10); D De Bièvre, Ilaria Espa and A Poletti, 'No Iceberg in Sight: On the Absence of WTO Disputes Challenging Fossil Fuel Subsidies' (2017) 17 International Environmental Agreements 411.

[44] AA Marhold, 'The World Trade Organization and Energy: Fuel for Debate' (2013) 2(8) ESIL Reflections; Selivanova (n 33).

restrictive measures to fossil fuels in the hope of creating a higher (artificially inflated) demand for such vital goods on the export market, causing the export price to rise above the domestic price.[45] It should be noted that the ultimate goal of using Article XI:1 to tackle dual pricing is not to bring the export price of the fossil fuel in question down to the same (artificially) low price level as maintained in the exporting country. For this would not solve the negative environmental impact of dual pricing: fossil fuels would continue to be wastefully burned. The idea is rather to even out domestic and export prices by ensuring that the fossil fuel in question is sold in the exporting country's domestic market at the same price as that prevailing on the global market. This will enable green energy to become more competitive and incentivize countries that apply dual pricing policies to switch to cleaner means.

A caveat is called for here, however: it is essential to determine at what stage in the process Article XI:1 becomes applicable to the natural resource in question (cf application of OPEC production quotas).[46] While case law (eg *Japan – Semiconductors*, *Argentina – Import Measures* and *India – Quantitative Restrictions*) suggests that the wording of Article XI:1 should be interpreted broadly, it is unclear to what extent it would cover production quotas and ceilings on fossil fuels in their natural state (ie before extraction, when still in the ground).[47] Many would argue that this is a matter falling within a member's sovereignty over its natural resources and therefore not subject to WTO disciplines.[48] With regard to natural resources, there is a fine line between quantitative export restrictions and production quotas, as evidenced by China's binding commitments on export duties on critical raw materials in its accession protocol. China agreed to bind its export duties on several raw materials and rare earths and to eliminate other export restrictions (such as licensing). This became a central issue in the *China – Raw Materials*

---

[45] Pogoretskyy (n 1) 219; AA Marhold, 'WTO Law and Economics and Restrictive Practices in Energy Trade: The Case of the OPEC Cartel' (2016) 9 Journal of World Energy Law and Business 475, 479–82.

[46] See Chapter 5. See also Marhold (n 45); M Cossy, 'Energy Trade and WTO Rules: Reflections on Sovereignty over Natural Resources, Export Restrictions and Freedom of Transit' in C Herrmann and JP Terhechte (eds), *European Yearbook of International Economic Law* (Springer 2012).

[47] *Japan – Semiconductors*, GATT panel report, paras 104–109; *Argentina – Hides and Leather*, panel report, para 11.17; *India – Quantitative Restrictions*, panel report, para 5.119; Marhold (n 45) 484–85. See also Chapters 1 and 5.

[48] UNGA Res 1803 (XVII) (18 December 1962) 'Permanent Sovereignty over Natural Resources'; see Chapters 1 and 5.

and *China – Rare Earths* cases.[49] The panels and the Appellate body found that China had breached its commitments, whereupon China transformed its export duties on these raw materials into production quotas, in much with the same way as OPEC's restrictive practices on petroleum.[50]

The issue becomes more difficult if dual pricing is administered through an export tax. In contrast to export restrictions, export taxes are admissible under GATT. Historically, GATT's preoccupations were access to markets and reducing protectionism rather than export restrictions, as GATT was originally negotiated to protect importers from protectionist measures.[51] Dual pricing by means of an export tax on an energy commodity favours the economy of the Member applying the tax in three possible ways: first, it can contribute to the general budget of the state in question; second, it can directly benefit the energy industry of that state; and third, it creates a discrepancy between the end price of a good on the export market and its domestic price, leading to cheaper inputs that make domestic energy-intensive industries more competitive. While export taxes may not be protectionist in the strict sense towards the industry of the exporting country, they nevertheless accord an advantage to the (industry of the) member applying the tax, and can therefore arguably be considered as protectionist in a wider sense. In this context, it is worth noting that the fact that export taxes are not explicitly regulated in GATT does not mean that a member cannot challenge them in dispute settlement. Since case law takes a very broad view of what constitutes a de facto quantitative restriction, a panel would have to decide whether the effect of the export tax in question amounts to a *de facto* export restriction contrary to GATT Article XI:1.

In this light, the implications of a partial WTO-wide reform of disciplines on export taxes should be explored. Generally speaking, taxes are levied domestically by governments on income, property and sales. A tariff, on the other hand, is a tax imposed on imported (or exported) goods and services as a tool available to shape international trade policy. It could, however, be argued that, although not regulated in GATT,

---

[49] *China – Raw Materials, China – Rare Earths*, panel and Appellate Body (AB) reports.

[50] See Chapter 5; SE Rolland, '*China-Raw Materials*: WTO Rules on Chinese Natural Resources Export Dispute' (2012) 16(21) *ASIL Insights* <www.asil.org/insights>; I Espa, *Export Restrictions on Critical Minerals and Metals: Testing the Adequacy of WTO Disciplines* (CUP 2015).

[51] K Bagwell, RW Staiger and AO Sykes, 'Border Instruments' in H Horn and PC Mavroidis (eds), *Legal and Economic Principles of World Trade Law* (CUP 2015) 129.

export taxes in effect function as export tariffs, as they restrict cross-border trade. An effective option could be to ensure that WTO members transform any export tax they maintain into an (export) tariff. This would significantly increase the transparency of the use of export taxes and dual pricing, as they would become subject to Article II:1 GATT (on schedules of concessions). It would also facilitate the negotiation and reduction of dual pricing maintained through export taxes.

Alternatively, members may try to compensate for export taxes on fossil fuels by imposing a carbon tax on the energy commodities in question. As fossil fuels are slowly losing their competitiveness owing to the rise of clean and renewable energy, export taxes may become a less attractive option, especially if the importing country is no longer so dependent on the fossil fuel due to a more varied energy mix, offering a broader choice in cleaner energy.

6.4.1.2   Article XVII (State Trading Enterprises)

Article XVII GATT on state trading enterprises (STEs) provides that if a WTO member maintains an STE, 'such enterprise shall, in its purchases or sales involving either imports or exports, act in a manner consistent with the general principles of non-discriminatory treatment prescribed in this Agreement for governmental measures affecting imports or exports by private traders'.[52] What exactly constitutes an STE remains unclear and open to interpretation, which may prove to be problematic. However, it may be assumed that traditional fossil fuel enterprises under government ownership or control (such as Saudi Aramco) would fall into this category.[53] Moreover, Article XVII also covers enterprises that have been granted 'exclusive or special privileges' by the government.[54] Selivanova is of the opinion that special rights and privileges can be assumed if 'it appears that rights or privileges can be considered exclusive or special if they enable the enterprise to influence trade flows'.[55] This is an important addition. Major energy exporting states often operate through state-owned energy enterprises and it is a fact that dual-pricing policies have significantly impacted on the terms of the global

---

[52] General Agreement on Tariffs and Trade, Marrakesh Agreement Establishing the World Trade Organization, Annex 1A (signed 15 April 1994) 1867 UNTS 187 (1994) 33 ILM 1153 (GATT 1994), art XVII:1. See also Chapter 3.

[53] Saudi Aramco, also known as the Saudi Arabian Oil Company, is the national petroleum and natural gas company of Saudi Arabia.

[54] Pogoretskyy (n 1) 220–22.

[55] ibid; Selivanova (n 1) 100.

trade in fossil fuels. So, if a WTO member owns an energy company that qualifies as an STE and that company operates dual-pricing policies, it is likely to be considered as behaving in a discriminatory manner contrary to Article XVII:1(a) GATT (and not solely in accordance with commercial considerations (Article XVII.1(b) GATT)).[56] WTO members wishing to act against members maintaining dual pricing would do well to explore this avenue, too.

6.4.2 Agreement on Subsidies and Countervailing Measures: Dual Pricing as a Prohibited or Actionable Subsidy

The Agreement on Subsidies and Countervailing Measures (SCM Agreement) is the most widely used agreement that is capable of effectively dealing with dual-pricing practices. Numerous scholars and policymakers, including Selivanova, Pogoretskky, Rolland and Espa, have explored ways of taming dual pricing by means of the SCM Agreement.[57] They will be discussed in this section, along with other options available under the agreement.

The rationale behind the SCM Agreement is to protect WTO members' national industries from the negative cross-border effects of state subsidization of the same industries in other WTO member countries. Article 1.1 of the SCM Agreement provides that a subsidy exists if there is (1) 'a financial contribution by a government or any public body within the territory of a Member' or (2) 'any form of income or price support in the sense of Article XVI of the GATT 1994' by a government or public body in a WTO member, through which a benefit is conferred upon its recipient.[58] Article 2 of the SCM Agreement further provides that, to be subject to the provisions of the agreement, a subsidy must be specific to an enterprise or industry

---

[56] It should be noted that, depending on the market, it might make commercial sense to charge a higher price abroad than domestically. If purchasing power is higher abroad than in the domestic market, then charging a higher price abroad is understandable.

[57] See n 2 above; Espa and Rolland (n 34) 6–7; AA Marhold 'WTO Subsidies Rules: Implications for Energy' in L Hancher, A De Hauteclocque and FM de Salerno (eds), *State Aid in the Energy Sector* (Hart 2018) 91; R Howse, *Securing Policy Space for Clean Energy under the SCM Agreement: Alternative Approaches* (E15 Initiative Think Piece, International Centre for Trade and Sustainable Development and World Economic Forum December 2013).

[58] Agreement on Subsidies and Countervailing Measures, Marrakesh Agreement Establishing the World Trade Organization, Annex 1A (signed 15 April 1994) 1869 UNTS 14 (SCM Agreement) art 1.1.

or group of enterprises or industries.[59] The SCM Agreement distinguishes between prohibited subsidies (Article 3) and actionable subsidies (Article 5).[60] Pursuant to Article 4 (Remedies), WTO members negatively affected by other members' subsidies have two options: they can refer their complaint to dispute settlement in the hope that a panel will judge the subsidy either prohibited or actionable and order that it be withdrawn or its adverse effects removed.[61] If the subsidizing member does not follow the recommendations made in the dispute settlement proceedings, the affected member may take countervailing measures as set out in part V of the SCM Agreement.[62] The affected member may initiate countervailing investigations pursuant to Article 11, possibly leading to the application of countervailing duties in accordance with Article 19.

Once it has been established that a certain measure qualifies as a subsidy as defined in the SCM Agreement, there are thus several options for redress available to WTO members. The difficulty, however, will be to ensure that dual pricing can be so qualified. Depending on the form a dual-pricing measure takes, there is a plausible argument to be made that it fits the definition of subsidy in Article 1 of the SCM Agreement. For instance, setting cheaper energy input prices for energy-intensive industries, made possible through dual-pricing practices, could be considered as government provision of goods and services, albeit in an unconventional, 'inverted' manner.[63] The argument would be that the government provision of a natural resource at less than fair market value (the dual-pricing practice) confers upon the member's domestic producers a benefit that qualifies as an actionable or prohibited subsidy. Intermediate consumers (firms) can be considered thereby to have been subsidized, as they benefit from lower input prices for their energy-intensive industries.[64] While this argument may not catch all dual-pricing schemes, it may be effective for some of them. Hence, a governmentally instituted dual-pricing programme could be seen as a form of financial contribution under Article 1.1 of the SCM Agreement.[65]

---

[59] ibid, art 1.1, 1.2.
[60] ibid, arts 3, 5.
[61] Note, however, that the case would need to meet the 'pass-through' test as expounded in *US – Softwood Lumber IV*, AB report, para 143. See Pogoretskyy (n 1) 226.
[62] SCM Agreement, pt V.
[63] *World Trade Report 2010* (n 1) 173–74; Pogoretskyy (n 1) 236.
[64] *World Trade Report 2010* (n 1) 173–74.
[65] SCM Agreement, art 1.1(a)(1)(iii); *World Trade Report 2010* (n 1) 173ff.

The challenge here is that if the financial gain from dual-pricing schemes can be understood as creating a general benefit or enhancing aggregate welfare for the member concerned, it may not be deemed specific within the meaning of Article 2 of the SCM Agreement and therefore fall outside the legal definition in Article 1. Consumer, as opposed to producer, subsidies are especially difficult to qualify as specific, as they often benefit a large category of consumers in a member country.[66] However, it could be argued that dual pricing confers a benefit specific to the energy industry (eg an upstream subsidy to the energy industry) and industries heavily reliant on energy inputs. Consequently, it would be sensible to focus on dual pricing as a subsidy to producers and attempt to prove that dual pricing gives them a benefit that is specific to them within the meaning of Article 2.

According to Article 5(c) of the SCM Agreement, a subsidy has an adverse effect on a WTO member when the subsidized imports cause 'serious prejudice' to the interests of another member; as a result, they become actionable.[67] Elaborating on this, Article 6 of the SCM Agreement lists the kinds of subsidies that may give rise to 'serious prejudice'. The panel in *Korea – Commercial Vessels* further elucidated the concept of 'serious prejudice' as being concerned with negative effects on a member's trade interests related to a particular product.[68] This may manifest as a drop in import or export volumes or market share, adverse price effects, or both, in the relevant market.[69]

If a complaining member can prove that dual pricing is a subsidy of a kind mentioned in Article 6, 'serious prejudice' is deemed to exist and will make the subsidy actionable. An illustration is the case the United States brought against China in 2017, *China – Subsidies to Producers of Primary Aluminium*. The United States complained that China's actions in the aluminium sector violate WTO rules on subsidies rules and cause 'serious prejudice' to other WTO members. The dispute can be considered as relating to dual pricing of aluminium, as China is accused of undercutting global prices for aluminium and forcibly expanding China's market share by providing the industry with state loans, coal, electricity and raw materials at artificially cheap rates. Although the case could

---

[66] PC Mavroidis, *Trade in Goods* (2nd edn, OUP 2012) 524; Quick (n 5) 195.

[67] P van den Bossche and W Zdouc, *Law and Policy of the World Trade: Texts, Cases and Materials* (3rd edn, CUP 2013) 785.

[68] ibid 786.

[69] ibid.

possibly set a precedent over dual pricing, for the moment it appears to have stalled at the consultations stage.

To summarize, if a certain dual-pricing measure falls within the definition of a subsidy in Article 1 SCM Agreement, a WTO member harmfully affected by the measure could argue that the practice is contrary to Articles 3 or 5 of the SCM Agreement. It could then initiate dispute settlement proceedings or countervailing duty (CVD) investigations. Countervailing duties would be a particularly effective means of counteracting the negative effects of dual pricing: they can be imposed unilaterally and deter countries from maintaining dual-pricing policies. However, it could be risky to use CVDs for environmental purposes, where they are likely to be applied in a discriminatory way. Moreover, they favour large markets, as uncompetitive local producers have no need to export. But, as already pointed out, this has not as yet been the subject of dispute settlement proceedings, and only a case decision could bring certainty to the matter.

Last but not least, it is important to mention Article 25 of the SCM Agreement ('Notifications') in relation to dual pricing and FFS more generally. Pursuant to Article 25.2, members 'shall notify any subsidy as defined in paragraph 1 of Article 1, which is specific within the meaning of Article 2, granted or maintained within their territories'. Although this should reinforce subsidy notification, especially with regard to FFS, including dual pricing[70] However, as observed earlier, FFS reform depends on collective action, yet the possibility that such a step could be perceived as self-inflicted harm may make self-notification difficult to enforce under current subsidy rules. Article 25.10 on counter-notification might offer a solution in this respect.[71] It states that:

> Any Member which considers that any measure of another Member having the effects of a subsidy has not been notified in accordance with the provisions of paragraph 1 of Article XVI of GATT 1994 and this Article may bring the matter to the attention of such other Member. If the alleged subsidy is not thereafter notified promptly, such Member may itself bring the alleged subsidy in question to the notice of the Committee.

This provision thus allows WTO members to bring FFS, including dual pricing, to the attention of the country imposing them, but also to alert the Committee on Subsidies and Countervailing Measures.

---

[70] Asmelash (n 16) 13–14.
[71] ibid.

6.4.3 Anti-Dumping Agreement: Countering Dual Pricing by Adjusting the Dumping Margin

Apart from the SCM Agreement, the Anti-Dumping Agreement (ADA) can also be a useful and – given existing case law – perhaps more realistic tool in countering the negative impact of dual pricing.[72] According to Article 2.1 ADA, a product is dumped if it is introduced into the commerce of another country at less than its normal value. Dumping exists where the 'normal value' (ie the price of the product in the domestic market) exceeds the 'export price'. Echoing the subsidies debate, it could be argued that dual pricing is a case of 'reversed input dumping' – that is, goods (eg steel products) which benefited from cheap energy inputs through below-market energy prices can and are dumped on the market of the importing country at prices made possible by the cheapness of those inputs domestically.[73] The logic here is that, without such anti-competitive practices, the product would have been sold at a higher price on the export market.

A WTO member may apply anti-dumping duties (ADDs) against members involved in dual pricing (Article 9 ADA).[74] For that, the member in question will have to prove that the dumping is causing it injury, and that there is a causal link between the dumping and that injury (Article 3.5 ADA). To that end, it is necessary to establish first the 'normal value' of the dumped product and then the relevant 'export price'. To prove that imports have been dumped because they benefited from domestic energy prices that had been kept artificially low, a member may use one of the alternative methods of calculating the normal value of the product. It would entail constructing the normal value of the product in question based on what the production cost in the domestic market of the exporting member would have been were it not for the cheap energy input. Thus, prices for the energy input would need to be adjusted to reflect the higher rates charged elsewhere. This would allow the anti-dumping authority to ascertain that the normal value of the imported product is higher than the export price, and on this basis establish a case of

---

[72] Agreement on Implementation of Article VI of the General Agreement on Tariffs and Trade 1994, Marrakesh Agreement Establishing the World Trade Organization, Annex 1A (signed 15 April 1994) 1868 UNTS 201 (ADA).

[73] Pogoretskyy (n 1) 239.

[74] Note, however, that, according to Article VI:5 GATT, a WTO member cannot apply both CVDs and ADDs in the same matter.

dumping. It is uncertain, however, whether the ADA allows the normal value to be determined in this manner.[75]

In the case of dual-pricing practices, the method can be adapted, as foreseen in Article 2.2, by incorporating a comparison with costs in third countries and, if necessary, substituting these for exporters' actual energy costs, so as to allow for a larger dumping margin that more accurately reflects the extent of the harm caused to the member adversely affected by the dumping. At present, there are two pending WTO cases in which this matter is at issue: *EU – Cost Adjustment Methodologies and Certain Anti-Dumping Measures on Imports from Russia* and *EU – Anti-Dumping Measures on Certain Cold-Rolled Flat Steel Products from Russia*. In essence, the EU acted against Russian dual-pricing policies by imposing ADDs on imports of ammonium nitrate and cold-rolled flat steel products, using an alternative method for establishing the normal value of the product.[76] In both instances, Russia is objecting to the way the EU has calculated the anti-dumping margin.

While they do not primarily target the environmentally adverse impacts of dual pricing, ADDs provide states with an effective means of countering dual-pricing practices. That said, they can be a double-edged sword, bearing in mind that an estimated two-thirds of EU ADDs have been imposed on renewable energy technology, such as solar panels from China. Not that this should be considered a problem if dumping is actually taking place. Indeed, if correctly applied, ADDs on renewable energy technology are a way of protecting domestic producers of clean energy from the harmful effects of dumped imports.

6.5   Beyond Existing Rules: How Can the WTO Curb Dual Pricing and Promote Fossil Fuel Subsidy Reform?

The options available in the current WTO legal toolkit discussed above can provide a WTO member, or group of WTO Members, with the wherewithal to challenge the dual-pricing policies of another member. At the very least, bringing such a case to the multilateral trading forum would certainly draw attention to the need to phase out dual-pricing policies. It would also send a strong signal that such policies are not

---

[75] When calculating costs, the actual costs paid cannot be disregarded. See esp *China – Broiler Products*, panel report; *EU – Biodiesel (Argentina)*, AB report.

[76] Based on Council Regulation (EC) 1225/2009 of 30 November 2009 on protection against dumped imports from countries not members of the European Community [2009] OJ L343/51, art 2(3), and Commission implementing regulations.

immune to being challenged in WTO dispute settlement proceedings. Moreover, it is likely that such a move would trigger the rapid inclusion of talks on broader FFS reform on the WTO agenda.

In addition to the possibilities under existing rules examined in the previous section, there are other avenues for addressing the issues of dual pricing and FFS reform that go beyond existing WTO rules. Below, we will suggest how subsidy rules could be reformed to curb dual pricing and explore what role the WTO could play in contributing to broader FFS reform. It is imperative that the organization and its membership recognize how important it is to phase out dual pricing and reform FFS and understand the crucial role the WTO can and should play in achieving this. The options put forward below would additionally help to ensure greater transparency in the way FFS and dual-pricing policies are instituted, which is a precondition for successful reform.

Many have called for the existing WTO rules on subsidies to be amended, as they have been outdated by recent developments in response to the need to scale up clean energy production and combat climate change.[77] In fact, they have led to irrational outcomes, as in the *Canada – Renewable Energy* case, where the Appellate Body had to resort to legal acrobatics to avoid deciding that a feed-in tariff (FIT) was a subsidy within the meaning of the SCM Agreement.[78] There are indeed several ways in which reform of WTO disciplines on subsidies could help to curb dual pricing.

6.5.1   Amending the SCM Agreement: Inspiration from TTIP Negotiations and the EU-Ukraine DCFTA

The foregoing section explained how dual pricing can be considered an inverted input subsidy that affects cross-border trade. Amending the SCM Agreement by adding dual pricing to the prohibited subsidies listed in Article 3.1 would therefore be a straightforward solution to discipline the practice under WTO law. As previously mentioned, the EU and the

---

[77] L Rubini, 'Rethinking International Subsidies Disciplines: Rationale and Possible Avenues for Reform' (E15 Initiative Overview Paper, International Centre for Trade and Sustainable Development and World Economic Forum, November 2015); R Howse, *Climate Mitigation Subsidies and the WTO Legal Framework: A Policy Analysis* (IISD 2010); G Horlick and P Clarke, 'Rethinking Subsidy Disciplines for the Future Synthesis of the Policy Options' (E15 Initiative Policy Options Paper, International Centre for Trade and Sustainable Development and World Economic Forum January 2016); Espa and Rolland (n 34).

[78] *Canada – Renewable Energy / Canada – Feed-in Tariff Program*, AB report, para 5.246.

United States have indeed proposed exactly this in the past.[79] However, as also noted, this and similar proposals by WTO members have so far not won through in the multilateral trading context. Nevertheless, efforts to include dual pricing in the list of prohibited subsidies in Article 3.1 should be revived, at least in the medium and longer term, for two reasons: first, because momentum has been created as a result of climate change mitigation commitments and the 2030 SDGs, and second, because there are recent example references to dual pricing having been included in other major treaty negotiations and, more importantly, in the provisions of the resulting treaties. These examples give us an indication of what form such an addition to the SCM Agreement might take. We will consider, in particular, the draft texts proposed in the EU-US Transatlantic Trade and Investment Partnership (TTIP) negotiations and the inclusion of a provision on dual pricing in the EU-Ukraine Deep and Comprehensive Free Trade Agreement (DCFTA) in the context of the EU-Ukraine Association Agreement.[80]

A possible prohibition on dual pricing has come up at several stages in the TTIP negotiations. Back in 2013, the EU proposed to include dual pricing in its talks with the United States, as it believed this could improve competitiveness and transparency in raw materials and energy markets.[81] In its initial position paper, the EU stated that:

---

[79] *World Trade Report 2010* (n 1) 174:

> Canuto and Fienberg [n 34] note that a provision specifically dealing with dual pricing of government-supplied inputs was included in an early draft of the SCM Agreement during the Uruguay Round negotiations. The provision, included in a November 1990 draft of Article 14, read as follows: 'When the government is the sole provider or purchaser of the good or service in question, the provision or purchase of such good or service shall not be considered as conferring a benefit, unless the government discriminates among users or providers of the good or service. Discrimination shall not include differences in treatment between users or providers of such goods or services due to normal commercial considerations.'

[80] European Commission, 'The Transatlantic Trade and Investment Partnership' <http://ec.europa.eu/trade/policy/in-focus/ttip/index_en.htm> accessed 20 July 2020; Office of the United States Trade Representative, 'Transatlantic Trade and Investment Partnership (T-TIP)' <https://ustr.gov/ttip> accessed 20 July 2020; Association Agreement between the European Union and Its Member States, of the one part, and Ukraine, of the other part' (signed 21 March 2014, entered into force 1 September 2017) [2014] OJ L161/3, ch 11.

[81] European Commission, 'EU-US Transatlantic Trade and Investment Partnership: Raw Materials and Energy' (Initial EU Position Paper, 2013) <http://trade.ec.europa.eu/doclib/docs/2013/july/tradoc_151624.pdf> accessed 20 July 2020, 3.

Government intervention in the price setting of energy goods on both the domestic market for industrial users and of energy goods destined for export purposes should be limited. A prohibition on dual pricing should further limit the possibility for resource rich countries to distort the market and subsidize sales to industrial users thus penalising foreign buyers and exports.[82]

Subsequently, in its first TTIP treaty text proposals in 2013, the EU included draft articles on export restrictions, domestic price regulation, dual pricing and trading and export monopolies.[83] The draft article on dual pricing (Article E) stated that:

'1 ... neither Party or regulatory authority thereof, shall adopt or maintain measures resulting in a higher price for exports of raw materials and energy goods to the other Party than the price charged for such goods and materials when intended for domestic industrial consumption.

2. The exporting Party shall upon request of the other Party provide the necessary information to substantiate that a different price for the same raw materials and energy goods sold on the domestic market and for export does not result from a measure prohibited by paragraph 1.[84]

In the draft treaty text proposed by the EU in 2016, this wording was replaced by an article on export pricing which amounted to the same as dual pricing:

A Party shall not adopt or maintain a higher price for exports of goods to the other Party than the price charged for such goods when destined for the domestic market, by means of any measure such as licenses or minimum price requirements.[85]

While TTIP negotiations are currently indefinitely on hold, the approach and text proposed by the EU could be partially used for a reform of the SCM Agreement to include dual pricing. Many of the issues identified by the EU in TTIP negotiations, including opposition to dual pricing and export restrictions, were championed by the United States.[86] These draft TTIP provisions were in fact inspired by successful commitments on dual

[82] ibid.
[83] European Commission, DG Trade, 'TTIP: Draft Non-Paper on Raw Materials and Energy' (EU-restricted) (20 September 2013), arts C–F.
[84] ibid, art E.
[85] European Commission, DG Trade, 'TTIP: EU's Proposal for a Chapter on Energy and Raw Materials in TTIP' (Note for the Attention of the Trade Policy Committee, 20 June 2016) art XXX ('Export pricing').
[86] KJ Benes, 'Considerations for the Treatment of Energy in the US-EU Transatlantic Trade and Investment Partnership' (September 2015) Columbia/SIPA Center on Global Energy Policy, 17.

pricing by acceding WTO members and a provision in the North American Free Trade Agreement (NAFTA).[87] The inclusion of such a provision in the SCM Agreement would therefore help to bring consistency to the regulation of dual pricing in international trade agreements.

More importantly, another example that could inspire reform of the SCM Agreement is the successful inclusion of a prohibition on dual pricing in the EU-Ukraine DCFTA. As discussed in Chapter 4, this EU FTA contains a chapter on trade-related energy.[88] Articles 269–71 of chapter 11 form its centre of gravity and explicitly prohibit any form of dual pricing and related discriminatory measures when trading in energy. Article 269(1) provides that the price for the supply of gas and electricity shall be determined on the basis of supply and demand only, although parties are allowed to regulate the price for purposes of 'general economic interest'.[89] If parties decide to do so, they must ensure that the method of calculating the regulated price is published prior to its entry into force.[90]

Dual pricing is prohibited altogether in Article 270. This GATT-plus requirement takes a very clear stance on the practice and is in line with the stance taken by the EU on dual-pricing policies in recent years. Although the prohibition does not link dual pricing with subsidization directly, it does so implicitly by including all measures that may result in dual pricing:

> 'neither Party or a regulatory authority thereof, shall adopt or maintain a measure resulting in a higher price for exports of energy goods to the other Party than the price charged for such goods when intended for domestic consumption.[91]

The same goes for customs duties and quantitative restrictions, which are prohibited unless justified on grounds of public policy or public security; protection of human, animal or plant life or health; or the protection of industrial and commercial property.[92] In such cases, the restrictions or measures may not be deemed to constitute arbitrary discrimination or a disguised restriction on trade between the parties. The EU-Ukraine

---

[87] Initial EU Position Paper, 2013 (n 81).
[88] EU-Ukraine DCFTA, ch 11.
[89] ibid, art 269(2).
[90] ibid, art 269(3).
[91] ibid, art 270(1).
[92] ibid, art 270(2).

DCFTA thus offers a very clear example of the legal form a prohibition on dual pricing could take in practice. If WTO members wish to include a rule on dual pricing in the SCM Agreement or in a potential plurilateral on (renewable) energy, the provisions in the EU-Ukraine DCFTA, plus those in the proposed TTIP text, may provide some guidance. Leastwise, it should be ensured that provisions of this kind are included in the accession protocols of new WTO Members. Additionally, when addressing subsidy disciplines more broadly, the way fishery and agricultural subsidies are being reformed could be instructive when it comes to FFS reform.[93]

The negative environmental impacts of dual pricing could also be offset by making room for policies that promote green energy, which existing WTO rules on subsidies do little to accommodate. The design of EU rules on state aid may serve as an inspiration here. In particular, the Commission Guidelines on State Aid for Environmental Protection provide a notable example on how EU members states can design their policies in support of green energy in a way that is consistent with the law on state aid.[94] The WTO could draft a similar set of guidelines for its members. Further, it should consider amending it subsidy rules so as to exempt certain forms of support for green energy. The EU's General Block Exemption Regulation (GBER) offers an elaborate model for the design of such exemptions.[95]

6.5.2   Including Fossil Fuel Subsidy Reform on the WTO Agenda

Although Section 6.3 pointed out that the trade-distorting aspects of dual pricing have been an ongoing subject of debate in the WTO for several decades, a wider discussion on the harmful effects and environmental impacts of FFS was long absent from the multilateral trading forum. Former Director-General Lamy emphasized in 2013 that the inability to include talks on FFS reform was a missed opportunity:

---

[93] See esp JP Trachtman, *Fossil Fuel Subsidies Reduction and the World Trade Organization* (2017) ICTSD Climate and Energy Issue Paper, s 3 ('Related Disciplines and Sources of Analogy'). For parallels with agricultural subsidies, see T Josling, *Rethinking the Rules for Agriculture Subsidies* (E15 Initiative Think Piece, International Centre for Trade and Sustainable Development and World Economic Forum January 2015).

[94] European Commission, 'Guidelines on State aid for environmental protection and energy 2014–2020' (Communication) [2014] OJ C200/1.

[95] Commission Regulation (EU) 651/2014 of 17 June 2014 declaring certain categories of aid compatible with the internal market in application of Articles 107 and 108 of the Treaty Text [2014] OJ L187/1 (General Block Exemption Regulation).

Similarly, the on-going political debate on reforming fossil fuel subsidies has largely bypassed the WTO. The surge in world energy prices in recent years has drawn high-level attention to fossil fuel subsidies, including by the G-20. The link between subsidies, consumption of energy and climate change has added a new dimension to the debate. Given that WTO members have decided to tackle the issue of environmentally harmful subsidies in the fisheries sector as part of the Doha Round, the absence of this topic from the WTO radar screen can be considered as a missed opportunity.[96]

However, WTO members are slowly but steadily realizing the contribution the organization can make to decarbonizing the energy sector, as well as to materializing the SDGs. At the eleventh ministerial conference in Buenos Aires in 2017, a group of twelve WTO members for the first time released a statement on fossil fuel subsidy reform,[97] in which they reached an understanding on (1) the rationalization and phase-out of inefficient fossil fuel subsidies that encourage wasteful consumption, and the need for the international community to join in these efforts; (2) the importance of taking full account of the specific needs and conditions of developing countries and of minimizing the possible adverse impacts on their development in a manner that protects the poor and the affected communities; and (3) the need to advance discussions within the WTO aimed at achieving ambitious and effective disciplines on inefficient fossil fuel subsidies that encourage wasteful consumption, including through enhanced WTO transparency and reporting that will enable proper evaluation of the effects of fossil fuel subsidy programmes on trade and resources.

Although, for the moment, the statement represents a modest initiative by a small group of WTO members, it may open the door to formalizing FFS reform discussions in the WTO. While some may argue – and correctly so – that the organization has more pressing matters on its plate and may need to reinvent itself completely, now may be the time not to waste a good crisis. It may offer the opportunity for the organization to reflect on the system and the space it allows in its

---

[96] WTO, 'Lamy Calls for Dialogue on Trade and Energy in the WTO' (29 April 2013) <www .wto.org/english/news_e/sppl_e/sppl279_e.htm> accessed 20 July 2020; P Lamy, *The Geneva Consensus: Making Trade Work for All* (CUP 2013) 121.

[97] Ministerial Conference, 11th Session, Buenos Aires, 10–13 December 2017 – Fossil Fuel Subsidies Reform Ministerial Statement (adopted 12 December 2017) WT/MIN(17)/54 (Chile; Costa Rica; Iceland; Liechtenstein; Mexico; New Zealand; Norway; Republic of Moldova; Samoa; Separate Customs Territory of Taiwan, Penghu, Kinmen and Matsu; Switzerland; and Uruguay).

substantive laws and institutional design for non-trade values such as sustainable development, including the phase-out of environmentally harmful fossil fuel subsidies. In terms of climate change mitigation, there could not be a better time, considering that oil prices are at a historic low and, more importantly, given the climate commitments that most of WTO members have made in the context of the 2015 Paris Agreement and the United Nations 2030 Sustainable Development Goals (SDGs).[98] To begin with, efforts should centre on awareness-raising rather than binding commitments: the initial goal should be to ensure that the issue of FFS reform is openly discussed in the forum, for instance within the framework of the Committee on Trade and Environment.

Apart from initiating discussions on FFS reform, the WTO could also contribute to more transparency on FFS through the Trade Policy Review Mechanism (TPRM). As Asmelash argues, members' trade policy reviews could include a section on FFS reform and restrictive practices in natural (energy) resources.[99] This would provide a means of monitoring countries' progress and actions in reforming FFS.

In addition, members should explore options for a plurilateral agreement on (sustainable) energy. Plurilateral agreements have a narrow group of signatories, although the issues they deal with can be of interest to a substantial number of WTO members. Those currently in force are the Trade in Civil Aircraft Agreement and the Government Procurement Agreement.[100] Several policy-makers and academics have pointed to the advantages such an agreement could have.[101] One of the main arguments in favour of such an agreement is that current WTO rules are not necessarily suited to dealing with the intricacies of the energy sector. A plurilateral agreement on (sustainable) energy would cater to like-minded WTO members interested in a better-equipped set of rules on energy and would moreover offer a perfect framework in which to draw up rules curbing FFS and constraining dual pricing. Such an agreement could contain a clause multilateralizing concessions if the required

---

[98] See A Eliason, 'Using the WTO to Facilitate the Paris Agreement: A Tripartite Approach' (2019) 52 Vanderbilt Journal of Transnational Law 545.

[99] Asmelash (n 16) 14.

[100] See WTO, 'Plurilaterals: Of Minority Interest' <www.wto.org/english/thewto_e/wha tis_e/tif_e/agrm10_e.htm> accessed 20 July 2020.

[101] G Marceau, 'The WTO in the Emerging Energy Governance Debate' in Pauwelyn (n 5) 26; International Centre for Trade and Sustainable Development (ICTSD), 'Fostering Low Carbon Growth: The Case for a Sustainable Energy Trade Agreement' (ICTSD Global Platform on Climate Change, Trade and Sustainable Energy 2011).

number of WTO members adhere to the agreement.[102] Besides policies constraining dual-pricing practices, the agreement could also focus on key trade-related issues for (sustainable) energy, such as tariffs, non-tariff barriers (NTBs), subsidies, government procurement, services, export restrictions, domestic energy regulation, trade facilitation and transit issues.[103] It should be mentioned, though, that all members – even those that do not participate in the plurilateral – would have to adopt such an agreement by consensus, as set out in Article X:9 of the WTO Agreement.[104]

For the abovementioned initiatives to gain ground, it is moreover essential that the WTO builds bridges with other organizations and initiatives focused on FFS reform. This will not only avoid duplication but also strengthen and streamline existing efforts in FFS reform, leading to a bigger political push. Such efforts should go beyond coordination between the WTO and the G7 and G20. FFS reform initiatives within the WTO could also be linked to the UNFCCC and the commitments included in the Paris Agreement, which requires countries to regularly submit nationally determined contributions (NDCs) detailing how they will contribute to prevent a global 1.5°C temperature rise.[105] These NDCs could contain sections on action undertaken in the area of FFS reform and could even be linked in this regard to members' trade policy reviews.

Other organizations with which the WTO should coordinate on FFS reform include the International Energy Agency and the International Monetary Fund. Coordination could begin as bottom-up exploratory talks on standardizing terminology, monitoring and notification methods, as well as the welfare policies needed if FFS are replaced.

6.6   Conclusion

Climate change mitigation is perhaps the most pressing challenge of our time and decarbonizing our energy markets could significantly contribute to that goal. To achieve this, however, the energy sector needs to be substantially reformed. The institutional framework of the WTO as well as its trade rules, even if not specifically designed to tackle FFS reform, could positively influence it. One way of doing so is to tackle

---

[102] ICTSD (n 101) 63.
[103] ibid.
[104] Marrakesh Agreement Establishing the World Trade Organization (signed 15 April 1994) 1867 UNTS 154 (1994) 33 ILM 1144.
[105] UNFCCC, art 2(a).

energy dual-pricing practices in the forum. Dual-pricing policies have been at the centre of heated debates in the multilateral trading forum for decades. Initiated mainly by the net energy importers among WTO members, discussions have predominantly focused on the trade-distorting aspects of dual pricing, neglecting the significant negative impact that these practices have on the environment. The adverse effects of dual pricing on the environment stem from the fact that countries sell their fossil fuel energy domestically at rates far below the global market price, thereby encouraging wasteful consumption and hampering diversification to cleaner energy sources.

Under existing rules, WTO members opposed to dual pricing could challenge those members that maintain such practices on the basis of Articles XI ('General Elimination of Quantitative Restrictions') and XVII ('State Trading Enterprises') GATT, for instance. Dual pricing could also be challenged under the SCM Agreement as an actionable or prohibited subsidy. The ADA0 would also provide an avenue for curbing the practice where the normal value of the dumped product is adjusted to take account of the cheapness of energy inputs in the dumping country.

In a second phase, the WTO could look beyond the existing rules of the multilateral trading system. The chapter revisited the idea of amending the SCM Agreement by adding dual pricing to the list of prohibited subsidies in Article 3.1. Negotiators would do well to consult the EU-Ukraine DCFTA provisions and the draft texts drawn up in the context of TTIP negotiations for concrete examples of the form provisions prohibiting of dual pricing could take.

For any such efforts to be fruitful in the WTO forum, however, it is of utmost importance that the organization include on its agenda the broader issue of FFS reform. While discussions may be initiated in a bottom-up, informal manner, they could path the way for the WTO to take tangible steps to increase transparency and, eventually, reform and reduce FFS. For instance, transparency in the administration of FFS could be considerably enhanced by including a section on fossil fuel subsidies in members' trade policy reviews.

The Emerging Concept of Energy Security in International Trade Law

7.1 Introduction

As pointed out in Chapters 2 and 3, the settlement of high-level disputes concerning trade in energy is a relatively new phenomenon in the multilateral trading system, although their number is steadily growing. The emergence of such disputes has brought to the fore energy-related concepts not previously faced by WTO panels and the Appellate Body (AB).

One such concept, of central importance, is 'energy security'. Although there is no internationally accepted legal definition of this multi-layered notion, which international relations literature has criticized for its vagueness, the term is widely used in energy-related treaties, as well as in preferential trade agreements (PTAs). In the WTO context, the term is rather novel but has recently started being used by states when referring to measures taken in connection with safeguarding their national energy supplies. On the ground, WTO panels and the AB have been required to interpret the meaning of the concept and to consider arguments connected to energy security in two disputes.[1] In *India – Solar Cells*, the AB examined India's attempt to avail itself of the Article XX(j) GATT exception ('essential to the acquisition or distribution of products in general or local short supply') on energy security grounds.[2] And in *EU – Energy Package*, the panel had to decide on issues related to energy in two instances: first, in connection with the EU's security of supply assessment accompanying third-country certification measures for

---

[1] For more on energy security see AA Marhold, 'Externalising Europe's Energy Policy in EU Free Trade Agreements: A Cognitive Dissonance between Promoting Sustainable Development and Ensuring Security of Supply?' (2019) 3 Europe and the World 1, 5–6; S Yergin, *The Quest: Energy, Security, and the Remaking of the Modern World* (Penguin 2011) 266ff.

[2] *India – Solar Cells*, AB report 34ff.

pipeline transport services, and second, in relation to Europe's 'gas diversification supply' criterion for gas infrastructure incentives. Both of these measures were ultimately held to be discriminatory under GATT and GATS, respectively.[3]

The goal of this chapter is to shed light on the emerging notion of energy security in international trade and WTO law. Taking a two-pronged approach, the chapter will start by studying the meaning of the concept of energy security and its evolving role in international (trade) law, and then go on to critically assess how panels and the AB have dealt with energy security in past cases and ponder the question of its treatment in future disputes.

7.2 The Concept of Energy Security and Its Role in International Law

7.2.1 *Energy Security as a Concept in International Relations*

Societies have been faced with energy interdependency for centuries. However, it is clear that in an era of technological and digital advancements and an evermore globalized world, our dependence on energy systems becomes increasingly complex. It is clear that a secure energy supply guaranteeing the proper and reliable functioning of those systems is of vital importance to our economies (and arguably also our national security). The expression 'energy security' is used frequently in the field of international relations, as well as in international and national policy debates about a country's energy supply. Yet, when asked, we may be hard-pressed to provide a precise definition of the term. One is likely to associate it with the idea that there should be no shortage in the energy supply needed to keep the economy going. As Daniel Yergin aptly remarked, '[e]nergy security may seem like an abstract concern – certainly important, yet vague, a little hard to pin down'.[4]

It is no coincidence that, despite being familiar with the term, we find it difficult to define. After all, in international relations literature and policy, its content has for decades been the subject of debate. The underlying cause of this difficulty is that in international relations

---

[3] *EU – Energy Package*, panel report, paras 7.1061–7.1063, 7.1296–7.1300. The panel report was not adopted by the DSB because it was appealed. An impasse over the appointment of new AB members has prevented the AB from issuing a report. See case summary at <www .wto.org/english/tratop_e/dispu_e/cases_e/ds476_e.htm> accessed 20 July 2020.

[4] Yergin (n 1) 266.

literature and policy, the content of term energy security has for decades been subject to fierce debate.[5] In essence, the issue lies in the fact that there are two major lines of thought on the notion of energy security. One is extremely narrow, focussing on the technical issues surrounding, inter alia, the energy infrastructure, demand and supply, energy mix, pricing and differing types of energy consumers and producers.[6] The other is very broad, taking into account geopolitical energy challenges and their various defence-related and historical narratives, arguably at the cost of precision and coherence.[7] While recognizing the complexity of the concept, Yergin nonetheless puts forward an 'everyday life' definition of the term – namely, 'the availability of sufficient supplies at affordable prices'.[8] He goes on to unpack the concept by discussing its various dimensions. These are: (1) the physical dimension (eg the need to protect energy assets, infrastructure and supply routes); (2) the crucial dimension of access to energy; (3) the regulatory dimension (ie ensuring a system of governance of energy supply and demand on a national and global level); and (4) the investment dimension and its importance for long-term energy security.[9] It thus becomes clear that energy security is a multifaceted concept with many practical and political implications. As things stand, however, despite the fact that a vast number of

---

[5] See A Johnston and G Block, *EU Energy Law* (OUP 2012) ch 9; Energy Charter Secretariat (ECS), *International Energy Security: A Common Concept for Energy Producing, Consuming and Transit Countries* (ECS 2015) 10ff; P Raillon, 'Energy Regulation and Security of Supply: The European Regulators' Approach' (ARIAE-CEER high-level meeting, Madrid April 2010) <www.ceer.eu>; I Dreyer and G Stang, 'What Energy Security for the EU' (2013) European Union Institute for Security Studies 1; J Lilliestam and A Patt, 'Conceptualising Energy Security in the European Context: A Policy-Perspective Bottom-Up Approach to the Cases of the EU, UK and Sweden' (June 2012) SEFEP Working Paper 2012–4; R Metais, 'Ensuring Energy Security in Europe: The EU between a Market-based and a Geopolitical Approach' (2013) College of Europe EU Diplomacy Paper 03/2013; A Goldthau, 'Conceptualizing Energy Security' (2012) 46 Energy Policy 36, BK Sovacool and MA Brown, 'Competing Dimensions of Energy Security: An International Perspective' (2010) 35 Annual Review of Environment and Resources 77; BK Sovacool and others 'Exploring Propositions about Perceptions of Energy Security: An International Survey' (2012) 16 Environmental Science and Policy 44; A Goldthau, 'A Public Policy Perspective on Global Energy Security' (2012) 13 International Studies Perspectives 65; A Goldthau and BK Sovacool, 'The Uniqueness of the Energy Security, Justice, and Governance Problem' (2012) Energy Policy 232; D Yergin, 'Ensuring Energy Security', (2006) 85(2) Foreign Affairs 69; L Chester, 'Conceptualising Energy Security and Making Explicit its Polysemic Nature'(2010) 38 Energy Policy 887.
[6] ECS (n 5) 10.
[7] ibid.
[8] Yergin (n 1) 268.
[9] ibid 269.

academics and policy-makers have discussed and attempted to frame definitions (legal or otherwise) of energy security and energy supply security, no clear consensus has yet emerged on the meaning of these concepts.[10] As a result, no legally binding definition of energy security exists, whether at international or regional (eg in EU law) level.[11]

In this author's opinion, the explanations given by the International Energy Agency (IEA), the OECD-affiliated body set up to balance the interests of energy importing and exporting countries in the wake of the 1970s oil crises, is the nearest one comes to an 'official' and internationally accepted definition of energy security.[12] Although the IEA's 1974 founding instrument, the Agreement on an International Energy Programme, does not mention energy security in so many words, it does contain a wide array of provisions emphasizing the importance of preventing 'supply emergencies' and reminds governments of their special responsibility for energy supply.[13] Today, the IEA describes energy security in broad terms as 'the uninterrupted availability of energy sources at an affordable price'.[14] The United Nations offers an additional description, characterizing energy supply security as 'the continuous availability of energy in varied forms, in sufficient quantities, and at reasonable prices'.[15]

It is important to distinguish between two aspects of energy security: long-term energy security, which is addressed by making timely investments that take account of sustainable development needs, and short-term energy security, which means that the system must be capable of reacting adequately to sudden changes in supply and demand (as when there are disruptions in supply).[16]

Despite the many issues that are left unresolved by attempts to frame a definition of energy security, it is commonly understood that the

[10] See n 5 above.

[11] The EU has confirmed that there is no legal definition of energy security at the European level; see EC, 'In-depth Study of European Energy Security' (Staff Working Document) SWD (2014) 330 final, 166, accompanying EC, 'European Energy Security Strategy' COM (2014) 330 final.

[12] International Energy Agency <www.iea.org> accessed 20 July 2020.

[13] OECD, Agreement on an International Energy Programme (signed 18 November 1974, entered into force 19 January 1976) 1040 UNTS 271, preamble.

[14] See International Energy Agency, 'What is Energy Security?' <www.iea.org/topics/energysecurity/subtopics/whatisenergysecurity/> accessed 20 July 2020.

[15] United Nations Development Programme, World Energy Assessment: Energy and the Challenge of Sustainability (UNDP 2015) 112.

[16] ibid. See International Energy Agency, World Energy Outlook 2016 (IEA 2016) 86.

concept refers to a supply that is reliable, accessible and affordable.[17] Crucially, the supply must also be sustainable in the long term. It follows that the ability of energy markets to guarantee energy security depends on them being resilient to shocks (an example of which, in the European context, are the recurring gas transit disputes that took place between Russia and Ukraine in the 2000s and which directly affected a great many EU member states[18]). In essence, energy security must go hand in hand with a sustainable energy supply, one that can be guaranteed for future generations. This is the thrust of Goal 7 of the United Nations Sustainable Development Goals, which calls for access to affordable, reliable, sustainable and modern energy for all.[19] Hence, sustainable development is inseparable from the concept of energy security.

7.2.2   The Role of Energy Security in Public International Law

Notwithstanding the lack of an international legal definition of energy security, the concept's relevance to international energy relations and international affairs more broadly means that it necessarily becomes regulated by international law. All sources of international law (ie treaties, custom, general principles, judicial decisions and writings of publicists, as per art 38.1 ICJ Statute[20]) are of importance for the regulation of international energy relations, and some are more particularly relevant to guaranteeing energy security.[21] Treaties perhaps offer us the most straightforward and searchable source in this respect and they will therefore be our focus here, before we turn to the treatment of energy security in international trade and WTO law. It should be mentioned, however, that other sources of international law besides treaties, as well as other principles of public international law (eg the principle of sovereignty over natural resources affirmed in UN General Assembly Resolution 1803[22]), can also be considered important to energy security

---

[17] See n 12 above.

[18] See AA Marhold, 'The Russo-Ukrainian Gas Disputes, the Energy Charter Treaty and the Kremlin Proposal: Is There Light at the End of the Gas Pipe?' [2011] 3 Oil, Gas and Energy Law Journal <www.ogel.org>.

[19] Target 7.a calls for greater access to and investment in clean energy technology.

[20] Statute of the International Court of Justice (entered into force 18 April 1946) 33 UNTS 993.

[21] See S Bruce, 'International Energy Law' in R Wolfrum (ed), The Max Planck Encyclopedia of Public International Law, (OUP 2008) online edn.

[22] UNGA Res 1803 (XVII) (18 December 1962) 'Permanent Sovereignty over Natural Resources'.

where the resources in question are primary energy commodities (ie fossil fuels) falling under national sovereignty.

With regard to treaties, two types of instruments have a particular bearing on safeguarding energy security: (a) treaties whose purpose is specifically to set multilateral or bilateral rules in the energy sector, and (b) treaties that are not expressly conceived to regulate energy matters but whose scope is considered to cover such matters. Regarding the former (energy-specific agreements), these can be further divided into three sub-types: (i) multilateral treaties regulating (economic) activity in the energy sector, such as the Energy Charter Treaty (which regulates international trade and investment in energy);[23] (ii) multilateral treaties establishing international organizations responsible for particular strands of energy regulation, such as the Treaty Establishing the European Atomic Energy Community (Euratom) Treaty,[24] the Statute of the Organization of Petroleum Exporting Countries (OPEC)[25] or the OECD's decision to establish the International Energy Agency;[26] and (iii) traités-contrats between two or more countries, such as those regulating trade in gas or joint development in the energy sector.[27]

In some types of treaties express reference is made to ensuring energy security as being part of their purpose.[28] Those not specifically on energy whose scope nonetheless extends to energy (security) include the COP 21 Paris Agreement, as well as the rules of the World Trade Organization and bilateral investment treaties (BITs).[29] Multilateral or bilateral preferential trade agreements (PTAs) that contain energy-specific chapters can

---

[23] Energy Charter Treaty (adopted 17 December 1994, entered into force 16 April 1998) 2080 UNTS 100.

[24] Treaty Establishing the European Atomic Energy Community (Euratom) (entered into force 1 January 1958) 294 UNTS 261.

[25] Statute of the Organization of Petroleum Exporting Countries (1 May 1965) 443 UNTS 427 (1965) 4 ILM 1175.

[26] See n 11 above.

[27] On an example of such an agreement – regulating the Nord Stream 2 pipeline – see L Hancher and AA Marhold, 'A Common EU Framework Regulating Import Pipelines for Gas? Exploring the Commission's Proposal to Amend the 2009 Gas Directive' (2019) 37 Journal of Energy and Natural Resources Law 289, 289–303.

[28] eg Energy Charter Treaty.

[29] The United Nations Framework Convention on Climate Change (UNFCCC), UN Doc FCCC/CP/2015/L.9/Rev.1, Decision 1/CP.21 (adopted 12 December 2015), art 2.1(c) ('Making finance flows consistent with a pathway towards low greenhouse gas emissions and climate-resilient development'), which could be understood as a basis for fossil fuel subsidy reform and thus as implicitly referring to long-term, sustainable energy security; Marrakesh Agreement Establishing the World Trade Organization (signed April 15 1994) 1867 UNTS 154 (1994) 33 ILM 1144.

also be included in this category, as they are part of more general treaties regulating economic relations between countries (eg the EU-Ukraine Deep and Comprehensive Free Trade Agreement, which contains a chapter on matters related to trade in energy).[30] Below, we will briefly discuss energy security in the various kinds of treaties belonging to the first category – those that deal specifically with energy. We will then turn to the second category and address the role of energy security in international trade law more generally. Lastly, we discuss the emergence of the concept in selected WTO case decisions.

7.2.3   Energy Security in Energy-Specific Treaties

7.2.3.1   Multilateral Treaties Regulating (Economic) Activity in the Energy Sector: The Example of the ECT

The Energy Charter Treaty (ECT) is the most comprehensive multilateral treaty regulating international economic activity in existence. It is currently undergoing a process of modernization. It was originally conceived to integrate the energy markets of the countries of the former Soviet Union into the global economic system and attract investment in this sector in that part of the world.[31] It could therefore legitimately be argued that the ECT was conceived with long-term energy security as its backdrop, although nowhere in the ECT's legal texts is the concept defined. Energy security nonetheless looms large in the ECT treaties and accompanying documents. For example, the founding document of the ECT, the 1991 European Energy Charter, states that the representatives of the signatories are 'willing to do more to attain the objectives of security of supply and efficient management and use of resources'. Title I of the ECT mentions as one of its objectives that '[t]he signatories are desirous of improving security of energy supply and of maximising the efficiency of production'. And the Energy Charter Protocol on Protection of Energy Efficiency and Related Environmental Aspects refers to energy security in relation to protection of the environment. Only later, however, was the multifaceted importance of energy security

---

[30] EU-Ukraine Deep and Comprehensive Free Trade Agreement (EU-Ukraine DCFTA), ch 12. This is part of the wider Association Agreement between the European Union and Its Member States, of the One Part, and Ukraine, of the Other Part (signed 21 March 2014, entered into force 1 September 2017) [2014] OJ L161/3 (provisionally in force).

[31] On the origin and purpose of the ECT see TW Wälde (ed), *The Energy Charter Treaty: An East-West Gateway to Investment and Trade* (Kluwer Law International 1996). See also Chapter 4.

truly recognized, when it took centre stage in the 2015 International Energy Charter, a political declaration building on the ECT.[32] In this document, a link is repeatedly made between supply security and the trilemma of energy security, economic development and environmental protection, though once again without venturing to offer a definition of the concept.[33]

7.2.3.2 Multilateral Treaties Concerning Specific Strands of the Energy Sector

International Energy Agency (IEA)   The IEA was initially a separate energy programme and then a standalone agency created under the auspices of the OECD to regulate relations between energy exporting and energy importing countries following the 1970s oil crises. The agency's purpose reveals that energy security was an inherent part of its remit. Although there is no express reference to energy security in the agency's founding instrument, the preamble stresses the importance of preventing supply emergencies and expresses the desire to 'promote secure oil supplies'.[34] Also, many of the core rules laid down in the agency's founding instrument are directly related to security of energy supply, especially the emergency reserve commitments (eg on oil stocks) required of signatories.[35]

Energy Community Treaty   The Energy Community Treaty is a noteworthy example of a regional energy treaty. The treaty extends the European Union energy acquis, especially the requirement to unbundle energy production and transmission from the sale of energy, to a group of non-EU countries – Ukraine, Moldova, Georgia and several Balkan states.[36] Here, too, one of the underlying purposes of the treaty was to enhance security of energy supply for both the European Union and the other parties to the treaty. This is indeed stated in so many words in the preamble: 'Desiring to enhance the security of supply of the single regulatory space by providing the stable regulatory framework necessary for the region in which connections to Caspian, North African and

---

[32] Agreed Text for Adoption in The Hague at the Ministerial Conference on the International Energy Charter on 20 May 2015.

[33] ibid 11.

[34] Agreement on an International Energy Programme (n 13) preamble.

[35] ibid, art 3.1 and annex ('Emergency Reserves').

[36] Treaty Establishing the Energy Community (signed 25 October 2005, entered into force 1 July 2006) [2006] OJ L198/18.

Middle East gas reserves can be developed and indigenous reserves of natural gas, coal and hydropower can be exploited.'[37] Article 35 of the treaty provides for the adoption of plans to this end and makes the link between security of supply and renewable energy.[38] However, the article remains limited in scope, imposing an obligation of conduct on the parties rather than an obligation of results.

International Atomic Energy Agency (IAEA) and Euratom   Needless to say, one of the areas of energy regulation where security is of the essence is the nuclear energy sector. Here, however, here, security is referred to mainly in connection with the safety of the technology used rather than security of supply. This can be seen in the treaties concluded under the auspices of the International Atomic Energy Agency (IAEA). The concept of energy security does not feature as such in these treaties; their security dimension is rather focused on nuclear safety and security and the safety of nuclear power workers and plants.[39] The same goes for the Euratom Treaty, which creates a specialized market for nuclear energy in Europe. Although security plays an important role there as well, it concerns the safety and security of nuclear energy policies rather that security of supply.

Organization of Petroleum Exporting Countries (OPEC)   As discussed in depth in Chapter 5, OPEC is a Vienna-based international organization set up in the 1960s to represent the interests of major petroleum producing and exporting countries.[40] Given the extent of its influence on the supply side of the market, one could say that OPEC members have had (and continue to have) a considerable impact on the energy security of net importing countries of petroleum. OPEC's statute is understandably phrased to reflect the flip side of energy security. Without mentioning the concept in so many words, the statute describes OPEC's goals as being to 'devise ways and means of ensuring the stabilization of prices in international oil markets with a view to *eliminating harmful and unnecessary fluctuations*'.[41] The

---

[37] ibid, preamble.

[38] ibid, art 35.

[39] See the various treaties on nuclear safety and nuclear security concluded under the auspices of the IAEA <www.iaea.org/resources/treaties/treaties-under-IAEA-auspices> accessed 20 July 2020.

[40] See <www.opec.org> accessed 20 July 2020.

[41] OPEC Statute, art 2(b) (emphasis added).

accent is on the importance of a steady income for producing nations, vis-à-vis the 'efficient, economic and regular supply of petroleum to consuming nations'.[42] Security of energy demand, meaning the guarantee of continuing income for the energy supplied, is thus the other side of the energy security coin.

7.2.3.3   *Traités-Contrats* in the Energy Sector

The last category of energy-specific treaties comprises the so-called *traités-contrats* relating to the energy sector, which come in various forms.[43] They often incorporate terminology from various legal traditions as well as legal-technical fields, giving them a distinctive character which has earned them the collective label *lex petrolea*.[44] Their coverage is broad, ranging from agreements on transportation by pipelines or joint development in the oil, gas or renewable energy sector to cooperation in energy research and development. Depending on the type of treaty, the nature of the cooperation and the energy sector concerned, energy security will inherently arise, implicitly or explicitly in such agreements. An example is the agreement concerning the development of the Turkey-Greece-Italy gas transportation corridor.[45]

A brief review of specialized treaties in the energy sector shows that, to varying degrees, energy security plays a role in energy-specific treaties. It would seem that the broader the scope of the treaty in question, the broader its understanding and use of the concept of energy security, as illustrated by the ECT. In more specialized regimes, such as the IEA or OPEC, energy security also comes into play, but in a way that will depend on the treaty's subject matter (eg constitution of minimum oil stocks to prevent disruptions or ensure a stable flow of energy supplies; procurement of steady income for producers).[46]

---

[42] ibid.

[43] For a comprehensive overview of such contracts, see T Morgandi, 'Bilateral State Practice Concerning Energy Activities in International Law' <www.energybilaterals.org> accessed 20 July 2020.

[44] For an excellent explanation of this phenomenon, see K Talus, S Looper and S Oitillar, '*Lex Petrolea* and the Internationalization of Petroleum Agreements: Focus on Host Government Contracts' (2012) 5 Journal of World Energy Law and Business 181.

[45] Agreement among the Hellenic Republic, the Republic of Turkey and the Italian Republic concerning the development of the Turkey-Greece-Italy Gas Transportation Corridor (signed 26 July 2007) 119; see Morgandi (n 43) (note, however, that the references to energy security are manifold).

[46] See text accompanying nn 38, 45 and 46 above.

7.2.4 Energy Security in International Trade Law: WTO and PTAs

Although not a core theme of international trade law, energy regulation falls within its broader scope where cross-border trade is concerned. Below, we consider energy security in the context of WTO law generally and in preferential trade agreements (PTAs), and then analyse recent WTO case law on the subject.

7.2.4.1 WTO

The WTO regulates international trade in goods, services and intellectual property. As this book has shown, for a long time cross-border energy trade was mostly dealt with outside the multilateral trading system, although nothing in the GATT 1947 or the WTO agreements excludes trade in energy from their scope. Debates surrounding energy security first entered GATT discussions through the back door in the Tokyo Round (1973–79) at the time of the 1970s oil crises.[47] Industrialized countries such as the United States experienced a shortage of fossil fuels, which led to the inclusion of talks on petroleum, and specifically on export restrictions and export taxes, in the agenda of the Tokyo Round.[48] Debates on energy dual pricing and restrictive practices in natural resources continued to resurface in the multilateral trading forum during the ensuing decades. However, as issues concerning energy regulation were regarded as only remotely relevant to GATT, and later the WTO, energy security as such was never at the centre of discussions. The Dispute Settlement Body began to be confronted with arguments concerning energy security when parties started bringing cases that linked trade measures with aspects of energy security (as discussed in Section 7.3).

7.2.4.2 Preferential Trade Agreements

Preferential Trade Agreements (PTAs) oftentimes take up matters on which a consensus has not been reached at the multilateral level. The recent batch of free trade agreements concluded by the European Union (EU) are a good example. Several of these include specialized chapters on energy and raw materials, in particular the EU-Singapore FTA, the

---

[47] On the history of dual pricing, see Chapter 6, Section 6.3.

[48] During the Tokyo Round, export restrictions were taken up in Group 3(b); see GATT and Export Restrictions – Technical Note by the Secretariat (1 May 1974) MTN/3B/9. See also GATT Secretariat, Export Restrictions and Charges – Background Note by the Secretariat (8 August 1989) MTN.GNG/NG2/W/40.

EU-Ukraine DCFTA and the current text of the new EU-Mexico FTA (undergoing legal-linguistic revision at the time of writing).[49] In chapter 7 of the EU-Singapore FTA, which focuses predominantly on non-tariff barriers in the renewable energy sector, the expression 'safety of energy supply' is mentioned only in relation to exceptions, which are the subject of Article 7.6.[50] Energy security played a much more prominent role in the EU-Ukraine DCFTA, no doubt on account of the disruptions to gas transit caused by tensions between Ukraine and Russia in the 2000s. In its preamble, the parties express their commitment 'to enhance energy security, facilitating the development of appropriate infrastructure and increasing market integration and regulatory approximation towards key elements of the EU acquis, promoting energy efficiency and the use of renewable energy sources as well as achieving a high level of nuclear safety and security'. Chapter 11 of the agreement, entitled 'Trade-Related Energy', contains several provisions that are pivotal for energy security, covering such matters as the prohibition of energy dual pricing (Article 269), cooperation on infrastructure (Article 274) and supply interruptions (Article 276).

The newly negotiated text of chapter X of the EU-Mexico FTA, entitled 'Energy and Raw Materials', also reaffirms the commitment to eliminate energy dual pricing and promote the diversification of energy resources and allows parties to 'preserve their right to adopt, maintain and enforce measures necessary to pursue legitimate public policy objectives, such as securing the supply of energy goods and raw materials, protecting society, the environment, public health and consumers and promoting public security and safety'.[51] This is concrete evidence that the EU, as the continent most dependent on energy imports, is making serious efforts to ensure that energy security is addressed in its relations with its trading partners.[52]

On the other side of the Atlantic, the newly negotiated US-Mexico-Canada Agreement (USMCA) no longer contains an energy-specific

---

[49] For more on these chapters, see AA Marhold 'Externalizing Europe's Energy Policy in EU Free Trade Agreements: A Cognitive Dissonance between Promoting Sustainable Development and Ensuring Security of Supply?' (2019) 3 Europe and the World 1.

[50] EU Free Trade Agreement between the European Union and the Republic of Singapore (entered into force 21 November 2019) [2019] OJ L294/3.

[51] EU-Mexico Free Trade Agreement: 'The Agreement in Principle' (26 April 2018, updated May 2020) arts 4, 1(2).

[52] The EU imports almost 60 per cent of its fossil fuels from abroad; see Eurostat, 'Energy Production and Imports' <https://ec.europa.eu/eurostat/statistics-explained/index.php/Energy_production_and_imports> accessed 20 July 2020.

chapter, as was the case with its predecessor, the North-American Free Trade Agreement (NAFTA).[53] However, in the accompanying bilateral US-Canada side letter on energy both the United States and Canada have reaffirmed the importance of energy security in their cooperation.[54]

7.3   Energy Security as an Emerging Concept in WTO Dispute Settlement: Lessons from *India – Solar Cells* and *EU – Energy Package*

Although the multilateral trading system may have long steered clear of matters pertaining to energy, let alone security of supply, the subject has nonetheless made its way into WTO case law. During the years following the founding of the WTO in 1995, the make-up of its membership gradually started changing, with an increasing number of major energy producing and exporting countries joining the organization.[55] This coincided with major technological developments and the commercialization of the renewable energy sector, and led to a steady rise in energy-related trade disputes before the WTO.

In two recent WTO disputes concerning energy trade, *India – Solar Cells* and *EU – Energy Package*, India and the EU introduced arguments based on energy security to justify measures that had the effect of restricting trade.[56] The two disputes represent opposite sides of the spectrum of energy sources – renewable (solar) energy on the one hand, and fossil fuels (natural gas) on the other. We will discuss each case in turn and analyse in the various ways in which the concept of energy security was used and how the panel and the AB interacted with the parties' arguments on the subject.

---

[53] Agreement between the United States of America, the United Mexican States and Canada (signed 30 November 2018) (USMCA); North American Free Trade Agreement, 1 January 1994, 1867 UNTS 14 (NAFTA) ch 6 ('Energy and Basic Petrochemicals').

[54] USMCA, annex ('Energy Regulatory Measures and Regulatory Transparency') art 3.

[55] See Chapter 2, Section 2.4.2. WTO's membership already included several major energy producing countries and more have joined during the last two decades, such as Russia, Saudi Arabia and Kazakhstan. On their accession commitments, see AA Marhold and F Weiss, 'Energy and Fossil Fuels as a Topic in WTO Accession Protocols' in M Bungenberg and others (eds), *European Yearbook of International Economic Law 2018* (Springer 2018) 61.

[56] *India – Solar Cells*, panel and AB reports; *EU – Energy Package*, panel report (appealed by both parties but, for the moment, unable to be reviewed).

7.3.1 India – Solar Cells: *Long-Term Energy Security as a Justification for Domestic Content Requirements?*

In *India – Solar Cells*, the United States complained against India's measures on solar cells and solar modules. India had taken the measures in the context of the deployment of solar energy in particular regions as part of its larger Jawaharlal Nehru National Solar Mission (JNNSM).[57] As part of this mission, India concluded long-term power purchase agreements (PPAs) with solar power developers.[58] Guidelines were issued setting out the terms and conditions to be taken up in the PPAs; they included a requirement to use solar cells and modules manufactured in India.[59] The United States argued that these measures were a domestic content requirement (DCR) inconsistent with GATT Article III:4 GATT on national treatment and Article 2.1 of the Agreement on Trade-Related Investment Measures, as indicated in paragraph 1(a) of the Illustrative List annexed to the latter agreement.[60]

India first sought to justify the measure by (unsuccessfully) invoking the Article III:8 GATT government procurement exemption. More importantly, however, it also attempted to defend the measure by invoking the Article XX(j) GATT exception ('essential to the acquisition or distribution of products in general or local short supply') and linking it to India's overall energy security. This was the first time a WTO panel had to decide on this exception.

---

[57] On the deployment of the mission, see IEA, 'Jawaharlal Nehru National Solar Mission (Phase I, II and III)' <www.iea.org/policies/4916-jawaharlal-nehru-national-solar-mission-phase-i-ii-and-iii> accessed 20 July 2020.

[58] *India – Solar Cells*, panel report, para 7.2.

[59] ibid, paras 7.4–7.14.

[60] Paragraph 1(a) of the Illustrative List reads as follows:

> TRIMs that are inconsistent with the obligation of national treatment provided for in paragraph 4 of Article III of GATT 1994 include those which are mandatory or enforceable under domestic law or under administrative rulings, or compliance with which is necessary to obtain an advantage, and which require:
>   (a) the purchase or use by an enterprise of products of domestic origin or from any domestic source, whether specified in terms of particular products, in terms of volume or value of products, or in terms of a proportion of volume or value of its local production

The United States also argued that the measures were inconsistent with the Agreement on Subsidies and Countervailing Measures.

According to India, the overarching goal of the JNNSM was to 'establish India as a global leader in solar energy, by creating the policy conditions for its diffusion across the country as quickly as possible'.[61] Energy security was the broader underlying objective of the JNNSM, which, in India's words, 'aims "to promote ecologically sustainable growth while addressing India's *energy security challenge*", and ... will "constitute a major contribution by India to the global effort to meet the challenges of climate change"'.[62] India argued that the Article XX (j) GATT exception applied on the grounds that the country's lack of domestic manufacturing capacity in solar cells and modules, and/or the risk of a disruption in imports, placed these 'products in general or local short supply' within the meaning of that provision.[63] US importation of solar cells would, in India's opinion, put local solar cell production in India at risk of being in general or local short supply.[64]

India also tried to avail itself of Article XX(d) GATT ('necessary to secure compliance with laws and regulations which are not inconsistent with the provisions of this agreement'), arguing that the measures were necessary in view of wider climate change mitigation and sustainable development commitments.

Energy security loomed large in both arguments put forward by India to justify its recourse to Article XX(j) and (d) GATT. On more than one occasion India referred to the IEA's and the UNDP's definition of energy security, and throughout it stressed the overall importance of ensuring

---

[61] *India – Solar Cells*, panel report, para 7.1, citing 'Resolution, Jawaharlal Nehru National Solar Mission, Ministry of New and Renewable Energy (11 January 2010), (Exhibit USA-4), paras 1 and 2'.

[62] ibid, para 7.15 (emphasis added); see also paras 7.16–7.19 on energy security.

[63] Article XX(j) GATT reads:

> Subject to the requirement that such measures are not applied in a manner which would constitute a means of arbitrary or unjustifiable discrimination between countries where the same conditions prevail, or a disguised restriction on international trade, nothing in this Agreement shall be construed to prevent the adoption or enforcement by any contracting party of measures: (j) essential to the acquisition or distribution of products in general or local short supply; Provided that any such measures shall be consistent with the principle that all contracting parties are entitled to an equitable share of the international supply of such products, and that any such measures, which are inconsistent with the other provisions of the Agreement shall be discontinued as soon as the conditions giving rise to them have ceased to exist.

[64] *India – Solar Cells*, panel report, para 6.6.2.

energy security.[65] It stated that the DCRs were 'the only way in which India can "guarantee" that manufacturing units for solar cells and modules are actually set up in India, and achieve the objective of energy security by creation of a manufacturing base for solar cells and modules'.[66] India argued that these DCR measures needed to be seen in the context of India's overall energy scenario and the challenges it was facing at the time, due to its rising energy deficit, as well as its dependence on fossil fuels and imported materials in meeting its energy requirements.[67] It stated, inter alia, that 'one of the main goals for India is to secure the assured supply of environmentally sustainable energy and technologies at all times'.[68]

India was unsuccessful in its endeavours, however, as the panel found that its DCRs were trade-related investment measures corresponding to the description in paragraph 1(a) of the Illustrative List annexed to the TRIMs Agreement.[69] The panel also held that the DCR did not fall within the government procurement exemption provided in Article III:8 GATT.[70]

The panel adopted a narrow reading of Article XX(j) GATT as being confined to products already in short supply, and that therefore India's attempt to avail itself of the exception could not succeed. The panel took the view that the words 'products in general or local short supply' refer to a situation in which the total quantity of a product actually available from all sources of supply does not meet demand in a particular geographical area or market.[71] It also found that those words did not cover products *at risk of becoming* in short supply (in the future) and that in any event India had not demonstrated the existence of an imminent risk of a supply shortage.[72] Having regard to Articles 31 and 32 of Vienna Convention on the Law of Treaties (VCLT), the panel moreover noted that the ordinary meaning of products *in* short supply implies that the products are already

---

[65] ibid, paras 7.16–7.17; India's first written submission, para 188, citing the definition given in UNDP, *World Energy Assessment* (n 15):'the continuous availability of energy in varied forms in sufficient quantities at reasonable prices'.

[66] *India – Solar Cells*, panel report, para 6.6.2 (India's request for review of the interim report).

[67] ibid, para 7.17.

[68] ibid, para 7.16.

[69] See GATT, art III:4; TRIMs Agreement, art 2.1.

[70] *India – Solar Cells*, panel report, para 7.135.

[71] ibid, para 7.207.

[72] ibid, para 7.238.

wanting.[73] To complete its analysis, the panel considered other possible approaches to interpreting the meaning of Article XX(j) based on the genesis of the provision.[74] Again, nothing suggested that the provision was intended to cover potential shortages. On the contrary, they confirmed the panel's position, as the provision was originally meant to remain in force only for a three-year transitional period to deal with shortages following the Second World War.[75]

If the foregoing is considered in relation to the two dimensions of energy security discussed in Section 7.2.1 (long-term/short-term), it seems that India attempted to build its arguments for the Article XX(j) defence around long-term (and, arguably, sustainable) security of supply, whereas the panel would appear to have been receptive only to arguments based on immediate and actual (ie short-term) security of supply only (eg a disruption that hampers the supply of power to a region).[76]

On appeal, India again lost, although the AB did go some way to recognizing the long-term dimension of security of supply by engaging in an interesting discussion on the relationship between energy security and Article XX(j) GATT.[77] It linked the exception to energy security when weighing various considerations for the purpose of assessing whether products are in 'in general or local short supply'.[78] While not overturning the panel's decision, the AB set out the following guidance for comparable future cases. First and foremost, the AB recommended that future panels should examine 'the extent to which a particular product is "available" for purchase in a particular geographical area or market, and whether this is sufficient to meet demand in the relevant area

---

[73] ibid, paras 7.243–7.244.

[74] ibid, para 7.249.

[75] ibid. The panel continued (emphasis added):

> Furthermore, when the decision was taken to retain the provision indefinitely, in what became Article XX(j), it was agreed that the scope of the exception was "not limited to shortages subsequent to the war, but might be needed in the event of a natural catastrophe". While the text of Article XX(j) refers to product shortages without limitation to war, natural catastrophe, or other particular situations, the foregoing does not suggest that the concept of "products in ... short supply" was envisaged as covering *prospective shortages*.

[76] On the different dimensions of energy security, see Section 7.2.1. See also G Isaac and T Menon, 'When Good Intentions Are Not Enough: Revisiting the US-India Solar Panels WTO Dispute' (2017) 10 OIDA International Journal of Sustainable Development 37, 41.

[77] *India – Solar Cells*, AB report, paras 5.2.3–5.2.4.

[78] ibid, para 5.7.

or market'.[79] This would enable panels to take into account 'such factors as the relevant product and geographic market, potential price fluctuations in the relevant market, the purchasing power of foreign and domestic consumers, and the role that foreign and domestic producers play in a particular market, including the extent to which domestic producers sell their production abroad'.[80]

While it could be argued that there is a plausible connection between the overarching objectives of Article XX (j) GATT and safeguarding long-term energy security, defences connected to long-term energy security – or, in this case, the prospect of an energy supply shortage – will likely not prevail if they are discriminatory. It can be inferred from the panel's and the AB's reasoning that only an actual disruption in energy supply is likely to be capable of satisfying these criteria.

In conclusion, in its arguments India explicitly linked (long-term) energy security to sustainability and its obligations under the COP21 Paris Agreement and in relation to the environment and renewable energy. Though enhancing energy security by encouraging renewable energy may be a noble goal, current WTO rules cannot accommodate such schemes if they are discriminatory. It is beyond the scope of this chapter to elaborate on this predicament. Suffice to say that it is a corollary of the problematic balance in the multilateral trading system between values that are strictly trade-related and those that are not, such as sustainable development and environment.[81]

7.3.2   EU – Energy Package: *Energy Security as an Exception under GATS or GATT?*

In *EU – Energy Package*, the WTO panel was confronted with a larger geopolitical conflict between the European Union and Russia which had been simmering for years (and arguably continues to

---

[79] ibid.

[80] ibid, para 5.89.

[81] On the WTO crisis and the space afforded to non-trade values, see G Marceau, 'Never Waste a Good Crisis: The End of the WTO Dream, or the Beginning of Something Greater?' (2020) 17 International Organizations Law Review 345; A van Aaken and J Kurtz, 'Beyond Rational Choice: International Trade Law and the Behavioral Political Economy of Protectionism' (2019) 22 Journal of International Economic Law 601; S Charnovitz, 'In Clinical Isolation: Is There a Meaningful Place for the World Trade Organization in the Future of International Economic Law? A WTO If You Can Keep It' (2019) 6 Questions of International Law 1.

simmer).[82] It concerned legislation designed to extend EU competition policy into the energy sector by means of the so-called Third-
Energy Package (TEP), a set of rules aimed at dismantling vertically
integrated energy companies and introducing competition into the
energy sector in EU member states.[83] The instrument central to
accomplishing this in the EU internal market for gas was the Gas
Directive.[84] The TEP turned on the key concept of full ownership
unbundling (OU) – that is, the mandatory separation of extraction,
transmission and sales activities, which Article 9 of the Gas Directive
imposed on energy companies active in the EU internal market.
Given the considerable variation between EU member states in how
they structure their respective energy sectors, and taking into
account the differences in their geographical locations, their access
to natural resources and their (recent) history, the TEP gave them
several options for achieving full ownership unbundling in their
legislation. Because several EU member states still had vertically
integrated energy sectors and would therefore be unable to immediately realize full ownership unbundling, the TEP provided for (temporary) milder forms of unbundling.[85] In practice, this led to three
possible models of unbundling: the ownership unbundling (OU)
model, whereby the pipeline transport service supplier (also known
as the transmission system operator or TSO) is completely separate
structurally from entities engaged in the production or supply of
natural gas;[86] the independent system operator (ISO) model,
whereby the transmission system is owned by a VIU but operated

[82] *EU – Energy Package*, panel report. On the geopolitical conflict between the EU and
Russia over the legal regimes governing pipelines for importing gas to Europe (eg Nord
Stream II pipeline), see Hancher and Marhold (n 27); V Chornyi and AA Marhold, 'In
Uncharted Waters: The Contested Legal and Political Landscape of Nord Stream 2' in
MM Roggenkamp and C Banet (eds), *European Energy Law Report XIV* (Intersentia,
forthcoming) <https://papers.ssrn.com/sol3/papers.cfm?abstract_id=3677001> accessed
30 August 2020; K Talus and M Wüstenberg, 'WTO Panel Report in the *EU – Energy
Package* dispute and the European Commission Proposal to Amend the 2009 Gas Market
Directive' (2018) 37 Journal of Energy and Natural Resources Law 327.
[83] See also the discussion on decentralization in Chapter 5.
[84] Directive 2009/73/EC of the European Parliament and of the Council of 13 July 2009
concerning common rules for the internal market in natural gas and repealing Directive
2003/55/EC [2009] OJ L211/94 (Gas Directive); Regulation (EC) 715/2009 of the
European Parliament and of the Council of 13 July 2009 on conditions for access to the
natural gas transmission networks and repealing Regulation (EC) 1775/2005 [2009] OJ
L211/36.
[85] Johnston and Block (n 5) 73ff.
[86] Gas Directive, art 9.

by a TSO that is separate from the VIU and complies with the OU rules;[87] and the independent transmission operator (ITO) model, whereby the VIU owns and operates the transmission system, but has to comply with certain behavioural and organizational require-ments concerning the relationship between transmission and its other activities.[88]

Russia, with a supplier of large quantities of natural gas and to the EU and active in the gas markets of several EU member states, objected to various aspects of the Third Energy Package, including the national laws of Croatia, Hungary and Lithuania that implemented the package, claim-ing that the TEP measures were discriminatory.[89] The bulk of Russia's claims targeted the transposition of the Gas Directive in these EU mem-ber states where Russia considered itself disadvantaged by the milder forms of unbundling. Two measures, in particular, to which Russia objected centred on the concept of energy security.

The first was the 'third-country certification measure'.[90] At the heart of this claim were Russia's larger objections to Article 11 of the Gas Directive, dubbed the 'Gazprom Clause'. This article, which requires third-country (non-EU) TSOs (in this case gas pipeline operators) active in the EU internal energy market to be certified, has been a thorn in Russia's side ever since the adoption of the Third Energy Package, as the Russian state-owned company Gazprom is active on the gas market in several EU member states and thus directly con-cerned by the requirement. A condition for receiving certification from the member state concerned (and, ultimately, the EU) is that it 'will not put at risk the security of supply of the Member State and the Community'.[91]

Since this is a matter relating to the supply of services, it has to be litigated under GATS, and must be connected to the services schedules of individual EU member states in their capacity as WTO members, instead of the EU-wide schedule on goods. Although arguably objecting to the application of the rule across the entire EU, Russia therefore had to connect its claim to the services schedule of individual WTO members, meaning that it had to object to the transposition of the directive in each

---

[87] ibid, art 9(8).
[88] ibid.
[89] See Eurostat (n 52); *EU – Energy Package*, panel report, s 2.2.
[90] *EU – Energy Package*, panel report, para 2.2.7.
[91] Gas Directive, art 11.

of the three member states in question.[92] Russia challenged the third-country certification measure as implemented in the national laws of Croatia, Hungary and Lithuania on the basis of Articles II:1, VI:1, VI:5(a) and XVII (GATS concerning MFN treatment, standards of domestic regulation and national treatment).

The panel was of the opinion that the only claim made by Russia that came within the scope of GATS was the transmission of natural gas via pipeline systems, excluding supply and LNG services.[93] With regard to this measure, the EU invoked the general exception provided for in Article XIV(a) GATS ('necessary to protect public morals or to maintain public order'). Footnote 5 states that '[t]he public order exception may be invoked only where a genuine and sufficiently serious threat is posed to one of the fundamental interests of society'. In defence of third-country certification, the EU argued that this measure was necessary to ensure the security of energy supply in the EU and hence to maintain public order.[94] The EU further claimed that security of energy supply was a fundamental interest of society, in that energy is 'one of the most basic necessities of modern societies' and supply disruptions can have 'severe social, economic and, ultimately, political consequences'.[95] It further maintained that its security of supply policy is reflected in various laws, regulations and strategies, and that the third-country certification measure in the Gas Directive is but one legal means to that end.[96] Like India in *India – Solar Cells* (although concerning fossil fuels instead of renewable energy), the EU put forward arguments centred on long-term energy security. Here, however, they were connected to ownership of energy infrastructure and the implications thereof.

Interestingly enough, Russia did not take issue with the claim that the security of energy supply was a fundamental interest of society.[97] However, it did object to the way the EU framed security of energy supply in such a way as to, in Russia's words, 'maximize [the European Union's] discretion to define security of supply in the manner most

[92] Article 24 of Croatia's Gas Market Act, Section 128/A of Hungary's Gas Act and Article 29 of Lithuania's Law on Natural Gas, but not Sections 123(5) and 123(6) of Hungary's Gas Act; see *EU – Energy Package*, panel report, para 7.1116.

[93] *EU – Energy Package*, panel report, para 7.322. See also V Pogoretskyy and K Talus, 'The WTO Panel Report in EU–Energy Package and Its Implications for the EU's Gas Market and Energy Security' (2020) 19 *World Trade Review* 531.

[94] *EU – Energy Package*, panel report, para 7.1135.

[95] ibid, para 7.1145.

[96] ibid.

[97] ibid, para 7.1146.

advantageous to its overall objectives, to include reducing reliance on Russian pipeline transport services and natural gas imports'.[98] In essence, Russia's criticism was that neither the directive nor any other EU legal source defined security of energy supply and that, more generally, the EU failed to provide a clear definition of security of energy supply in its defence based on Article XIV(a) GATS.[99]

The EU's defence was not successful. Admittedly, the panel did agree with the EU that energy security 'is a fundamental interest of society within the meaning of footnote 5 to Article XIV(a) of the GATS'.[100] It also agreed that 'foreign control of TSOs poses a genuine and sufficiently serious threat to a fundamental interest of the EU society, namely its security of energy supply'.[101] But the panel reiterated that the responding member must show that the measure is both designed and necessary to protect public morals or maintain public order.[102] In short, the panel was not convinced by the EU's attempt to link energy security with the Article XIV(a) exception as a defence against Russia's claim.[103] First and foremost, the panel decided that similar threats to the security of gas supply were posed by both foreign and domestic TSOs.[104] Moreover, the panel saw 'no reason to conclude that there is no risk of domestic persons having commercial interests and/or personal and family links in foreign countries, which would render them vulnerable to requirements and inducements emanating from foreign governments'.[105] In conclusion, the panel found that the measure did not pass the legal test of the chapeau of Article XIV, and thus decided that under WTO rules it was discriminatory to subject non-EU TSOs to security of supply certification.[106]

Russia's second claim relating to security of energy supply concerned the so-called Trans-European Networks for Energy (TEN-E) measure,

---

[98] ibid, and Russia's opening statement at the second meeting of the panel, para 153.
[99] *EU – Energy Package*, panel report, para 7.1147.
[100] ibid, para 7.1156.
[101] ibid, para 7.1202; see also para 7.1239.
[102] ibid, para 7.230, citing *US – Gambling*, AB report, para 292. The AB relied on a similar legal standard when upholding a challenged measure on the basis of the general exception contained in Article XX(a) GATT (measures 'necessary to protect public morals') in *Colombia – Textiles*, AB report, para 5.67 and *EC – Seal Products*, AB report, para 5.169.
[103] *EU – Energy Package*, panel report, para 7.1217.
[104] ibid.
[105] ibid, para 7.1250; Pogoretskyy and Talus (n 93) 16. In the present author's opinion, one way of dealing with the issue would be for the EU to make intra-EU TSOs subject to a degree of risk assessments in relation to security of supply.
[106] *EU – Energy Package*, panel report, para 7.1254.

which it challenged under Articles I:1 and III:4 GATT.[107] The EU TEN-E Regulation sets out the criteria for designating certain cross-border infrastructure projects as projects of common interest (PCIs).[108] These projects benefit from certain advantages accorded by the EU, including concessions to facilitate their timely implementation and financial incentives.[109] For a project to benefit from the TEN-E Regulation, it must fulfil several requirements, some of which are aimed at enhancing energy security within the EU. Article 4(2)(b) of the TEN-E Regulation provides that the projects must contribute to '(i) market integration'; '(ii) security of supply, inter alia through appropriate connections and diversification of supply sources, supplying counterparts and routes'; '(iii) competition, inter alia through diversification of supply sources, supplying counterparts and routes'; and '(iv) sustainability'.[110] Russia was of the opinion that these diversification criteria and the benefits accorded to earmarked energy infrastructure projects constituted de facto discrimination against imports of Russian gas under GATT.[111]

In its defence, the EU, much in the same vein as India, invoked Article XX(j) GATT, arguing that the TEN-E measure was necessary as natural gas could become a product in local short supply in the event of disruption of the gas supply, given that 'the transmission of gas requires especially dedicated fixed infrastructure that is costly and time-consuming to build'.[112] Recalling the analysis of the AB in *India - Solar Cells*, the panel found that Article XX(j) GATT only covered situations where a product is 'presently in short supply' and not situations where a product is at risk of becoming in short supply in the future.[113] The panel thus rejected the EU's defence and held that the EU had not proven that natural gas is a product in short supply in the European Union.[114] Confirming the findings of *India - Solar Cells*, *EU - Energy Packages*

---

[107] *EU - Energy Package*, panel report, s 3.

[108] *EU - Energy Package*, panel report, s 2.2.8; Regulation (EU) 347/2013 of the European Parliament and of the Council of 17 April 2013 on guidelines for trans-European energy infrastructure and repealing Decision 1364/2006/EC and amending Regulations (EC) 713/2009, (EC) 714/2009 and (EC) 715/2009 [2013] OJ 115/39 (TEN-E Regulation) art 1.2.

[109] *EU - Energy Package*, panel report, s 2.2.8.

[110] TEN-E Regulation, art 4(2)(b); *EU - Energy Package*, panel report, para 2.56.

[111] Pogoretskyy and Talus (n 93) 16–17.

[112] *EU - Energy Package*, panel report, para 7.1336.

[113] *EU - Energy Package*, panel report, paras 7.1331–7.1335, summarizing AB's position in *India - Solar Cells*.

[114] ibid, para 7.1382.

strengthens the assumption that Article XX(j) GATT defences connected to long-term security of supply will not prevail.

In sum, energy security was a crucial concept in *EU – Energy Package.* The overall take-away with regard to energy security is that measures taken by WTO members to safeguard (long-term) energy security of supply are more likely to be successful under Article XIV(a) GATS than under Article XX(j) GATT. The reason for this is that the threshold for constituting a genuine and sufficiently serious threat to a fundamental interest of society (in the sense of energy security) under Article XIV(a) GATS is easier to meet than the threshold the prospect of a supply shortage must meet under Article XX(j) GATT. The former shows that energy security measures can be accommodated within the public policy exception, while arguments concerning an impending shortage of goods are harder to square with Article XX(j) GATT. While in the present cases, both India and the EU were not successful, the AB in *India – Solar Cells* did open the door to a stronger connection between long-term security of supply and subparagraph (j), and the panel in *EU – Energy Package* was receptive to the possibility of considering energy security measures as falling within the ambit of the public policy exception. The treatment of the concept of energy security by the panel and the AB therefore gives some guidance for future cases concerning energy security measures taken in connection with cross-border trade in renewable energy, as well as fossil fuels. Yet many questions remain open, such as the (theoretical) relationship between energy security measures and national security exceptions in the WTO.

7.4   Conclusion

Energy security is undoubtedly a crucial concept in international relations and international law. Although there is as yet no internationally accepted legal definition of the concept, it is generally understood to cover the continuous availability of energy resources at affordable prices. This chapter first discussed the different dimensions of energy security – short-term, long-term and sustainability – as well as debates over the content of the concept in international relations. It then discussed the place of energy security in various categories of energy-specific treaties and its treatment in international trade law more generally (WTO and preferential trade agreements). Although in the past energy security played only a limited role in the multilateral trading system – mainly related to restrictive practices concerning natural resources in the

1970s – contemporary EU and US PTAs have chapters devoted exclusively to energy, which invariably contain provisions concerning energy security. Recently, the WTO Dispute Settlement Body has been confronted with the concept of energy security as a result of its being raised by members in defence of measures relating to renewable energy (solar) and fossil fuels (gas). The panel and AB reports in *India – Solar Cells* and *EU – Energy Package* show that while energy security may be a valid concern, it will not serve as an effective defence if the measure is applied in a discriminatory manner. This confronts us with significant issues, as it could be argued that one of the prime purposes of safeguarding a WTO Member's energy security is to allow for the possibility of discriminating against energy supplies from other members on the basis of geo-political and strategic considerations. In particular, measures concerning long-term security of supply are unlikely to qualify for the Article XX(j) GATT exception, as this provision seems to have been intended for present shortages rather than the prospect of impending shortages. On the other hand, according to the position adopted by the panel in *EU – Energy Package* energy security measures claimed to have been introduced on public policy grounds are more likely to be considered as falling under the exception provided in Article XIV(a) GATS. While this gives an indication of how future disputes concerning these matters may be litigated, important questions remain unresolved – notably the impact of national security exceptions – which future dispute settlement proceedings may help to clarify.

8

General Conclusion and Recommendations

8.1 International Trade Law, Energy and the Challenges of Changing Markets

The first part of this book studied the concepts, history and regulation of energy in international trade law. The second part probed the challenges of changing markets through case studies bearing on the trilemma of decentralization, decarbonization and energy security. One conclusion to be drawn from the discussions undertaken in the book is that while international trade law regulates some aspects of cross-border trade in energy, this remains a complicated sector to regulate, especially in view of those challenges. In connection with decentralization, how to deal comprehensively with global energy cartels and to ensure diversification away from market domination by a single energy supplier remain challenges under current international trade rules. Concerning decarbonization, although fossil fuel subsidization by means of dual pricing can in theory be curbed under current rules, practice is lagging behind. And exceptions related to long term energy security goals have so far not won through in WTO dispute settlement proceedings, dimming policy prospects in this field. It is safe to say that at the multilateral level there is a pressing need for rules that address the realities of cross-border trade in energy and tackle energy trade regulation in a proper and proactive manner.

This concluding chapter therefore offers suggestions for enhanced energy governance from an institutional angle. It will explore the question at three levels. First of all, it will discuss the advantages and disadvantages of the WTO as a forum for tackling energy issues more proactively. Next, it will contemplate the possible forms of interaction between the WTO and the ECT in this respect. Finally, it will briefly consider the possibility of innovatory energy regulation through PTAs.

8.2   Enhanced Global Energy Governance: Is the WTO the Right Forum?

This section considers the pros and cons of the WTO acting as a forum for global energy governance. Is the WTO the right body to tackle pressing global energy issues more proactively? If energy, and trade in fossil fuels in particular, is such a sensitive topic, should the WTO be accorded a bigger governance role in for global trade in energy?

The answer would appear to lie in one of three possible options. The most radical would be to abandon any such aspiration altogether by completely excluding energy from the WTO's remit. The main reason for taking such a drastic stance would be the subject's geopolitical sensitivity, as a result of which changes of substance and hard commitments from stakeholders are difficult to achieve. Besides, WTO agreements were not tailored to deal with the realities of energy trade, so what's the good of trying to square the circle?

That said, excluding energy from the WTOs purview would be a difficult task, given that it has already received some coverage within the forum, has been the subject of several WTO dispute settlement proceedings, and some intermediate solutions have already been found within the organization to some of the challenges it raises. Additionally, given the far-reaching trade ramifications of energy regulation, it is nigh impossible to isolate energy from other trade-related issues.

Second, one could argue that things should be left as they are, even though important questions concerning WTO agreements and their relationship to energy remain unanswered under current rules. Members might even find that situation satisfactory. Vital questions concerning WTO law and energy would be investigated only on a case-by-case basis as and when disputes between members are referred to the Dispute Settlement Body (DSB).

The third option would be for the WTO to regulate energy matters in a more comprehensive and proactive manner This would represent a conscious choice to use the WTO in a changed trade landscape as a means of introducing clarity into energy trade rules by actively tackling problems, identifying gaps in the law and finding the necessary answers. This could be accomplished through interpretation, adaptation and elaboration. Perhaps the WTO could even draft specialized agreements on energy trade. Such efforts would not have to be confined to the WTO, but could involve cooperation with other relevant institutions (eg Energy

Charter Treaty, UNFCCC). No matter what form such initiatives would take, they would be conditional upon energy at the very least being integrated as an official topic of discussion in the WTO.

Even if the WTO and WTO agreements are not geared towards energy, the organization's institutional machinery offers a promising platform for future energy trade architecture. The reasons for this are manifold and will be briefly explained in this section. They include the WTO's very purpose, its wide membership, its negotiation and trade policy review functions, its dispute settlement system and its existing involvement with issues inseparably linked to energy such as the environment, climate change and sustainable development. However, there are also considerable drawbacks to promoting more active energy regulation within the WTO, not least because the WTO is itself undergoing the biggest crisis it has experienced since its inception.[1] Moreover, multilateral solutions are currently being undermined by the proliferation of plurilateral trade agreements. This section will therefore set out the advantages as well as some disadvantages of equipping the WTO with rules specific to the energy sector.

8.2.1 Arguments in Favour of More Proactive Energy Regulation in the WTO

8.2.1.1 Subject Matter of the WTO

When entrusting the negotiation of comprehensive energy policies to intergovernmental organizations, a consideration to bear in mind is that those with an economic focus are more likely to succeed than those with an environmental focus.[2] One reason for this is that economic institutions tend to function better, as the transaction costs for decision-making and enforcing compliance are lower.[3] An illustration of this is the limited success of measures aimed at meeting the goals of

---

[1] The Appellate Body effectively ceased to function in December 2019 as a result of US discontent over its modus operandi; see R Howse, 'Making the WTO (Not So) Great Again: The Case Against Responding to the Trump Trade Agenda through Reform of WTO Rules on Subsidies and State Enterprises' (2020) 32 Journal of International Economic Law 371; S Charnovitz, 'In Clinical Isolation: Is There a Meaningful Place for the World Trade Organization in the Future of International Economic Law? A WTO If You Can Keep It' (2019) 6 Questions of International Law 1.

[2] TL Meyer, 'The Architecture of International Energy Governance' (2013) 106 ASIL Proceedings 5.

[3] ibid.

the UNFCCC, an environmental institution, compared to the achieve-ments of the WTO.[4]

The WTO clearly has an economic focus as it governs trade relations among its members.[5] Its objective is to promote free trade by reducing tariffs and other trade barriers and eliminating discriminatory treatment in international trade relations.[6] In the words of the preamble to the WTO Agreement, it does so by 'allowing for the optimal use of the world's resources in accordance with the objective of sustainable devel-opment, seeking both to protect and preserve the environment'.[7]

There is a case for arguing quite simply that, as trade in energy qualifies as multilateral trade between nations, then it falls squarely within the scope of the WTO and so there is no better place in which to regulate it. Moreover, given the objective stated above, the WTO can exert a positive influence on trade in energy commodities and technology by bringing it into line with the requirements of sustainable development and environ-mental protection.[8] Of course, the preambular language should not give rise to overly idealistic expectations, but it is a simple fact that trade in energy has taken on huge proportions, transforming from a purely national matter over a century ago to a global phenomenon today. With global trade increasing, the number of WTO members engaged in energy trade, production or transportation on the rise and an ever-growing corpus of rules governing the (clean and renewable) energy sector, the number of disputes is likely to mushroom, and these disputes need a forum in which to be solved. Considering the uneven global distribution of fossil fuels, the WTO can help in two ways. First, it can alleviate disparities in natural endowments by promoting smooth(er) international trade flows enabling resources to move from places with excess supply to areas that have shortages, and thereby reduce the risk of friction between nations.[9] Second, the organization can offer a system for effectively settling conflicts when they arise.

---

[4] See X Wang and G Wiser, 'The Implementation and Compliance Regimes under the Climate Change Convention and its Kyoto Protocol' (2002) 11 Review of European Comparative and International Environmental Law 181.

[5] Agreement Establishing the World Trade Organization (signed 15 April 1994) 1867 UNTS 154 (1994) 33 ILM 1144 (WTO Agreement) art II:1.

[6] ibid, preamble.

[7] ibid.

[8] R Leal-Arcas and A Filis, 'The Fragmented Governance of the Global Energy Economy' (2013) 6 Journal of World Energy Law and Business 1, 9.

[9] WTO, World Trade Report 2010: Trade in Natural Resources (WTO 2010) 48.

8.2.1.2 Involvement with Closely Related Issues

Another argument in support of giving the WTO a greater role in the formulation and refinement of international rules on energy is the close link between energy and several issues already on the WTO's agenda.

The WTO's mission has gone beyond the traditional aim of promoting free trade to include – without making it a principal objective – the promotion of sustainable development and environmental protection and preservation.[10] These issues are inseparably linked to energy in that a successful legal framework on energy cannot be built without addressing sustainable development and environmental matters and, vice versa, the challenges posed by global sustainable development, environmental issues and climate change cannot be resolved without taking energy into account. Energy does not exist in a vacuum.[11]

Pursuant to the 1994 Decision on Trade and Environment, the WTO set up the Committee on Trade and Environment, whose terms of reference required it, inter alia, 'to identify the relationship between trade measures and environmental measures'.[12] In addition, the committee was required to make appropriate recommendations on whether modifications to the multilateral trading system were necessary in order to 'enhance positive interaction between trade and environmental measures' and thereby foster sustainable development and to prevent protectionism.[13] These efforts were strengthened in the appropriately named Doha Development Round (DDA 2001), which required negotiations to be undertaken to eliminate tariff barriers and non-tariff barriers on environmental goods and services.[14] The ambition to provide better access to the goods and technologies that protect the environment and

---

[10] WTO Agreement, preamble.

[11] ibid. On discussions around issues on the WTO agenda, see S Charnovitz, 'Triangulating the World Trade Organization' (2002) 96 AJIL 28.

[12] Decision of Trade Negotiation Committee of 15 December 1993, cited in WTO, Decision on Trade and Environment (1994).

[13] ibid.

[14] Negotiations on environmental goods and services are part of the Doha Development Agenda (DDA) pursuant to Doha Ministerial Declaration (DMD) (adopted 20 November 2001) WT/MIN(01)/DEC/1, para 31(iii). Environmental goods and services have been discussed for many years in the context of the Special Session of the Committee on Trade and Environment (CTESS), though no agreed list of environmental products has so far been drawn up. See WTO, 'Eliminating Trade Barriers on Environmental Goods and Services' <www.wto.org/english/tratop_e/envir_e/envir_neg_serv_e.htm> accessed 20 July 2020.

combat climate change was taken to the next level after the 2014 World Economic Forum in Davos, at which a group of fourteen WTO members (including the European Union, the United States and China) launched negotiations on so-called green goods with a view to reaching a plurilateral deal completely eliminating tariffs.[15] At the time of writing, eighteen participants representing forty-six WTO members were involved in these ongoing negotiations.[16] What exactly constitutes environmental goods and services is not clear-cut, but wind turbines, solar panels and other goods and services closely linked to energy production could arguably be classified as such. Goods like solar panels and biogas plant equipment are used to produce clean energy production and contribute to energy efficiency. Trade in agricultural goods also has a bearing on energy, as some biofuels (eg ethanol) are classified as agricultural products and therefore subject to different import tariffs than other fuels.[17] The wider debate on climate change also reveals the extent to which energy and the environment are intertwined and raises important questions regarding fossil fuel subsidies, as discussed in Chapter 6.

How and where energy interlocks with these closely related issues within the WTO, and what the consequences of this interconnectedness are, needs to be explored in greater depth. It would be beneficial if the environment and energy debates were merged into one, given that they share a common concern – namely, sustainable use of the world's resources.[18]

8.2.1.3   Breadth of WTO's Membership

Another reason for the WTO to become more involved in energy trade is that there is no other international trade organization with such a wide membership.[19] The WTO has 164 members at present. They include major fossil fuel producing, exporting and transporting countries. The fact that these key stakeholders in the global energy landscape are full-fledged participants in the multilateral trade system is likely to aid

---

[15] European Commission, 'EU in Joint Launch of WTO Negotiations for Green Goods Agreement' (Press Release, 24 January 2014) <https://ec.europa.eu/commission/presscor ner/detail/en/IP_14_71>, accessed 24 February 2021.

[16] See WTO, 'Environmental Goods Agreement (EGA)' <www.wto.org/english/tratop_e/ envir_e/ega_e.htm> accessed 20 July 2020.

[17] See Chapter 3, Section 3.2.2.

[18] WTO Agreement, preamble.

[19] On the WTO's broad membership, see Chapter 4.

negotiations between energy producing and exporting members and energy transporting and importing members.

As pointed out in Chapter 4, although the Energy Charter Treaty (ECT) was specifically designed for the energy sector, its membership is narrower than that of the WTO.[20] This leads to the conclusion that, although in theory the ECT might provide a better framework for global trade in energy, the WTO is likely to have a much broader reach and to provide a more solid basis for cooperation as its members include major energy players . And, even better, if the ECT and the WTO were to pool their efforts, this could create a win-win situation (see Section 8.3).

8.2.1.4 Negotiation and Trade Policy Review Function of the WTO

This argument is directly linked to that of the WTO's broad membership. One of the WTO's chief functions is to offer an inclusive platform for trade negotiations between its members.[21] The WTO is itself is a product of negotiations, and everything it does is based on negotiations, from commitments to lower tariffs and curb other trade barriers to measures opening up service markets.[22] The organization is not static, however, meaning that existing agreements can be renegotiated and new agreements added. The platform offered by the WTO lends itself to energy negotiations aimed, for example, at lowering barriers in energy trade or concluding a plurilateral agreement on energy. Agreements of this kind usually have a narrower group of signatories and are sector-specific.[23] They may have to limit themselves to weaker commitments at the outset, given that hard commitments in the energy field are likely to prove difficult to obtain, at least initially, but weak commitments are better than no commitments at all and they are capable of paving the way to stronger commitments in the future.

Furthermore, the WTO has a so-called Trade Policy Review Mechanism (TPRM), [24] which allows it to monitor members' observance

---

[20] Energy Charter Treaty (adopted 17 December 1994, entered into force 16 April 1998) 2080 UNTS 100 (ECT).

[21] WTO Agreement, art III:2.

[22] See WTO, 'What We Do' <www.wto.org/english/thewto_e/whatis_e/what_we_do_e.htm > accessed 20 July 2020.

[23] See WTO Agreement, annex 4; see also WTO, 'Plurilaterals: Of Minority Interest' <www .wto.org/english/thewto_e/whatis_e/tif_e/agrm10_e.htm> accessed 20 July 2020.

[24] WTO Agreement, art III:4, annex 3; Trade Policy Review Mechanism as Amended by the General Council (amended, effective 1 January 2019) <www.wto.org/english/docs_e/ legal_e/29-tprm_e.htm#tprm_d> accessed 24 February 2021.

of the commitments they undertake. Under the TPRM, members must keep the WTO and their trade partners informed of their practices, and the WTO is empowered to conduct regular reviews of members' trade policies. The ultimate aim of this mechanism is to enhance transparency and improve understanding of countries' trade policies, enlighten public and intergovernmental debates on these issues and allow a better multilateral assessment of the effects of WTO policies. This mechanism could offer a valuable means of achieving greater transparency in multilateral discussions on trade in energy.

8.2.1.5   WTO Dispute Settlement System

Another advantage the WTO offers over other options is its dispute settlement system, which is governed by the rules of the Dispute Settlement Understanding (DSU).[25] Article 3.2 DSU describes the dispute settlement mechanism as being central to ensuring security and predictability in the multilateral trading system.[26] WTO members must settle any trade dispute, including those related to energy, in this forum alone. In other words, they are precluded from settling their trade disputes elsewhere. There are two reasons for this: it ensures that members' disputes are settled a multilateral setting and prevents unilateral rulings on breaches of WTO law.[27] Notwithstanding the crisis in which it currently finds itself, the WTO dispute settlement system has clearly been one of the WTO's success stories, with some 600 cases having been settled during the organization's twenty-five-year history.[28]

---

[25] WTO Agreement, art III:3; Understanding on Rules and Procedures Governing the Settlement of Disputes, Marrakesh Agreement Establishing the World Trade Organization, Annex 2 (signed 15 April 1994) 1869 UNTS 401 (1994) 33 ILM 1226 (DSU).

[26] DSU, art 3.2.

[27] *US – Section 301 Trade Act*, panel report, para 7.43:

> Article 23.1 [DSU] is not concerned only with specific instances of violation. It prescribes a general duty of a dual nature. First, it imposes on all Members to 'have recourse to' the multilateral process set out in the DSU when they seek the redress of a WTO inconsistency. In these circumstances, Members have to have recourse to the DSU dispute settlement system to the exclusion of any other system, in particular a system of unilateral enforcement of WTO rights and obligations. This, what one could call 'exclusive dispute resolution clause', is an important new element of Members' rights and obligations under the DSU.

[28] See D McRae, 'What is the Future of the WTO Dispute Settlement?' (2004) 7 *Journal of International Economic Law* 3; WTO, 'Chronological List of Disputes Cases' <www.wto.org/english/tratop_e/dispu_e/dispu_status_e.htm> accessed 20 July 2020.

A comparison can again be made with the Energy Charter Treaty. Although the ECT provides for the settlement of state-state,[29] investor-state,[30] transit,[31] energy trade,[32] environmental[33] and competition[34] disputes, the ECT system has so far been used only for investor-state disputes.[35] The settlement mechanism for disputes between ECT member countries (at least one of whom must not be a WTO member) closely follows the WTO model but as yet remains completely untested.[36] Paradoxically, therefore, although lacking specialized rules on energy, the WTO has been far more active and effective in resolving energy trade disputes than the ECT, which again confirms the latter's rather dormant state. It also again shows that the WTO can be, and should continue to be, an appropriate forum for settling disputes related to energy.

8.2.2 Obstacles to More Proactive Energy Regulation in the WTO

While the section above presented several arguments in support of a more active role for the WTO with respect to energy regulation, it is important not to ignore the counterarguments, which are twofold. The first is (understandably) the WTO's current standstill. The second turns on the politically sensitive nature of trade in energy.

As pointed out in the course of this book, the multilateral trading system is facing many challenges at the moment. A blockage within the Appellate Body and the failure to conclude the Doha Round (which has been ongoing for twenty years) are perhaps the most obvious but not the only manifestations of this crisis.[37] It remains unclear when or indeed whether those two problems will be resolved. In the meantime, however, there are other, more urgent matters that need resolving.

Since the establishment of the WTO, the world has changed significantly. Those changes are not only geopolitical, but also concern the way

---

[29] ECT, art 27.

[30] ECT, art 26.

[31] ECT, art 7(7).

[32] ECT, art 29 ('Interim Provisions on Trade-Related Matters'), annex D ('Interim Provisions for Trade Dispute Settlement').

[33] ECT, art 19.

[34] ECT, art 6.

[35] International Energy Charter, 'List of Cases' <www.energychartertreaty.org/cases/list-of-cases/> accessed 20 July 2020.

[36] On the ECT and trade disputes, see Chapter 4, Section 4.2.5.

[37] B Hoekman and PC Mavroidis, 'WTO "à la carte" or "menu du jour"? Assessing the Case for More Plurilateral Agreements' (2015) 26 European Journal of International Law 319.

we trade. The countries that have newly joined the multilateral trading system are major trading partners whose idiosyncrasies cannot be overlooked. Also, trade has evolved from the simple sale and purchase of goods and services trade and now embraces the more complex phenomenon of global value chains resulting from increasing globalization.

Aside from this paradigm shift, Van den Bossche and Zdouc mention other pressing issues that need to be addressed in the WTO context. They include: (1) further liberalization of trade in goods and services to cover not just tariffs but also non-tariff barriers; (2) development of the dispute settlement system; (3) trade and climate change (energy inevitably comes into play here); (4) trade and labour standards; (5) trade and food security; (6) integration of more developing countries within the WTO; and,(7) the expansion of the WTO's mandate in the areas of investment, currency policy and, last but not least, energy.[38] The need to address these issues has also given rise to an additional challenge: the proliferation of preferential trade agreements and the urgency of reframing their relationship with the WTO.[39]

Given the many trials and tribulations the multilateral trading system is currently facing and the difficulty it has finding a consensus on the matters already under discussion, why add the even more contentious issue of energy to its negotiating plate, one might ask? This is a valid question, though it is a defeatist stance to take and would prevent any new matters from ever being addressed until conditions are right.

The second argument against giving the WTO a more active role in energy regulation is connected to the politically sensitive nature of energy discussions in general. We have seen that energy was a topic largely avoided in the WTO's early years, and that when it did start becoming a topic of discussion, a consensus was difficult to achieve. For instance, the opposition to dual pricing voiced by WTO members did not yield any concrete results.[40] In addition to this, energy was not given an official place in WTO discussions, and this continues to be the case today, suggesting that WTO members simply lack the political willingness to make it an integral part of the WTO agenda.

This, too, could be a valid argument against giving the WTO a more proactive role in energy regulation. However, such reluctance is unlikely

---

[38] P Van den Bossche and W Zdouc, *Law and Policy of the World Trade: Texts, Cases and Materials* (3rd edn, CUP 2013) 1018–1019; WTO, *World Trade Report 2013: Factors Shaping the Future of World Trade over the Next Decades* (WTO 2013).

[39] Hoekman and Mavroidis (n 37).

[40] See Chapter 6.

to continue forever. For one thing, the WTO's membership has changed dramatically and now includes most major energy producers and exporters. They will want to have a say on these matters. And energy importers, for their part, will want to secure concessions. Based on the findings of the present study, it is highly probable that an increasing number of energy disputes will be brought to the WTO, especially in view of the increasing regulation of renewable energy technologies in domestic law. What is more, the energy trading landscape is changing: renewables are starting to outcompete fossil fuels, whose prices have fallen to an historic low. This may mean that we are entering a new era in which the WTO will no longer give fossil fuels special treatment (as it has done in the past by leaving fossil fuel subsidies untouched). What is certain is that energy issues will continue knocking on the WTO's door, so the least the organization can do is to include the subject on its official agenda.

Based on the above discussion, the arguments in favour of the WTO serving as an active forum for global energy governance negotiations outnumber those against. The subject matter of the WTO, its existing involvement in closely related matters, its broad membership, its TPRM and dispute settlement system all lay a solid foundation for a more proactive stance on pressing issues in general, and energy regulation more specifically – and not least because there is every reason to hope that the WTO will become relevant again. Indeed, if it were to tackle twenty-first-century issues more proactively, this could be the way to reinvent itself.

8.2.3 A Plurilateral Framework on Energy in the WTO?

There are some who believe that the right way for the WTO to address the challenges posed by energy is by initiating comprehensive negotiations on the subject.[41] In their view, the ultimate aim would be a framework agreement on energy, similar to the agreement on agriculture produced during the Uruguay Round.[42] Such agreements, permitted by Article II:3 of the WTO Agreement, allow a subset of WTO members to agree on disciplines that are in their sole interest. Currently, there are only two active plurilateral agreements, one on government procurement and the other on civil aircraft.[43]

---

[41] eg T Cottier and others, 'Energy in WTO Law and Policy' in T Cottier and P Delimatsis (eds), *The Prospects of International Trade Regulation: From Fragmentation to Coherence* (CUP 2011).

[42] ibid.

[43] There have also been plurilaterals on beef and dairy, but they were terminated in 1997.

The author is of the opinion that comprehensive negotiations on energy giving rise to a framework agreement could be of benefit to interested members. Moreover, it would be a way of attracting the necessary attention to energy issues in the WTO. Whilst a plurilateral framework agreement on energy would therefore be the preferred option, allowing members to address all pertinent issues in a comprehensive manner, we have seen that the WTO has so far been unable to bring such initiatives to fruition. Even simply initiating comprehensive negotiations, not to mention discussing the terms of a framework agreement, could prove a difficult and lengthy process, especially as all members, even those that do not participate in the plurilateral, have to adopt such an agreement by consensus.[44]

It may therefore be wiser and more realistic to start by broaching energy matters within the WTO in a more modest manner (eg through cooperation in specific areas). Whilst a framework agreement could be kept as a possible option for dealing with energy more comprehensively, some other alternatives, not incompatible with concluding a framework agreement, will be considered in the following sections. They are oriented towards working more closely with the Energy Charter Secretariat and possibly setting up a joint WTO/ECT committee or working group on energy trade and transit in that context.

Another option would be to reach out to other relevant energy-related international organizations (IOs). Cottier and colleagues have suggested that comprehensive negotiations would be an opportunity to authoritatively define the relationship of the WTO with other relevant IOs in the field, such as the UNFCCC and OPEC.[45]

Cooperation and coordination with other relevant IOs involved in the energy sector seems unavoidable in the long run. But rather than trying to solidify relations with other organizations through comprehensive energy negotiations, it might prove more fruitful to start working with these organizations in more informal settings, for instance by holding themed workshops and consultations. This could be a way of exploring where there is common ground and solutions could be found, before envisaging comprehensive energy negotiations at an official level, if that is an option at all.[46]

[44] WTO Agreement, art X:9.
[45] Cottier (n 41).
[46] N Lamp, 'The Receding Horizon of Informality in WTO Meetings' (2015) Queen's University Faculty of Law Research Paper Series 2015–060.

To conclude, the author proposes three possible avenues for ensuring that energy finds its way onto the WTO agenda: (1) active discussion of energy issues within the WTO, at the initiative of the WTO and its members; (2) closer cooperation, coordination and, potentially, amalgamation with the ECT on energy issues and the possible creation of joint working groups and committees on topics of common interest; and (3) informal outreach to other relevant IOs, such as the United Nations Economic Commission for Europe (UNECE), UNFCCC and OPEC, through the organization of workshops on topics of common interest, discussions and consultations.

8.3   WTO-ECT Synergy: Scenarios of Competition, Integration and Complementarity

The previous section weighed the pros and cons of the WTO serving as a forum for international energy regulation. It concluded that the WTO could indeed be a suitable platform for more actively pursuing energy trade regulation. Even if the political willingness is there, this should not, however, be seen as a matter solely for the WTO and its members. On the contrary, the WTO should join hands with the ECT to reap the benefits of closer cooperation in areas of common interest, thereby creating synergies conducive to a higher standard of energy regulation. In Chapter 4 we saw that there is a risk of tension between the WTO and ECT due to the concurrent applicability of some of their provisions. How can these institutions best manage the unresolved clashes caused by overlaps in substance and procedure? This largely depends on how the two treaty regimes develop in the future, not only in terms of their mutual interaction but, more importantly, their respective positions on global energy trade governance, given the potential both organizations have to actively contribute to promoting sustainable development and climate change mitigation.

This section will contemplate three potential scenarios for their future relationship and role. One thing is clear, however: whatever path each regime takes in the future, it should be against a background of greater cooperation and coordination so as to minimize governance gaps and duplication.

8.3.1   *Unproductive Scenario: Competition*

While it was clear from the moment the WTO was founded in 1995 that the multilateral trading system would be an undertaking for the long term, the feasibility of similar ambitions for the ECT was questioned from the start in some quarters. In April 1996, even before the ECT had entered into force, Thomas Wälde expressed doubts over its chances of success:

> There is serious competition, mainly from the European Union's further integration and association strategies eastwards, but also from the US, the expansion of the GATT/WTO, the International Energy Agency and a talked-about global investment code. Perhaps these forces will overshadow and deny to the Energy Charter Treaty any significant future growth.[47]

Wälde thus saw the relationship between the WTO and the ECT as above all one of competition and menace. This is surprising, given that one of the ECT's main objectives was to acquaint non-WTO countries with the rules of the multilateral trading system. It is therefore unclear why Wälde saw the WTO as a danger to the ECT, rather than as an opportunity to introduce ECT parties to the WTO, and conversely to introduce WTO-type laws to the energy sector. His view is all the more surprising as the WTO was only marginally interested in actively engaging with energy issues at the time.

For these reasons, it seems neither constructive nor desirable to view the relationship between the WTO and the ECT – whether in the past or in the future – in this way. To consider them as being in competition with each other would be anathema to modern and effective energy trade governance, leading to unnecessary duplication of work to no proven benefit. A competitive relationship would therefore be a missed opportunity and an unproductive way forward. Rather, the treaties would do far better to recognize the unique potential each regime possesses and build on their respective strengths to reach wider common objectives.

8.3.2   Productive Scenario 1: (Partial) Integration

Historically, it seems more accurate to view the nexus between the WTO and the ECT as one of (partial) integration of the ECT. At the ECT's inception, integration lay in the objective of introducing former socialist countries to the global trading system of the WTO through the ECT. Although this gave rise to practical difficulties caused by competing

---

[47] TW Wälde (ed), *The Energy Charter Treaty – An East-West Gateway to Investment and Trade* (Kluwer Law International 1996) xxi.

competence and parallel applicability, they were mitigated to some extent by the rules of conflict issued by the Energy Charter Secretariat.

Since then, integration between the WTO and ECT has moved into a second and much more promising phase. The last twenty-five years have seen huge changes in the membership of both treaty regimes, not to mention the trading landscape in which they operate. When the WTO and the ECT were established, renewable energy was confined to the fringes of the energy debate. Since then increasing insistence on sustainable development and climate change mitigation has brought about a sea-change, with clean energy technologies now claiming their much-deserved place centre-stage.

In this second phase of integration, the two regimes should not shy away from reassessing the situation and taking steps towards regulatory reform, where needed. This could mean cutting treaty provisions that are duplicative and collaborating where the two regimes can both contribute to a common goal. For example, there needs to be a critical assessment of the continuing relevance of ECT trade provisions once ECT parties have joined the WTO (which they have).

But integration between the regimes should go even further, beyond the mere removal of duplication to truly fruitful cooperation, with the WTO and the ECT making joint efforts to tackle issues of common interest. Energy trade and transit will remain pertinent issues that need further clarification sooner rather than later. Enhanced energy governance with a view to promoting sustainable development should be in everybody's interest, as well.

To take maximum advantage of the opportunity to further energy regulation, the WTO should invite input from the ECT. The WTO and ECT made a modest step in the direction of increased cooperation and coordination by organizing a joint conference at the WTO's headquarters in Geneva in 2013. The event focused on legal challenges concerning energy facing the WTO and the ECT and interaction between their respective legal instruments.[48] More effort is needed to maximize the gains that cooperation between the WTO and the ECT can bring.

A logical next step would, for example, be to establish a WTO/ECT working group to address pressing issues of common interest relating to energy trade and transit. Its mandate could range from harmonizing

---

[48] WTO, 'Lamy Calls for Dialogue on Trade in Energy in WTO' <http://wto.org/english/news_e/sppl_e/sppl279_e.htm> accessed 20 July 2020; WTO, 'Workshop on the Role of Intergovernmental Agreements in Energy Policy' <www.wto.org/english/tratop_e/envir_e/wksp_envir_apr13_e/wksp_envir_apr13_e.htm> accessed 20 July 2020.

WTO and ECT concepts and policies on energy trade to exploring new key topics such as a comprehensive approach to trade in clean energy. Such a platform could also help to accelerate the search for common ground on more politically sensitive issues, such as the interrelationship between the gas transport and transit obligations laid down in the two treaties and the imbalance between subsidies for fossil fuels and renewables.

The WTO has a broad membership which includes most major energy producing and exporting countries. This is something the ECT lacks. The WTO also serves as a forum for trade negotiations and offers an avenue for improving market access (through members' schedules of bound tariff concessions). The ECT, on the other hand, has shown itself to be a constructive platform for energy trade and transit discussions and offers an investor-state dispute resolution mechanism. These are features that have so far been (largely) absent from the WTO. If they were brought under the umbrella of a joint initiative, it would be to the benefit not only of the treaty regimes themselves but also the countries that have adhered to them, and would facilitate work towards common goals and the avoidance of overlaps.

8.3.3 Productive Scenario 2: Complementarity in Global Energy Governance

The second productive scenario builds on the first but places it in the bigger picture of global energy governance. Although not incompatible with the previous one, it apprehends the nexus between the ECT and the WTO in terms of complementarity. In other words, the WTO and the ECT would each contribute to strengthening energy architecture in distinct but complementary ways.

Global energy governance generally revolves around five broad pillars – trade, energy security climate change mitigation, transit and investment[49] – which have hitherto been dealt with separately under a plethora of different regimes. Think of the UN Sustainable Energy for All initiative and the International Energy Agency's engagement with energy security, for example, in addition to the WTO and ECT regimes. Yet the five pillars are clearly interlinked and not hermetically closed off from each other. A more coherent and comprehensive energy governance architecture that takes all five pillars into account

---

[49] Leal-Arcas and Filis (n 8) 19.

would undoubtedly be beneficial to sustainable development and climate change mitigation. The pressing environmental and energy challenges we are facing today seem set to grow, and it is clear that a more holistic approach to energy regulation is needed if they are to be properly addressed.

Harnessing the complementarities of the WTO and the ECT - as well as other treaty regimes and mechanisms – would lead to a more coherent system of global energy and environmental resources management. The WTO's focus is obviously on trade. The ECT, on the other hand, is particularly relevant to the investment pillar of energy governance by virtue of its investment protection and dispute resolution provisions. It also plays an active role in energy transit negotiations. The ECT can thus make a contribution to energy governance that complements that of the WTO, as energy investment and energy transit are areas in which the WTO falls short.

However, a holistic solution - for instance, in the form of a multilateral and multi-stakeholder instrument covering the whole spectrum of energy regulation – presupposes that other aspects of energy governance (eg decarbonization, energy security) are adequately covered, too. The gains for sustainable development will be all the greater if non-renewable and renewable energy governance are addressed together. Where WTO and the ECT coverage is currently insufficient, links could be established with other instruments of energy governance. Take, for example, the ECT Protocol on Energy Efficiency and Related Environmental Aspects (PEEREA). Its provisions are mostly of the nature of soft law –a menu of good practices on energy efficiency and environmental policies. One could imagine bridges being built so that the fundamentals set out in this protocol apply in other relevant fora, such as the UN Sustainable Energy for All initiative or a potential future environmental goods agreement. Some of the best practices set out in the PEEREA could be transformed into harder commitments in the field of climate change mitigation.

Only through cooperation and coordination can the true potential of using energy governance to advance sustainable development be unlocked – through what we might call 'energy synergy'. If the objective is to create a holistic framework with firm rules covering all five pillars of global energy governance, an approach that cuts across the various regimes is needed. A multifaceted framework for energy governance could be drawn up under the auspices of the WTO or ECT umbrella, but not necessarily so.

8.4 Alternative Route: Innovating Energy Regulation through PTAs

In the optimal scenario, the WTO, the ECT and their respective members would actively contribute to improving the international legal framework for energy regulation, drawing on input from IOs tasked with related topics.

As we saw in Chapter 4, energy regulation is increasingly being crystallized in PTAs, a new generation of agreements that incorporate one or more of the pillars of energy governance. At a bilateral level, one can think of the sustainable development chapters with a renewable energy focus that the EU has been including in its FTAs. A good example the recently concluded EU-Singapore FTA, which covers both trade and investment. It contains a chapter entitled 'Non-Tariff Barriers to Trade and Investment in Renewable Energy Generation', the spirit of which is conveyed in the following words:

> In line with global efforts to reduce greenhouse gas emissions, the Parties share the objective of promoting, developing and increasing the generation of energy from renewable and sustainable non-fossil sources, particularly through facilitating trade and investment.[50]

Far from treating the promotion of trade and investment flows and the promotion of environmental protection and renewable energy as irreconcilable objectives, the chapter sees facilitation of trade and investment flows as a way of scaling up renewable energy generation and hence reducing greenhouse gas emissions. This goes to show that these objectives are perfectly compatible and can be united in a single instrument covering more than one pillar of energy governance. What is more, they create synergies between trade, investment and sustainable development objectives, from which all three will emerge stronger.

8.5   Conclusion

This concluding chapter has sketched some scenarios suggesting how international trade law might adapt global energy governance to respond to current challenges. It made the case for greater involvement by the WTO in regulating energy trade – despite the fact that the organization has had a historically troublesome relationship with this field.

---

[50] Free Trade Agreement between the European Union and the Republic of Singapore (entered into force 21 November 2019) [2019] OJ L294/3, art 7.1.

Notwithstanding its current crisis, the WTO is better suited to the task than first impressions might suggest.

At the negotiating level, the WTO has the advantage of having been involved in matters closely related to energy, such as the environment, (sustainable) development, natural resources and agriculture. What it lacks at present in order to realize its potential in the energy field is the readiness to embrace energy at official level in policy discussions the technical expertise needed to navigate this complex field and support particularly from stakeholders, in the energy industry.[51]

That said, work on a more efficient system of global energy regulation should not be confined to the WTO. Increased cooperation and coordination with the ECT should be envisaged. The chapter discussed three modes of interaction: an unproductive scenario of competition between the two treaty-regimes, and the more fruitful options of (partial) integration and complementarity. Together, the two treaty regimes can generate synergies important to the search for solutions.

If such efforts are absent or fail, current trends suggest that enhanced energy regulation will proceed through bilateral, regional and sector-specific initiatives, as illustrated in recent EU FTAs with Singapore, Ukraine and Mexico[52]

---

[51] D Crosby, 'Energy Discrimination and International Rules in Hard Times: What's New This Time Around, and What Can Be Done' (2012) 5 Journal of World Energy Law and Business 325, 342.

[52] See Chapter 4 Section 4.3.

BIBLIOGRAPHY

1 Books, Articles, Research Papers and Studies

Oman: Energy Policy, Laws and Regulations Handbook, vol 1 *Strategic Information and Basic Laws* (International Business Publications 2015)

Aaken A van and Kurtz J, 'Beyond Rational Choice: International Trade Law and the Behavioral Political Economy of Protectionism' (2019) 22 Journal of International Economic Law 601

Asmelash HB, 'Energy Subsidies and WTO Dispute Settlement: Why Only Renewable Energy Subsidies Are Challenged' (2015) 18 Journal of International Economic Law 261

    Phasing Out Fossil Fuel Subsidies in the G20: Progress, Challenges, and Ways Forward (ICTSD,2017)

Azaria D, 'Energy Transit under the Energy Charter Treaty and the General Agreement on Tariffs and Trade' (2009) 27 Journal of Energy and Natural Resources Law 559

    Treaties on Transit of Energy via Pipelines and Countermeasures (OUP 2015)

Bagwell K and Staiger RW, 'An Economic Theory of the GATT' (1999) 89 American Economic Review 215

    'Domestic Policies, National Sovereignty and International Economic Institutions' (2001) 116 Quarterly Journal of Economics 519

    The Economics of the World Trading System (MIT Press 2002)

    and Sykes AO, 'Border Instruments' in H Horn and PC Mavroidis (eds), *Legal and Economic Principles of World Trade Law* (CUP 2015)

Behn D, 'The Potential Problem with Dual Gas Pricing Practices at the WTO" (17 December 2007) <https://ssrn.com/abstract=1151553>

Benes KJ, 'Considerations for the Treatment of Energy in the US-EU Transatlantic Trade and Investment Partnership' (September 2015) Columbia/SIPA Center on Global Energy Policy

Besson S, 'Sovereignty' in R Wolfrum (ed), *The Max Planck Encyclopedia of Public International Law* (OUP 200) online edn

Beyerlin U and Holzer V, 'Conservation of Natural Resources' in R Wolfrum (ed), *Max Planck Encyclopedia of Public International Law* (OUP 2008) online edn

284

Bordoff J and Houser T, 'Navigating the US Oil Export Debate' (January 2015) Columbia/SIPA Center on Global Energy Policy

Bruce S, 'International Energy Law' in R Wolfrum (ed), *The Max Planck Encyclopedia of Public International Law* (OUP 2008) online edn

Brundtland Commission, *Report of the World Commission on Environment and Development: Our Common Future* (OUP 1987)

Canuto C and Fienberg TC, 'Natural Resource-Based Products' in TP Stewart (ed), *The GATT Uruguay Round: A Negotiating History (1986–1992)* (Kluwer Law and Taxation 2003) vol 1a

Carey T, 'Cartel Price Controls vs. Free Trade: A Study of Proposals to Challenge OPEC's Influence in the Oil Market through WTO Dispute Settlement' (2009) 24 American University International Law Review 786

Chalabi F, *Oil Policies, Oil Myths: Analysis and Memoir of an OPEC 'Insider'* (IB Tauris 2010)

Charnovitz S, 'In Clinical Isolation: Is There a Meaningful Place for the World Trade Organization in the Future of International Economic Law? A WTO If You Can Keep It' (2019) 6 Questions of International Law 1

—— 'Triangulating the World Trade Organization' (2002) 96 American Journal of International Law 28

Chauhan SK and Shukla A, 'Environmental Impacts of Production of Biodiesel and Its Use in Transportation Sector' in MA Dos Santos Bernardes (ed), *Environmental Impact of Biofuels* (In Tech Open 2011)

Chester L, 'Conceptualising Energy Security and Making Explicit Its Polysemic Nature' (2010) 38 Energy Policy 887

Chornyi V and Marhold A-A, 'In Uncharted Waters: The Contested Legal and Political Landscape of Nord Stream 2' in MM Roggenkamp and C Banet (eds), *European Energy Law Report XIV* (Intersentia forthcoming) <https://papers .ssrn.com/sol3/papers.cfm?abstract_id=3677001>

Clements B and others (eds), *Energy Subsidy Reform: Lessons and Implications* (IMF 2013)

Coady D and others, 'Defining and Measuring Energy Subsidies' in B Clements and others, *Energy Subsidy Reform: Lessons and Implications* (IMF 2013)

Cosbey A and Mavroidis PC, 'A Turquoise Mess: Green Subsidies, Blue Industrial Policy and Renewable Energy; The Case for Redrafting the Subsidies Agreement of the WTO' (2014) Robert Schuman Centre for Advanced Studies 2014/17

Cossy M, 'Energy Transport and Transit in the WTO' in J Pauwelyn (ed), *Global Challenges at the Intersection of Trade, Energy and Environment* (Graduate Institute of International and Development Studies/Centre for Trade and Economic Integration 2010)

—— 'Energy Services under the General Agreement on Trade in Services' in Y Selivanova (ed), *Regulation of Energy in International Trade Law: WTO, NAFTA and Energy Charter* (Wolters Kluwer 2011)

'Energy Trade and WTO Rules: Reflections on Sovereignty over Natural Resources, Export Restrictions and Freedom of Transit' in C Herrmann and JP Terhechte (eds), *European Yearbook of International Economic Law* (Springer 2012)

Cottier T and others, 'Energy in WTO Law and Policy' in T Cottier and P Delimatsis (eds), *The Prospects of International Trade Regulation: From Fragmentation to Coherence* (CUP 2011)

Cottier T and Espa I (eds), *International Trade in Sustainable Electricity* (CUP 2017)

Crosby D, 'Energy Discrimination and International Rules in Hard Times: What's New This Time Around, and What Can Be Done' (2012) 5 Journal of World Energy Law and Business 325

Daintith T and Hancher L, *Energy Strategy in Europe: The Legal Framework* (De Gruyter 1986)

Dale S, 'The New Economics of Oil' (October 2015) Oxford Institute for Energy Studies

Dam-de Jong D, *International Law and Governance of Natural Resources in Conflict and Post-Conflict Situations* (CUP 2015)

De Bièvre D, Espa I and Poletti A, 'No Iceberg in Sight: On the Absence of WTO Disputes Challenging Fossil Fuel Subsidies' (2017) 17 International Environmental Agreements: Politics, Law and Economics 411

Defilla S, 'Energy Trade under the ECT and Accession to the WTO' (2003) 21 Journal of Energy and Natural Resources Law 428

Desta MG, 'The GATT/WTO System and International Trade in Petroleum: An Overview' (2003) 21 Journal of Energy and Natural Resources Law 385
  'The Organization of Petroleum Exporting Countries, the World Trade Organization, and Regional Trade Agreements' (2003) 37 Journal of World Trade 523

Dogaheh KJ, 'Integrating Energy into the World Trading System: Law and Policy' (PhD thesis, University of Warwick 2007)

Dolzer R and Schreuer C, *Principles of International Investment Law* (OUP 2008)

Drabek Z and Mavroidis PC (eds), *Regulation of Foreign Investment: Challenges to International Harmonization* (2013) World Scientific Studies in International Economics, vol 21

Dralle TM, *Ownership Unbundling and Related Measures in the EU Energy Sector* (Springer 2018)

Dreyer I and Stang G, 'What Energy Security for the EU' (2013) European Union Institute for Security Studies 1

Ehring L and Chianale CF, 'Export Restrictions in the Field of Energy' in Y Selivanova (ed), *Regulation of Energy in International Trade Law: WTO, NAFTA and Energy Charter* (Wolters Kluwer 2011)

Eisen JB and others, *Energy, Economics and the Environment: Cases and Materials* (4th edn, Foundation Press 2015)

Eliason A, 'Using the WTO to Facilitate the Paris Agreement: A Tripartite Approach' (2019) 52 Vanderbilt Journal of Transnational Law 545

Energy Charter Secretariat, *Trade in Energy: WTO Rules Applying under the Energy Charter Treaty* (ECS 2001)

Applicable Trade Provisions of the Energy Charter Treaty (ECS 2003)

International Energy Security: A Common Concept for Energy Producing, Consuming and Transit Countries (ECS 2015)

Espa I, *Export Restrictions on Critical Minerals and Metals: Testing the Adequacy of WTO Disciplines* (CUP 2015)

Espa I and Rolland SE, 'Subsidies, Clean Energy and Climate Change' (E15 Initiative Think Piece, International Centre for Trade and Sustainable Development and World Economic Forum February 2015)

Ethier WJ, 'Political Externalities, Nondiscrimination, and a Multilateral World' (2004) 12 Review of International Economics 303

European Commission, 'European Energy Security Strategy' COM (2014) 330 final 'In-depth Study of European Energy Security' (Staff Working Document) SWD (2014) 330 final

Farah PD and Cima E, 'Energy Trade and the WTO: Implications for Renewable Energy and the OPEC Cartel' (2013) 16 Journal of International Economic Law 707

Fliess B and Mård T, 'Taking Stock of the Measures Restricting the Export of Raw Materials: Analysis of OECD Inventory Data' (2012) OECD Trade Policy Paper 140

Frasl I, 'The Trade Rules of the GATT and Related Instruments and the Energy Charter Treaty' in TW Wälde (ed), *The Energy Charter Treaty: An East-West Gateway for Investment and Trade* (Kluwer Law International 1996)

Garner BA, *Garner's Dictionary of Legal Usage* (OUP 2011)

Gautier P, 'Non-Binding Agreements' in R Wolfrum (ed), *The Max Planck Encyclopedia of Public International Law* (OUP 2008) online edn

Gibbs M, 'Energy Services, Energy Policies and the Doha Agenda' in UNCTAD, 'Energy and Environmental Services: Negotiating Objectives and Development Priorities' (2003) UN Doc UNCTAD/DITC/TNCD/2003/3

Global Intelligence Alliance, 'Russia's Accession to the WTO and its Impact on Her Energy and Commodities Industries' (March 2012) GIA Industry White Paper 1/2012

Gnutzmann H and Gnutzmann-Mkrtchyan A, 'The Silent Success of Customs Unions' (2019) 52 Canadian Journal of Economics 178

Goldthau A, 'A Public Policy Perspective on Global Energy Security' (2012) 13 International Studies Perspectives 65

Goldthau A and Sovacool BK, 'The Uniqueness of the Energy Security, Justice, and Governance Problem' (2012) 41 Energy Policy 232

Goldthau A and Witte JM (eds), *Global Energy Governance: The New Rules of the Game* (Brookings Institution Press 2010)

Graham TR, 'Reforming the International Law Trading System: The Tokyo Round Trade Negotiations in the Final Stage' (1979) 12 Cornell International Law Journal 1

'Results of the Tokyo Round' (1979) 6 Georgia Journal of International and Comparative Law 153

'The Reorganization of Trade Policymaking: Prospects and Problems' (1980) 13 Cornell International Law Journal 221

Haghighi SS, *Energy Security: The External Legal Relations of the European Union with Major Oil and Gas Supplying Countries* (Hart 2007)

Hancher L and Marhold A, 'A Common EU Framework Regulating Import Pipelines for Gas? Exploring the Commission's Proposal to Amend the 2009 Gas Directive' (2019) 37 Journal of Energy and Natural Resources Law 289

and Salerno FM, 'Energy Policy after Lisbon' in A Biondi, P Eeckhout and S Ripley (eds), *EU Law after Lisbon* (OUP 2012)

Hayer S, *Fossil Fuel Subsidies* (Directorate-General for Internal Policies in-depth analysis PE 595.372, European Parliament 2017)

Hoda A, *Tariff Negotiations and Renegotiations under the GATT and the WTO: Procedures and Practices* (CUP 2002)

Hoekman B and Kostecki M, *The Political Economy of the World Trading System: From GATT to WTO* (3rd edn, OUP 2009)

Hoekman B and Matoo A, 'Liberalizing Trade in Services: Lessons from Regional and WTO Negotiations' (2013) 18 International Negotiation 131

Hoekman B and Mavroidis PC, *The World Trade Organization: Law, Economics and Politics* (Routledge 2007)

'WTO "à la carte" or "menu du jour"? Assessing the Case for More Plurilateral Agreements' (2015) 26 European Journal of International Law 319

Holzer K, *Carbon-Related Border Adjustment and WTO Law* (Edward Elgar 2014)

Horlick G and Clarke P, 'Rethinking Subsidy Disciplines for the Future' (E15 Initiative Policy Options Paper, International Centre for Trade and Sustainable Development and World Economic Forum January 2016)

Horn H and Mavroidis PC (eds), *Legal and Economic Principles of World Trade Law* (CUP 2015)

Hossain K and Chowdhury SR (eds), *Permanent Sovereignty over Natural Resources in International Law* (Frances Pinter 1984)

Howse R, *Climate Mitigation Subsidies and the WTO Legal Framework: A Policy Analysis* (IISD 2010)

Securing Policy Space for Clean Energy under the SCM Agreement: Alternative Approaches (E15 Initiative Think Piece, International Centre for Trade and Sustainable Development and World Economic Forum December 2013)

'Making the WTO (Not So) Great Again: The Case against Responding to the Trump Trade Agenda through Reform of WTO Rules on Subsidies and State Enterprises' (2020) 32 Journal of International Economic Law 371

and Bork BP van, 'Options for Liberalising Trade in Environmental Goods in the Doha Round' (2006) International Centre for Trade and Sustainable Development Issue Paper 2

and Eliason AL, 'Domestic and International Strategies to Address Climate Change: An Overview of the WTO Legal Issues' in T Cottier, O Nartova and SZ Bigdeli, *International Trade Regulation and the Mitigation of Climate Change: World Trade Forum* (CUP 2009)

Hudec RE, *The GATT Legal System and World Trade Diplomacy* (2nd edn, Butterworth 1990)

International Centre for Trade and Sustainable Development, 'Fostering Low Carbon Growth: The Case for a Sustainable Energy Trade Agreement' (ICTSD Global Platform on Climate Change, Trade and Sustainable Energy, November 2011)

International Energy Agency, *World Energy Outlook 2016* (IEA 2016)

Nuclear Power in a Clean Energy System (IEA 2019)

World Energy Outlook 2019 (IEA 2019)

OECD and World Bank, 'The Scope of Fossil-Fuel Subsidies in 2009 and a Roadmap for Phasing Out Fossil Fuel Subsidies' (Joint Report for G-20 Summit Seoul, 11–12 November 2010)

International Monetary Fund, *Energy Subsidy Reform: Lessons and Implications* (IMF 2013)

International Organization on Standardization, *ISO and Energy* (ISO 2018)

Isaac G and Menon T, 'When Good Intentions Are Not Enough: Revisiting the US-India Solar Panels WTO Dispute' (2017) 10 OIDA International Journal of Sustainable Development 37

Jiménez-Guerra A, *The World Trade Organization and Oil* (Oxford Institute for Energy Studies SP 12, October 2001)

Johnston A and Block G, *EU Energy Law* (OUP 2012)

Josling T, *Rethinking the Rules for Agriculture Subsidies* (E15 Initiative Think Piece, International Centre for Trade and Sustainable Development and World Economic Forum January 2015)

Konoplaynik A and Wälde T, 'Energy Charter Treaty and Its Role in International Energy' (2006) 24 Journal of Energy and Natural Resources Law 523

Lamp N, 'The Receding Horizon of Informality in WTO Meetings' (2015) Queen's University Faculty of Law Research Paper Series 2015–060

Lamy P, *The Geneva Consensus: Making Trade Work for All* (CUP 2013) ch 8 'Trade and Energy: The Case for a Greater WTO Role'

Lang K-O and Westphal K, 'Nord Stream 2: A Political and Economic Contextualization' (2017) SWP Research Paper 3/2017

Lauterpacht E, 'Gentlemen's Agreements' in W Flume (ed), *Internationales Recht und Wirtschaftsordnung: Festschrift für F. A. Mann zum 70. Geburtstag am 11. August 1977* (CH Beck 1977)

Leal-Arcas R and Filis A, 'The Fragmented Governance of the Global Energy Economy: A Legal-Institutional Analysis' (2013) 6 Journal of World Energy Law and Business 348

    and Abu Gosh ES, *International Energy Governance: Selected Legal Issues* (Edward Elgar 2014)

Lehrman RL, 'Energy Is Not the Ability to Do Work' (1973) 11 *Physics Teacher* 15

Lifshitz Y, 'Gone with the Wind? The Potential Tragedy of the Common Wind' (2010) 28 UCLA Journal of Environmental Law and Policy 435

Lilliestam J and Patt A, 'Conceptualising Energy Security in the European Context: A Policy-Perspective Bottom-Up Approach to the Cases of the EU, UK and Sweden' (June 2012) SEFEP Working Paper 2012-4

Marceau G, 'Never Waste a Good Crisis: The End of the WTO Dream, or the Beginning of Something Greater?' (2020) 17 International Organizations Law Review 345

    'The WTO in the Emerging Energy Governance Debate' in J Pauwelyn (ed), *Global Challenges at the Intersection of Trade, Energy and the Environment* (Graduate Institute of International and Development Studies/Centre for Trade and Economic Integration 2011)

Marhold AA, 'The Russo-Ukrainian Gas Disputes, the Energy Charter Treaty and the Kremlin Proposal: Is There Light at the End of the Gas Pipe?' (2011) 3 Oil, Gas and Energy Law Journal <www.ogel.org>

    'The World Trade Organization and Energy: Fuel for Debate' (2013) 2(8) ESIL Reflections

    'Fragmentation and the Nexus between the WTO and the ECT in Global Energy Governance: A Legal-Institutional Analysis Twenty Years Later' (2015) 16 Journal of World Investment and Trade 389

    'EU Regulatory Private Law in the Energy Community: The Synergy between the CEER and the ECRB in Facilitating Customer Protection' in M Cremona and H-W Micklitz (eds), *Private Law in the External Relations of the EU* (OUP 2016)

    'WTO Law and Economics and Restrictive Practices in Energy Trade: The Case of the OPEC Cartel' (2016) 9 Journal of World Energy Law and Business 475

    'Fossil Fuel Subsidy Reform in the WTO: Options for Constraining Dual Pricing in the Multilateral Trading System' (E15 Initiative Issue Paper, International Centre for Trade and Sustainable Development and World Economic Forum, December 2017)

    'The Interplay between Liberalization and Decarbonization in the European Internal Energy Market for Electricity' in K Mathis and BR Huber (eds), *Energy Law and Economics* (Springer 2018)

'WTO Subsidy Rules: Implications for Energy' in L Hancher, A de Hauteclocque and FM Salerno (eds), *State Aid in the Energy Sector* (Hart 2018)

'Externalising Europe's Energy Policy in EU Free Trade Agreements: A Cognitive Dissonance between Promoting Sustainable Development and Ensuring Security of Supply?' (2019) 3 Europe and the World 1

and Weiss F, 'Energy and Fossil Fuels as a Topic in WTO Accession Protocols' in M Bungenberg and others (eds), *European Yearbook of International Economic Law 2018* (Springer 2018)

Mavroidis PC, 'No Outsourcing of Law? WTO Law as Practiced by WTO Courts' (2008) 102 American Journal of International Law 421

Trade in Goods (2nd edn, OUP 2012)

The Regulation of International Trade, vol 1 *GATT* (MIT Press 2015)

Bermann G and Wu M, *The Law of the World Trade Organization: Documents, Cases and Analysis* (West 2010)

McRae D, 'What Is the Future of WTO Dispute Settlement?' (2004) 7 Journal of International Economic Law 3

Metais R, 'Ensuring Energy Security in Europe: The EU between a Market-Based and a Geopolitical Approach' (2013) College of Europe EU Diplomacy Paper 03/2013

Meyer TL, 'The Architecture of International Energy Governance' (2013) 106 ASIL Proceedings 5

'Energy Subsidies and the World Trade Organization' (2013) 17(22) ASIL Insights <www.asil.org/insights>

Milthorp P and Christy D, 'Energy Issues in Selected WTO Accessions' in Y Selivanova (ed), *Regulation of Energy in International Trade Law: WTO, NAFTA and Energy Charter* (Wolters Kluwer 2011)

Molinuevo M, *Protecting Investment in Services: Investor-State Arbitration versus WTO Dispute Settlement* (Wolters Kluwer 2011)

Nychay N and Shemelin D, 'Interpretation of Article 7(3) of the Energy Charter Treaty' (2012) Graduate Institute of International and Development Studies/ Centre for Trade and Economic Integration, Trade and Investment Law Clinic Paper

OECD, IEA and Eurostat, *Energy Statistics Manual* (OECD/IEA 2005)

Osborne MJ and Rubinstein A, *A Course in Game Theory* (MIT 1994)

Osmańczyk EJ, *Encyclopedia of the United Nations and International Agreements*, (A Mango ed, 3rd edn, Routledge 2003)

Øvergaard S, 'Definition of Primary and Secondary Energy' (September 2008) Oslo Group on Energy Statistics Issue Paper

Owen NA, Inderwildi OR and King DA, 'The Status of Conventional World Oil Reserves: Hype or Cause for Concern?' (2010) 38(8) Energy Policy 4743

Oxman BH, 'Jurisdiction' in R Wolfrum (ed), *The Max Planck Encyclopedia of Public International Law* (OUP 200) online edn

Paparinskis M, 'Investment Arbitration and the Law of Countermeasures' (2008) 79 British Yearbook of International Law 264

Pauwelyn J, *Conflict of Norms in Public International Law: How WTO Law Relates to Other Rules of International Law* (CUP 2003)

'Fragmentation in International Law' in R Wolfrum (ed), *The Max Planck Encyclopedia of Public International Law* (OUP 2008) online edn

(ed), *Global Challenges at the Intersection of Trade, Energy and Environment* (Graduate Institute of International and Development Studies/Centre for Trade and Economic Integration 2010)

Pindyck RS and Rubinfeld DL, *Microeconomics* (8th edn, Pearson 2013)

Pogoretskyy V, 'The System of Energy Dual Pricing in Russia and Ukraine: The Consistency of the Energy Dual Pricing System with the WTO Agreement on Anti-Dumping' (2009) 4 Global Trade and Customs Journal 313

'Energy Dual Pricing in International Trade: Subsidies and Anti-Dumping Perspectives' in Y Selivanova (ed), *Regulation of Energy in International Trade Law: WTO, NAFTA and Energy Charter* (Wolters Kluwer 2011)

Freedom of Transit and Access to Gas Pipeline Networks under WTO Law (CUP 2017)

and Melnyk S, 'Russian Energy and the WTO: Overview of the Accession Negotiations of the Russian Federation and Final Commitments' (2018) 1 Oil, Gas and Energy Law Journal <www.ogel.org>

and Talus K, 'The WTO Panel Report in EU–Energy Package and Its Implications for the EU's Gas Market and Energy Security' (2020) 19 World Trade Review 531

Pollitt M, 'The Role of Energy Policy in Energy Transitions: Lessons from the Energy Liberalisation Era' (2012) 50 Energy Policy 128

Quick R, 'Dual Pricing' in J Pauwelyn (ed), *Global Challenges at the Intersection of Trade, Energy and Environment* (Graduate Institute of International and Development Studies/Centre for Trade and Economic Integration 2010)

Raillon P, 'Energy Regulation and Security of Supply: The European Regulators' Approach' (ARIAE-CEER high-level meeting, Madrid April 2010) <www .ceer.eu>

Redgwell C, 'International Regulation of Energy Activities' in MM Roggenkamp and others (eds), *Energy Law in Europe* (OUP 2007)

Rios Herrán R and Poreti P, 'Energy Trade and Investment under the North American Free Trade Agreement' in Y Selivanova (ed), *Regulation of Energy in International Trade Law: WTO, NAFTA and Energy Charter* (Wolters Kluwer 2011)

Ripinsky S, 'The System of Gas Dual Pricing in Russia: Compatibility with WTO Rules' (2004) 3 World Trade Review 463

Roggenkamp MM, 'Transit of Network-Bound Energy: The European Experience' in TW Wälde (ed), *The Energy Charter Treaty: An East-West Gateway to Investment and Trade* (Kluwer Law International 1996)

Rolland SE, '*China – Raw Materials*: WTO Rules on Chinese Natural Resources Export Dispute' (2012) 16(21) ASIL Insights <www.asil.org/insights>

Rubini L, 'Rethinking International Subsidies Disciplines: Rationale and Possible Avenues for Reform' (E15 Initiative Overview Paper, International Centre for Trade and Sustainable Development and World Economic Forum, November 2015)

Rusnák U, 'Modernisation of the Energy Charter: The Long Story Told Short' (Kluwer Arbitration Blog, 21 July 2020)

Ruta M and Venables AJ, 'International Trade in Natural Resources' (March 2012) WTO Staff Working Paper ERDS-2012-07

Sakmar SL, 'Bringing Energy Trade into the WTO: The Historical Context, Current Status, and Potential Implications for the Middle East Region' (2008) 18 Indiana International and Comparative Law Review 89

Schrijver NJ, 'Natural Resources, Permanent Sovereignty over' in R Wolfrum (ed), *The Max Planck Encyclopedia of Public International Law* (OUP 2008) online edn

Development without Destruction: The UN and Global Resource Management (United Nations Intellectual History Project Series, Indiana University Press 2010)

Schwebel SM, 'The Story of the UN's Declaration on Permanent Sovereignty over Natural Resources' (1963) 49 American Bar Association Journal 463

Selivanova Y, 'The WTO and Energy: WTO Rules and Agreements of Relevance to the Energy Sector' (2007) International Centre for Trade and Sustainable Development Issue Paper 1

Energy Dual Pricing in the WTO: Analysis and Prospects in the Context of Russia's Accession to the World Trade Organization (Cameron May 2008)

'Managing the Patchwork of Agreements in Trade and Investment' in A Goldthau and JM Witte (eds), *Global Energy Governance: The New Rules of the Game* (Brookings Institution Press 2010)

'Energy Challenges for International Trade Rules' (2011) 8 Transnational Dispute Management 3

(ed), *Regulation of Energy in International Trade Law: WTO, NAFTA and Energy Charter* (Wolters Kluwer 2011)

Shen Y, Moomy R and Eggert RG, 'China's Public Policies toward Rare Earths, 1975–2018' (2019) 33 Mineral Economics 127

Shih W-C, 'Energy Security, GATT/ WTO, and Regional Agreements' (2009) 49 Natural Resources Journal 433

Simma B and Pulkowski D, 'Of Planets and the Universe: Self-Contained Regimes in International Law' (2006) 17 European Journal of International Law 483

Smil V, *Energy Transitions: History, Requirements, Prospects* (Praeger 2010)

Sørensen B, 'A History of Renewable Energy Technology' (1991) 19 Energy Policy 8

Sovacool BK and others, 'Exploring Propositions about Perceptions of Energy Security: An International Survey' (2012) 16 Environmental Science and Policy 44

    and Brown MA, 'Competing Dimensions of Energy Security: An International Perspective' (2010) 35 Annual Review of Environment and Resources 77

Steenblik R, 'Subsidies in the Traditional Energy Sector' in J Pauwelyn (ed), *Global Challenges at the Intersection of Trade, Energy and Environment* (Graduate Institute of International and Development Studies/Centre for Trade and Economic Integration 2010)

Stewart TP and McDonough PJ, *Opportunities and Challenges from Russia's 2012 Accession to the WTO* (Stewart and Stewart 2011)

Sykes A, Mavroidis PC and Irwin DA, *The Genesis of the GATT* (CUP 2008)

Talus K, *Introduction to EU Energy Law* (OUP 2016)

    Looper S and Oitillar S, '*Lex Petrolea* and the Internationalization of Petroleum Agreements: Focus on Host Government Contracts' (2012) 5 Journal of World Energy Law and Business 181

Talus K and Wüstenberg W, 'WTO Panel Report in the *EU – Energy Package* Dispute and the European Commission Proposal to Amend the 2009 Gas Market Directive' (2018) 37 Journal of Energy and Natural Resources Law 327

Tarr D and Thomson PD, 'The Merits of Dual Pricing of Russian Natural Gas' (2004) 27 World Economy 1173

Tomain JP, *Energy Law in a Nutshell* (2nd edn, West Academic 2011)

    and Cudahy RD, *Energy Law in a Nutshell* (3rd edn, West Academic 2016)

Trachtman JP, Review of *Conflict of Norms in Public International Law: How WTO Law Relates to Other Rules of International Law* by J Pauwelyn (2004) 98 American Journal of International Law 855

    Fossil Fuel Subsidies Reduction and the World Trade Organization (2017) ICTSD Climate and Energy Issue Paper

Trebilcock MJ and Howse R, *The Regulation of International Trade* (3rd edn, Routledge 2002)

UNCTAD, 'Trade Agreements, Petroleum and Energy Policies' (2000) UNCTAD/ITCD/TSB/9

    'WTO Accession and Development Policies' (2001) UNCTAD/DITC/TNCD/11

United Nations Development Programme, *World Energy Assessment: Energy and the Challenge of Sustainability* (UNDP 2015)

Van den Bossche P, *The Law and Policy of the World Trade Organization* (2nd edn, CUP 2008)

and Zdouc W, *Law and Policy of the World Trade: Texts, Cases and Materials* (3rd edn, CUP 2013)

The Law and Policy of the World Trade Organization (4th edn, CUP 2017)

Voon T, 'Modernizing the Energy Charter Treaty: What about Termination?' (*Investment Treaty News*, 2 October 2009) <https://cf.iisd.net/itn/2019/10/02/modernizing-the-energy-charter-treaty-what-about-termination-tania-voon/> accessed 20 July 2020

Vooren B van and Wessel RA, *EU External Relations Law: Text, Cases and Materials* (CUP 2014)

Wälde TW, *The Energy Charter Treaty: An East-West Gateway for Investment and Trade* (Kluwer Law International 1996)

Wang X and Wiser G, 'The Implementation and Compliance Regimes under the Climate Change Convention and Its Kyoto Protocol' (2002) 11 Review of European, Comparative and International Environmental Law 181

Weekes JM and others, 'NAFTA 2.0: Drilling Down – The Impact of the CUSMA/USMCA on Canadian Energy Stakeholders' (2019) 7(1) Energy Regulation Quarterly <www.energyregulationquarterly.ca>

Wernar L, *Blood Oil: Tyrants, Violence and the Rules that Run the World* (OUP 2016)

Winzer C, 'Conceptualizing Energy Security' (2012) 46 Energy Policy 36

Wolfrum R and Matz N, *Conflicts in International Environmental Law* (Springer 2003)

WTO, *The Legal Texts: The Results of the Uruguay Round of Multilateral Trade Negotiations* (WTO 1999)

World Trade Report 2010: Trade in Natural Resources (WTO 2010)

World Trade Report 2013: Factors Shaping the Future of World Trade over the Next Decades (WTO 2013)

World Trade Statistical Review (WTO 2019)

Yafimava Y, *The OPAL Exemption Decision: Past, Present and Future* (Oxford Institute for Energy Studies Paper NG 117, January 2017)

Yanovich A, 'WTO Rules and the Energy Sector' in Y Selivanova (ed), *Regulation of Energy in International Trade Law: WTO, NAFTA and Energy Charter* (Wolters Kluwer 2011)

Yergin D, 'Ensuring Energy Security' (2006) 85(2) *Foreign Affairs* 69

The Prize: The Epic Quest for Oil, Money and Power (Free Press 2008)

The Quest: Energy Security and the Remaking of the Modern World (Penguin Press 2011)

Yermakov V and Henderson J, 'The New Deal for Oil Markets: Implications for Russia's Short-Term Tactics and Long-Term Strategy' (2020) Oxford Institute for Energy Studies Energy Insight 67

Zarilli S, 'The Doha Work Programme: Possible Impact on Energy Trade and on Domestic Policies in Energy-Producing Developing Countries' (2003) 21 Journal of Energy and Natural Resources Law 399

2 Legal Sources

Treaties and Contracts

WTO

ADA (Agreement on Anti-Dumping): Agreement on Implementation of Article VI of the General Agreement on Tariffs and Trade 1994, Marrakesh Agreement Establishing the World Trade Organization, Annex 1A (signed 15 April 1994) 1868 UNTS 201

AoA: Agreement on Agriculture, Marrakesh Agreement Establishing the World Trade Organization, Annex 1A (signed 15 April 1994) 1867 UNTS 410

ASCM: Agreement on Subsidies and Countervailing Measures, Marrakesh Agreement Establishing the World Trade Organization, Annex 1A (signed 15 April 1994) 1869 UNTS 14

DSU (Dispute Settlement Rules): Understanding on Rules and Procedures Governing the Settlement of Disputes, Marrakesh Agreement Establishing the World Trade Organization, Annex 2 (signed 15 April 1994) 1869 UNTS 401 (1994) 33 ILM 1226

GATS: General Agreement on Trade in Services, Marrakesh Agreement Establishing the World Trade Organization, Annex 1B (signed 15 April 1994) 1869 UNTS 183 (1994) 33 ILM 1167

GATT 1947: General Agreement on Tariffs and Trade (signed 30 October 1947) 61 Stat A-11, TIAS 1700, 55 UNTS 194

GATT 1994: General Agreement on Tariffs and Trade, Marrakesh Agreement Establishing the World Trade Organization, Annex 1A (signed 15 April 1994) 1867 UNTS 187 (1994) 33 ILM 1153

TBT Agreement: Agreement on Technical Barriers to Trade, Marrakesh Agreement Establishing the World Trade Organization, Annex 1A (signed 15 April 1994) 1868 UNTS 120

TRIMs Agreement: Agreement on Trade-Related Investment Measures, Marrakesh Agreement Establishing the World Trade Organization, Annex 1A (signed 15 April 1994) 1868 UNTS 186

TRIPs Agreement: Agreement on Trade-Related Aspects of Intellectual Property Rights, Marrakesh Agreement Establishing the World Trade Organization, Annex 1C (signed 15 April 1994) 1869 UNTS 299 (1994) 33 ILM 1197

WTO Agreement: Marrakesh Agreement Establishing the World Trade Organization (signed 15 April 1994) 1867 UNTS 154 (1994) 33 ILM 1144

Other

COP21 Paris Agreement: United Nations Framework Convention on Climate Change (UNFCCC) UN Doc FCCC/CP/2015/L.9/Rev.1, Decision 1/CP.21 (adopted 12 December 2015)

ECT: Energy Charter Treaty (adopted 17 December 1994, entered into force 16 April 1998) 2080 UNTS 100

Energy Community Treaty: Treaty Establishing the Energy Community (signed 25 October 2005, entered into force 1 July 2006) [2006] OJ L198/18

EU-Mexico Free Trade Agreement: 'The Agreement in Principle' (26 April 2018, updated May 2020 <trade.ec.europa.eu>)

EU-Singapore Free Trade Agreement: Free Trade Agreement between the European Union and the Republic of Singapore (entered into force 21 November 2019) [2019] OJ L294/3

EU-Ukraine Association Agreement: Association Agreement between the European Union and Its Member States, of the one part, and Ukraine, of the other part (signed 21 March 2014, entered into force 1 September 2017) [2014] OJ L161/3

Euratom: Treaty Establishing the European Atomic Energy Community (Euratom) (entered into force 1 January 1958) 294 UNTS 261

HS Convention (Harmonized System Convention): International Convention on the Harmonized Commodity Description and Coding System (adopted 14 June 1983) 1503 UNTS 167

ICCPR: International Covenant on Civil and Political Rights (adopted 19 December 1966, entered into force 23 March 1976, rectified 25 October 1977) 999 UNTS 171, 1057 UNTS 407

ICJ Statute: Statute of the International Court of Justice (entered into force 18 April 1946) 33 UNTS 993

ITGI Project Agreement: Agreement among the Hellenic Republic, the Republic of Turkey and the Italian Republic concerning the development of the Turkey-Greece-Italy Gas Transportation Corridor (signed 26 July 2007)

NAFTA: North American Free Trade Agreement (entered into force 1 January 1994) 1867 UNTS 14

OECD/IEA: Agreement on an International Energy Programme (signed 18 November 1974, entered into force 19 January 1976) 1040 UNTS 271

OPEC Statute: Statute of the Organization of Petroleum Exporting Countries (entered into force 1 May 1965) 443 UNTS 427 (1965) 4 ILM 1175

TEU: Consolidated Version of the Treaty on European Union [2010] OJ C83/01

TFEU: Consolidated Version of the Treaty on the Functioning of the European Union [2008] OJ C115/47

United Nations Convention on Biological Diversity (adopted 5 June 1992, entered into force 29 December 1993) 1760 UNTS 79

UNCLOS: United Nations Convention on the Law of the Sea (adopted 10 December 1982, entered into force 14 November 1994) 1833 UNTS 379

USMCA: Agreement between the United States of America, the United Mexican States and Canada (signed 30 November 2018, entered into force 1 July 2020)

VCLT: Vienna Convention on the Law of Treaties (adopted 23 May 1969, entered into force 27 January 1980) 1155 UNTS 331

EU Secondary Legislation

Commission Regulation (EU) 651/2014 of 17 June 2014 declaring certain categories of aid compatible with the internal market in application of Articles 107 and 108 of the Treaty [2014] OJ L187/1 (General Block Exemption Regulation)

Council Regulation (EC) 1225/2009 of 30 November 2009 on protection against dumped imports from countries not members of the European Community [2009] OJ L343/51 (Basic Regulation)

Directive 2003/54/EC of the European Parliament and of the Council of 26 June 2003 concerning common rules for the internal market in electricity and repealing Directive 96/92/EC [2003] OJ L176/37

Directive 2003/55/EC of the European Parliament and of the Council of 26 June 2003, concerning common rules for the internal market in natural gas and repealing Directive 98/30/EC [2003] OJ L176/57

Directive 2009/72/EC of the European Parliament and of the Council of 13 July 2009 concerning common rules for the internal market in electricity and repealing Directive 2003/54/ EC [2009] OJ L211/69

Directive 2009/73/EC of the European Parliament and of the Council of 13 July 2009 concerning common rules for the internal market in natural gas and repealing Directive 2003/55/EC [2009] OJ L211/94

Directive (EU) 2018/2001 of the European Parliament and of the Council of 11 December 2018 on the promotion of the use of energy from renewable sources (recast) [2018] OJ L328/82

Regulation (EC) 715/2009 of the European Parliament and of the Council of 13 July 2009 on conditions for access to the natural gas transmission networks and repealing Regulation (EC) 1775/2005 [2009] OJ L211/36

Regulation (EU) 347/2013 of the European Parliament and of the Council of 17 April 2013 on guidelines for trans-European energy infrastructure and repealing Decision 1364/2006/EC and amending Regulations (EC) 713/ 2009, (EC) 714/2009 and (EC) 715/2009 [2013] OJ L115/39(TEN-E Regulation)

WTO Accession Documents

China: Accession Protocol (23 November 2001) WT/L/431; Report of the Working Party on the Accession of China (10 November 2001) WT/MIN(01)/3

Ecuador: Accession Protocol (21 January 1996) WT/L/432; Report of the Working Party on the Accession of Ecuador (21 January 1996) WT/L/77 and Corr.1

Kazakhstan: Accession Protocol (30 November 2015) WT/L/957; Report of the Working Party on the Accession of Kazakhstan (23 June 2015) WT/ACC/KAZ/93

Oman: Accession Protocol (9 November 2000) WT/ACC/OMN/28; Report of the Working Party on the Accession of Oman (28 September 2000) WT/ACC/OMN/26

Russian Federation: Accession Protocol (22 August 2012) WT/L/839, WT/MIN(11)/27; Report of the Working Party on the Accession of the Russian Federation (17 November 2011) WT/ACC/RUS/70, WT/MIN(11)/2

Saudi Arabia: Accession Protocol (11 December 2005) WT/L/627; Report of the Working Party on the Accession of the Kingdom of Saudi Arabia, (1 November 2005) WT/ACC/SAU/61

Ukraine: Accession Protocol (16 May 2008) WT/L/718; Report of the Working Party on the Accession of Ukraine (25 January 2008) WT/ACC/UKR/152

GATT Tariff Schedules

1947 Geneva Schedules to GATT (1950) 56–61 UNTS

Schedule II – Benelux, pt 1 (1950) 56 UNTS 128–29

Schedule IV – Burma (1950) 57 UNTS 92

Schedule V – Canada, pt 1 (1950) 57 UNTS 132

Schedule VII – Chile, pt 1 (1950) 58 UNTS 17

Schedule IX – Cuba, pt 2 (1950) 58 UNTS 49

Schedule XI – France (1950) 59 UNTS 39–41

Schedule of the United States to GATT (1950) 61 UNTS 183

Tokyo Round Schedules: Geneva (1979) Protocol to GATT (30 June 1979) vols I, II, III, IV

International Resolutions and Declarations

UNGA

UNGA Res 523 (VI) 'Integrated Economic Development and Commercial Agreements' (12 January 1952)

UNGA Res 626 (VII) 'Right to Exploit Freely Natural Wealth and Resources' (21 December 1952)

UNGA Res 1803 (XVII) 'Permanent Sovereignty over Natural Resources' (18 December 1962) <http://legal.un.org/avl/ha/ga_1803/ga_1803.html> (Procedural History) accessed 20 July 2020

WTO

Doha Ministerial Declaration (DMD) (adopted 20 November 2001) WT/MIN(01)/DEC/1

Doha Work Programme – Ministerial Declaration, Annex C – Services (adopted 18 December 2005) WT/MIN(05)/DEC

Ministerial Conference, 11th Session, Buenos Aires, 10–13 December 2017 – Fossil Fuel Subsidies Reform Ministerial Statement (adopted 12 December 2017) WT/MIN(17)/54

GATT

GATT, Punta del Este Ministerial Declaration (20 September 1986)

Energy Charter Secretariat

Concluding Document of the Hague Conference on the European Energy Charter (1991 European Energy Charter)

Final Act of the International Conference and Decision by the Energy Charter Conference in respect of the Amendment to the Trade-Related Provisions of the Energy Charter Treaty (24 April 1998) Joint Declaration on Trade-Related Intellectual Property Rights

Agreed Text for Adoption in The Hague at the Ministerial Conference on the International Energy Charter on 20 May 2015

Other

G20 Leaders' Statement, Pittsburgh Summit (24–25 September 2009)

G7 Leaders' Declaration, Ise-Shima Summit (26–27 May 2016)

Decisions and Miscellaneous Documents of International Organizations

WTO

Decision on Trade and Environment (1994)

Rules of Procedure for Sessions of the Ministerial Conference, (25 July 1996) WT/L/161, Annex 3 – Observer Status for International Intergovernmental Organizations in the WTO

Council for Trade in Services – Energy Services – Background Note by the Secretariat (9 September 1998) Doc S/C/W/52

Committee on Trade and Development – Report of the Committee on Trade and Development' (14 November 2000) WT/COMTD/M/29

General Council – Minutes of Meeting (October 2001) WT/GC/M/69

Council for Trade in Services – Special Session – Report by the Chairman to the Trade Negotiations Committee (28 November 2005) TN/S/23, Annex B – Sectoral and Modal Objectives as Identified by Members, s 11 – Energy Services

Council for Trade in Services – Energy Services – Background Note by the Secretariat (12 January 2010) Doc S/C/W/311

Committee on Trade and Development – Note on the Meeting of 21 June and 5 July 2011 (19 October 2011) WT/COMTD/M/82

GATT Secretariat

Committee on Trade and Development – The Impact of Higher Petroleum Prices on Developing Countries – Note by the Secretariat (28 January 1974) COM. TD/W/208

Export Restrictions and Charges – Background Note by the Secretariat (8 August 1989) MTN.GNG/NG2/W/40

Services Sectoral Classifications List – Note by the Secretariat' (10 July 1991) MTN. GNS/W/120

Energy Charter Secretariat

Transit Protocol (Draft) (22 October 2010) TT87 22/01/2010

Roadmap for the Modernisation of the Energy Charter Treaty Process (24 November 2010)

Modernisation of the Energy Charter Treaty (Decision of the Energy Charter Conference, 27 November 2018) CCDEC 2018 18 STR

EU

European Commission, 'EU-US Transatlantic Trade and Investment Partnership: Raw Materials and Energy' (Initial EU Position Paper, 2013)

European Commission DG Trade, 'TTIP: Draft Non-Paper on Raw Materials and Energy' (EU-restricted) (20 September 2013)

European Commission, 'Non-Paper on a Chapter on Energy and Raw Materials in TTIP' (leaked) (27 May 2014)

European Commission, 'EU-US Transatlantic Trade and Investment Partnership: Raw Materials and Energy (Initial EU Position Paper, 2015)

European Commission DG Trade, 'TTIP: EU's Proposal for a Chapter on Energy and Raw Materials in TTIP' (Note for the Attention of the Trade Policy Committee, 20 June 2016)

Council of the EU, 'Negotiating Directives for the Modernisation of the Energy Charter Treaty: Adoption' (2 July 2019) 10745/19 Add 1

Other

OECD, 'Glossary of Statistical Terms', Glossary of Environment Statistics, Studies in Methods, Series F, No 67 (UN 1997)

United Nations Statistics Division, 'Manual of the Basic Set of Environmental Statistics of the FDES 2013' (28 December 2016)

United Nations Standard International Trade Classification (UNSITC) Revision 3, Statistical Papers Series M, No 34/Rev 3, ST/ESA/STAT/SER.M/34/Rev.3 (2006)

Decisions of Domestic Jurisdictions

Bundesnetsagentur (Germany), Decision in the administrative proceedings concerning non-compliance with the OPAL exemption decision of 25 February 2009 as amended by the decision of 7 July 2009 (BK7-08–009-E2) (in German).

Negotiating History Documents

Energy Charter Secretariat

'Legal Sub-Group's Report on Inter-relationship of the Charter Treaty with the GATT' (European Energy Charter, Conference Secretariat, Room Document 1, Plenary Session, 14–18 December 1993) (ECT *travaux préparatoires*)

GATT Secretariat

Group on Non-Tariff Measures – Sub-Group on Subsidies and Countervailing Measures (31 May 1976) MTN/NTM/W/43/Add.6

Situation of Schedules of Contracting Parties to the GATT (18 June 1980) TAR/W/7

Protocol for the Accession of Mexico to the General Agreement on Tariffs and Trade (Basic Instruments and Selected Documents Series, 33rd Supplement, 17 July 1986)

Group of Negotiations on Goods – Negotiating Group on Natural Resource-Based Products – Energy Products – Note by the Secretariat (27 September 1988) MTN.GNG/NG3/W/16

Negotiating Group on Natural Resources-Based Products – Note by the Secretariat' (10 August 1989) MTN.GNG/NG3/11

Group of Negotiations on Goods – Negotiations on Natural Resource-Based Products – Submission from the United States (8 February 1990) MTN. GNG/NG3/W/2

Group of Negotiations on Goods – Negotiations on Natural Resource-Based Products – Natural Resource-Based Products: Two-Tier Pricing Issue – Submission from the United States (8 February 1990) MTN.GNG/NG3/W/13

Group of Negotiations on Goods – Negotiations on Natural Resource-Based Products – Natural Resource-Based Products: Submission from the United States (8 February 1990) MTN.GNG/NG3/W/23

Group of Negotiations on Goods – Negotiations on Natural Resource-Based Products – Submission from the European Communities (8 February 1990) MTN.GNG/NG3/W/37

Group of Negotiations on Goods, Negotiating Group on Natural Resource-Based Products – Meeting of 11 February 1987 – Note by the Secretariat (26 February 1990) MTN.GNC/NG3/1

Group of Negotiations on Goods – Negotiating Group on Natural Resource-Based Products – Procedures for the Negotiations (27 March 1990) MTN.GNG/NG3/W/16

Status of Schedules of Contracting Parties to the GATT (16 October 1992) TAR/W/85

UN

Economic and Social Council – Preparatory Committee of the International Conference on Trade and Employment (13 November 1946) UN Doc E/PC/T/C.II/50

WTO

Council for Services – Special Session – Report by the Chairman to the Trade Negotiations Committee (28 November 2005) TN/S/23

Negotiating Group on Rules – New Draft Consolidated Chair Texts of the AD and SCM Agreements – Draft SCM Agreement, Art 2.1(c) (Specificity) and Art 14 (Calculation of the Amount of Subsidy) (19 December 2008) TN/RL/W/326

INDEX

Lightning Source UK Ltd.
Milton Keynes UK
UKHW020649170223
417189UK00015B/461

9 781108 445917